George Stephenson.

LIFE OF GEORGE STEPHENSON.

THE LIFE

OF

GEORGE STEPHENSON,

RAILWAY ENGINEER.

BY

SAMUEL SMILES.

FROM THE FOURTH LONDON EDITION.

COLUMBUS, OHIO:
FOLLETT, FOSTER AND COMPANY.
1859.

PREFACE.

The Invention of the Locomotive Engine and its application to the working of Railways, is one of the most remarkable events of the present century.

Within a period of about thirty years, railways have been adopted as the chief means of internal communication in all civilized countries.

The expenditure involved in their construction has been of an extraordinary character. In Great Britain alone, at the end of the year 1856, not less than 308,775,894*l.* had been raised and expended in the construction of 8,635 miles of railway, which were then open for public traffic.

This great work has been accomplished under the eyes of the generation still living; and the vast funds required for the purpose have been voluntarily raised by private individuals, without the aid of a penny from the public purse.

The system of British Railways, whether considered in point of utility or in respect of the gigantic character and extent of the works involved in their construction, must be regarded as the most magnificent public enterprise yet accomplished in this country — far surpassing all that has been achieved by any government, or by the combined efforts of society, in any former age.

But railways have proved of equal importance to other countries, and been adopted by them to a large extent. In the United States, there are at present not less than 26,000 miles in active operation; and when the Grand Trunk system of Canada has been completed, that fine colony will possess railroad communications 1500 miles in extent.

Railways have also been extensively adopted throughout Europe—above 10,000 miles being already at work in the western continental countries, whilst large projects are in contemplation for Russia, Austria, and Turkey.

Railways for India and Australia are the themes of daily comment; and before many years have elapsed, London will probably be connected by an iron band of railroads with Calcutta, the capital of our Eastern Empire.

Their important uses need not here be discussed. As constituting a great means of social inter-communication, they are felt to enter into almost all the relations between man and man. Trade, manufactures, agriculture, postal communication, have alike been beneficially influenced by this extraordinary invention.

The following facts as respects railway communication in Great Britain, must be regarded as eminently significant: The number of passengers conveyed by railway, in 1856, amounted to not less than 129,347,592; and of these, more than one half traveled by third-class trains, at an average cost of eight-tenths of a penny per mile, the average fare for all classes of passengers not exceeding one penny farthing per mile. The safety with which this immense traffic was conducted is not the least remarkable feature of the system; for it appears, from Captain Galton's report to the Board of Trade, that the proportion of accidents to passengers, from causes beyond their own control, was only one person killed to 16,168,449 conveyed.* Those who desire statistical evidence as to the extent to which this new means of communication is employed for the conveyance of manufactures, minerals, and agricultural produce, will find abundant proofs in the same report.

In Canada and the United States, the railroad is of greater value even than in England; it is there regarded as the pioneer of colonization, and as instrumental in opening up new and fertile territories of vast extent — the food-grounds of future nations.

What may be the eventual results of the general adoption of railways in the civilized countries of Europe, remains to be seen; but it is probable that, by abridging distance, bringing nations into closer communication, and enabling them more freely to exchange the products of their industry, they may tend to abate national antipathies and bind together more closely the great families of mankind.

Disastrous though railway enterprises and speculations have proved to many concerned in them, and mixed up though they have been with much fraud and folly, the debt which the public at large owe to railways cannot be disputed; and after all temporary faults and blots have been admitted and disposed of, they must, nevertheless, be recognized as the most magnificent system of public inter-communication that has yet been given to the world.

* Captain Galton's Report to the Committee of Council for Trade, etc., 21st July, 1857

What manner of men were they by whom this great work was accomplished? How did the conception first dawn upon their minds? By what means did railways grow and quicken into such vigorous life? By what moral and material agencies did the inventors and founders of the system work out the ideas whose results have been so prodigious?

These questions the Author has endeavored to answer in the following Biography of George Stephenson, to whose labors the world is mainly indebted for the locomotive railway system. Indeed, he has been so closely identified with its origin, progress, and eventual establishment on a sound practical basis, that his life may be said to include the history of Railway Locomotion almost down to the present time.

Independently, however, of these considerations, the life of George Stephenson will be found to furnish subject of interest as well as instruction. Strongly self-reliant, diligent in self-culture, and of indomitable perseverance, the characters of such men — happily numerous in England — are almost equivalent to institutions. And if the Author have succeeded in delineating, however imperfectly, the life and character of George Stephenson, the perusal of this book may not be without some salutary influence.

The Author's acknowledgments are due to the following gentlemen, amongst others, for much valuable information as to the successive improvements effected by Mr. Stephenson in the locomotive engine, and also with reference to the various railways, at home and abroad, with which he was professionally connected: Mr. Robert Stephenson, M.P.; Mr. Edward Pease, of Darlington; Mr. John Dixon, C.E.; Mr. John Bourne, C.E.; Mr. Thomas Sopwith, C.E.; Sir Joshua Walmsley; Mr. Jonathan Foster, of Wylam; Mr. Charles Parker; Mr. William Kell, and Mr. Clephan, of Gateshead.

Many interesting facts, relating to Mr. Stephenson's early career, have been obtained from William Coe and other humble persons, who were only too proud to have the opportunity of communicating what they remembered of their distinguished fellow-workman.

The Author is also under obligations to Mr. F. Swanwick, C.E.; Mr. C. Binns, of Clay Cross, and Mr. Vaughan, of Snibston, for various particulars, introduced in the present edition, illustrative of Mr. Stephenson's private life and habits while residing at Liverpool, Alton Grange, and Tapton House, and which supply an admitted defect in the earlier editions of this biography.

8, Glenmohr Terrace,
Hyde Vale, Blackheath.

CONTENTS.

CHAPTER VI.

CHAPTER VII.

CHAPTER VIII.

CHAPTER IX.

CHAPTER X.

CHAPTER XI.

CHAPTER XII.

CHAPTER XIII.

CHAPTER XIV.

CHAPTER XV.

CHAPTER XVI.

CHAPTER XVII.

CHAPTER XVIII.

CHAPTER XIX.

CHAPTER XX.

CHAPTER XXI.

CHAPTER XXII.

CHAPTER XXIII.

CHAPTER XXIV.

CHAPTER XXV.

CHAPTER XXVI.

CHAPTER XXVII.

CHAPTER XXVIII.

CHAPTER XXIX.

CHAPTER XXX.

CHAPTER XXXI.

CHAPTER XXXII.

CHAPTER XXXIII.

CHAPTER XXXIV.

CHAPTER XXXV.

CHAPTER XXXVI.

RESUME OF THE RAILWAY SYSTEM AND ITS RESULTS.

BY R. STEPHENSON, ESQ., M.P.

Birthplace of George Stephenson.

LIFE OF GEORGE STEPHENSON.

CHAPTER I.

EARLY YEARS.

ABOUT eight miles west of Newcastle-on-Tyne stands the colliery village of Wylam, consisting of a number of mean cottages, situated on the north bank of the river Tyne. The Newcastle and Carlisle railway runs along the opposite bank; and the traveler by that line sees only the usual signs of a colliery in the unsightly pumping-engine surrounded by heaps of ashes, coal-dust and slag; while a neighboring iron-furnace, in full blast, throws out dense smoke and loud jets of steam by day, and lurid flames at night. These works form the nucleus of the village, which is almost entirely occupied by coal miners and iron-furnace men.

There is nothing to interest one in the village itself. But, a few hundred yards from its eastern extremity stands a humble detached dwelling, which will be interesting to many as the birthplace of George Stephenson, the Railway Engineer. It is a common, two-storied, red-tiled building, portioned off into four laborers' apartments. The house is known by the name of High Street House, and was originally so called because it stands by the side of what used to be the old riding Post Road or Street, between Newcastle and Hexham, along which the post was carried on horseback within the memory of people still living. At an earlier period, this road used to be so unsafe that the Judges, when on circuit, were escorted along it by a considerable body of armed men, as a protection against the freebooters who invested the district. A sum of money, denominated "dagger money," was annually contributed by the Sheriff of Newcastle, for the purpose of providing daggers and other weapons for the escort; and it is a curious fact that this tribute still continues to be paid in broad gold pieces of Charles the First's coinage, though the necessity for it has long since ceased.*

The lower room in the west end of the humble cottage referred to, was the home of the Stephenson family; and there George Stephenson was born on the 9th of June, 1781. The apartment is now, what it was then, an ordinary laborer's dwelling—its walls unplastered, its floor of clay, and the bare rafters are exposed overhead.

Robert Stephenson, or "Old Bob," as the neighbors familiarly called him, and his wife Mabel, were a respectable couple, careful and hard working. They belonged to the ancient and honorable family of Workers—that extensive family which constitutes the backbone of our country's greatness—the common working people of England. A tradition is, indeed, preserved in the family, that old Robert Stephenson's father and mother came across the border from Scotland, on the loss of considerable property there. Miss Stephenson, daughter of Robert Stephenson's third son John, states that a suit was even commenced for the recovery of the property, but was dropt for want of means to prosecute it. Certain it is, however, that Robert Stephenson's position throughout life was that of an humble workman. After marrying at Walbottle, a village situated between Wylam and Newcastle, he removed with his wife Mabel to Wylam, where

* *Notes and Queries*, December 27th, 1856.

he found employment as fireman of the old pumping-engine at that colliery. The engine which he "fired" has long since been removed: as an old villager said of it, "she stood till she grew fearsome to look at, and then she was pulled down."

Mabel Stephenson was the only daughter of Robert Carr, a dyer at Ovingham. Her family had dwelt in the neighborhood of Newcastle for generations. The author, when engaged in tracing the early history of George Stephenson, casually entered into conversation one day with an old man near Dewley, a hamlet close adjoining Walbottle. Mabel Stephenson, he said, had been his mother's cousin; and all their "forbears" belonged to that neighborhood. It appears that she was a woman of somewhat delicate constitution, nervous in temperament, and troubled occasionally, as her neighbors said, with the "vapors." But those who remember her, concur in asserting that "she was a rale canny body." And a woman of whom this is said, by general consent, in the Newcastle district, may be pronounced a worthy person indeed. It is about the highest praise of a woman which Northumbrians can express. The meaning of the word "canny" with them is quite different from that which it bears in Yorkshire or the Scotch Lowlands. To be "canny," amongst the Scotch, is to be somewhat innocuous and rather soft; in Yorkshire, it means sly and knowing, with an assumed simplicity of manner; but in Northumberland, it means goodness itself—something closely approaching to perfection. Applied to a woman, it "caps" every other compliment, and is a climax to them all.

The Northumbrian people, generally, exhibit many striking and characteristic qualities, inherited, most probably, from the hardy and energetic Northmen, who settled in such numbers along the north-eastern coasts many centuries ago. Taking them as a whole, they are bigger and hardier men*—more enter-

* Their tenacity of life would seem to be greater. The locomotive engineer of a large railway informs me, as the result of a long experience, that the north-country engine-drivers and stokers usually recover from injuries to body and limb, which, to south-country workmen, are almost invariably fatal.

prising, energetic and laborious—and of more marked individuality—than the inhabitants of our more southern counties. They are rougher in manner and more difficult to polish; but they are full of shrewdness and mother wit, and possessed of great strength of character, of which, indeed, their remarkable guttural speech is but a type. The name Stephenson or Stevenson is said to signify, in the Norse tongue, the son of Steeve, or the strong; and certainly the subject of this story exhibited, in a remarkable manner, this characteristic quality of his family.

George Stephenson was the second of a family of six children. The family Bible of Robert and Mabel Stephenson, which seems to have come into their possession in November, 1790, contains the following record of the births of these children, evidently written by one hand and at one time:—

"A Rechester of the children belonging Robert and Mabel Stepheson—
"James Stepheson Was Born March the 4 day 1779
"George Stepheson Was Born June 9 day 1781
"Elender Stepheson Was Born April the 16 day 1784
"Robert Stepheson Was Born March the 10 day 1788
"John Stepheson Was Born November the 4 day 1789
"Ann Stepheson Was Born July the 19 day 1792." *

As the wages earned by Robert Stephenson as fireman, when in full work, did not amount to more than twelve shillings a week, it may be inferred that, even with the most rigid economy, there was very little to spare for the clothing, and nothing for the schooling, of the children. As an aged neighbor, who remembers them well, says of the parents: "They had very little to come and go upon; they were honest folk, but sore hauddea doon in the world."

Robert Stephenson was a slender man, of attenuated frame. He was an exceedingly amiable person, and was long remem-

* Of the two daughters, Eleanor married Stephen Liddell, afterwards employed in the Locomotive Factory in Newcastle; and Anne married John Nixon, with whom she emigrated to the United States. John Stephenson was accidently killed at the Locomotive Factory, in January, 1831.

bered for his curious love of nature as well as of romance. He was accustomed, while tending his engine-fire in the evenings, to draw around him the young people of the village, and to feast their imaginations with his wonderful stories of Sinbad the Sailor, and Robinson Crusoe, besides others of his own invention. Hence he was an immense favorite with all the boys and girls of the place, and "Bob's engine-fire" was always their favorite resort. Another feature in his character, by which he was long remembered, was his strong affection for birds and animals of all sorts. In the winter time, he had usually a flock of tame robins about him, and they would come hopping familiarly round the engine-fire, to pick up the crumbs which he saved for them out of his slender dinner. In summer time, he went bird-nesting in his leisure hours; and one day he took his little boy George to see a blackbird's nest for the first time. Holding him up in his arms, the boy gazed with wonder into the nest full of young birds—a sight which he never forgot, but used to speak of with delight to his intimate friends, when he himself had grown an old man.

While a boy at Wylam, George led the ordinary life of working-people's children. He played about the doors; went bird-nesting when he could; and ran errands to the village. In course of time he was promoted to the office of carrying his father's dinner to him while at work; and he helped to nurse his younger brothers and sisters at home—for in the poor man's dwelling every hand must early be turned to useful account. None of the children ever went to school; the family was too poor, and food too dear, to admit of that.

One of the duties of the elder children was to see that the younger ones were kept out of the way of the chaldron wagons which were then dragged by horses along the wooden tramroad immediately in front of the cottage door. Wooden railways were early used in Northumberland; and this at Wylam was destined to be the first on which a locomotive engine traveled regularly between the coal-pit and the loading-quay. At the time, how ever, of which we speak, locomotives had scarcely been dreamt of; horses were still the only tractive power; and one of the daily sights of young Stephenson was the coal-wagons dragged by their means along this wooden railway at Wylam.

Thus eight years passed; after which, the coal having been worked out on the north side, the old engine was pulled down, and the Stephenson family, following the work, removed from Wylam to Dewley Burn. The Duke of Northumberland, (to whom most of the property in the neighborhood belongs,) had opened a new pit there. An engine was erected, of which Robert Hawthorn, father of the afterwards celebrated Newcastle engineers, was the plugman or engineman; and Robert Stephenson was appointed to act as his fireman.

Dewley Burn, at this day, consists of a few old-fashioned low-roofed cottages, standing on either side of a babbling little stream. They are connected by a rustic wooden bridge, which spans the rift in front of the doors. In the central one-roomed cottage of this group, on the right bank, Robert Stephenson settled for a time with his family. The pit at which he was employed stood in the rear of the cottages. It has long since been worked out and closed in; and only the marks of it are now visible—a sort of blasted grass covering, but scarcely concealing the scoriæ and coal-dust, accumulated about the mouth of the old pit. Looking across the fields, one can still discern the marks of the former wagon-way, leading in the direction of Walbottle. It was joined on its course by another wagon-road leading from the direction of Black Callerton. Indeed, there is scarcely a field in the neighborhood that does not exhibit traces of the workings of former pits. But grass now grows over all the wagon-roads there. The coal has all been "won;" and pit engines, apparatus and workmen, have long since passed away.

CHAPTER II.

BEGINS A CAREER OF LABOR.

As EVERY child in a poor man's house is a burden until his little hands can be turned to profitable account and made to earn money towards supplying the indispensable wants of the family, George Stephenson was put to work as soon as an opportunity of employment presented itself. A widow, named Grace Ainslie, then occupied the neighboring farmhouse of Dewley. She kept a number of cows, and had the privilege of grazing them along the wagon-ways. She needed a boy to herd the cows, to keep them out of the way of the wagons, and prevent their straying or trespassing on the neighbors' "liberties;" the boy's duty was also to bar the gates at night after all the wagons had passed. George petitioned for this post, and to his great joy he was appointed, at the wage of two-pence a day.

It was light employment, and he had plenty of spare time on his hands, which he spent in bird-nesting, making whistles out of reeds and scrannel straws, and erecting Lilliputian mills in the little water-streams that ran into the Dewley bog. But his favorite amusement at this early age was erecting clay engines, in conjunction with his chosen playmate, Tom Thirlaway. They found the clay for their engines in the adjoining bog; and the hemlock, which grew about, supplied them with abundance of imaginary steampipes. The place is still pointed out, "just aboon the cut-end," as the people of the hamlet describe it, where the future engineer made his first essays in modeling. This early indication of a mechanical turn may remind the reader of a similar anecdote of the boy Smeaton, who, when missed one day by his parents, was found mounted on the roof of the cottage fixing a puny windmill.

As the boy grew older and more able to work, he was set to lead the horses when ploughing, though scarce big enough to stride across the furrows; and he used afterwards to say that he rode to his work in the mornings, at an hour when most other children of his age were fast asleep in their beds. He was also employed to hoe turnips, and do similar farm work, for which he was paid the advanced wage of four-pence a day. But his highest ambition was to be taken on at the colliery where his father worked; and he shortly joined his elder brother James there as a "corf-bitter," or "picker," where he was employed in clearing the coal of stones, bats and dross. His wages were now advanced at sixpence a day, and afterwards to eightpence when he was set to drive the gin-horse.

Shortly after, he went to Black Callerton Colliery to drive the gin there. And as that colliery lies about two miles across the fields from Dewley Burn, the boy walked that distance early in the morning to his work, returning home late in the evening. Some of the old people of Black Callerton still remember him as a "grit bare-legged laddie," and they describe him as being then "very quick-witted, and full of fun and tricks." As they said, "there was nothing under the sun but he tried to imitate." He was usually foremost in the sports and pastimes of youth.

Among his first strongly developed tastes, was the love of birds and animals, which he inherited from his father. Blackbirds were his especial favorites. The hedges between Dewley and Black Callerton were capital bird-nesting places; and there was not a nest there that he did not know of. When the young birds were old enough, he would bring them home with him, feed them, and teach them to fly about the cottage unconfined by cages. One of his blackbirds became so tame that, after flying about the doors all day, and in and out of the cottage, it would take up its roost upon the bed-head at night. And most singular of all, the bird would disappear in the spring and summer months, when it was supposed to go into the woods to pair and rear its young, after which it would reäppear at the cottage and resume its social habits during the winter. This went on for several years. George had also a stock of tame rabbits, for which he built a little house behind the cottage, and for many years he continued to pride himself upon the superiority of his breed.

After he had driven the gin for some time at Dewley and Black Callerton, he was taken on as an assistant to his father in firing the engine at Dewley. This was a step of promotion which he had anxiously desired; his only fear being lest he should be found too young for the work. Indeed, he afterwards used to relate how he was wont to hide himself from sight when the owner of the colliery went around, lest he should be thought too little a boy thus to earn his small wages. Since he had modeled his clay engines in the bog, his young ambition was to be an engine-man. And to be an assistant fireman was the first step towards this position. Great, therefore, was his exultation when, at about fourteen years of age, he was appointed assistant fireman, at the wage of a shilling a day.

But the coal at Dewley Burn being at length worked out, and the pit being about to be "laid in," the family prepared for another removal. This time their removal was to Jolly's Close, a few miles to the south, close behind the village of Newburn, where another coal mine of the Duke's called "the Duke's Winnin," had recently been opened out.

Jolly's Close then consisted of a small row of cottages situated upon a flat space of ground enclosed by lofty banks on either side, at the bottom of the narrow rift called Walbottle Dean. Jolly's Close, however, no longer exists, and only a few of the oldest people in the neighborhood are aware that such a place ever was. A mountain of earth, shale and débris, the accumulation of fifty years, lies tumbled over its site—the rubbish, or "deeds," having been shot over from the hillside, once a green hill, but now a scarified, blasted rock, along which furnaces blaze and engines labor night and day. The stream in the hollow, which used to run in front of old Robert Stephenson's cottage door, is made to pay tribute in the form of water power at every wheel in the Dean; and only a narrow strip now remains of what was once a green meadow.

One of the old persons in the neighborhood, who knew the family well, describes the dwelling in which they lived, as a poor cottage of only one room, in which the father, mother, four sons and two daughters lived and slept. It was crowded with three low-poled beds. This one apartment served for parlor, kitchen, sleeping-room and all. The cottage went with the work, and the use of it formed part of the workman's wage—the Duke being both the employer and the landlord.

The children of the Stephenson family were now growing up apace, and were most of them of an age to be able to earn money at various kinds of colliery work. James and George, the two eldest sons, worked as assistant firemen; and the younger boys worked as wheelers or pickers on the banktops. The two girls helped their mother with the household work.

So far as weekly earnings went, the family were at this time pretty comfortable. Their united earnings amounted to from 35*s.* to 40*s.* a week; and they were enabled to command a fair share of the necessaries of life. But it will be remembered that in those days, from 1797 to 1802, it was much more difficult for the working classes to live than it is now; for money did not go near so far. The price of bread was excessive. Wheat, which for three years preceding 1795, had averaged only 54*s.*, now advanced to 76*s.* a quarter; and it continued to rise until in December, 1800, it had advanced to 130*s.*, and barley and oats in proportion. There was a great dearth of provisions; corn riots were of frequent occurrence; and the taxes on all articles of consumption were very heavy. The war with Napoleon was then raging; derangements of trade were frequent, causing occasional suspensions of employment in all departments of industry, from the pressure of which working people are always the first to suffer.

During this severe period, George Stephenson continued to live with his parents at Jolly's Close. Other workings of the coal were opened out in the neighborhood; and to one of these he was removed as fireman on his own account. This was called the "Mid Mill Winnin;" there he had for his mate a young man named Bill Coe, and to these two was entrusted the working of the little engine put up at Mid Mill. They worked together there for about two years, by twelve-hour shifts, George firing the engine at the wage of a shilling a day.

He was now fifteen years old. His ambition was as yet limited to attaining the standing of a full workman, at a man's wages; and with that view he endeavored to attain such a knowledge of his engine as would eventually lead to his employment as an engine-man, with its accompanying advantage of higher pay. He was a steady, sober, hard-working young man, and nothing more, according to the estimate of his fellow-workmen.

One of his favorite pastimes in by-hours was trying feats of strength with his companions. Although in frame he was not particularly robust, yet he was big and bony, and considered very strong for his age. His principal competitor was Robert Hawthorn, with whom he had frequent trials of muscular strength and dexterity, such as lifting heavy weights, throwing the hammer, and putting the stone. At throwing the hammer George had no compeer; but there was a knack in putting the stone which he could never acquire, and here Hawthorn beat him. At lifting heavy weights off the ground from between his feet—by means of a bar of iron passed through them, the bar placed against his knees as a fulcrum, and then straightening the spine and lifting them sheer up—Stephenson was very successful. On one occasion, they relate, he lifted as much as sixty stone weight in this way—a striking indication of his strength of bone and vigor of muscle.

When the pit at Mid Mill was closed, George and his companion Coe were sent to work another pumping-engine, erected near Throckley Bridge, where they continued for some months. It was while working at this place, that his wages were raised to 12*s*. a week—an event of no small importance in his estimation. On coming out of the foreman's office that Saturday evening on which he received the advance, he announced the fact to his fellow-workmen, adding triumphantly, "I am now a made man for life!"

The pit opened at Newburn, at which old Robert Stephenson worked, proving a failure, it was closed; and a new pit was sunk at Water-row, on a strip of land lying between the Wylam wagon-way and the river Tyne, about half a mile west of Newburn Church. A pumping-engine was erected there by Robert Hawthorn, now the Duke's engineer at Walbottle; and old Stephenson went to work it as fireman, his son George acting as the engineman or plugman. At this time he was about seventeen years old—a very youthful age for occupying so responsible a post. He had thus already got ahead of his father in his station as a workman; for the plugman holds a higher grade than the fireman, requiring more practical knowledge and skill, and usually receiving higher wages.

The duty of the plugman was to watch the engine and to see that it kept well in work, and that the pumps were efficient in drawing the water. When the water-level in the pit was lowered, and the suction became incomplete through the exposure of the suction holes, then his business was to proceed to the bottom of the shaft, and plug the tube so that the pump should draw;

hence the designation of Plugman. If a stoppage in the engine took place through any defect in it which he was incapable of remedying, then it was his duty to call in the aid of the chief engineer of the colliery to set the engine to rights.

But from the time when George Stephenson was appointed fireman, and more particularly afterwards as engine-man, he applied himself so assiduously and so successfully to the study of the engine and its gearing—taking the machine to pieces in his leisure hours for the purpose of cleaning and mastering its various parts—that he very soon acquired a thorough practical knowledge of its construction and mode of working, and thus he very rarely needed to call to his aid the engineer of the colliery. His engine became a sort of pet with him, and he was never wearied of watching and inspecting it with devoted admiration.

There is indeed a peculiar fascination about an engine, to the intelligent workman who watches and feeds it. It is almost sublime in its untiring industry and quiet power; capable of performing the most gigantic work, yet so docile that a child's hand may guide it. No wonder, therefore, that the workman, who is the daily companion of this life-like machine, and is constantly watching it with anxious care, at length comes to regard it with a degree of personal interest and regard, speaking of it often in terms of glowing admiration. This daily contemplation of the steam-engine, and the sight of its steady action, is an education of itself to the ingenious and thoughtful workman. It is certainly a striking and remarkable fact, that nearly all that has been done for the improvement of the steam-engine has been accomplished, not by philosophers and scientific men, but by laborers, mechanics, and engine-men. It would appear as if this were one of the departments of practical science in which the higher powers of the human mind must bend to mechanical instinct. The steam-engine was but a mere toy, until it was taken in hand by workmen. Savery was originally a working miner, Newcomen a blacksmith, and his partner Cawley a glazier. In the hands of Watt, the instrument maker, who devoted almost a life to the subject, the condensing engine acquired gigantic strength; and George Stephenson, the colliery engine-man, was certainly not the least of those who have assisted to bring the high-pressure engine to its present power.

While studying to master the details of his engine, to know its weaknesses, and to quicken its powers, George Stephenson gradually acquired the character of a clever and improving workman. Whatever he was set to do, that he endeavored to do well and thoroughly; never neglecting small matters, but aiming at being a complete workman at all points; thus gradually perfecting his own mechanical capacity, and securing at the same time the respect of his fellow-workmen and the increased confidence and esteem of his employers.

CHAPTER III.

ENGINEMAN AT NEWBURN—SELF-CULTURE.

GEORGE STEPHENSON was eighteen years old before he learnt to read. He was now almost a full-grown workman, earning his twelve shillings a week, and having the charge of an engine, which occupied his time to the extent of twelve hours every day. He had thus very few leisure moments that he could call his own. But the busiest man will find them if he watch for them; and if he be careful in turning these moments to useful account, he will prove them to be the very "gold-dust of time," as Young has so beautifully described them.

To his poor parents George Stephenson owed a sound constitution and vigorous health. They had also set before him an example of sobriety, economy, and patient industry—habits which are in themselves equivalent to principles. For habits are the most inflexible of all things; and principles are, in fact, but the names which we assign to them. If his parents, out of their small earnings and scanty knowledge, were unable to give their son any literary culture, at all events they had trained him well, and furnished him with an excellent substratum of character. Unquestionably, however, he labored under a very serious disadvantage in having to master, at a comparatively advanced age, those simple rudiments of elementary instruction, which all children in a country calling itself civilized ought to have imparted to them at school. The youth who reaches manhood, and enters, by necessity, upon a career of daily toil, without being able to read his native language, does not start on equal terms with others who have received the benefits of such instruction. It is true that he who, by his own voluntary and determined efforts, overcomes the difficulties early thrown in his way, and succeeds in eventually teaching himself, will value the education thus acquired much more than he to whom it has been imparted as a mere matter of duty, on the part of parents or of society. What the self-educated man learns, becomes more thoroughly his own, makes a more vivid impression upon his mind, and fixes itself more enduringly there. It usually also exercises a more powerful influence in the formation of his character, by disciplining his spirit of self-help, and accustoming him to patient encounter with, and triumph over, difficulties.

We have seen how Stephenson's play-hours were occasionally occupied — in a friendly rivalry with his fellows in feats of strength. Much also of his spare time, when he was not actually employed in working the engine, was devoted to cleaning it and taking it to pieces, for the purpose of mastering its details. At this time he was also paying some attention to the art of braking, which he had expressed to Coe his desire to learn, in order that he might improve his position, and be advanced to higher wages.

Not many of his fellow-workmen had learnt to read; but those who could do so, were placed under frequent contribution by George and the other laborers at the pit. It was one of their greatest treats to induce some one to read to them by the engine-fire, out of any book or stray newspaper which might find its way into the village of Newburn. Bonaparte was then overrunning Italy, and astounding Europe by his brilliant succession of victories; and there was no more eager auditor of these exploits, when read from the newspaper accounts, than the young engineman at the Water-row Pit.

There were also numerous stray bits of information and intelligence contained in these papers, which excited Stephenson's interest. One of these related to the Egyptian art of hatching birds' eggs by means of artificial heat. Curious about everything relating to birds, he determined to test the art by experiment. It was spring time, and he forthwith went a bird-nesting in the adjoining woods and hedges, where there were few birds' nests of which he did not know. He brought a collection of eggs of all kinds into the engine-house, set them in flour in a warm place, covering the whole over with wool, and then waited the issue of his experiment. But though the heat was kept as steady as possible, and the eggs were carefully turned every twelve hours, they never hatched. The eggs chipped, and some of them exhibited well-grown chicks; but none of the birds came forth alive, and thus the experiment failed. This incident, however, shows that the inquiring mind of the youth was now fairly at work.

Another of his favorite occupations continued to be the modeling of clay engines. He not only tried to model engines which he had himself seen, but he also attempted to form models in clay of engines which were described to him as being in existence; and doubtless his modeling at this time, imperfect though his knowledge was, exhibited considerable improvement upon his first attempts in the art when a herd-boy in the bog at Dewley Burn. He was told, however, that all the wonderful engines of Watt and Boulton, about which he was so anxious to know, were to be found described in books, and that he must satisfy his curiosity by searching the publications of the day for a more complete description of them. But, alas! Stephenson could not read; he had not yet learnt even his letters.

Thus he shortly found, when gazing wistfully in the direction of knowledge, that to advance further as a skilled workman, he must master this wonderful art of reading—the key to so many other arts. He would thus be enabled to gain an access to books, the depositories of the experience and wisdom of all times. Although now a grown man, and doing the work of a man, he was not ashamed to confess his ignorance and go to school, big as he was, to learn his letters. Perhaps, too, he foresaw that in laying out a little of his spare earnings for this purpose, he was investing money judiciously, and that every hour he spent at school, he was really working for better wages. At all events, he determined to make a beginning—a small beginning, it is true, but still a right one, and a pledge and assurance that he was in earnest in the work of self-culture. He desired to find a road into knowledge; and no man can sincerely desire this but he will eventually succeed. He possessed that will and purpose which are the invariable forerunners of success.

His first schoolmaster was Robin Cowens, a poor teacher in the village of Walbottle. He kept a night-school, which was attended by a few of the colliers and laborers' sons in the neighborhood. George took lessons in spelling and reading three nights in the week. Tommy Musgrove, the lad who "sled out" the engine at the Water-row Pit, usually went with him to the evening lesson. This teaching of Robin Cowens cost three-pence a week; and though it was not very good, yet George, being hungry for knowledge, and eager to acquire it, soon learnt to read. He also practiced "pot-hooks," and at the age of nineteen he was proud to be able to write his own name.

A Scotch dominie, named Andrew Robertson, set up a night school in the village of Newburn, in the winter of 1799. It was more convenient for George Stephenson to attend this school, as it was nearer to his work, and not more than a few minutes' walk from Jolly's Close. Besides, Andrew had the reputation of being a skilled arithmetician; and this was a branch of knowledge that Stephenson was now desirous of acquiring. He accordingly began taking lessons from him, paying four pence a week. Andrew Gray, the junior fireman at the Water-row Pit, began arithmetic at the same time; and he has since told the writer, that George learnt "figuring" so much faster than he did, that he could not make out how it was—"he took to figures so wonderful." Although the two started together from the same point, at the end of the winter George had mastered "reduction," while Andrew Gray was still grappling with the difficulties of simple division. But George's secret was his perseverance. He worked out the sums in his by-hours, improving every minute of his spare time by the engine fire, there solving the arithmetical problems set for him upon his slate by his master. In the evenings, he took to Andrew Robertson the sums which he had thus "worked," and new ones were "set" for him to study out the following day. Thus his progress was rapid, and, with a willing heart and mind, he soon became well advanced in arithmetic. Indeed, Andrew Robertson became somewhat proud of his pupil; and shortly afterwards, when the Water-row Pit was closed, and George removed to Black Callerton to work there, the poor schoolmaster, not having a very extensive connection in Newburn, went with his pupils, and set up his night school at Black Callerton, where they continued their instructions under him as before.

George still found time to attend to his favorite animals while working at the Water-row Pit. He kept up his breed of rabbits, and even drove a small trade in them, selling portions of his stock from time to time. Like his father, he used to tempt the robin-redbreast to hop and fly about him at the engine fire, by the bait of bread-crumbs saved from his dinner. But his favorite animal was his dog — so sagacious that he performed the office of a servant, in almost daily carrying his dinner to him at the pit. The tin containing the meal was suspended from the dog's neck; and thus laden he proudly walked the road from Jolly's Close to Water-row Pit, quite through the village of Newburn. He turned neither to the left nor right, nor minded for the time the barking of curs at his heels. But his course was not unattended with perils. One day the big strange dog of a passing butcher espied the engine-man's messenger, ran after him, and fell upon him with the tin can about his neck. There was a terrible tussle and worrying between the dogs, which lasted for a brief while, and shortly after, the dog's master, anxious for his dinner, saw his faithful servant approaching, bleeding but triumphant. The tin can was still round his neck, but the dinner had escaped in the struggle. Though George went without his dinner that day, yet when the circumstances of the combat were related to him by the villagers who had seen it, he was prouder of his dog than ever.

It was while working at the Water-row Pit that Stephenson first learnt the art of braking an engine. This being one of the higher departments of colliery labor, and amongst the best paid, George was very anxious to learn it. A small winding engine having been put up for the purpose of drawing the coals from the pit, Bill Coe, his friend and fellow-workman, was appointed the brakesman. He frequently allowed George to try his hand at the brake, and instructed him how to proceed. But in this course Coe was opposed by several of the other workmen—one of whom, a brakesman named William Locke,* went so far as to stop the working of the pit because Stephenson had been called in to the brake. But one day as Mr. Charles Nixon, the manager of the pit, was observed approaching, Coe adopted an experiment which had the effect of putting a stop to the opposition. He forthwith called upon George Stephenson to "come into the brake-house, and take hold of the machine." No sooner had he done this, than Locke, as usual, sat down, and the working of the pit was stopped. "What's the meaning of this?" asked Mr. Nixon; "what's wrong that the pit is standing?" Coe's answer was that Locke had refused to take the corf. "And why?" asked Nixon. "Because Locke objects to my learning George there (pointing to Stephenson) to brake." Locke, when requested to give an explanation, said that "young Stephenson couldn't brake, and, what was more, never would learn to brake: he was so clumsy

* He afterwards removed to Barnsley in Yorkshire; he was the father of Mr. Locke, the celebrated engineer.

that he was like to rive his arms off." Mr. Nixon, however, ordered Locke to go on with the work, which he did; and Stephenson, after some further practice, acquired the art of braking.

After working at the Water-row Pit, and in the neighborhood of Newburn, for about three years, George, with his companion Coe, was removed to Black Callerton Colliery, in the year 1801. The pit there belonged to the same masters, Nixon and Cramlington, and George was regularly appointed brakesman at the Dolly Pit.

CHAPTER IV.

BRAKESMAN AT BLACK CALLERTON.

GEORGE STEPHENSON was now a young man of twenty years of age—a well knit, healthy fellow—a sober, steady, and expert workman. Beyond this, and his diligence and perseverance, and the occasional odd turns which his curiosity took, there was nothing remarkable about him. He was no precocious genius. As yet he was comparatively untaught, and had but mastered the mere beginnings of knowledge. But his observant faculties were active, and he diligently turned to profitable account every opportunity of exercising them. He had still only the tastes and ambitions of an ordinary workman, and perhaps looked not beyond that condition.

His duties as a brakesman may be briefly described. The work was somewhat monotonous, and consisted in superintending the working of the engine and machinery by means of which the coals were drawn out of the pit. Brakesmen are almost invariably selected from those who have had considerable experience as engine firemen, and borne a good character for steadiness, punctuality, watchfulness, and "mother wit." In George Stephenson's day, the coals were drawn out of the pit in corves, or large baskets made of hazel rods. The corves were placed two together in a cage, between which and the pit ropes there was usually from fifteen to twenty feet of chain. The approach of the corves towards the pit mouth was signaled by a bell, brought into action by a piece of mechanism worked from the shaft of the engine. When the bell sounded, the brakesman checked the speed, by taking hold of the hand-gear connected with the steam valves, which were so arranged that by their means he could regulate the speed of the engine, and stop or set it in motion when required. Connected with the fly-wheel was a powerful wooden brake, acting by pressure against its rim, something like the brake of a railway carriage against its wheels, and the brakesman was enabled, by applying his foot to a foot-step near him, on catching sight of the chain attached to the ascending corve cage, at once, and with great precision, to stop its revolutions, and arrest the ascent of the corves at the pit mouth, when they were forthwith landed on the "settle board." On the full corves being replaced by empty ones, it was then the duty of the brakesman to reverse the engine, and send the corves down the pit to be filled again.

The monotony of George Stephenson's occupation as a brakesman was somewhat varied by the change which he made, in his turn, from the day to the night shift. This duty, during the latter stage, chiefly consisted in sending the men and materials into the mine, and in drawing other men and materials out. Most of the workmen enter the pit during the night shift, and leave it in the latter part of the day, whilst coal-drawing is proceeding. The requirements of the work at night are such, that the brakesman has a good deal of spare time on his hands, which he is at liberty to employ in his own way. From an early period, Stephenson was accustomed to employ those vacant night hours in working the sums set for him by Andrew Robertson upon his slate, in practicing writing in his copy-book, and also in mending the shoes of his fellow-workmen. His wages while working at the Dolly Pit amounted to from 1*l.* 15*s.* to 2*l.* in the fortnight;* but he

* William Coe has furnished me with an abstract of the wages book of Black Callerton, from which it appears that George Stephenson's earnings for the fortnight were as follows: On June 18th, 1801, he was paid 1*l.* 19*s.* 4*d.*, and a ticket for two shillings worth of rye;

gradually added to them as he became more expert at shoe-mending, and afterwards at shoemaking. Probably he was stimulated to take in hand this extra work, by the attachment which he had at this time formed for a respectable young woman of the village, named Fanny Henderson. Fanny was a servant in a neighboring farm house; and George, having found her a high principled young woman of excellent character, courted her with the intention of making her his wife and setting up in a house of his own. The personal attractions of Fanny Henderson, though these were considerable, were the least of her charms. Her temper was of the sweetest; and those who knew her speak of the charming modesty of her demeanor, her kindness of disposition, and withal her sound good sense.

Amongst his various mendings of old shoes at Callerton, George Stephenson was on one occasion favored with the shoes of his sweetheart, Fanny Henderson, to sole. One can imagine the pleasure with which he would linger over such a piece of work, and the pride with which he would execute it. A friend of his, still living, relates that, after he had finished the shoes, he carried them about with him in his pocket on the Sunday afternoon, and that from time to time he would whip them out and hold them up to sight—the tiny little shoes that they were—exhibiting them with exultation to his friend, and exclaiming, "what a capital job he had made of them!" Other lovers have carried about with them a lock of their fair one's hair, a glove, or a handkerchief; but none could have been prouder of their cherished love-token than was George Stephenson of his Fanny's shoes, which he had just soled, and of which he had made such a "capital job."

Out of his earnings from shoe-mending at Callerton, George contrived to save his first guinea. The first guinea saved by a

on June 17th, 1802, he was paid 1*l*. 15*s*. But bread was so dear in those days, that the wages paid to workmen were not really so high as they appear: in 1801, wheat was selling at 5*l*. 18*s*. 3*d*., and rye at 3*l*. 19*s*. 9*d*. the quarter.

working man is no trivial thing. If, as in Stephenson's case, it has been the result of prudent self-denial, of extra labor at by-hours, and of sound resolutions to save and economize for worthy purposes, the first guinea saved is an earnest of better things. It is a nest-egg—a token of increase—the beginning, it may be, of prosperity and wealth. When Stephenson had saved this guinea, he was somewhat proud of the achievement, and expressed the opinion to a friend, who many years after reminded him of it, that he was "now a rich man."

At Callerton, Stephenson—habitually sober and steady—was a standing example of character to the other workmen. He never missed a day's wages by being off work in consequence of a drinking-bout, as many others did. William Coe says of him, that, though he knew Stephenson intimately, he never saw him "the worse for drink" in his life. On pay Saturday afternoons, when the workmen at the pit kept their fortnightly holiday, some spending their afternoon and evening in the public house, and others in the adjoining fields, cock-fighting and dog-fighting, Stephenson, instead of either drinking or playing, used to take his engine to pieces for the purpose of obtaining "insight" and practical acquaintance with its details; and he invariably cleaned all the parts and put the machine in thorough working order before leaving her. Thus his engine was always clean and in excellent condition, and his knowledge of its powers and its mechanism became almost complete.

In the winter evenings Stephenson proceeded with his lessons in arithmetic under Andrew Robertson. But Robertson had soon taught his pupil all that he himself knew, which probably did not amount to much. He even admitted that he could carry Stephenson no further in arithmetic, the pupil having outstripped the master. He went on, however, with his writing lessons; and by the year following, when he signed his name in the parish registry of Newburn, on the occasion of his marriage to

Fanny Henderson, he was able to write a good, legible round hand.

Not long after he began to work at Black Callerton as brakesman, he had a quarrel with a pitman named Ned Nelson, a roistering bully, who was the terror of the village. Nelson was a great fighter; and it was therefore considered dangerous to quarrel with him. Stephenson was so unfortunate as not to be able to please this pitman by the way in which, as brakesman, he drew him out of the pit; and Nelson swore at him grossly because of his alleged clumsiness. George defended himself, and appealed to the testimony of the other workmen as to his braking. But Nelson had not been accustomed to George's style of self-assertion; and after a great deal of abuse, he threatened to kick the brakesman, who defied him to do so. Nelson ended by challenging Stephenson to a pitched battle; and the latter accepted the challenge, when a day was fixed on which the fight was to come off.

Great was the excitement at Black Callerton when it was known that George Stephenson had accepted Nelson's challenge. Everybody said that he would be killed. The villagers—the young men, and especially the boys of the place, with whom George was an especial favorite—all wished that he might beat Nelson, but they scarcely dared to say so. They came about him while he was to work in the engine-house, to inquire if it was really true that he was "goin' to feight Nelson?" "Ay; never fear for me; I'll feight him." And "feight" him he did. For some days previous to the appointed day of battle, Nelson went entirely off work for the purpose of keeping himself fresh and strong, whereas Stephenson went on doing his daily work, as usual, and appeared not in the least disconcerted by the prospect of the affair. So, on the evening appointed, after George had done his day's labor, he went into the Dolly Pit field, where his already exulting rival was ready to meet him. George stripped, and "went in" like a practiced pugilist—though it was his first and last fight. After a few rounds, George's wiry muscles and practiced strength enabled him severely to punish his adversary, and to secure for himself an easy victory.

This circumstance is related in illustration of Stephenson's personal pluck and courage; and it was thoroughly characteristic of the man. He was no pugilist, and the very reverse of quarrelsome. But he would not be put down by the bully of the colliery, and he fought him. There his pugilism ended; they afterwards shook hands, and continued good friends. In after life, Stephenson's mettle was often as hardly tried, though in a different way; and he did not fail to exhibit the same resolute courage, in contending with the bullies of the railway world, as he had thus early shown in his encounter with Ned Nelson the fighting pitman of Black Callerton.

CHAPTER V.

MARRIAGE AND HOUSEKEEPING AT WILLINGTON QUAY.

By dint of thrift, sobriety and industry, George Stephenson managed to save as much money at Black Callerton as enabled him, on leaving it for Willington Ballast Quay, to take a house and furnish it in a very humble style, for the reception of his young bride, Fanny Henderson.

Willington Quay, whither Stephenson now went to act as brakesman at the Ballast Hill, lies on the north bank of the Tyne, about six miles below Newcastle. It consists of a line of houses straggling along the river side; and high behind it towers up the huge mound of ballast emptied out of the ships which resort to the quay for their cargoes of coal for the London market. The ballast is thrown out of the ship's hold into wagons laid alongside. When filled, a train of these is dragged up the steep incline which leads to the summit of the Ballast Hill, where the wagons are run out and their contents emptied to swell the monstrous accumulation of earth, chalk and Thames mud already laid there, probably to form a puzzle for future antiquaries and geologists, when the origin of these immense hills along the Tyne has been forgotten. On the summit of the Willington Ballast Hill was a fixed engine, which drew the trains of laden wagons up the incline; and of this engine George Stephenson now acted as brakesman.

The cottage in which he took up his abode is a small two-storied dwelling, standing a little back from the quay, with a bit of garden ground in front. The Stephenson family occupied the upper room in the west end of the cottage. Close behind rises the Ballast Hill.

When the cottage dwelling had been made snug, and prepared for the young wife's reception, the marriage took place. It was celebrated in Newburn Church, on the 28th of November, 1802.

George Stephenson's signature, as it stands in the books, is that of a person who seems to have just learned to write. Yet it is the signature of a man, written slowly and deliberately, in strong round hand. With all this care, however, he had not been able to avoid a blotch; the word "Stephenson" has been brushed over before the ink was dry.

After the ceremony, George and his newly wedded wife proceeded to the house of old Robert Stephenson and his wife Mabel, at Jolly's Close. The old man was now becoming infirm, though he still worked as an engine fireman, and contrived with difficulty "to keep his head above water." When the visit had been paid, the bridal party prepared to set out for their new home at Willington Quay. They went in a homely old-fashioned style, though one quite usual in those days, before macadamized roads had been adopted, or traveling by railway so much as dreamt of. Two stout farm horses were borrowed from Mr. Burn, of the Red House farm, Wolsingham, where Anne Henderson, the bride's sister, lived as servant. The two horses were each provided with a saddle and a pillion; and George having mounted one, his wife seated herself on the pillion behind him, holding on by her arms round his waist. Robert Gray and Anne Henderson in like manner mounted the other horse; and in this wise the wedding party rode across the country, passing through the old streets of Newcastle, and then by Wallsend to their home at Willington Quay—a long ride of about fifteen miles.

We may here mention that Mr. Burn, the farmer at Wolsingham, shortly after married Anne Henderson; and a good wife she proved. In those times the farmer and his servant did not stand so far apart, in point of social position, as they do now. Household servants were themselves generally the daughters of small farmers, and there was no great condescension in the master taking to wife one who had proved herself a clever and thrifty housekeeper. Paterson, the small farmer of Black Callerton, with whom George Stephenson had lodged while working at the Dolly Pit, in like manner married another sister, Betty; and she too, like her sisters, proved a valuable and worthy helpmate.

George Stephenson's daily life at Willington was that of a regular, steady workman. By the manner, however, in which he continued to improve his spare hours in the evening, he was silently and surely paving the way for being something more than a mere workman. While other men of his class were idling in public-houses, he set himself down to study the principles of mechanics, and to master the laws by which his engine worked. For a workman, he was even at that time more than ordinarily speculative—often taking up strange theories, and trying to sift out the truth that was in them. While sitting by the side of his young wife in his cottage dwelling, in the winter evenings, he was usually occupied in making mechanical experiments, or in modeling experimental machines. Amongst his various speculations while at Willington, he occupied himself a good deal in endeavoring to discover perpetual motion. Although he failed, as so many others had done before him, the very efforts he made tended to whet his inventive faculties, and to call forth his dormant powers. He actually went so far as to construct the model of a machine by which he thought he would secure perpetual motion. It consisted of a wooden wheel, the periphery of which was furnished with glass tubes filled with quicksilver; as the wheel rotated, the quicksilver poured itself down into the lower tubes, and thus a sort of self-acting motion was kept up in the apparatus, which, however, did not prove to be perpetual. Where he had first obtained the idea of this machine—whether from conversation, or reading, or his own thoughts, is not now remembered; but possibly he may have heard of an apparatus of a similar kind which is described in the "History of Inventions." As he had then no access to books, and indeed could barely read with ease, it is possible that he may have been told of the invention, and then set about testing its value according to his own methods.

Much of his spare time continued to be occupied by labor more immediately profitable, regarded in a pecuniary point of view. From mending shoes he proceeded to making them, and he also drove a good trade in making shoe-lasts, in which he was admitted to be very expert. William Coe, who continued to live at Willington in 1851, informed the writer that he bought a pair of shoes from George Stephenson for 7*s.* 6*d.*, and he remembered that they were a capital fit, and wore well. But an accident occurred in his household about this time, which had the effect of directing his industry into a new and still more profitable channel. The cottage chimney took fire one day in his absence; the alarmed neighbors rushing in, threw bucketsfull of water upon the fire; some in their zeal mounted on the ridge of the house and poured volumes of water down the chimney. The fire was soon put out, but the house was thoroughly soaked. When George came home he found the water running out of the door, everything in disorder, and his new furniture covered with soot. The eight-day clock, which hung against the wall—one of the most highly prized articles in the house—was grievously injured by the steam with which the room had been filled. Its wheels were so clogged by the dust and soot, that it was brought to a complete stand-still. George was always ready to turn his hand to anything, and his ingenuity never at fault, immediately set to work for the repair of the unfortunate clock. He was advised to send it to the clockmaker, but that would have cost money;

and he declared that he would repair it himself—at least he would try. The clock was accordingly taken to pieces and cleaned; the tools which he had been accumulating by him for the purpose of constructing the perpetual motion machine, enabled him to do this; and he succeeded so well that, shortly after, the neighbors sent him their clocks to clean, and he soon became one of the most famous clock-doctors in the neighborhood.

It was while living at Willington Quay that George Stephenson's only son Robert was born, on the 16th of December, 1803. The child was from his earliest years familiarized with the steady industry of his parents; for there were few, if any, idle moments spent in that cottage. When his father was not busy in making or mending shoes, cutting out shoe-lasts, or cleaning clocks, he was occupied with some drawing or model, in constructing which he sought to improve himself. The child was from the first, as may well be imagined, a great favorite with his father, whose evening hours were made happier by his presence. George Stephenson's strong "philoprogenitiveness," as phrenologists call it, had in his boyhood expended itself on birds, and dogs, and rabbits, and even on the poor old gin-horses which he had driven at the Callerton Pit; and now he found in his child a more genial object on which to expend the warmth of his affection.

The christening of the child took place in the school-house at Wallsend, the old parish church being at the time in so dilapidated a condition from the "creeping" * of the ground underneath, consequent upon the excavation of the coal, that it was considered dangerous to enter it. On this occasion, Robert Gray and Anne Henderson, who had officiated as bridesman and bridesmaid at the wedding, came over again to Willington, and stood as

* The congregation in a church near Newcastle were one Sunday morning plentifully powdered with chips from the white ceiling of the church, which had been *crept under*, being above an old mine. "It's only the pit a-creeping," said the parish clerk, by way of encouragement to the people to remain. But it would not do; for there was a sudden *creep out* of the congregation. The clerk went at last, with a powdered head, crying out, "It's only a creep."—*Our Coal Fields and our Coal Pits.*

godfather and godmother to little Robert, as the child was named, after his grandfather.

After working for about three years as a brakesman at the Willington machine, George Stephenson was induced to leave his situation there for a similar one at the West Moor Colliery, Killingworth. It was while residing at Killingworth that his remarkable practical qualities as a workman were first recognized by his employers, and that he slowly but surely acquired that reputation as an Engineer and Inventor by which he afterwards became so extensively known and honored.

CHAPTER VI.

BRAKESMAN AT WEST MOOR, KILLINGWORTH.

The village of Killingworth lies about seven miles north of Newcastle, and is one of the best known collieries in that neighborhood. The workings of the coal are of vast extent, giving employment to a large number of work-people. The colliery stands high and commands an extensive view of the adjacent country; it overlooks the valley of the Tyne on the south, and the pinnacles of the Newcastle spires may be discerned in the distance, when not obscured by the clouds of smoke which rise up from that vast hive of manufacturing industry.

To this place George Stephenson first came as a brakesman in the year 1804. He had scarcely settled down in his new home, ere he sustained a heavy loss in the death of his wife, for whom he cherished the sincerest affection. Their married life had been happy, sweetened as it was by daily successful toil. The husband was sober and hard-working, and his young wife made his hearth so bright and his home so snug, that no attraction could draw him from her side in the evening hours. But this domestic happiness was all to pass away; and the twinkling feet, for which the lover had made those tiny shoes at Callerton, were now to be hidden for evermore from his eyes. It was a terrible blow, but he bore it as he best could. There was work before him to do —work, which Stephenson, like many more, found to be a balm for even the heaviest sorrow. But he long lamented his bereavement, and continued tenderly to cherish his dear wife's memory.

Shortly after this event, while his grief was still fresh, he received an invitation from some gentlemen concerned in large works near Montrose, in Scotland, to proceed thither and superintend the working of one of Boulton and Watt's engines. He accepted the offer, and made arrangements to leave Killingworth for a time.

Having left his boy in charge of a worthy neighbor, he set out upon his long journey to Scotland, on foot, with his kit upon his back. While in Scotland, he was paid good wages, and contrived to save 28*l*., which he brought back to Killingworth with him, after an absence of about a year. His friend Coe states that while in the North, George Stephenson had tried to make some alterations in the engine which he worked, but without success, and that this led to a disagreement between him and the colliery owners. Longing to get back to his own kindred—his heart yearning for the son he had left behind, Stephenson took leave of his Montrose employers, and trudged back to Killingworth on foot, as he had gone. He related to his friend, on his return, that when on the borders of Northumberland, late one evening, footsore and wearied with his long day's journey, he knocked at a small farmer's cottage door, and requested shelter for the night. It was refused, and then he entreated that, being sore, tired, and unable to proceed any further, they would permit him to lie down in the outhouse, for that a little clean straw would serve him. The farmer's wife appeared at the door, looked at the traveler, then retiring with her husband, the two confabulated a little apart, and finally they invited Stephenson into the cottage. Always full of conversation and anecdote, he soon made himself at home in the farmer's family, and spent with them a few pleasant hours. He was hospitably entertained for the night, and when he left the cottage in the morning, he pressed them to make some charge for his lodging, but they would not hear of such a thing. They asked him to remember them kindly, and if he ever came that way, to be sure and call again. Many years after, when Stephenson had become a thriving man, he did not forget the humble pair who had thus succored and entertained him on his way; he sought their cottage again, when age had silvered their hair; and when he left the aged couple, on that occasion, they may have been reminded of the old saying that we may sometimes "entertain angels unawares."

Reaching home, Stephenson found that his father had met with a serious accident at the Blucher Pit, which had reduced him to great distress and poverty. While engaged in the inside of an engine, making some repairs, a fellow-workman accidentally let in the steam upon him. The blast struck him full in the face—he was terribly scorched, and his eyesight was irretrievably lost. The helpless and infirm man had struggled for a time with poverty; his sons who were at home, poor as himself, were little able to help him, while George was at a distance in Scotland. On his return, however, with his savings in his pocket, his first step was to pay off his father's debts, amounting to about 15*l.*; soon afterwards he removed the aged pair from Jolly's Close to a comfortable cottage adjoining the tram-road near the West Moor at Killingworth, where the old man lived for many years, supported entirely by his son. He was quite blind, but cheerful to the last. One of his greatest pleasures, towards the close of his life, was to receive a visit from his grandson Robert, who would ride straight into the cottage mounted on his "cuddy," and call upon his grandfather to admire the points of the animal. The old man would then dilate upon the ears, fetlocks, and quarters of the donkey, and generally conclude by pronouncing him to be a "real blood."

Stephenson was again taken on as a brakesman at the West Moor Pit. He does not seem to have been very hopeful as to his prospects in life about the time (1807–8). Indeed, the condition of the working class generally was then very discouraging.

England was engaged in a great war, which pressed heavily upon the industry, and severely tried the resources of the country. Heavy taxes were imposed upon all the articles of consumption that would bear them. Incomes of 50*l.* a year and upwards were taxed 10 per cent. There was a constant demand for men to fill the army, navy, and militia. Never before had England heard such drumming and fifing for recruits. In 1805, the gross forces of the United Kingdom amounted to nearly 700,000 men, and early in 1808 Lord Castlereagh carried a measure for the establishment of a local militia of 200,000 men. These measures produced great and general distress amongst the laboring classes. There were serious riots in Manchester, Newcastle, and elsewhere, through scarcity of work and lowness of wages. Every seventh person in England was a pauper, maintained out of the poor-rates—there being, in 1807, 1,234,000 paupers to 7,636,000 persons who were not paupers. Those laborers who succeeded in finding employment were regularly mulcted of a large portion of their earnings to maintain the unemployed, and at the same time to carry on the terrible war in which Britain contended single-handed against Napoleon, then everywhere victorious. The working people were also liable to be pressed for the navy, or drawn for the militia; and though men could not fail to be discontented under such circumstances, they scarcely dared, in those perilous times, even to mutter their discontent to their neighbors.

George Stephenson was one of those drawn at that time for the militia. He must therefore either quit his work and go a soldiering, or find a substitute. He adopted the latter course, and paid a considerable sum of money to a militia-man to serve in his stead. Thus nearly the whole of his hard won earnings were swept away at a stroke. He was almost in despair, and contemplated the idea of leaving the country, and emigrating to the United States. A voyage thither was then a more formidable thing for a working man to accomplish than a voyage to Australia is now. But he seriously entertained the project, and had all but made up his mind. His sister Ann, with her husband, emigrated about that time, but George could not raise the requisite money, and they departed without him. After all, it went sore against his heart to leave his home and his kindred—the scenes of his youth and the friends of his boyhood; but he struggled long with the idea, brooding over it in sorrow. Speaking afterwards to a friend of his thoughts at the time, he said: "You know the road from my house at the West Moor to Killingworth? I remember when I went along that road I wept bitterly, for I knew not where my lot would be cast." But Providence had better and greater things in store for George Stephenson than the lot of a settler in the wilds of America. It was well that his poverty prevented him from prosecuting further the idea of emigration, and rooted him to the place where he afterwards worked out his great career so manfully and victoriously.

Many years after, when addressing a society of young men at Belper, in Derbyshire, on the necessity of Perseverance — his favorite text—he said: "Well do I remember the beginning of my career as an engineer, and the great perseverance that was required for me to get on. Not having served an apprenticeship, I had made up my mind to go to America, considering that no one in England would trust me to act as engineer. However, I was trusted in some small matters, and succeeded in giving satisfaction. Greater trusts were reposed in me, in which I also succeeded. Soon after, I commenced making the locomotive engine; and the results of my perseverance you have this day witnessed."*

In 1808, Stephenson, with two other brakesmen, named Robert Wedderburn and George Dodds, took a small contract under the colliery lessees, for braking the engines at the West Moor Pit. The brakesmen found the oil and tallow; they divided the work amongst them, and were paid so much per score for their labor.

* Speech to Mechanics' Institute at Belper, July 6th, 1841, the members of the Chesterfield Institute having traveled thither by railway train over the line constructed by Mr. Stephenson.

There being two engines working night and day, two of the three men were always at work; the average earnings of each amounting to from 18*s.* to 20*s.* a week. But Stephenson resorted to his usual mode of ekeing out his earnings. His son Robert would soon be of an age to be sent to school; and the father, being but too conscious, from his own experience, of the disadvantages arising from the want of instruction, determined that his boy should at least receive the elements of a good education. Stinted as he was for means at the time, maintaining his parents, and struggling with difficulties, this early resolution to afford his son proper culture, must be regarded as a noble feature in his character, and strikingly illustrative of his thoughtfulness and conscientiousness. Many years after, speaking of the resolution which he thus early formed, he said: "In the earlier period of my career, when Robert was a little boy, I saw how deficient I was in education, and I made up my mind that he should not labor under the same defect, but that I would put him to a good school, and give him a liberal training. I was, however, a poor man; and how do you think I managed? I betook myself to mending my neighbors' clocks and watches at nights, after my daily labor was done, and thus I procured the means of educating my son."*

Besides mending clocks and watches at this time, he also continued to make and mend shoes, and to manufacture shoe-lasts for the shoemakers of the neighborhood. He even cut out the pitmen's clothes for their wives to make up; and it is said that to this day there are clothes worn at Killingworth which have been made after "Geordy Steevie's cut."

Perhaps the secret of every man's best success in life is the readiness with which he takes advantage of opportunities. George Stephenson was an eminent illustration of this readiness in turning all his time to profit, and everything that he knew to useful account. Every spare minute was laid under contribution,

* Speech at Newcastle, on the 18th June, 1844, on the occasion of celebrating the opening of the Newcastle and Darlington Railway.

either for the purpose of adding to his earnings or to his knowledge. The smallest fragments of his time were regarded by him as precious; and he was never so happy as when improving them. He missed no opportunity of extending his observations, more especially in his own immediate department; he was always acquiring new facts, and aiming at improvements in his own calling. Sometimes he failed, but his very failures only served to strengthen his hardy nature, and they eventually conducted him to success.

The "small matters" intrusted to George Stephenson, in which he succeeded, as referred to in his speech at Belper, were these: Soon after he became a brakesman at the West Moor, he observed that the ropes with which the coal was drawn out of the pit by the winding-engine were badly arranged, as he thought, and he suggested an improvement. The ropes "glued," and wore each other to tatters by perpetual friction. There was thus great wear and tear, and a serious increase in the expenses of the pit. George found that the ropes which, at other pits in the neighborhood, lasted about three months, at the West Moor Pit became worn out in about a month. As there was at that time an interruption of the trade with Russia in consequence of the war, and ropes were exceedingly dear, (about 1*s.* 5*d.* the pound,) it was obvious to him that any improvement by which a saving in the wear of ropes could be effected, would be of considerable advantage to the owners. His suggestions were approved by the head engineer of the pit, and he was encouraged to carry them into effect. He accordingly did so, and by shifting the pulley-wheels so that they worked immediately over the centre of the pit, and by an entire reärrangement of the gearing of the machine, he shortly succeeded in greatly lessening the wear and tear of the ropes, much to the advantage of the owners as well as of the workmen, who were thus enabled to labor more continuously and profitably.

He also, about the same time, attempted to effect an improvement in the winding-engine, which he worked, by placing a valve between the air-pump and condenser. This expedient, although it led to no practical results, showed that his mind was actively at work in mechanical adaptations. It continued to be his regular habit, on Saturdays, to take the engine to pieces, for the purpose, at the same time, of familiarizing himself with its action, and of placing it in a state of thorough working order. And by thus diligently mastering the details of the engine, he was enabled, as opportunity occurred, to turn to practical account the knowledge thus patiently acquired.

Such an opportunity was not long in presenting itself. In the year 1810, a pit was sunk by the "Grand Allies," (the lessees of the pit,) at the village of Killingworth, now known as the Killingworth High Pit. An atmospheric or Newcomen engine, originally made by Smeaton, was fixed there for the purpose of pumping out the water from the shaft; but somehow or other the engine failed to clear the pit. As one of the workmen has since described the circumstance—"She couldn't keep her jack-head in water; all the enginemen in the neighborhood were tried, as well as Crowther of the Ouscburn, but they were clean bet."

Good working engineers were then rarely to be met with; and many even of those who were most in repute, worked very much in the dark, without any knowledge of the principles of mechanics. The tools used in the construction of engines were of the rudest description, the fabrication of the parts being, for the most part, done by hand. A few ill-constructed lathes, with drills and boring-machines of rude construction, constituted the principal tools. The mechanics were also very clumsy, and for the most part, ill-trained. Indeed, there were only three or four establishments at that time in the kingdom that could turn out a respectable steam engine. It is not, therefore, surprising that this engine should have proved a failure, and that neither the master engineer nor any of the workmen in the neighborhood could set her to rights.

The engine went on fruitlessly pumping for nearly twelve

months, and began to be looked on as a total failure. Stephenson had gone to look at it when in course of erection, and then observed to the over-man that he thought it was defective; he also gave it as his opinion that, if there were much water in the mine, the engine would never keep it under. Of course, as he was only a brakesman, his opinion was considered to be worth very little on such a point, and no more was thought about it. He continued, however, to make frequent visits to the engine, to see "how she was getting on." From the bank-head where he worked his brake he could see the chimney smoking at the High Pit; and as the workmen were passing to and from their work, he would call out and inquire "if they had gotten to the bottom yet?" And the reply was always to the same effect—the pumping made no progress, and the workmen were still "drowned out."

One Saturday afternoon he went over to the High Pit to examine the engine more carefully than he had yet done. He had been turning the subject over in his mind; and after a long examination, he seemed to satisfy himself as to the cause of the failure. Kit Heppel, who was a sinker at the mine, said to him: "Weel, George, what do you mak' o' her? Do you think you could do anything to improve her?" "Man," said George in reply, "I could alter her and make her draw; in a week's time from this I could send you to the bottom."

Forthwith Heppel reported this conversation to Ralph Dodds, the head viewer; and Dodds being now quite in despair, and hopeless of succeeding with the engine, determined to give George's skill a trial. George had already acquired the character of a very clever and ingenious workman; and at the worst he could only fail, as the rest had done. In the evening, Mr. Dodds went towards Stephenson's cottage in search of him. He met him on the road, dressed in his Sunday's suit, about to proceed to "the preachings" in the Methodist Chapel, which he at that time attended. "Well, George," said Mr. Dodds, accosting him, "they tell me you think you can put the engine at the High

Pit to rights." "Yes sir," said George, "I think I could." "If that's the case, I'll give you a fair trial, and you must set to work immediately. We are clean drowned out, and cannot get a step further. The engineers hereabout are all bet; and if you really succeed in accomplishing what they cannot do, you may depend upon it I will make you a man for life."

It is said that George, the same evening, borrowed the "howdie horse," * and rode over to Duke's Hall, near Walbottle, where his old friend Hawthorn, the engineer to the Duke of Northumberland, then resided, and consulted him as to the improvements which he proposed to make in the pumping-engine. And next morning, Sunday though it was, (for the work must be commenced forthwith,) Stephenson entered upon his labors. The only condition that he made, before setting to work, was that he should select his own workmen. There was, as he knew, a good deal of jealousy amongst the "regular" men that a colliery brakesman should pretend to know more about their engine than they themselves did, and attempt to remedy defects which the most skilled men of their craft, including the engineer of the colliery, had failed to do. But George made the condition a *sine quâ non.* "The workmen," said he, "must neither be all Whigs or all Tories." There was no help for it, so Dodds ordered the old hands to stand aside. The men grumbled, but gave way; and George and his party went in.

The engine was taken entirely to pieces. The injection cap, being considered too small, was enlarged to nearly double its former size, the opening being increased to about twice the area. The cylinder having been found too long, was packed at the bottom with pieces of timber; these and other alterations were necessarily performed in a rough way, but, as the result proved, on true principles. The repairs occupied about four days, and by the following Wednesday the engine was carefully put together

* One of the pit horses generally employed in case of emergency in bringing the midwife to the rescue.

again and set to work. It was kept pumping all Thursday, and by the Friday afternoon the pit was cleared of water, and the workmen were "sent to the bottom," as Stephenson had promised. The alterations thus effected in the engine and in the pumping apparatus proved completely successful, and Stephenson's skill as a pump-curer became the marvel of the neighborhood.

Mr. Dodds was particularly gratified with the manner in which the job had been done, and he made Stephenson a present of ten pounds, which, though very inadequate when compared with the value of the work performed, was accepted by him with gratitude. He was proud of the gift as the first marked recognition of his skill as a workman; and he used afterwards to say that it was the biggest sum of money he had up to that time earned in one lump. Ralph Dodds, however, did more than this. He appointed Stephenson engineman at High Pit, at good wages, during the time the pit was sinking—the job lasting for about a year; and he also kept him in mind for further advancement.

Stephenson's skill as an engine-doctor soon became noised abroad, and he was called upon to prescribe remedies for all the old, wheezy, and ineffective pumping machines in the neighborhood. In this capacity he soon left the "regular" men far behind, though they in their turn were very much disposed to treat the Killingworth brakesman as no better than a quack. Nevertheless, his practice was really founded upon a close study of the principles of mechanics, and on an intimate practical acquaintance with the details of the pumping-engine.

Another of his smaller achievements in the same line is still told by the people of the district. While passing to and from his work at High Pit, he observed that the workmen in the quarry in the corner of the road leading to Long Benton, were considerably interrupted by the accumulation of water. A windmill was put up for the purpose of driving a pumping apparatus, but it failed to draw the water. Stephenson was asked what they were to do in order to clear the quarry. He said "he would set up for them an engine no bigger than a kail-pot that would clear them out in a week." And he did so. A little engine was speedily erected by him, and by its means the quarry was pumped dry in the course of a few days. Thus his local celebrity very soon became considerable.

CHAPTER VII.

COLLIERY ENGINE-WRIGHT AT KILLINGWORTH.

WHILE thus daily engaged in the curing and working of pumping-engines, George Stephenson continued diligently to employ his evenings in self-improvement. When not occupied in cleaning clocks and watches, he was busy contriving models of steam-engines and pumping-engines, or attempting to master the mysteries of perpetual motion (which he had not yet given up), or endeavoring to embody in a tangible shape the mechanical inventions which he found described in the odd volumes on mechanics which came in his way.

Many of those evenings were spent in the society of John Wigham, whose father occupied the Glebe farm at Benton, close at hand. John was a good penman and a good arithmetician, and Stephenson frequented his society chiefly for the purpose of improving himself in these points. Under Andrew Robertson, he had never thoroughly mastered the rule of three, and it was only when Wigham took him in hand that he made any decided progress towards the higher branches of arithmetic. He generally took his slate with him to Wigham's cottage, when he had his sums set, that he might work them out while tending the engine on the following day. When too busy with other work to be able to call upon Wigham in person, he sent the slate by a fellow-workman to have the former sums corrected and new ones set. So much patient perseverance could not but eventually succeed; and by dint of practice and study, Stephenson was enabled successively to master the various rules of arithmetic.

John Wigham was of great use to his pupil in many ways. He was a good talker, fond of argument, an extensive reader, as country reading went in those days, and a very suggestive thinker. Though his store of information might be comparatively small when measured with that of more highly cultivated minds, much of it was entirely new to Stephenson, who regarded him as a very clever and extraordinary person. Young as John Wigham was, he could give much useful assistance to Stephenson at that time, and his neighborly services were worth untold gold to the eager pupil. Wigham taught him to draw plans and sections; though in this branch Stephenson proved so apt that he soon surpassed his master. Wigham was also a little versed in Chemistry and Natural Philosophy, and a volume of Ferguson's Lectures on Mechanics which he possessed was a great treasure to both the students. One who remembers their evening occupations, says he used to wonder what they meant by weighing the air and water in their odd way. They were trying the specific gravities of objects; and the devices which they employed, the mechanical shifts to which they were put, were often of the rudest kind. In these evening entertainments, the mechanical contrivances were supplied by Stephenson, whilst Wigham found the scientific rationale. The opportunity thus afforded to the former of cultivating his mind by contact with one wiser than himself proved of great value, and in after-life Stephenson gratefully remembered the assistance which, when an humble workman, he had derived from John Wigham, the farmer's son.

His leisure moments thus carefully improved, it will be inferred that Stephenson was necessarily a sober man. Though his notions were never extreme on this point, he was systematically temperate. It appears that on the invitation of his master, Ralph Dodds — and an invitation from a master to a workman is not easy to resist — he had on one or two occasions, been induced to join him in a forenoon glass of ale in the public-house of the village. But one day, about noon, when Mr. Dodds had got him as far as the public-house door, on his invitation to "come and take a glass o' yill," Stephenson made a dead stop, and said firmly, "No, sir, you must excuse me; I have made a resolution to drink no more at this time of day." And he went back. He desired to retain the character of a steady workman; and the instances of men about him who had made shipwreck of their character through intemperance, were then, as now, unhappily, but too frequent. Perhaps, too, he was sober with an eye to thrift. He still steadily kept in mind the resolution which he had formed to give his son a good education, and Robert was now of an age to be sent to a better school than that which the neighboring village of Long Benton provided. There he had been some time under the charge of Rutter, the parish clerk, who kept a road-side school, where the instruction was of a very limited kind—scarcely extending beyond the child's primer and "pot-hooks." About the year 1814, Robert was accordingly sent to Bruce's academy at Newcastle, where he commenced a course of sound elementary instruction.

By dint of extra labor during his by-hours, with this object, George Stephenson had managed to save a sum of £100, which he accumulated in *guineas*, each of which he afterwards sold to Jews, who went about buying up gold coins (then dearer than silver), at twenty-six shillings a piece; and he lent out the proceeds at good interest. He was now, therefore, a comparatively thriving man. The first guinea which he had saved with so much difficulty at Black Callerton, had proved the nest-egg of future guineas; and the habits of economy and sobriety which he had so early cultivated, now enabled him to secure a firmer foothold in the world, and to command the increased esteem and respect of his fellow-workmen and employers.

At this time, and for many years after, Stephenson dwelt in a cottage standing by the side of the road leading from the West

Moor Pit to Killingworth. The railway from the West Moor Pit crosses this road close by the easternmost end of the cottage. The dwelling originally consisted of but one apartment on the ground floor, with a garret overhead, to which access was obtained by means of a step-ladder. But with his own hands Stephenson built an oven; and in course of time he added rooms to the cottage, until it grew into a comfortable four-roomed dwelling, in which he continued to live as long as he resided at Killingworth.

There was a little garden attached to the cottage, in which, while a workman, Stephenson took a pride in growing gigantic leeks and astounding cabbages. There was great competition amongst the villagers in the growth of vegetables, all of whom he excelled, excepting one of his neighbors, whose cabbages sometimes outshone his.

In the protection of his garden crops from the ravages of the birds, he invented a strange sort of "fley-craw," which moved its arms with the wind; and he fastened his garden door by means of a piece of ingenious mechanism, so that no one but himself could enter it. Indeed, his odd and eccentric contrivances excited much marvel amongst the Killingworth villagers. Thus, he won the women's admiration by connecting their cradles with the smoke-jack, and making them self-acting! Then he astonished the pitmen by attaching an alarm to the clock of the watchman, whose duty it was to call them betimes in the morning. The cottage of Stephenson was a sort of curiosity shop of models, engines, self-acting planes, and perpetual motion machines—which last contrivance, however, baffled him as effectually as it had done hundreds of preceding inventors. He also contrived a wonderful lamp which burned under water, with which he was afterwards wont to amuse the Brandling family at Gosforth—going into the fish-pond at night, lamp in hand, attracting and catching the fish, which rushed wildly towards the subaqueous flame.

Dr. Bruce tells of a competition which Stephenson had with

the joiner at Killingworth, as to which of them could make the best shoe-last; and when the former had done his work, either for the humor of the thing, or to secure fair play from the appointed judge, he took it to the Morrisons in Newcastle, and got them to put their stamp upon it. So that it is possible the Killingworth brakesman, afterwards the inventor of the safety-lamp and the originator of the railway system, and John Morrison, the last-maker, afterwards the translator of the Scriptures into the Chinese language, may have confronted each other in solemn contemplation over the successful last, which won the verdict coveted by its maker.

Sometimes he would endeavor to impart to his fellow-workmen the results of his scientific reading. Every thing that he learnt from books was so new and so wonderful to him, that he regarded the facts he drew from them in the light of discoveries, as if they had been made but yesterday. Once he tried to explain to some of the pitmen how the earth was round, and kept turning round. But his auditors flatly declared the thing to be impossible, as it was clear that "at the bottom side they must fall off!" "Ah!" said George, "you don't quite understand it yet."

In elastic muscular vigor, George Stephenson was now in his prime, and he still continued to be zealous in measuring his strength and agility with his fellow-workmen. The competitive element in his nature was strong; and his success was remarkable in these feats of rivalry. Few, if any, could lift such weights, throw the hammer and put the stone so far, or cover so great a space at a standing or running leap. One day, between the engine hour and the rope-rolling hour, Kit Heppel challenged him to leap from one high wall to another, with a deep gap between them. To Heppel's surprise and dismay, George took the standing leap, and cleared the eleven feet at a bound. Had his eye been less accurate, or his limbs less agile and sure, the feat must have cost him his life.

But so full of redundant muscular vigor was he, that leaping, putting and throwing the hammer, were not enough for him. He was also ambitious of riding on horseback, and as he had not yet been promoted to the honor of keeping a riding horse of his own, (which, however, he was shortly afterwards,) he sometimes contrived to ride for "the howdie," when the services of that official were required in the village. He would volunteer his services on such occasions, when the fleetest of the gin-horses were usually put in requisition. Sometimes, also, he borrowed the animal for a pleasure ride. On one of these latter occasions, he brought the horse back reeking; on which Tommy Mitcheson, the bank horse-keeper, a rough-spoken fellow, exclaimed to him:—"Set such fellows as you on horseback, and you'll soon ride to the de'il." But Tommy Mitcheson lived to tell the joke, and confess that, after all, there had been a better issue to George's horsemanship than that which he so hastily predicted.

Old Cree, the engine-wright at Killingworth, having been killed by an accident, George Stephenson was, in 1812, appointed engine-wright of the colliery, at the salary of £100 a year. He was also allowed the use of a galloway to ride upon, in his visits of inspection to the collieries leased by the "Grand Allies" in that neighborhood. The "Grand Allies" were a company of gentlemen, consisting of Sir Thomas Liddell (afterwards Lord Ravensworth), the Earl of Strathmore, and Mr. Stuart Wortley (afterwards Lord Wharncliffe), the lessees of the Killingworth collieries. Having been informed of the merits of Stephenson, of his indefatigable industry, and the skill which he had displayed in the repairs of the pumping-engines, they readily acceded to Mr. Dodd's recommendation, that he should be appointed the colliery engineer; and, as we shall see, they continued to honor him by distinguished marks of their approval.

He was now in a measure relieved from the daily routine of manual labor, and advanced to the grade of a higher class workman. He was no less a worker, but only in a different way. It might be inferred that he had now the command of greater leisure; but his leisure hours were more than ever given to work, either necessary or self-imposed.

When the High Pit had been sunk, and the coal was ready for working, Stephenson erected his first winding-engine, to draw the coals out of the pit, and also a pumping-engine for Long Benton colliery, both of which proved quite successful. Amongst other works of this time, he projected and laid down a self-acting incline, along the declivity which fell towards the coal-loading place near Willington, where he had formerly officiated as brakesman; and he so arranged it, that the full wagons descending drew the empty wagons up the incline. This was one of the first self-acting inclines laid down in that district.

Afterwards, in describing his occupations at this period of his life before a Committee of the House of Commons,* he said: "After making some improvements in the steam-engines above ground, I was then requested by the manager of the colliery to go under ground along with him, to see if any improvements could be made in the mines, by employing machinery as a substitute for manual labor and horse-power, in bringing the coals out of the deeper workings of the mine. On my first going down the Killingworth Pit, there was a steam-engine under ground for the purpose of drawing water from a pit that was sunk at some distance from the first shaft. The Killingworth coal-field is considerably dislocated. After the colliery was opened, at a very short distance from the shaft, one of those dislocations, or dykes as they are called, was met with. The coal was thrown down about forty yards. Considerable time was spent in sinking another pit to this depth. And on my going down to examine the work, I proposed making the engine (which had been erected some time previously) to draw the coals up an inclined plane, which descended immediately from the place where it was fixed. A considerable change was accordingly made in the mode of working the colliery, not only in applying the machinery, but

* Evidence given before the Select Committee on Accidents in Mines, 1835.

employing putters instead of horses in bringing the coals from the hewers; and by those changes, the number of horses in the pit was reduced from about one hundred to fifteen or sixteen. During the time I was engaged in making these important alterations, I went round the workings in the pit with the viewer, almost every time that he went into the mine—not only at Killingworth, but at Mountmoor, Derwentcrook, Southmoor, all of which collieries belonged to Lord Ravensworth and his partners; and the whole of the machinery in all these collieries was put under my charge."

Mr. Stephenson had now many more opportunities for improving himself in mechanics than he had hitherto possessed. His familiar acquaintance with the steam-engine proved of great value to him. The practical study which he had given to it when a workman, and the patient manner in which he had groped his way through all the details of the machine, gave him the power of a master in dealing with it, as applied to colliery purposes. His shrewd insight, together with his intimate practical acquaintance with its mechanism, enabled him to apprehend, as if by intuition, its most abstruse and difficult combinations.

Sir Thomas Liddell was frequently about the works, and he encouraged Stephenson greatly in his efforts after improvement. The subject of the locomotive engine was already closely occupying his attention; although as yet it was regarded very much in the light of a curious and costly toy, of comparatively small practical use. But Stephenson from the first detected the value of the machine, and formed an adequate conception of the gigantic might which as yet slumbered within it, and he was not slow in bending the whole faculties of his mind to the development of its extraordinary powers.

Meanwhile, the education of his son Robert at the Newcastle school proceeded apace, and the father contrived to make his progress instrumental in promoting his own improvement. The youth was entered a member of the Newcastle Literary and

Philosophical Institution, the subscription to which was *3l. 3s.* a year. He spent much of his leisure time there, reading and studying; and on Saturday afternoons, when he went home to his father's at Killingworth, he usually carried with him a volume of the Repertory of Arts and Sciences, or of the Edinburgh Encyclopædia, which furnished abundant subjects for interesting and instructive converse during the evening hours. Then John Wigham would come over from the Glebe farm to join the party, and enter into the lively scientific discussions which occurred on the subjects of their mutual reading. But many of the most valuable works belonging to the Newcastle Library were not permitted to be removed from the room; these Robert was instructed to read and study, and bring away with him descriptions and sketches for his father's information. His father also practiced him in the reading of plans and drawings, without at all referring to the written descriptions. He used to observe to his son, "A good drawing or plan should always explain itself;" and, placing a drawing of an engine or machine before the youth, he would say, "There, now, describe that to me—the arrangement and the action." Thus he taught him to read a drawing as easily as he would read a page of a book. This practice soon gave to both the greatest facility in apprehending the details of even the most difficult and complicated mechanical drawing.

The son, like his father, was very fond of reducing his scientific reading to practice. On one occasion, after reading Franklin's description of the lightning experiment, he expended all his hoarded Saturday's pennies in purchasing about half a mile of copper wire, at a brazier's shop in Newcastle. After privily preparing his kite, he sent it up at the cottage door, insulating the wire by means of a silk handkerchief. His father's pony was standing near, waiting for the master to mount. Bringing the end of the wire just over the pony's crupper, so smart an electric shock was given it, that the brute was almost knocked down. At this juncture the father issued from the door with riding-whip in hand, and was witness to the scientific trick just played off upon his galloway. "Ah! you mischievous scoundrel!" cried he to the boy, who ran off. But he inwardly chuckled with pride, nevertheless, at his son's successful experiment.

The connection of Robert with the Philosophical and Literary Society of Newcastle brought him into communication with the Rev. William Turner, one of the secretaries of the institution. That gentleman was always ready to assist the inquirer after knowledge, and took an early interest in the studious youth from Killingworth, with whose father also he soon became acquainted. Mr. Turner cheerfully and even zealously helped them in their joint inquiries, and excited, while he endeavored to satisfy, their eager thirst for scientific information. Many years afterwards, towards the close of his life, Mr. Stephenson expressed most warmly the gratitude and esteem he felt towards his revered instructor. "Mr. Turner," he said, "was always ready to assist me with books, with instruments and with counsel, gratuitously and cheerfully. He gave me the most valuable assistance and instruction, and to my dying day I can never forget the obligations which I owe to my venerable friend."

Mr. Turner's conduct towards George Stephenson was all the more worthy of admiration, because at that time the object of his friendly instruction and counsel occupied but the position of a comparatively obscure workman, of no means or influence, who had become known to him only through his anxious desire for information on scientific subjects. He could little have dreamt that the object of his almost fatherly attention would achieve a reputation so distinguished as that to which he afterwards reached, and that he would revolutionize by his inventions and improvements the internal communications of the civilized world The circumstance is encouraging to those who, like Mr. Turner, are still daily devoting themselves with equal disinterestedness to the education of the working-classes in our schools and mechanics' institutes. Though the opportunity of lending a helping hand to such men as George Stephenson may but rarely occur, yet the labors of such teachers are never without excellent results.

CHAPTER VIII.

THE BEGINNINGS OF RAILWAYS AND LOCOMOTIVES.

RAILWAYS, like most other important inventions, had very humble beginnings. The first railway, properly so called, consisted of a rude line of wooden or iron rails, laid down for the easier guidance of wagons in which coal was hauled from the pit to the shipping place. This germ of the modern railroad, planted by some unknown hand, grew to maturity gradually and slowly. Progress, in this as in almost all branches of mechanics, was effected through the exertions of many; one generation entering upon the labors of that which preceded it, and carrying onward their improvements.

There is, doubtless, a vast difference between the old road track, on which pack-horses carried the main traffic of the country down to a comparatively recent date, and the modern railroad worked by powerful locomotives: yet the change was effected by comparatively easy stages. From an early period the growing trade and commerce of the country demanded constantly increased facilities for the transport of heavy articles. This was especially necessary in the mining districts, where it is to be observed that nearly all the modern improvements in road-making have had their origin.* The prime object of all the

* "We owe," said Captain Laws, "all our railways to the collieries in the North; and the difficulty which their industry overcame, taught us to make railways, and to make locomotives to work them."—*Evidence upon the Gauge Commission*, 1845.

improvements made in the road was, so to diminish friction by increasing the smoothness of the surface, that the haulage of the coal-wagons by horses should be rendered as easy as possible. With this object, wooden rails were first laid down by one Master Beaumont* between his coal pits near Newcastle, and the staithes by the river side, probably about the year 1630. On these rails a large loaded wagon could be drawn by one horse.

The same mode of transport was shortly after generally employed in the principal colliery districts. Old Roger North thus describes the railroads as they were laid down in the neighborhood of the Tyne, in 1676:

"Another remarkable thing is their *way-leaves;* for when men have pieces of ground between the colliery and the river, they sell the leave to lead coal over their ground, and so dear that the owner of a rood of ground will expect 20*l.* per annum for this leave. The manner of the carriage is, by laying rails of timber from the colliery down to the river exactly straight and parallel, and bulky carts are made with four rowlets fitting these rails, whereby the carriage is so easy that one horse will draw down some four or five chaldron of coals, and is an immense benefit to the coal merchants." †

A century later (in 1770–1772) the same roads were found in general use by Arthur Young. The roadway was little improved, but the works on which the road was formed were sometimes of a formidable character. Speaking of wagon roads near Newcastle, Mr. Young observes: "The coal-wagon roads, from the pits to the water, are great works, carried over all sorts of inequalities of ground, so far as the distance of nine or ten miles. The tracks of the wheels are marked with pieces of wood let into

* This enterprising gentleman expended not less than 30,000*l.* in his mining speculations, the result of which is described by a local chronicler, one Mr. Gray, writing in 1649, who quaintly observes, that "within a few years he consumed all his money, and *rode home upon his light horse.*"

† Roger North's Life of Lord Keeper Guilford, A. D. 1676.

the road for the wheels of the wagons to run on, by which means one horse is enabled to draw, and that with ease, fifty or sixty bushels of coals." *

An intelligent French traveler, named Saint-Fond, who visited Newcastle in 1791, speaks in terms of high admiration of the colliery wagon ways, as superior to everything of the kind that he had seen. He describes the wooden rails as formed with a rounded upper surface, like a projecting moulding, and the wagon wheels as being "made of cast-iron, and hollowed in the manner of a metal pulley," that they might fit the rounded surface of the rails. The economy with which the coal was thus hauled to the shipping places was strongly urged upon his own countrymen, as an inducement to them to adopt a similar mode of transit.†

Similar wagon roads were laid down in the colliery districts of Scotland at a comparatively early period. At the time of the Scotch rebellion, in 1745, a railway existed between the Tranent coal pits and the small harbor of Cockenzie in East Lothian; and a portion of the line had the honor of being selected as a position for General Cope's cannon at the battle of Prestonpans.

In these rude wooden tracks we find the germ of the modern railroad. Improvements were gradually made in them. Thus at some collieries, thin plates of iron were nailed upon their upper surface, for the purpose of protecting the parts most exposed to friction. Cast-iron rails were also tried, the wooden rails having been found liable to rot. The first iron rails are supposed to have been laid down at Whitehaven as early as 1738. This cast-iron road was denominated a "plate-way," from the plate-like form in which the rails were cast. In 1767, as appears from the books of the Coal-brookdale Iron Works, in Shropshire, five or six tons of rails were cast as an experiment, on the suggestion of

* Six Months' Tour, vol. iii, p. 9.

† Travels in England, Scotland and the Hebrides, translated from the French, vol. i, pp. 142-6.

Mr. Reynolds, one of the partners; and they were shortly after laid down to form a road. In 1776, a cast-iron railway, nailed to wooden sleepers, was laid down at the Duke of Norfolk's colliery near Sheffield. The person who designed and constructed this coal line was Mr. John Curr, whose son has erroneously claimed for him the invention of the cast-iron railway. He certainly adopted it early, and thereby met the fate of men before their age; for his plan was opposed by the laboring people of the colliery, who got up a riot in which they tore up the road and burnt the coal staith, whilst Mr. Curr fled into a neighboring wood for concealment, and lay there *perdu* for three days and nights, to escape the fury of the populace.* In 1789, Mr. Wm. Jessop constructed a railway at Loughborough, in Leicestershire, and there introduced the cast-iron edge-rail, with flanches cast upon the tire of the wagon wheels to keep them on the track, instead of having the margin or flanch cast upon the rail itself; and this plan was shortly after adopted in other places. In 1800, Mr. Benjamin Outram, of Little Eaton in Derbyshire, used stone props instead of timber for supporting the ends and joinings of the rails. As this plan was pretty generally adopted, the roads became known as "Outram roads," and subsequently, for brevity's sake, "tram-roads." From this time the use of tram-roads rapidly extended, until at length they were generally adopted in the mining districts.

The progress of railways was, indeed, such that the canal interests became somewhat uneasy respecting them. The Duke of Bridgewater, when congratulated by Lord Kenyon on the successful issue of his scheme, made answer, with far-sighted shrewdness—"Yes, we shall do well enough if we can keep clear of these d—d tram-roads—there's misehief in them!" It

* Railway Locomotion and Steam Navigation, their principles and practice, by John Curr, of New South Wales. London, Williams & Co., 1847. The author of this book was son of the John Curr of Sheffield, who laid down the above railway, and who also wrote a book, which was printed in 1797, entitled "The Coal Viewer and Engine Builder's Practical Companion."

will be observed, however, that the improvements thus far effected had been confined almost entirely to *the road.* The railway wagons still continued to be drawn by horses. The gradual improvements made in the rail, by improving the firmness and smoothness of the track, had, indeed, effected considerable economy in horse-power; but that was all. What was further wanted was, the adoption of some mechanical agency applicable to the purpose of railway traction. Unless some such agency could be invented, it was clear that railway improvement had almost reached its limits. Inventors and projectors, however, presented themselves in numbers, and various schemes were proposed. One suggested the adoption of sails, supposing that the wagons might be impelled along the tram-ways like ships before the wind.* But the most favorite scheme was the application of steam power on the high-pressure principle, for the purpose of railway traction.

Solomon de Caus, who was shut up for his supposed madness in the Bicêtre at Paris, seems to have been the first to conceive the idea of employing steam for moving carriages on land, as well as ships at sea. Marion de Lorme, in a letter to the Marquis de Cinq-Mars, dated Paris, February, 1641, thus describes a visit paid to this celebrated mad-house, in the company of the English Marquis of Worcester:—"We were crossing the court, and I, more dead than alive with fright, kept close to my companion's side, when a frightful face appeared behind some immense bars, and a hoarse voice exclaimed, 'I am not mad! I am not mad! I have made a discovery that would enrich the country that adopted it.' 'What has he discovered?' asked our guide. 'Oh!'

* "Upon a long extent of iron railway, in an open country, carriages properly constructed might make profitable voyages from time to time with sails instead of horses; for though a constant or regular intercourse could not be thus carried on, yet goods of a certain sort, that are saleable at any time, might be staid till wind and weather were favorable."—*Memoirs of R. L. Edgeworth*, vol. i, p. 153. Mr. Edgeworth made several experimements with a *sailing carriage* of his invention on Hare Hatch Common, but the experiments were abandoned in consequence of the dangerous results which threatened to attend them.

answered the keeper, shrugging his shoulders, 'something trifling enough: you would never guess it; it is the use of the steam of boiling water.' I began to laugh. 'This man,' continued the keeper, 'is named Solomon de Caus; he came from Normandy four years ago, to present to the king a statement of the wonderful effects that might be produced from his invention. To listen to him, you would imagine that with steam you could navigate ships, move carriages; in fact, there is no end to the miracles which, he insists upon it, could be performed. The Cardinal sent the madman away without listening to him. Solomon de Caus, far from being discouraged, followed the Cardinal wherever he went, with the most determined perseverance, who, tired of finding him forever in his path, and annoyed at his folly, shut him up in the Bicêtre. He has even written a book about it, which I have here.'" * It appears that the Marquis of Worcester was greatly struck by the appearance of De Caus, and afterwards studied his book, portions of which he embodied in his "Century of Inventions." The Marquis is also said to have entertained the idea of moving carriages by steam power, but never embodied it in any practical form.

Savery, the Cornish miner and engineer, who did so much to develop the powers of the high-pressure engine, also proposed it as a method of propelling carriages along ordinary roads. But he took no practical measures with the view of carrying out his suggestion. The subject was shortly after, in 1759, introduced to the powerful mind of James Watt, by Dr. Robinson, then a young man studying at Glasgow College. "He threw out," says Watt, "the idea of applying the power of the steam-engine to the moving of wheel-carriages, and to other purposes; but the scheme was not matured, and was soon abandoned, on his going abroad." †

* The book is entitled "Les Raisons des Forces Mouvantes, avec diverses machines tant utiles que puissantes." Paris, 1615.

† Narrative of James Watts's Invention, in Robinson's Mechanical Philosophy, vol. ii art. *Steam-Engine.*

Watt however afterwards, in the specification of his patent of 1769, gave a description of an engine of the kind suggested by his friend Robinson, in which the expansive force of steam was proposed as the motive power. It also appears that other inventors were in the field about the same time; for in a letter written by Dr. Small to Mr. Watt, on the 18th of April, 1769, it is stated that "one Moore, a linen-draper of London, had taken out a patent for moving wheel-carriages by steam;"* but no steps were taken to reduce the invention to practice. Watt again, in his patent of 1784, described a similar engine to that indicated in his first patent, specifying the mode of applying steam to the moving of wheel-carriages. The plan proposed by Watt, although a curiosity at the present day, bears the impress of his original mind. The boiler was to be of wooden staves, hooped together with iron; the iron furnace inside the boiler, and almost entirely surrounded with water; the whole being placed on a carriage, the wheels of which were to be worked by a piston, the reciprocatory action being converted into a rotary one by toothed wheels and a sun and planet motion. The cylinder was to be seven inches in diameter, the number of strokes sixty per minute, and their length one foot. The carriage was to carry two persons. But no such carriage was ever built, Watt being too busily occupied with the perfecting of his condensing engine to proceed further with his proposed locomotive.

The first actual model of a steam-carriage, of which we have any written account, was constructed by a Frenchman named Cugnot, who exhibited it before the Marshal de Saxe in 1763.† He afterwards built an engine on the same model, at the cost of the French monarch. But when set in motion, it projected itself onward with such force, that it knocked down a wall which stood in its way; and its power being considered too great for ordinary

* The Mechanical Inventions of James Watt, by J. P. Muirhead, M.A.

† Stuart's Historical and Descriptive Anecdotes of Steam-Engines, and of their Inventors and Improvers, pp. 208, 209.

use, it was put aside as being a dangerous machine, and was stowed away in the Arsenal Museum at Paris.*

An American inventor, named Oliver Evans, was also occupied with the same idea; for, in 1772, he invented a steam-carriage to travel on common roads; and in 1787 he obtained from the State of Maryland the exclusive right to make and use steam-carriages. His invention, however, never came into practical use.

It also appears that, in 1784, William Symington, the inventor of the steam-boat, conceived the idea of employing steam power in the propulsion of carriages; and in 1786 he had a working model of a steam-carriage constructed, which he submitted to the professors and other scientific gentlemen of Edinburgh. But the state of the Scotch roads was at that time so horrible, that he considered it impracticable to proceed further with his scheme, and he shortly gave it up in favor of his project of steam-navigation.†

The first English model of a steam-carriage was made in 1784, by William Murdoch, the friend and assistant of Watt. It was on the high-pressure principle, and ran on three wheels. The boiler was heated by a spirit-lamp; and the whole machine was of very diminutive dimensions, standing little more than a foot high. Yet, on one occasion, the little engine went so fast that it outran the speed of its inventor. Mr. Buckle‡ says, that one night, after returning from his duties in the mine at Redruth, in Cornwall, Murdoch determined to try the working of his model locomotive. For this purpose, he had recourse to the walk leading to the church, about a mile from the town. The walk was rather narrow, and was bounded on either side by high edges. It

* It is now preserved in the Conservatoire des Arts et Metiers.

† See a pamphlet entitled "A Brief Narrative, proving the Right of the late William Symington, Civil Engineer, to be considered the Inventor of Steam Land Carriage Locomotion; and also the Inventor and Introducer of Steam Navigation." By Robert Bowie. London: Sherwood, Gilbert and Piper, 1833.

‡ Biographical paper on William Murdoch, read by Mr. William Buckle, of Soho, before the Institute of Mechanical Engineers, October, 1850.

was a dark night, and Murdoch set out alone to try his experiment. Having lit his lamp, the water shortly began to boil, and off started the engine with the inventor after it. He soon heard distant shouts of despair. It was too dark to perceive objects; but he shortly found, on following up the machine, that the cries for assistance proceeded from the worthy pastor of the parish, who, going towards the town on business, was met on this lonely road by the hissing and fiery little monster, which he subsequently declared he had taken to be the Evil One *in propriâ personâ.* No further steps, however, were taken by Murdoch to embody his idea of a locomotive carriage in a more practical form.

A few years later, in 1789, one Thomas Allen, of London, published "A Plan of a new-invented Machine to convey goods, merchandise, passengers, etc., from one place to another, without horses, and by the power or force of steam only." Mr. Allen proceeded upon the idea, that if steam could be applied to the turning of wheels for one purpose, such as grinding corn, it could for another, such as the haulage of carriages. From his Plan, which is in the possession of the Society of Antiquaries of Newcastle-upon-Tyne,* it appears that he intended the wheels of his machine to be cogged, and that he anticipated a speed upon a common road of "somewhat better than ten miles an hour." The plan, however, was a very crude one, and not even a model of the machine seems to have been made.

Towards the end of the last century, the adoption of rail and tram-roads, worked by horses, had become general in the colliery and mining districts. There could be no doubt as to the great economy secured by this mode of moving heavy loads, as compared with the ordinary method of haulage on common roads. As trade and manufactures were extending with great rapidity—Watt's invention of the steam-engine having given an immense impetus to industry in all its branches—it was proposed to extend

* Presented by Lord Ravensworth, August 6th, 1856.—*Proceedings of Society of Antiquaries of Newcastle-upon-Tyne*, vol. i, p. 152.

the application of railroads to the transit of merchandise and goods from town to town, especially in those districts where canals were not considered practicable. The first suggestion to this effect was published by a Northumbrian gentleman, who was daily familiar with the working of the extensive coal traffic over the railways in the neighborhood of Newcastle-upon-Tyne. On the 11th of February, 1800, Mr. Thomas, of Denton, read a paper on the subject before the Literary and Philosophical Society of Newcastle, entitled "Observations on the propriety of introducing Roads on the principle of the Coal Wagon Ways, for the general carriage of Goods, Merchandise, etc." *

In the course of the following year, the same idea was taken up by Dr. James Anderson, of Edinburgh, who proposed, in his "Recreations of Agriculture," the general adoption of railways, worked by horse-power, to be carried along the existing turnpike roads. Dr. Anderson dilated upon his idea with glowing enthusiasm. "Diminish carriage expense but one farthing," said he, "and you widen the circle of intercourse; you form, as it were, a new creation, not only of stones and earth, and trees and plants, but of men also, and, what is more, of industry, happiness, and joy." The cost of all articles of human consumption would, he alleged, be thus reduced, agriculture promoted, distances diminished, the country brought nearer to the town, and the town to the country. The number of horses required to carry on the traffic of the kingdom would be greatly diminished, and a general prosperity would, he insisted, be the result of the adoption of his system. "Indeed," said he, "it is scarcely possible to contemplate an institution from which would result a greater quantity of harmony, peace, and comfort, to persons living in the country, than would naturally result from the introduction of railroads."

That the same idea was taking hold of the more advanced minds of the country, is further evident from the fact, that in the following year (1802) Mr. Edgeworth urged the adoption of a

* Minute Books of the Literary and Philosophical Society of Newcastle, 1800.

similar plan for the transit of passengers. "Stage-coaches," he said, "might be made to go at six miles an hour, and post-chaises and gentlemen's traveling carriages at eight—both with one horse; and small stationary steam-engines, placed from distance to distance, might be made, by means of circulating chains, to draw the carriages, with a great diminution of horse-labor and expense."

While this discussion was going forward, Richard Trevethick, a captain in a Cornish tin mine, and a pupil of William Murdoch's—influenced, no doubt, by the successful action of the model engine which the latter had constructed—determined to build a steam-carriage adapted for use on common roads. He took out a patent, to secure the right of his invention, in the year 1802. Andrew Vivian, his cousin, joined with him in the patent—Vivian finding the money, and Trevethick the brains. The patent was dated the 24th March, 1802, and described as "A grant unto Richard Trevethick and Andrew Vivian, of the parish of Cranbourne, in the county of Cornwall, engineers and miners, for their invented methods of improving the construction of steam-engines, and the application thereof for driving carriages, and for other purposes." * The steam-carriage built by Trevethick on this patent presented the appearance of an ordinary stage-coach on four wheels. It had one horizontal cylinder, which, together with the boiler and the furnace-box, was placed in the rear of the hind axle. The motion of the piston was transmitted to a separate crank-axle, from which, through the medium of spur-gear, the axle of the driving-wheel (which was mounted with a fly-wheel) derived its motion. It is also worthy of note, that the steam-cocks and the force-pump, as also the bellows used for the purpose of quickening combustion in the furnace, were worked off the same crank-axle.

This was the first successful high-pressure engine constructed on the principle of moving a piston by the elasticity of steam against the pressure only of the atmosphere. Such an engine

* The number of the patent in the Record of Patents Office is 2599.

had been described by Leopold, though in his apparatus the pressure acted only on one side of the piston. In Trevethick and Vivian's engine, the piston was not only raised, but was also depressed by the action of the steam, being in this respect an entirely original invention, and of great merit. The steam was admitted from the boiler under the piston moving in a cylinder, impelling it upward. When the motion had reached its limit, the communication between the piston and the under side was shut off, and the steam allowed to escape into the atmosphere. A passage was then opened between the boiler and the upper side of the piston, which was pressed downwards, and the steam again allowed to escape into the atmosphere. Thus the power of the engine was equal to the difference between the pressure of the atmosphere and the elasticity of the steam in the boiler.

This first steam-carriage adapted for actual use on common roads, was, on the whole, tolerably successful. It excited considerable interest in the remote district, near to the Land's End, where it had been constructed. Being so far removed from the great movements and enterprise of the commercial world, Trevethick and Vivian determined upon exhibiting their machine in the metropolis, with a view, if possible, to its practical adoption for the purpose intended. In furtherance of this object, they set out with the locomotive to Plymouth, whence a sea-captain, named Vivian, was to convey it in his vessel to town. Coleridge relates, that whilst the vehicle was proceeding along the road towards the port, at the top of its speed, and had just carried away a portion of the rails of a gentleman's garden, Andrew Vivian descried ahead of them a closed toll-gate, and called out to Trevethick, who was behind, to slacken speed. He immediately shut off the steam; but the momentum was go great, that the carriage proceeded some distance, coming dead up, however, just on the right side of the gate, which was opened like lightning by the toll-keeper. "What have us got to pay here?" asked Vivian. The poor toll-man, trembling in every limb, his teeth chattering in his head, essayed a reply—"Na-na-na-na"—"What have us got to pay, I say?" "No-noth-nothing to pay! My de-dear Mr. Devil, do drive on as fast as you can! nothing to pay!"

The carriage safely reached the metropolis, and was there publicly exhibited in an inclosed piece of ground near Euston Square, where the London and Northwestern Station now stands; and it dragged behind it a wheel-carriage full of passengers. On the second day of the performance, crowds flocked to see the machine; but Trevethick, in one of his odd freaks, shut up the place, and shortly after removed the engine. While in the metropolis he secured the support of Lord Stanhope, Davies Gilbert, and other distinguished men. Sir Humphry Davy took much interest in the invention of his countryman, and, writing to his friend David Giddy, in Cornwall, shortly after the machine had reached town, he said—"I shall hope soon to hear that the roads of England are the haunts of Captain Trevethick's dragons—a characteristic name." It was felt, however, that the badness of the English roads at the time rendered it next to impossible to bring the steam-carriage into general use; so that, after having been successfully exhibited as a curiosity, it was abandoned by Trevethick as a practical failure.

In the year following the exhibition of the steam-carriage, a gentleman was laying heavy wagers as to the weight which could be hauled by a single horse on the Wadsworth and Croydon iron tram-way; and the number and weight of wagons drawn by the horse were something surprising. Trevethick very probably put the two things together—the steam-horse and the iron-way—and proceeded to construct his second or railway locomotive. The idea, however, was not entirely new to him; for although his first steam-carriage had been constructed with a view to its employment on common roads, the specification of his patent distinctly alludes to the application of his engine to traveling on railroads. In 1804 he proceeded to construct a locomotive after an improved plan for this special purpose; and in the course of the same year it was completed, and tried on the Merthyr Tydvil Railway in South Wales. On the occasion of its first trial, the engine succeeded in dragging after it several wagons containing ten tons of bar-iron, at the rate of about five miles an hour. The boiler of this engine was cylindrical, flat at the ends, and constructed of cast-iron. The furnace and flue were inside the boiler, within which the single cylinder, of eight inches in diameter and four feet six inches stroke, was immersed upright. As in the first engine, the motion of the wheels was produced by spur-gear, to which was also added a fly-wheel on one side. The waste steam was thrown into the chimney through a tube into it at right angles; but it will be obvious that this arrangement was not calculated to produce any result in the way of a steam-blast in the chimney. In fact, the waste steam seems to have been turned into the chimney in order to get rid of the nuisance caused by throwing the jet directly into the air. Trevethick was here hovering on the verge of a great discovery; but that he was not aware of the action of the blast in contributing to increase the draught, and thus quicken combustion, is clear, from the fact that he employed bellows for this special purpose; and at a much later date (in 1815) he took out a patent which included a method of urging the fire by means of fanners.

Although the locomotive tried upon the Merthyr Tydvil Railway succeeded in drawing a considerable weight, and traveled at a fair speed, it nevertheless proved, like the first steam-carriage, a practical failure. It was never employed to do regular work, but was abandoned after a few experiments. Its jolting motion champed up the cast-iron road, which was little calculated to bear so heavy a weight—though it was very light as compared with modern engines—and it was consequently dismounted from its wheels, and the engine was subsequently fixed and used to pump one of the largest pumps on the mine, for which work it was found well adapted.

Trevethick was satisfied with merely making a few experiments with his steam carriage and engine; and being a volatile genius, fond of new projects, he seems to have thought no more of the locomotive, but left it to take care of itself. Yet his machine, although unfitted for actual work, was a highly meritorious production, and its invention may be said to constitute an important link in the history of the mechanism of the steam-engine.

Trevethick having abandoned the locomotive for more promising schemes, no further progress was made with it for some years. An imaginary difficulty seems to have tended, amongst other obstacles, to prevent its adoption and improvement. This was the supposition that, if any heavy weight were placed behind the engine, the "grip" or "bite" of the smooth wheels of the locomotive upon the equally smooth iron rail, must necessarily be so slight that the wheels would slip round upon the rail, and, consequently, that the machine would not make any progress. Hence Trevethick, in his patent, recommended that the periphery of the driving-wheels should be made rough by the projection of bolts or cross-grooves, so that the adhesion of the wheels to the road might be secured. This plan was adopted in Trevethick's engine tried on the Merthyr Tydvil Railway, and its progress must therefore necessarily have been a succession of jolts, very trying to the cast-iron plates of the colliery tram-road.

Following up the presumed necessity for a more effectual adhesion between the wheels and the rails than that presented by their mere smooth contact, Mr. Blenkinsop, of Leeds, in 1811, took out a patent for a racked or tooth-rail laid along one side of the road, into which the toothed-wheel of his locomotive worked as pinions work into a rack. The boiler of his engine was supported by a carriage with four wheels without teeth, and rested immediately upon the axles. These wheels were entirely independent of the working parts of the engine, and therefore merely supported its weight on the rails, the progress being effected by means of the cogged wheel working into the cogged rail. The engine had two cylinders instead of one, as in Trevethick's engine. The invention of the double cylinder was due to Matthew Murray, of Leeds, one of the best mechanical engineers of his time, Mr. Blenkinsop, who was not himself a mechanic, having consulted him as to all the practical arrangements of his locomotive. The connecting-rods gave the motion to two pinions by cranks at right-angles to each other; these pinions communicating the motion to the wheel which worked into the toothed-rail.

Mr. Blenkinsop's engines began running on the railway extending from the Middleton collieries to the town of Leeds, a distance of about three miles and a half, on the 12th of August, 1812.* They continued for many years to be one of the principal curiosities of the neighborhood, and were visited by strangers from all parts. In the year 1816, the Grand Duke Nicholas (afterwards Emperor) of Russia observed the working of Blenkinsop's locomotive with curious interest and expressions of no slight admiration. An engine dragged behind it as many as thirty coal-wagons at a speed of about three miles and a quarter per hour. These engines continued for many years to be thus employed in the haulage of coal, and furnish the first instance of the regular employment of locomotive power for commercial purposes.

The Messrs. Chapman, of Newcastle, in 1812, endeavored to overcome the same fictitious difficulty of the want of adhesion between the wheel and the rail, by patenting a locomotive to work along the road by means of a chain stretched from one end of it tc the other. This chain was passed once round a grooved barrel-wheel under the centre of the engine: so that, when the wheel turned, the locomotive, as it were, dragged itself along the railway. An engine, constructed after this plan, was tried on the Heaton Railway, near Newcastle; but it was so clumsy in its action, there was so great a loss of power by friction, and it was found to be so expensive and difficult to keep in repair, that

* Annals of Leeds, vol. ii, p. 222.

it was very soon abandoned. Another remarkable expedient was adopted by Mr. Brunton of the Butterly Works, Derbyshire, who, in 1813, patented his Mechanical Traveler to go *upon legs*, working alternately like those of a horse!* But the engine never got beyond the experimental state, for, in one of its trials, it unhappily blew up and killed several of the bystanders. These, and other similar contrivances with the same object, projected about the same time, show that invention was actively at work, and that many minds were now anxiously laboring to solve the important problem of locomotive traction upon railways.

But the difficulties contended with by these early inventors, and the step-by-step progress which they made, will probably be best illustrated by the experiments conducted by Mr. Blackett, of Wylam, whose persevering efforts in some measure paved the way for the labors of George Stephenson, who, shortly after him, took up the question of steam locomotion, and brought it to a successful issue.

The Wylam wagon-way is one of the oldest in the north of England. Down to the year 1807, it was formed of wooden spars or rails, laid down between the colliery at Wylam—where old Robert Stephenson had worked—and the village of Lemington, some four miles down the Tyne, where the coals were loaded in keels or barges, and floated down the river past Newcastle, thence to be shipped for the London market. Each chaldron wagon was originally drawn by one horse, with a man to each horse and wagon. The rate at which the journey was performed was so slow that only two journeys were performed by each man and horse in one day, and three on the day following, the driver being allowed 7*d.* for each journey. This primitive wagon-way passed, as before stated, close in front of the cottage in which George Stephenson was born; and one of the earliest sights

* A description of Mr. Brunton's locomotive is given by Dr. Lardner in his work on 'The Steam Engine," 7th edition, p. 338.

which met his infant eyes was this wooden tram-road worked by horses.

Mr. Blackett was the first colliery owner in the North who took an interest in the locomotive engine. He went so far as to order one direct from Trevethick to work his wagon-way, about the year 1811. The engine came down to Newcastle; but for some reason or other, perhaps because of the imperfect construction of the wagon-way as compared with the weight of the engine, it was never put upon the road. Mr. Blackett eventually sold it to a Mr. Winfield, of Gateshead, by whom it was employed for many years in blowing the cupola of his iron-foundry.

Mr. Blackett had taken up the wooden road in 1808, and laid down a "plateway" of cast-iron—a single line, with sidings. The wagons continued to be drawn by horses; but the new iron road proved so much smoother than the former wooden one, that one horse, instead of drawing one chaldron wagon was now enabled to draw two. Still determined to make the experiment of working his plate-way by locomotive power, Mr. Blackett, in 1812, ordered another engine, after Trevethick's patent, which had yet two years to run. He also resolved to employ the rack-rail and toothed driving-wheel, like Blenkinsop's, and he had the road altered accordingly. The locomotive was constructed by Thomas Waters, of Gateshead, who executed the work for Trevethick on commission. This engine was of the most awkward construction imaginable. It had a single cylinder six inches in diameter, with a fly-wheel working at one side to carry the cranks over the dead points. The boiler was of cast-iron. Jonathan Foster, the Wylan engine-wright, who superintended its construction, described the machine to the writer as having "lots of pumps, cog-wheels and plugs, requiring constant attention while at work." The weight of the whole was about six tons. When completed it was conveyed to Wylam on a wagon, and there mounted upon the wooden frame supported by four pairs of wheels, which had previously been constructed for it.

A barrel of water placed on a rude frame supported by other two pairs of wheels, served as a tender. After a great deal of labor, the cumbrous and unsightly machine was got upon the road. But the engine would not move an inch! When the machinery was set in motion, Jonathan Foster says, "She flew all to pieces, and it was the biggest wonder i' the world that we were not all blewn up." The useless engine was taken off the road and sold; and Mr. Blackett's efforts were thus far in vain.

He was still, however, desirous of testing the practicability of employing locomotive power in railway traction, and he determined upon making yet another trial. Accordingly, he proceeded to build another engine, under his own and Jonathan Foster's immediate inspection, in the Wylam work-shops. The new engine had a single eight-inch cylinder, and was fitted with a fly-wheel; the driving-wheel on one side being cogged, in order to enable it to travel in the rack-rail. This engine proved more successful than its predecessors. Although it was clumsy and unsightly, it was found capable of dragging eight or nine loaded wagons down to the shipping-place at Lemington. Its weight was, however, too great for the road, and the cast-iron plates were constantly breaking.

Although this new locomotive was considered by Mr. Blackett to be an improvement upon horse traction, its working was by no means satisfactory. It crept along at a snail's pace, sometimes taking six hours to travel the five miles down to the loading-place. It was also very apt to get off the rack-rail, and then it stuck. On these occasions, the horses had to be sent out to drag on the wagons, as before. The engine itself, constructed by incompetent workmen, often broke down; its plugs, pumps, or cranks got wrong; and then the horses were sent out to drag it back to the shop. Indeed, it became so cranky, that the horses were very frequently sent out following the engine, to be in readiness to draw it along when it gave up; and at length the workmen declared it to be "a perfect plague."

Mr. Blackett did not obtain any credit amongst his neighbors for these expensive experiments. Many laughed at his machines, regarding them only in the light of costly crotchets—frequently quoting the proverb of "A fool and his money." Others regarded them as absurd innovations on the established method of hauling coal; and pronounced that they would "never answer." To some, indeed, they were the cause of considerable apprehension and alarm.

A story is still current at Wylam, of a stranger who was proceeding one dark evening down the High Street Road, as the "Black Billy" (for so the locomotive was called) was seen advancing, puffing and snorting its painful and laborious way up from Newburn. The stranger had never heard of the new engine, and was almost frightened out of his senses at its approach. An uncouth monster it must have looked, coming flaming on in the dark, working its piston up and down like a huge arm, snorting out loud blasts of steam from either nostril, and throwing out smoke and fire as it panted along. No wonder that the stranger rushed terrified through the hedge, fled across the fields, and called out to the first person he met that he had just encountered "a terrible deevil on the High Street Road."

Notwithstanding the comparative failure of his locomotive thus far, Mr. Blackett persevered with his experiments. About 1813 he took out a patent, in the name of William Hedley, his viewer, for a frame on four wheels, on which to mount the locomotive engine. One of the first experiments which he made with this frame was, to test the adhesion of the smooth wheels of a carriage, properly weighted, upon the smooth rails of the road. Six men were placed upon the frame, which was fitted up with windlasses, attached by gearing to the several wheels. When the men were set to work the windlasses, Mr. Blackett found that the adhesion of the wheels on the smooth rails was sufficient to enable them to propel the machine without slipping. Having then found the proportion which the power bore to the weight, he demonstrated, by successive experiments, that the weight of the engine would of itself produce sufficient adhesion to enable it to drag after it, on a smooth tram-road, the requisite number of wagons in all kinds of weather. Thus was the fallacy which had heretofore prevailed on this subject completely dissipated, and it was satisfactorily proved that rack-rails, toothed-wheels, endless chains, and legs, were alike unnecessary for the efficient traction of loaded wagons upon a moderately level road.

As may readily be imagined, the jets of steam from the piston, blowing off into the air at high pressure while the engine was in motion, caused considerable annoyance to horses passing along the Wylam road, at that time a public highway. The nuisance was felt to be almost intolerable, and a neighboring gentleman threatened to have it put down. To diminish the nuisance as much as possible, Mr. Blackett gave orders that so soon as any horse, or vehicle drawn by horses, came in sight, the locomotive was to be stopped, and the frightful blast of the engine thus suspended until the passing animals had got out of sight. Much interruption was caused to the working of the railway by this measure; and it excited considerable dissatisfaction amongst the workmen. The following plan was adopted to abate the nuisance: A reservoir was provided immediately behind the chimney, into which the waste steam was thrown after it had performed its office in the cylinder; and from this reservoir, the steam gradually escaped into the atmosphere without noise.* This arrangement was devised expressly for the purpose of preventing any blast in the chimney, the value of which was not detected until George Stephenson, adopting it with a preconceived design and purpose, demonstrated its importance and value—as being, in fact, the very life-breath of the locomotive engine.

* A drawing of the Wylam engine is given in the first edition of Nicholas Wood's Treatise on Railroads, 1825. The engine was placed on eight wheels, having seven rack-wheels working inside them, distributing the motion; while a barrel fixed behind the engine on two other wheels, contained the water—an exceedingly clumsy, uncouth-looking machine.

CHAPTER IX.

GEORGE STEPHENSON'S FIRST LOCOMOTIVES.

WHILE Mr. Blackett was thus experimenting and building locomotives at Wylam, George Stephenson was anxiously brooding over the same subject at Killingworth. He was no sooner appointed engine-wright of the collieries, than his attention was directed to the more economical haulage of the coal from the pits to the river side. We have seen that one of the first important improvements which he made, after being placed in charge of the colliery machinery, was to apply the surplus power of a pumping steam-engine, fixed under ground, for the purpose of drawing the coals out of the deeper workings of the Killingworth mines—by which he succeeded in effecting a large reduction in the expenditure on manual and horse labor.

The coals, when brought above ground, had next to be laboriously dragged by means of horses to the shipping staiths on the Tyne, several miles distant. The adoption of a tram-road, it is true, had tended to facilitate their transit; nevertheless, the haulage was both tedious and expensive. With the view of economizing labor, inclined planes were laid down by Mr. Stephenson, where the nature of the ground would admit of this expedient being adopted. Thus, a train of full wagons let down the incline by means of a rope running over wheels laid along the tram-road, the other end of which was attached to a train of empty wagons placed at the bottom of the parallel road on the same incline, dragged them up by the simple power of gravity—an exceedingly economical mode of working the traffic. But this applied only to a comparatively small portion of the entire length of road. An economical method of working the coal trains, instead of by means of horses—the keep of which was at the time very costly in consequence of the high price of corn—was still a great desideratum; and the best practical minds in the collieries were actively engaged in the attempt to solve the problem. Although Mr. Stephenson from an early period entertained and gave utterance to his sanguine speculations as to the "traveling engine," this was his first practical object in studying it, and endeavoring to make it an effective power; and he now proceeded to devote the entire energy of his strong practical intellect to the subject.

First, he endeavored to make himself thoroughly acquainted with what had already been done. Mr. Blackett's engines were working daily at Wylam, past the cottage in which he had been born; and thither he frequently went, sometimes in the company of Nicholas Wood, to inspect Trevethick's patent engine, and observe the improvements which were from to time made by Mr. Blackett, both in the locomotive and in the plate-way along which it worked. He carefully inspected the "Black Billy," with its single cylinder and fly-wheel, its pumps, plugs, and spur gear. After mastering its arrangements and observing the working of the machine, he did not hesitate to declare to Jonathan Foster, on the spot, his firm conviction that he could make a much better engine than Trevethick's — one that would draw steadier and work more cheaply and effectively.

In the meantime, he had also the advantage of seeing one of Blenkinsop's Leeds engines, constructed by Fenton Murray and Wood, of that town. The engine was a very excellent piece of workmanship, and a great improvement upon the clumsy machines which Mr. Stephenson had inspected at Wylam. It was placed on the tram-way, leading from the collieries of Kenton and Coxlodge, on the second of September, 1813; and a large concourse of spectators assembled to witness its first performances. This locomotive drew sixteen chaldron wagons, containing an aggregate weight of seventy tons, at the rate of about three miles an hour. George Stephenson and several of the Killingworth men were amongst the crowd of spectators that day; and after examining the engine and observing its performances, he observed to his companions, as related by Heppel, who was present, that "he thought he could make a better engine than that to go upon legs." Probably he had heard of the invention of Brunton, whose patent had by this time been published, and proved the subject of much curious speculation in the colliery districts. Certain it is that, shortly after the inspection of the Coxlodge engine, Stephenson contemplated the construction of a new locomotive, which was to surpass all which had preceded it. He observed that those engines which had been constructed up to this time, however ingenious in their arrangements, had proved practical failures. Mr. Blackett's were both clumsy and expensive. Chapman's had been removed from the Heaton tram-way in 1812, and was regarded as a total failure. And the Blenkinsop engine at Coxlodge was found very unsteady and costly in its working; besides, it pulled the rails to pieces, the entire strain being upon the rack-rail, on one side of the road. The boiler, however, having shortly blown up, there was an end of the engine; and the colliery owners did not feel encouraged to try any further experiment.

An efficient and economical working locomotive engine, therefore, still remained to be invented; and to accomplish this object Mr. Stephenson now applied himself. Profiting by what his predecessors had done, warned by their failures, and encouraged by their partial successes, he commenced his important labors. There was still wanting the man who should accomplish for the locomotive what James Watt had done for the steam-engine, and combine in a complete form the separate plans of others, embodying with them such original inventions and adaptations of his own as to entitle him to the merit of inventing the working locomotive, in the same manner as James Watt is regarded as the inventor of the working condensing engine. This was the great work upon which George Stephenson now entered, probably without any adequate idea of the immense consequences of his labors to society and civilization.

He proceeded to bring the subject of constructing a "Traveling Engine," as he then denominated the locomotive, under the notice of the lessees of the Killingworth colliery, in the year 1813. Lord Ravensworth, the principal partner, had already formed a very favorable opinion of Stephenson, from the important improvements which he had effected in the colliery engines, both above and below ground; and, after considering the matter, and hearing Stephenson's statements, he authorized him to proceed with the construction of a locomotive—though his lordship was, by some, called a fool for advancing money for such a purpose. "The first locomotive that I made," said Mr. Stephenson, many years after,* when speaking of his early career, at a public meeting in Newcastle, "was at Killingworth colliery, and with Lord Ravensworth's money. Yes, Lord Ravensworth and partners were the first to entrust me with money to make a locomotive engine. That engine was made thirty-two years ago, and we called it 'My Lord.' I said to my friends, there was no limit to the speed of such an engine, if the works could be made to stand it."

Mr. Stephenson had, however, many serious difficulties to encounter before he could get fairly to work with the erection of his locomotive. His chief difficulty was in finding mechanics sufficiently skilled in the knowledge of machinery, and in the use of tools, to follow his instructions and embody his designs, in a practical shape. Skilled mechanics were few in number in those days, and were for the most part confined to Birmingham, Manchester, Leeds, and London. The tools in use about the collieries

* Speech at the opening of the Newcastle and Darlington Railway, June 18th, 1844.

were rude and clumsy; and there were then no such facilities as now exist for turning out machinery of an entirely new character. Mr. Stephenson was thus under the necessity of working with such men and tools as were at his command; and he had in a great measure to train and instruct his workmen himself. The engine was built in the workshops at the West Moor, the leading mechanic being John Thirlwall, the colliery blacksmith, an excellent workman in his way, though quite new to the work now entrusted to him.

In this first locomotive constructed at Killingworth, Mr. Stephenson to some extent followed the plan of Blenkinsop's engine. The boiler was cylindrical, eight feet in length, and thirty-four inches in diameter, with an internal flue-tube twenty inches wide passing through the boiler. The engine had two vertical cylinders of eight inches diameter and two feet stroke let into the boiler, working the propelling gear with cross-heads and connecting rods The power of the two cylinders was continued by means of spur-wheels, which communicated the motive power to the wheels supporting the engine on the rail, instead of, as in Blenkinsop's engine, to cog-wheels which acted on the cogged rail, independent of the four supporting wheels. This adoption of spur-gear was the chief peculiarity of the new engine: it worked upon what is termed the second motion. The chimney was of wrought iron, around which was a chamber extending back to the feed-pumps, for the purpose of heating the water previous to its injection into the boiler. The engine had no springs whatever, and was mounted on a wooden frame supported on four wheels. In order, however, to neutralize as much as possible the jolts and shocks which such an engine would necessarily encounter from the obstacles and inequalities of the then very imperfect plate-way, the water barrel which served for a tender was fixed to the end of a lever and weighted, the other end of the lever being connected with the frame of the locomotive carriage. By this means the weight of the two was more equally distributed, though the contrivance did not by any means compensate for the total absence of springs.

The wheels of the new locomotive were all smooth—and it was the first engine that had been so constructed. From the first, Mr. Stephenson was convinced that the adhesion between a smooth wheel and an edgerail would be as efficient as Mr. Blackett had proved it to be between the wheel and the tramroad. And, although every one at that time argued that the adhesion upon a tramrail was by no means a criterion of what the adhesion would be upon an edgerail, Mr. Stephenson felt confident that there was no essential difference between the one and the other. Before, however, constructing the smooth wheels for his locomotive, he had the adhesion between the wheels of a carriage, properly loaded, and the rails, tested and satisfactorily proved by experiment. He made a number of workmen mount upon the wheels of a wagon moderately loaded, resting their entire weight upon the spokes on one side, and found that the wagon could thus be easily propelled forward without the wheels slipping. He then determined to fix smooth wheels upon his locomotive, in the firm belief that the weight of the engine would of itself be of sufficient adhesion for the purpose of traction.

The engine was, after much labor and anxiety, and frequent alterations of parts, at length brought to completion, having been about ten months in hand. It was first placed upon the Killingworth Railway on the 25th of July, 1814; and its powers were tried on the same day. On an ascending gradient of 1 in 450, the engine succeeded in drawing after it eight loaded carriages of thirty tons weight at about four miles an hour; and for some time after, it continued regular at work. It was indeed the most successful working engine that had yet been constructed.

Although a considerable advance upon all previous locomotives, "Blucher" (as the engine was popularly called) was nevertheless a somewhat cumbrous and clumsy machine. The parts were huddled together. The boiler constituted the principal feature; and being the foundation of the other parts, it was made to do duty not only as a generator of steam, but also as a basis for the fixings of the machinery and for the bearings of the wheels and axles. The want of springs was seriously felt; and the progress of the engine was a succession of jolts, causing considerable derangement of the machinery. The mode of communicating the motive power to the wheels by means of the spur gear also caused frequent jerks, each cylinder alternately propelling or becoming propelled by the other, as the pressure of the one upon the wheels became greater or less than the pressure of the other; and when the teeth of the cogwheel became at all worn, a rattling noise was produced during the traveling of the engine.

As the principal test of the success of the locomotive was its economy as compared with horse power, careful calculations were made with the view of ascertaining this important point. The result was, that it was found the working of the engine was at first barely economical; and at the end of the year the steam power and the horse power were ascertained to be as nearly as possible upon a par in point of cost. The fate of the locomotive in a great measure depended on this very engine. Its speed was not beyond that of a horse's walk, and the heating surface presented to the fire being comparatively small, sufficient steam could not be raised to enable it to accomplish more on an average than about three miles an hour. The result was anything but decisive; and the locomotive might have been condemned as useless, had not Mr. Stephenson at this juncture applied the steam-blast, and at once more than doubled the power of the engine.

Although Trevethick, in the engine constructed by him in 1804, allowed the waste steam to escape into the chimney, there was no object in the arrangement except to get rid of a nuisance and to avoid the unsightliness of the escape steam blowing off in jets into the open air. The exit pipe adopted by Mr. Trevethick, as we have already observed, was not contrived with the view of producing any effect; nor does any seem to have been produced, for it is certain that he afterwards abandoned the arrangement. It is remarkable that a man so ingenious as Trevethick should not have discerned its advantages; but it is clear that he could not have done so, for as late as 1815, after George Stephenson had discovered and successfully adopted the steam-blast, Trevethick took out a patent, the principal object of which was to "produce a current of air in the manner of a winnowing machine, to *blow the fire*." "Flat plates or leaves," revolving in a case, were the means adopted by him for this purpose; and in the same patent he proposed to "place in the flue a screw or set of vanes, somewhat similar to a smoke-jack," which were "to revolve by connection with the steam-engine, for the purpose of *creating an artificial draught in the chimney*." This contrivance was, however, a useless one, as Mr. Stephenson's mode of applying the blast already threw it far into the shade as a means of stimulating combustion by artificial means.

It is remarkable how little Trevethick really accomplished for railway progress, notwithstanding his ingenuity and skill as an inventor and mechanician. Instructed by Murdoch and assisted by Vivian, he was enabled to erect his first steam carriage, after which he constructed his first railway locomotive. But Trevethick was one of those men who are satisfied with making a beginning. He was not endowed with the gift of continuance—the quality of perseverance. With half the cleverness and double the application he might have successfully worked out the problem of railway locomotion, and kept ahead of all competitors.

George Stephenson was a man of an entirely different fibre. His patience was never baffled by failure; his faith was never shaken by opposition. When he became fully possessed by a conviction, he held to it with dogged tenacity, and braved the shafts of ridicule, the arguments of opponents, and the shrugs and the sneers of the utterly indifferent. Above all, he was an accurate and careful observer; and the improvements which he was enabled to effect in the locomotive were mainly due to the care with which he noted facts, and the patient reflection which he bestowed upon them, with the object of turning them to useful account.

Thus, his adoption of the steam-blast in the chimney was in no way the issue of accident; but it was an invention the result of careful observation and patient reflection. In his first locomotive the eduction steam was allowed to escape into the open atmosphere, with a hissing blast, which was the terror of horses and cattle, and was generally complained of as a nuisance. A neighboring squire even threatened an action against the colliery lessees if it were not put an end to. But Mr. Stephenson's attention had already been drawn to the circumstance of the much greater velocity with which the steam issued from the exit pipe, compared with that at which the smoke escaped from the chimney of the engine. He then thought that, by conveying the eduction steam into the chimney, by means of a small pipe, after it had performed its office in the cylinders, and allowing it to escape in a vertical direction, its velocity would be imparted to the smoke from the fire, or to the ascending current of air in the chimney,* thereby increasing the draught, and consequently the intensity of combustion in the furnace.

* Mr. Nicholas Wood gives the following account of the circumstances which led to the invention of the steam-blast by Mr. Stephenson: "When the engines were first made, the steam escaped into the atmosphere, and made comparatively little noise. It was found difficult thus to produce steam in sufficient quantity to keep the engine constantly working, or rather to obtain an adequate rapidity of current in the chimney to give sufficient intensity to the fire. To effect a greater rapidity or to increase the draught of the chimney, Mr. Stephenson thought that, by causing the steam to escape into the chimney through a pipe with its end turned upwards, the velocity of the current would be accelerated; and such was the effect." (*Practical Treatise on Railroads*, by Nicholas Wood, C.E. Ed. 1825, p. 292.) This passage clearly shows the preconceived design and purpose of Mr. Stephenson in inventing the steam-blast. A claim has, nevertheless, been set up in behalf of Timothy Hackworth, as its inventor in 1829, although the design, mechanism and rationale of the invention, as effected by Mr. Stephenson in 1815, and

The experiment was no sooner made than the power of the engine was at once more than doubled: combustion was stimulated by the blast; consequently the capability of the boiler to generate steam was greatly increased, and the effective power of the engine augmented in precisely the same proportion, without in any way adding to its weight.

This simple but beautiful expedient, though it has hitherto received but slight notice as an original idea on the part of its author, was really fraught with the most important consequences to railway communication; and it is not too much to say that the success of the locomotive depended upon its adoption. Without the steam-blast, the advantages of the "multitubular boiler" could never have been fairly tested; and it was these two improvements, working together, which afterwards secured the triumph of the locomotive on the opening of the Liverpool and Manchester Railway. Without the steam-blast, by which the intensity of combustion was kept up to the highest point, and the evolution of steam thus rapidly effected, high rates of speed by means of the combustion of coke could not have been attained, and locomotives might still have been dragging themselves unwieldily along at a little more than five or six miles an hour.

The steam-blast had scarcely been adopted, with so decided a success, when Mr. Stephenson, observing the numerous defects in his engine, and profiting by the experience which he had already acquired, determined to construct a second engine, in which to embody his improvements in their best form. Careful and cautious observation of the working of his locomotive had convinced him that the complication arising out of the action of the two cylinders being combined by spur-wheels would prevent its coming into practical use. He accordingly directed his attention to an entire change in the construction and mechanical arrangements of the machine; and in the following year, con-

adopted by him in all the Killingworth engines from that year downwards, were clearly described by Mr. Wood in 1825!

jointly with Mr. Dodds, who provided the necessary funds, he took out a patent, dated the 28th of February, 1815,* for an engine which combined in a remarkable degree the essential requisites of an economical locomotive; that is to say, few parts, simplicity in their action, and directness in the mode by which the power was communicated to the wheels supporting the engine.

This locomotive, like the first, had two vertical cylinders, which communicated *directly* with each pair of the four wheels that supported the engine, by means of a cross head and a pair of connecting-rods. But in attempting to establish a direct communication between the cylinders and the wheels that rolled upon the rails, considerable difficulties presented themselves. The ordinary joints could not be employed to unite the parts of the engine, which was a rigid mass, with the wheels rolling upon the irregular surface of the rails; for it was evident that the two rails of the line of way—more especially in those early days of imperfect construction of the permanent road—could not always be maintained at the same level—that the wheel at one end of the axle might be depressed into one part of the line which had subsided, whilst the other wheel would be comparatively elevated; and, in such a position of the axles and the wheels, it was obvious that a rigid communication between the cross head and the wheels was impracticable. Hence it became necessary to form a joint at the top of the piston-rod where it united with the cross head, so as to permit the cross head to preserve complete parallelism with the axles of the wheels with which it was in communication.

In order to obtain that degree of flexibility, combined with direct action, which was essential for insuring power and avoiding needless friction and jars from irregularities in the road, Mr.

* A grant to Ralph Dodds and George Stephenson, both of Killingworth, engineers, for their various Improvements in the Construction of Locomotive Engines Patent Office, No. 3887.

Stephenson made use of the "ball and socket" joint (so called from its resemblance to the hip-joint of the human body) for effecting a union between the ends of the cross heads where they united with the connecting rods, and between the ends of the connecting rods where they were united with the crank-pins attached to each driving wheel. By this arrangement the parallelism between the cross head and the axle was at all times maintained and preserved, without producing any serious jar or friction on any part of the machine.

The next important point was to combine each pair of wheels by means of some simple mechanism, instead of by the cog-wheels which had formerly been used. And, with this object, Mr. Stephenson began by inserting each axle into two cranks at right angles to each other, with rods communicating horizontally between them.

A locomotive was accordingly constructed upon this plan in the year 1815, and it was found to answer extremely well. But at that period the mechanical skill of the country was not equal to the task of forging crank axles of the soundness and strength necessary to stand the jars incident to locomotive work. Mr. Stephenson was accordingly compelled to fall back upon a substitute, which, although less simple and efficient, was within the mechanical capabilities of the workmen of that day, in respect of construction as well as repair. He adopted a chain which rolled over indented wheels placed on the centre of each axle, and so arranged that the two pairs of wheels were effectually coupled and made to keep pace with each other. The chain, however, after a few years use, became stretched; and then the engines were liable to irregularity in their working, especially in changing from working back to working forward again. Eventually, the chain was laid aside, and the front and hind wheels were united by rods on the outside, instead of by rods and crank axles inside, as specified in the original patent. This expedient completely answered the purpose required, without involving any expensive or difficult workmanship.

Thus, in the year 1815, Mr. Stephenson, by dint of patient and persevering labor—by careful observation of the works of others, and never neglecting to avail himself of their suggestions—had succeeded in manufacturing an engine which included the following important improvements on all previous attempts in the same direction — viz: simple and direct communication between the cylinder and the wheels rolling upon the rails; joint adhesion of all the wheels, attained by the use of horizontal connecting rods; and finally, a beautiful method of exciting the combustion of the fuel by employing the waste steam, which had formerly been allowed uselessly to escape into the air. Although many improvements in detail were afterwards introduced in the locomotive by Mr. Stephenson himself, as well as by his equally distinguished son, it is perhaps not too much to say that this engine, as a mechanical contrivance, contained the germ of all that has since been effected. It may, in fact, be regarded as the type of the present locomotive engine.

CHAPTER X.

INVENTS THE "GEORDY" SAFETY LAMP.

Explosions of fire-damp were unusually frequent in the coal mines of Northumberland and Durham about the time when George Stephenson was engaged in the construction of his first locomotives. These explosions were frequently attended with fearful loss of life and dreadful suffering to the colliery workers. Killingworth Colliery was not free from such deplorable calamities; and during the time that Stephenson was employed as a brakesman at the West Moor, several "blasts" took place in the pit, by which many workmen were scorched and killed, and the owners of the colliery sustained heavy losses. One of the most serious of these accidents occurred in 1806, not long after he had been appointed brakesman, by which ten persons were killed. Stephenson was working at the mouth of the pit at the time, and the circumstances connected with the accident seem to have made a deep impression on his mind, as will appear from the following graphic account, which he gave to a committee of the House of Commons, some thirty years after the event: *

"The pit had just ceased drawing coals, and nearly all the men had got out. It was sometime in the afternoon, a little after mid-day. There were five men that went down the pit; four of them for the purpose of preparing a place for the furnace. The fifth

* Evidence given before the Select Committee on Accidents in Mines, 26th June, 1835.

was a person who went down to set them to work. I sent this man down myself, and he had just got to the bottom of the shaft about two or three minutes, when the explosion took place. I had left the mouth of the pit, and had gone about fifty or sixty yards away, when I heard a tremendous noise, looked round, and saw the discharge come out of the pit like the discharge of a cannon. It continued to blow, I think, for a quarter of an hour, discharging everything that had come into the current. There was wood came up, stones came up, and trusses of hay that went up into the air like balloons. Those trusses had been sent down during the day, and I think they had in some measure injured the ventilation of the mine. The ground all round the top of the pit was in a trembling state. I went as near as I durst go; everything appeared cracking and rending about me. Part of the brattice, which was very strong, was blown away at the bottom of the pits. Very large pumps were lifted from their places, so that the engine could not work. The pit was divided into four by partitions; it was a large pit, fourteen feet in diameter, and partitions were put down at right angles, which made four compartments. The explosion took place in one of those four quarters, but it broke through into all the others at the bottom, and the brattice or partitions were set on fire at the first explosion. After it had continued to blow for a quarter of an hour the discharge ceased, and the atmosphere all round poured into the pit to fill up the vacant place that must have been formerly occupied by the flame. In one of the other pits, that was connected by some doors in a drift with that in which the explosion took place, were several men, some of whom succeeded in getting up safe. The ropes in the first pit were shattered to pieces by the force of the blasts, but the ropes in the other pits were still left comparatively uninjured. Nobody durst go near the shafts for some time, for fear of another explosion taking place. At last we considered it necessary to run the rope backwards and forwards, and give the miners, if there were any at the bottom of the shaft, an opportunity of catching the rope as it came to the bottom. Whenever the rope went to the bottom it was allowed to remain a short time, till we considered the men had time to cling to it. Several were safely got up in this way; and another man had got hold of the rope, and was being drawn up, when a further explosion took place at the time he was in the shaft, but it was merely like the discharge of a gun, and it did not continue like the former blast. This man, it appeared, had been helped up so far by the increased current which came about him, that, the rope running up at a great velocity, he was projected up the shaft, yet he was landed without injury; it was a singular case. Four out of the five men who had been sent down just before the explosion took place, were not seen again for three or four-and-twenty weeks, when they were found buried amongst the corves, or baskets and little carriages, at the bottom of the shafts. The overlooker, who had gone to set these men to work, knew the situation they were likely to be placed in; and, hearing the noise of the explosion before it reached the shaft, he threw himself behind some pillars near the pits, so that the current went past him; but the flame came about him, and nearly all his clothes were burnt off his back, though he laid himself down flat upon his face for safety. After the blast ceased, this person got up and found his way round to the other pit, when he got up by the rope in the manner stated. The pit continued to blast every two or three hours for about two days. It appears that the coal had taken fire, and as soon as the carburetted hydrogen gas collected in sufficient quantity to reach the part where it was burning, it ignited again; but none of the explosions were equal to the first, on account of many parts of the mine having become filled with azotic gas, or the after-damp of the mine. All the ditches in the country-side were stopped to get water to pour into the pit. We had extinguishing or fire-engines brought from Newcastle, and the water was poured in till it came above the fire, and then it was extinguished. The loss to the owners of the colliery by this accident must have been about £20,000."

Another explosion of a similar kind occurred in the same pit in 1809, by which twelve persons lost their lives. George Stephenson was working at the pit when the accident occurred, but the blast did not reach the shaft as in the former case; the unfortunate persons in the pit having been suffocated by the after-damp. But more calamitous explosions than these occurred in the neighboring collieries; one of the worst being that which took place in May, 1812, in the Felling Pit, near Gateshead, a mine belonging to Mr. Brandling, by which no fewer than ninety men and boys were suffocated or burnt to death. And a similar accident occurred in the same pit in the year following, by which twenty-two men and boys perished.

It was natural that George Stephenson, when appointed to the responsible office of colliery engine-wright, should devote his attention to the causes of these deplorable accidents, and to the means by which they might if possible be prevented. His daily occupation led him to think much and deeply on the subject. As the engineer of a colliery so extensive as that of Killingworth, where there were nearly 160 miles of gallery excavation, and in which he personally superintended the formation of inclined planes for the conveyance of the coal to the pit entrance, he was necessarily very often under ground, and brought face to face with the dangers of fire-damp. From fissures in the roofs of the galleries, carburetted hydrogen gas was constantly flowing; in some of the more dangerous places it might be heard escaping from the crevices of the coal with a hissing noise. Ventilation, firing, and all conceivable modes of drawing out the foul air had been adopted, and the more dangerous parts of the galleries were built up. Still the danger could not be wholly prevented. The miners must necessarily guide their steps through the extensive underground pathways with lighted lamps or candles, the naked flame of which, coming in contact with the inflammable air, daily exposed them, and their fellow-workers in the pit, to the risk of death in one of its most dreadful forms.

One day, in the year 1814, a workman hurried into Mr. Stephenson's cottage with the startling information that the deepest main of the colliery was on fire! He immediately hastened to the pit-mouth, about a hundred yards off, whither the women and children of the colliery were fast running, with wildness and terror depicted in every face. In an energetic voice, Stephenson ordered the engineman to lower him down the shaft in the corve. There was danger, it might be death, before him—but he must go. As those about the pit-mouth saw him descend rapidly out of sight, and heard from the gloomy depths of the shaft the mingled cries of despair and agony rising from the work people below, they gazed on the heroic man with breathless amazement.

He was soon at the bottom, and in the midst of his workmen, who were paralyzed at the danger which threatened the lives of all in the pit. Leaping from the corve on its touching the ground, he called out, "Stand back! Are there six men among you who have courage enough to follow me? If so, come, and we will put the fire out."

The Killingworth men always had the most perfect confidence in George Stephenson, and instantly they volunteered to follow him. Silence succeeded to the frantic tumult of the previous minute, and the men set to work. In every mine, bricks, mortar and tools enough are at hand, and by Stephenson's direction materials were forthwith carried to the required spot, where, in a very short time the wall was raised at the entrance to the main, he himself taking the most active part in the work. The atmospheric air was by this means excluded, the fire was extinguished, the people were saved from death, and the mine was preserved.

This anecdote of Mr. Stephenson was related to the writer, near the pit-mouth, by one of the men, Kit Heppel, who had been an eye-witness to it, and helped to build up the brick wall by which the fire was stayed, though several workmen were suffocated in the pit. Heppel relates that, when down the pit some days after, seeking out the dead bodies, the cause of the accident was the subject of some conversation between himself and Stephenson, and Heppel then asked him, "Can nothing be done to prevent such awful occurrences?" Stephenson replied that he thought something might be done. "Then," said Heppel, "the sooner you start the better; for the price of coal-mining now is *pitmen's lives.*"

The chief object to be attained was, to devise a lamp that would burn and give forth sufficient light to guide the miner in his underground labors, without communicating flame to the inflammable gas which accumulated in certain parts of the pit.* Something had already been attempted towards the invention of a colliery lamp by Dr. Clanny, of Sunderland, who, in 1813, contrived an apparatus to which he gave air from the mine through water, by means of bellows. This lamp went out of itself in inflammable gas. It was found, however, too unwieldy to be used by the miners for the purposes of their work. A committee of gentlemen was formed at Sunderland to investigate the causes of the explosions, and to devise, if possible, some means of preventing them. At the invitation of that committee, Sir Humphry Davy, then in the full zenith of his reputation, was requested to turn his attention to the subject. He accordingly visited the collieries near Newcastle on the 24th of August, 1815;† and at the close of that year, on the 9th of November, 1815, he read his celebrated paper "On the Fire-Damp of Coal Mines, and on methods of lighting the Mines so as to prevent its Explosion," before the Royal Society of London.‡

* The common means employed by the miners for lighting those parts of the mine where danger was apprehended from the fire-damp, was by a steel wheel, which, being made to revolve in contact with flint, afforded a succession of sparks; but the apparatus always required a person to work it; and though much less liable to explode the fire-damp than a common candle, yet its use was not altogether free from danger, and the light which it gave forth was very inefficient.

† Paris's Life of Davy, 4to ed., p. 310.

‡ Ibid., p. 315.

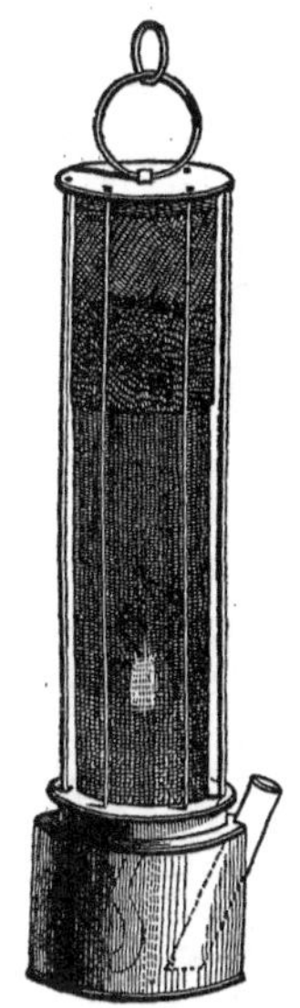
DAVY'S SAFETY LAMP.

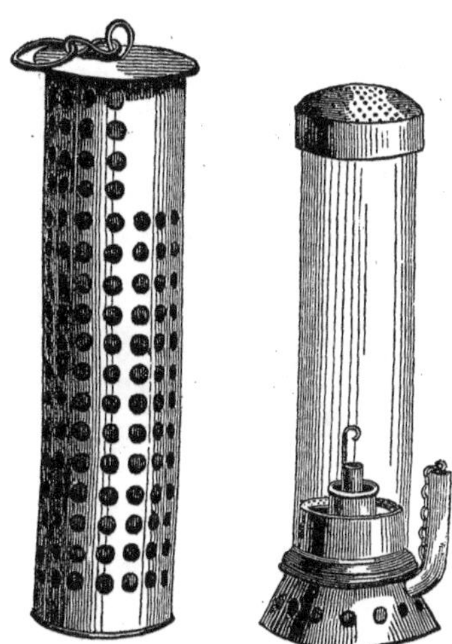
STEPHENSON'S SAFETY LAMP.

But an humbler, though not less diligent and original thinker, had been to work before him, and had already practically solved the problem of the Safety Lamp. Stephenson was of course well aware of the anxiety which prevailed in the colliery districts as to the invention of a lamp which should give light enough for the miner's work without exploding the fire-damp. The painful incidents above described only served to quicken his eagerness to master the difficulty. Let the reader bear in mind the comparative obscurity of Stephenson's position, for he was as yet but one step removed from the grade of a manual laborer —the meagreness of his scientific knowledge, all of which he had himself gathered, bit by bit, during his leisure moments, which were but few—his almost entire lack of teachers, excepting his own keen and observant eye, and his shrewd and penetrating judgment; let these things be remembered, and the invention of the Geordy Safety Lamp by Stephenson, will be regarded as an achievement of the highest merit.

For several years he had been engaged, in his own rude way, in making experiments with the fire-damp in the Killingworth mine. The pitmen used to expostulate with him on these occasions, believing that the experiments were fraught with danger. One of the sinkers, called M'Crie, observing him holding up lighted candles to the windward of the "blower" or fissure from which the inflammable gas escaped, entreated him to desist; but Stephenson's answer was, that "he was busy with a plan by which he could make his experiments useful for preserving men's lives." * On these occasions the miners usually got out of the way before he lit the gas.

In 1815, although he was very much occupied with the business of the collieries and with the improvements in his new locomotive engine, he was also busily engaged in making experi-

* Evidence given before the Committee appointed to report upon the claims of George Stephenson, relative to the invention of his Safety Lamp. Hodgson: Newcastle, 1817, p. 21

ments on inflammable gas in the Killingworth pit. As he himself afterwards related to the Committee of the House of Commons,* which sat on the subject of Accidents in Mines in 1835, the nature and object of those experiments, we cannot do better than cite his own words:

"I will give the Committee," said he, "my idea mechanically, because I knew nothing of chemistry at the time. Seeing the gas lighted up, and observing the velocity with which the flame passed along the roof, my attention was drawn to the contriving of a lamp, seeing it required a given time to pass over a given distance. My idea of making a lamp was entirely on mechanical principles; and I think I shall be found quite correct in my views, from mechanical reasoning. I knew well that the heated air from the fire drove round a smoke-jack, and that caused me to know that I could have a power from it. I also knew very well that a steam-engine chimney was built for the purpose of causing a strong current of air through the fire. Having these facts before me, and knowing the properties of heated air, I amused myself with lighting one of the blowers in the neighborhood of where I had to erect machinery. I had it on fire; the volume of flame was coming out the size of my two hands, but was not so large but that I could approach close to it. Holding my candle to the windward of the flame, I observed that it changed its color. I then got two candles, and again placed them to the windward of the flame; it changed color still more, and became duller. I got a number of candles, and placing them all to the windward, the blower ceased to burn. This then gave me the idea, that if I could construct my lamp so as, with a chimney at the top, to cause a current, it would never fire at the top of the chimney; and by seeing the velocity with which the ignited fire-damp passed along the roof, I considered that, if I could produce a current through tubes in a lamp equal to the

* Report.—Accidents in Mines, with Evidence. (Parliamentary Paper, 603. Session 1835.)

current that I saw passing along the roof, I should make a lamp that could be taken into an explosive mixture without exploding externally."

Such was Mr. Stephenson's theory, when he proceeded to embody his idea of a miner's safety lamp in a practical form. In the month of August, 1815, he requested his friend Mr. Nicholas Wood, the head viewer of the colliery, to prepare a drawing of a lamp, according to the description which he gave him. After several evenings' careful deliberations, the drawing was prepared, and it was shown to several of the head men about the works. "My first lamp," said Mr. Stephenson, describing it to the Committee above referred to, "had a chimney at the top of the lamp, and a tube at the bottom, to admit the atmospheric air, or fire-damp and air, to feed the burner or combustion of the lamp. I was not aware of the precise quantity required to feed the combustion; but to know what quantity was necessary, I had a slide at the bottom of the first tube in my lamp, to admit such a quantity of air as might eventually be found necessary to keep up the combustion." Stephenson then, accompanied by his friend Wood, went to Newcastle, and ordered a lamp to be made according to the prepared plan, by Messrs. Hogg, tinmen, at the head of the Side—a well known street in Newcastle. At the same time, they ordered a glass to be made for the lamp, at the Northumberland Glass House, in the same town. This lamp was received from the makers on the 21st of October, and was taken to Killingworth for the purpose of immediate experiment.

George Stephenson arrived home about dusk, and found Moodie, the under viewer, all anxiety, waiting for him at the cottage. The lamp was immediately filled with oil, trimmed and lighted; and all was now ready for its trial in the pit. But Mr. Wood had not yet arrived, and it was thought necessary that he should be present. He was known to be at Benton, about a mile distant. "Robert," said George, turning to his son, "you must go over for Wood, and tell him to come directly." It was a dark night; but the boy had learned implicitly to obey his father, and he set out forthwith. On his way he had to pass through Benton churchyard, and as he cautiously approached the wicket-gate and opened it, he thought he saw a white figure standing amongst the tombs! He started back, his heart fluttering, and, making the circuit of the wall of the burying-ground, he came round on the other side; and then he saw that the supposed white figure had been caused by a lanthorn flashing its light upon the grave-digger, who was busy plying his vocation at that late hour. Mr. Wood was soon found, and, mounting his horse, he rode over to Killingworth at once. When Robert reached the cottage, he found his father had just left, (it was then near eleven o'clock,) and gone down the shaft for the purpose of trying the lamp in one of the most dangerous parts of the mine!

Arrived at the bottom of the shaft with the lamp, the party directed their steps towards one of the foulest galleries in the pit, where the explosive gas was issuing through a blower in the roof of the mine with a loud hissing noise. By erecting some deal boarding around that part of the gallery into which the gas was escaping, the air was thus made more foul for the purpose of the experiment. After waiting for about an hour, Moodie, whose practical experience of fire-damp in pits was greater than that of either Stephenson or Wood, was requested by them to go into the place which had thus been made foul; and, having done so, he returned, and told them that the smell of the air was such, that if a lighted candle were now introduced an explosion must inevitably take place. He cautioned Stephenson as to the danger, both to themselves and to the pit, if the gas took fire. But Stephenson declared his confidence in the safety of his lamp, and, having lit the wick, he boldly proceeded with it towards the explosive air. The others, more timid and doubtful, hung back when they came within hearing of the blower; and, apprehensive of the danger, they retired into a safe place, out of sight of the lamp, which gradually disappeared with its bearer, in the recesses of the mine. It was a critical moment; and the danger was such as would have tried the stoutest heart. Stephenson advancing alone, with his yet untried lamp, in the depths of those underground workings—calmly venturing his own life in the determination to discover a mode by which the lives of many might be saved and death disarmed in these fatal caverns—presented an example of intrepid nerve and manly courage, more noble even than that which, in the excitement of battle and the collective impetuosity of a charge, carries a man up to the cannon's mouth.

Advancing to the place of danger, and entering within the fouled air, his lighted lamp in hand, Stephenson held it firmly out, in the full current of the blower, and within a few inches of its mouth! Thus exposed, the flame of the lamp at first increased, and then flickered and went out; but there was no explosion of the gas. Stephenson returned to his companions, who were still at a distance, and told them what had occurred. Having now acquired somewhat more confidence, they advanced with him to a point from which they could observe him repeat his experiment—but still at a safe distance. They saw that when the lighted lamp was held within the explosive mixture, there was a great flame; the lamp was almost full of fire; and then it smothered out. Again returning to his companions, he relighted the lamp, and repeated the experiment. This he did several times, with the same result. At length Wood and Moodie ventured to advance close to the fouled part of the pit; and, in making some of the later trials, Mr. Wood himself held up the lighted lamp to the blower. Such was the result of the first experiments with the *first practical Miner's Safety Lamp;* and such the daring resolution of its inventor in testing its valuable qualities.

Before leaving the pit, Stephenson expressed his opinion that, by an alteration of the lamp, which he then contemplated, he could make it burn better. This was by a change in the slide through which the air was admitted into the lower part of the lamp, under the flame. After making some experiments on the air collected at the blower, by means of bladders which were mounted with tubes of various diameters, he satisfied himself that, when the tube was reduced to a certain diameter, the explosion would not pass through; and he fashioned his slide accordingly, reducing the diameter of the tube until he conceived it was quite safe. In the course of about a fortnight the experiments were repeated in the pit, in a place purposely made foul as before. On this occasion, a large number of persons ventured to witness the experiments, which again proved perfectly successful. The lamp was not yet, however, so efficient as he desired. It required, he observed, to be kept very steady when burning in the inflammable gas, otherwise it was very liable to go out, in consequence, as he imagined, of the contact of the burnt air, (as he then called it,) or azotic gas, that lodged round the exterior of the flame. If the lamp was moved backwards and forwards, the azote came in contact with the flame and extinguished it. "It struck me," said he, "that if I put more tubes in, I should discharge the poisonous matter that hung round the flame, by admitting the air to its exterior part." Although, as he afterwards explained to the committee,* he had no access to scientific works, nor intercourse with scientific men, nor anything that could assist him in his inquiries on the subject, besides his own indefatigable spirit of inquiry, he contrived a rude apparatus by means of which he proceeded to test the explosive properties of the gas, and the velocity of current (for this was the direction of his inquiries) required to permit the explosion to pass through tubes of different diameters. His own description of these experiments, in the course of which he had several "blows up," is interesting:

"I made several experiments (and Mr. Wood was with me at

* House of Commons' Report and Evidence, already quoted, p. 97.

the time) as to the velocity required in tubes of different diameters, to prevent explosion from fire-damp. We made the mixtures in all proportions of light carburetted hydrogen with atmospheric air, in the receiver; and we found by the experiments, that when a current of the most explosive mixture that we could make was forced up a tube four-tenths of an inch in diameter, the necessary current was nine inches in a second to prevent its coming down that tube. These experiments were repeated several times. We had two or three blows up in making the experiments, by the flame getting down into the receiver, though we had a piece of very fine wire gauze put at the bottom of the pipe, between the receiver and the pipe through which we were forcing the current. In one of these experiments I was watching the flame in the tube, my son was taking the vibrations of the pendulum of the clock, and Mr. Wood was attending to give me the column of water as I called for it, to keep the current up to a certain point. As I saw the flame descending in the tube, I called for more water, and he unfortunately turned the cock the wrong way; the current ceased, the flame went down the tube, and all our implements were blown to pieces, which at the time we were not very well able to replace."

The explosion of this glass receiver, which had been borrowed from the stores of the Philosophical Society at Newcastle, for the purpose of making the experiments, caused the greatest possible dismay amongst the party; and they dreaded to inform Mr. Turner, the Secretary, of the calamity which had occurred. Fortunately none of the experimenters were injured by the explosion.

Mr. Stephenson followed up those experiments by others of a similar kind, with the view of ascertaining whether ordinary flame would pass through tubes of a small diameter; and with this object he filed off the barrels of several small keys. Placing these together, he held them perpendicularly over a strong flame, and ascertained that it did not pass upward. This served as further proof to his mind of the soundness of the principle he was pursuing.

In order to correct the defect of his first lamp, Mr. Stephenson accordingly resolved to alter it so as to admit the air to the flame by several tubes of reduced diameter, instead of by one tube. He inferred that a sufficient quantity of air would thus be introduced into the lamp for the purposes of combustion, whilst the smallness of the apertures would still prevent the explosion passing downwards—and at the same time, the "burnt air" (the cause, in his opinion, of the lamp going out) would be more effectually dislodged. He accordingly took the lamp to the shop of Mr. Matthews, a tinman in Newcastle, and had it altered so that the air was admitted by three small tubes inserted in the bottom of the lamp, the openings of which were placed on the outside of the burner, instead of having (as in the original lamp) one tube opening directly under the flame.

This second or altered lamp was tried in the Killingworth pit on the fourth of November, and was found to burn better than the first lamp, and to be perfectly safe. But as it did not yet come up entirely to the inventor's expectations, he proceeded to contrive a third lamp, in which he proposed to surround the oil vessel with a number of capillary tubes. Then it struck him, that if he cut off the middle of the tubes, or made holes in metal plates, placed at a distance from each other equal to the length of the tubes, the air would get in better, and the effect in preventing the communication of explosion would be the same. "I thought," he says, "that the air would have easier access, and the effect might be the same if I cut away the middle of the tubes; and that the flame, if it passed through the apertures at top, would not communicate the explosion to the hydrogen beyond the plate below. I constructed a lamp upon this principle, and found that, the holes having been punched very small, the flame never passed even through the first plate." *

* A Description of the Safety Lamp, invented by George Stephenson, and now in use in the Killingworth Colliery. London: Baldwin, Craddock and Joy, 1817, p. 8.

Stephenson was encouraged to persevere in the completion of his safety lamp, by the occurrence of several fatal accidents about this time in the Killingworth pit. On the 9th of November, a boy was killed by a blast in the *A* pit, at the very place where Stephenson had made the experiments with his first lamp; and, when told of the accident, he observed that if the boy had been provided with his lamp, his life would have been saved.

The third safety lamp, as finally designed by Stephenson, was in the hands of the manufacturer on the 24th of November, before he had heard of Sir Humphry Davy's experiments, or of the lamp which that gentleman proposed to construct. And this third lamp was finished, and tried in the Killingworth pit, on the 30th of the same month. On the 5th of December, Stephenson exhibited it before the Literary and Philosophical Society of Newcastle; and shortly after it came into practical use in the Killingworth collieries. To this day it is in regular use there, under the name of the "Geordy Lamp," as contradistinguished from the "Davy;" and the Killingworth pitmen have expressed to the writer their decided preference for the "Geordy." It is certainly a strong testimony in its favor, that no accident is known to have arisen from its use, since it was first introduced into the Killingworth mines. With the addition of the wire-gauze over the glass cylinder, Mr. Stephenson expressed his conviction, before the committee above referred to, that, so altered, his lamp is the safest for use, and superior to every other.*

* Report on Accidents in Coal Mines, 1835, p. 103.

CHAPTER XI.

CONTROVERSY AS TO THE INVENTION OF THE SAFETY LAMP.

Although the first safety lamp, adapted for practical use in the every-day work of coal-mining, was contrived by George Stephenson, the name of Sir Humphry Davy, as most readers are aware, has been generally identified with the invention. But a Committee of the House of Commons, which sat in 1835, after making a careful and detailed inquiry into the whole subject, distinctly stated that "the principles of its construction appear to have been practically known to Clanny and Stephenson, previously to the period when Davy brought his powerful mind to bear upon the subject." * Not only, however, were the principles of its construction known to Stephenson, but he actually made a lamp, the safety of which he demonstrated by repeated experiments, several months before Sir Humphry Davy had produced his Miner's Lamp, or published his views upon the subject.

Dr. Clanny had also constructed a Safety Lamp, before Stephenson had made the attempt, after a plan first suggested and tried by Humboldt. It was, to insulate the air within the lamp from the foul air in the mine, by means of water, and to keep up the supply of atmospheric air by the action of bellows. But this lamp, though safe, was found impracticable, and consequently was not adopted. What was wanted was a lamp that the miners could easily carry about with them; that would give light enough

* Report on Accidents in Mines, Session 1835, p. vii. (Parliamentary Paper, 603.)

to enable them to work by in dangerous places, and yet be safe. And such a lamp Stephenson was unquestionably the first to invent, construct, and prove. It will be observed, from what has been stated, that the plan which Stephenson adopted was to supply air to the flame of the lamp by means of small *tubes*. It afterwards appeared, from a paper published by Sir Humphry Davy in the following year,* that this was the idea which he contemplated embodying in his first lamp. But Stephenson had already ascertained the same fact, and confirmed it by repeated experiments with the two Safety Lamps which were constructed for him, after the designs which he furnished. It is true, his theory of the "burnt air," and of "the draught," was wrong; but his lamp was right. Torricelli did not know the rationale of his Tube, nor Otto Gürike that of his Air-pump; yet no one thinks of denying them the merit of their inventions on that account. The discoveries of Volta and Galvani were in like manner independent of theory; the greatest discoveries consisting in bringing to light certain grand facts, on which theories are afterwards framed. Mr. Stephenson pursued the Baconian method, though he did not think of that, but of inventing a safe lamp, which he knew could only be done through a process of repeated experiment. He experimented upon the fire-damp at the blowers in the mine, and also by means of the apparatus which was blown up in his cottage, as above described by himself. By experiment he distinctly ascertained that the explosion of fire-damp could not pass through small tubes; and he also effected what had not before been done by any inventor—he constructed a lamp on this principle, and repeatedly proved its safety at the risk of his life. In a letter published by Mr. Stephenson in the Philosophical Magazine† — the editor of which had given expression to the opinion, that his attempts at safety tubes and apertures had been borrowed from what he heard of Sir Humphry Davy's researches

* Philosophical Transactions for 1816, part i, p. 11.

† Philosophical Magazine for March, 1817.

—he challenged the editor to bring the evidence of facts and dates before the public, before venturing to dispute his veracity. "If fire-damp," said he, "were admitted to the flame of a lamp through a small tube—that it would be consumed by combustion, and that explosion would not pass and communicate with the external gas, was the idea I had embraced as the principle on which a safety lamp might be constructed, and this I stated to several persons long before Sir H. Davy came into this part of the country. The plan of such a lamp was seen by several, and the lamp itself was in the hands of the manufacturer during the time he was here; at which period it is not pretended he had formed any correct idea upon which he intended to act. . . . . That I pursued the principle thus discovered and applied, and constructed a lamp with three tubes, and one with small perforations, without knowing that Sir Humphry Davy had adopted the same idea, and without receiving any hint of his experiments, is what I solemnly assert."

Indeed it is perfectly clear, from the dates at which the results of Sir Humphry Davy's experiments with fire-damp were published, that it was simply impossible for Mr. Stephenson to have borrowed any of his ideas or plans. The latter, it will be remembered, had prepared the plan of his first safety lamp as early as August, 1815, at which time Sir Humphry Davy had not given much consideration to the subject, nor formed any definite ideas upon it. On the 29th of September following, Davy wrote to the Rev. Mr. Hodgson, requesting a supply of fire-damp from a blower, and informing him, at the same time, that "he had thought a good deal on the prevention of explosions from fire-damp, and entertained *strong hopes* of being able to effect something satisfactory on the subject." * It is obvious, then, that at that date Sir Humphry had not discovered the tube principle, nor applied it in the invention of a lamp. Sir H. Davy, shortly

* Letter published by the Rev. Mr. Hodgson in support of Sir H. Davy's claims, in the *Newcastle Courant* of February 1st, 1817.

after this time, is found in correspondence with the Rev. Mr. Hodgson as to the principle afterward enunciated by him, that explosion would not pass down small tubes; and on the 19th of October he wrote a *private* letter, communicating his views on the subject; but Mr. Hodgson regarded this letter as strictly confidential, and did not in any way communicate it to the public.

Mr. Stephenson, it will be remembered, placed the plan of his lamp in the hands of the Newcastle tinman in the beginning of October; and it was made and delivered to him on the 21st of October, after which it was tested at the blower in the Killingworth pit, on the evening of the same day. Up to this time nothing was known of the nature or results of Sir H. Davy's experiments. But on the 31st of October Davy communicated the fact which he had now discovered to the Rev. Dr. Gray, then Rector of Bishop Wearmouth (afterwards Bishop of Bristol), in a communication intended to be private,* but which was inadvertently read at a public meeting of coal-miners, held at Newcastle, on the 3d of November following. In that letter he stated, "When a lamp or candle is made to burn in a close vessel, having apertures only above and below, an explosive mixture of gas admitted merely enlarges the light, and then gradually extinguishes it without explosion. Again; the gas mixed in any proportion with common air, I have discovered, will not explode in a small tube, the diameter of which is not less than one-eighth of an inch, or even a larger tube, if there is a mechanical force urging the gas through the tube." This was the first public intimation of the result of Sir H. Davy's investigations; and it has been stated as probable, that the information was conveyed to Mr. Stephenson by some of his friends who might have attended the meeting. Supposing this to be so, it contained nothing which he had not already verified by repeated experiments. The fact that explosion would not pass through small tubes was by this time perfectly well known to him. He had been continuing his

* Paris's Life of Davy, 4to ed., p. 314.

experiments during the end of October and the beginning of November; his second and improved lamp, constructed on this very principle, was already completed, and it was actually tried in the Killingworth mine on the 4th of November, the very day following the meeting at which Sir Humphry Davy's discovery was first announced. Whereas the Tube Safety Lamp, which the latter had constructed on the principle above stated, was not presented to the Royal Society until the 9th of November following. Thus, Mr. Stephenson had invented and tested two several tube lamps before Sir Humphry Davy had presented his first lamp to the public.

The subject of this important invention was exciting so much interest in the northern mining districts, and Mr. Stephenson's numerous friends considered his lamp so completely successful—having stood the test of repeated experiments—that they urged him to bring his invention before the Philosophical and Literary Society of Newcastle, of some of whose apparatus he had availed himself in the course of his experiments on fire-damp. After much persuasion, he consented to do so; and a meeting was appointed for the purpose of receiving his explanations, on the evening of the 5th of December, 1815. Mr. Stephenson was at that time so diffident in manner and unpracticed in speech, that he took with him his friend, Mr. Nicholas Wood, to act as his interpreter and expositor on the occasion. From eighty to a hundred of the most intelligent members of the Society were present at the meeting, when Mr. Wood stood forward to expound the principles on which the lamp had been formed, and to describe the details of its construction. Several questions were put, to which Mr. Wood proceeded to give replies to the best of his knowledge. But Stephenson, who up to that time had stood behind Wood, screened from notice, observing that the explanations given were not quite correct, could no longer control his reserve; and standing forward, he proceeded, in his strong Northumbrian dialect, to describe the lamp, down to its minutest details. He then produced several bladders full of carburetted hydrogen, which he had collected from the blowers in the Killingworth mine, and proved the safety of his lamp by numerous experiments with the gas, repeated in various ways; his earnest and impressive manner exciting in the minds of his auditors the liveliest interest both in the inventor and his invention.

Sir Humphry Davy had not, at this time, sent down to his friends in Newcastle a specimen of his lamp; but on the 14th of December he wrote thus to the Rev. Dr. Gray: "I trust I shall be able in a very few days to send you a model of a lanthorn nearly as simple as a common glass lanthorn, and which cannot communicate explosion to the fire-damp." He further explained that the lamp was to be constructed on the principle, that "the fire-damp will not explode in tubes or feeders of a certaim small diameter," and that "the ingress into and egress of air, from this lanthorn, is through such small tubes or feeders." * Shortly after, Sir H. Davy's model lamp was received, and exhibited to the coal-miners at Newcastle, on which occasion the observation was made by several gentlemen, "Why, it is the same as Stephenson's!"

Notwithstanding Mr. Stephenson's claim to be regarded as the first inventor of the Tube Safety Lamp, his merits do not seem to have been recognized at the time beyond the limits of his own district. Sir Humphry Davy carried off all the *éclat* which attached to the discovery. What chance had the unknown workman of Killingworth with so distinguished a competitor? The one was as yet but a colliery engine-wright, scarce raised above the manual-labor class, without chemical knowledge or literary culture, pursuing his experiments in obscurity, with a view only to usefulness; the other was the scientific prodigy of his day, the pet of the Royal Society, the favorite of princes, the most brilliant of lecturers, and the most popular of philosophers. Davy had not in him much of the patient plodding of the experi-

* Paris's Life of Davy, 4to ed., pp. 314, 315.

mentalist, but he divined science as if by inspiration. He had the temperament and genius of a poet, which blazed forth in dazzling eloquence, winning for him alike the admiration of fashionable ladies, and of learned philosophers, and making his lectures and experiments "the rage" of the hour. The press blazoned forth his discoveries and enhanced his magnificent reputation; and when he presented his Davy Lamp to the world, it was regarded as but one of the many brilliant achievements which his grand and original genius had conquered.

But George Stephenson, though a less brilliant, was a no less useful and original worker; and when the merit of inventing the safety lamp became the subject of discussion, it was only reasonable and proper that his claims should be fairly considered. He had risked his life in testing the safety of his lamp, before Sir Humphry Davy had even formed a definite opinion on the subject. And though the theory on which Stephenson constructed his lamp was erroneous, he had proved it to be a safety lamp to all intents and purposes. He had discovered the lamp, though not its rationale. Such being the case, he calmly yet firmly asserted his claims as its inventor.

No small indignation was expressed by the friends of Sir Humphry Davy at this "presumption" on Stephenson's part. The scientific class united to ignore him entirely in the matter. Like many other select corporations, your men of the scientific societies were then too ready to set their shoulders together to keep out any new and self-raised man, who obtruded himself as an inventor or discoverer, in what they regarded as their special domain. Stephenson afterwards had the same battle to fight with the civil engineers, who, even for some time after he had been a constructor of gigantic railway works, refused to recognize "the colliery engine-wright" as entitled to rank amongst the class of scientific engineers.

In 1831, Dr. Paris, in his "Life of Sir Humphry Davy," *

* P. 328, 4to ed., 1831. London: Colburn and Bentley.

thus spoke of Stephenson, in connection with his claims as an inventor of the safety lamp:—"It will hereafter be scarcely believed that an invention so eminently scientific, and which could never have been derived but from the sterling treasury of science, should have been claimed on behalf of an engine-wright of Killingworth, of the name of Stephenson—a person not even possessing a knowledge of the elements of chemistry."

But Stephenson was really far above claiming for himself an invention which did not belong to him. He had already accomplished a far greater thing than even the making of a safety lamp—he had constructed the first successful locomotive, which was to be seen daily at work upon the Killingworth railway. By the important improvements he had made in the engine, he might almost be said to have *invented* it; but no one—not even the philosophers—detected as yet the significance of that wonderful machine. It excited no scientific interest, called forth no leading articles in the newspapers or the reviews, and formed the subject of no eloquent lectures at the Royal Society; for railways were, as yet, comparatively unknown, and the might which slumbered in the locomotive was scarcely, as yet, even dreamt of. What railways were to become, rested in a great measure with that "engine-wright of Killingworth, of the name of Stephenson," though he was scarcely known as yet beyond the limits of his own district.

As to the value of the invention of the safety lamp, there could be no doubt; and the colliery owners of Durham and Northumberland, to testify their sense of its importance, determined to present a testimonial to its inventor. A meeting of coal-owners was called to consider the subject; but, previous to its taking place, Mr. Robert William Brandling, of Gosforth, a warm friend of Stephenson, although he could not attend the meeting, anxious that justice should be done in the matter, addressed a letter to the committee, dated the 22d August, 1816, in which he expressed the wish that a strict examination should take place previous to

8

the adoption of any measure which might carry a decided opinion to the public, as to the person to whom the invaluable discovery of the safety lamp was actually due. "The conviction," said he, "upon my mind is, that Mr. George Stephenson, of Killingworth Colliery, is the person who first discovered and applied the principle upon which safety lamps may be constructed; for, whether the hydrogen gas is admitted through capillary tubes, or through the apertures of wire-gauze, which may be considered as merely the orifices of capillary tubes, does not, as I conceive, in the least affect the principle." * The subsequent publication of this letter formed the commencement of an animated controversy, which proceeded for some time in the local papers, and from them became transferred to the scientific journals of the day.

On the 31st of August following, a meeting of the coal-owners was held at Newcastle, for the purpose of presenting Sir Humphry Davy with a reward for "the invention of *his* Safety Lamp." To this no objection could be taken; for though the principle on which the first safety lamps of Stephenson and Davy were constructed was the same; and although Stephenson's lamp was, unquestionably, the first successful lamp that was constructed on such principle, and proved to be efficient—yet Sir H. Davy did invent a safety lamp, no doubt quite independent of all that Stephenson had done; and, having directed his careful attention to the subject, and elucidated the true theory of explosion of carburetted hydrogen, he was entitled to all praise and reward for his labors. But when the meeting of coal-owners proposed to raise a subscription for the purpose of presenting Sir H. Davy with a reward for "his invention of *the* safety lamp," the case was entirely altered; and Mr. Stephenson's friends then proceeded to assert his claims to be regarded as its first inventor.

Considerable discussion took place at the meeting referred to, after which it was adjourned until the 11th of October, when the coal-owners again met, John George Lambton, Esq., afterwards

* Durham County Advertiser, October 19th, 1816.

Earl of Durham, occupying the chair. Mr. Brandling proposed a further adjournment "until, by a comparison of dates, and an inquiry into facts, it shall be ascertained whether the merit of the invention of the safety lamp is due to Sir Humphry Davy or to George Stephenson."* Mr. Brandling, himself an inventor of a safety lamp, and a gentleman thoroughly conversant with the subject, declared his conviction that Stephenson was entitled to be regarded as "the inventor of the safety lamp;" and he was supported by Mr. Arthur Mowbray and other coal-owners present. The proposition was, however, negatived; on which Mr. Brandling and others retired from the meeting, and a committee was formed for the purpose of collecting subscriptions towards a testimonial to be presented to Sir Humphry Davy. The result was that a sum of £2000 was presented to that distinguished gentleman, as "the inventor of the safety lamp;" but, at the same time, a purse of 100 guineas was voted to George Stephenson, in consideration of what he had done in the same direction. This result was, however, very unsatisfactory to Stephenson, as well as to his friends.

The advocates of Sir Humphry Davy's claim, in their zeal for him, went so far as to insinuate that Stephenson had borrowed or pirated Davy's idea. Humble though his position was, Stephenson felt that, when brought forward as the man entitled to the credit of inventing the lamp—remembering, moreover, how much of his time and labor he had given to the work, and knowing that he had risked his life in testing the efficiency of his invention—it was due to himself, firmly but modestly, to vindicate his claims, and to repudiate the charge brought against him of having stolen the idea of another. His friend, Mr. Brandling, of Gosforth, then suggested to him that, the subject being now fairly before the public, he should publish a statement of the facts on which his claim was founded.

* A Collection of all the Letters which have appeared in the Newcastle Papers, with other Documents, relating to Safety Lamps. London: Baldwin, Cradock and Joy, 1817

This was not at all in George Stephenson's line. He had never appeared in print before; and it seemed to him to be a more formidable thing to write a letter for publication in "the papers," than even to invent a safety lamp or to design a locomotive. However, he called to his aid his son Robert, set him down before a sheet of foolscap, and when all was ready, told him to "put down there just what I tell you." The writing of this letter occupied more evenings than one; and when it was at length finished after many corrections, and fairly copied out, the father and son set out—the latter dressed in his Sunday's round jacket—to lay the joint production before Mr. Brandling, at Gosforth House. Glancing over the letter, Mr. Brandling said, "George, this will not do." "It is all true, sir," was the reply. "That may be; but it is badly written." Robert blushed, for he thought it was the penmanship that was called in question, and he had written his very best. Mr. Brandling requested his visitors to sit down, while he put the letter in a more polished form, which he did, and it was shortly after published in the local papers.

In that and subsequent communications, Mr. Stephenson treated as an ungenerous insult the insinuations made against him, that he was pretending to run a race of science with Sir Humphry Davy. "With means," said he, "too limited to allow me to indulge myself by purchasing many of those beautiful instruments that facilitate the labors of the experimental philosopher — with not always one day's respite in the week from a laborious employment — it is impossible that Mr. Hodgson (his controversial opponent) could have imagined I had the folly and presumption to enter the lists with a gentleman of talents and fortune, whose time has long been and still is devoted to the pursuit, who has an opportunity of having his ideas brought immediately to the test of experiment, and who for that purpose (an advantage beyond all others) can command the assistance of such an artist as Mr. Newman.

"Whether or not Mr. Brandling be justified in the opinion he has expressed, it appears to me may easily be decided; and if it can be proved that I took advantage, in the formation of the Safety Lamp, of any suggestions, except the printed opinions of scientific men, I deserve to lose the confidence of my honorable employers and the good opinion of my fellow men, which I feel an honest pride in declaring, even in my humble situation in life, is of more value in my estimation than any reward that generous but indiscriminating affluence can bestow." *

As a vehement controversy continued to be carried on in the Newcastle papers as to the relative merits of the respective claimants, Mr. Stephenson, in the year 1817, consented to publish the detailed plans, with descriptions, of the several safety lamps which he had contrived for use in the Killingworth Colliery. The whole forms a pamphlet of only sixteen pages of letter-press. † He there says:

"Several of my friends having expressed a wish that I would lay an engraved plan of my safety lamp before the public, with as correct an account of the dates of the invention as I am able, I have resolved to do so. I was, at the same time, advised to publish the steps by which I was led to this discovery, and the theory I had formed in my own mind upon the subject, which, with the facts from which I drew my conclusions, were freely communicated to several persons during the time I was engaged in the pursuit. With this I cannot persuade myself to comply; my habits as a practical mechanic, make me afraid of publishing theories; and I am by no means satisfied that my own reasons, or any of those I have seen published, why hydrogen gas will not explode through small apertures, are the true ones. It is sufficient for our present purpose that that fact has been dis-

* A Collection of Letters, etc., relating to the Safety Lamp, p. 38.

† A Description of the Safety Lamp, invented by George Stephenson, and now in use in the Killingworth Colliery; to which is added, an account of the lamp constructed by Sir Humphry Davy: with Engravings. London: Baldwin, Cradock and Jov, 1817.

covered, and that it has been successfully applied in the construction of a lamp that may be carried with perfect safety into the most explosive atmosphere.

"I have had frequent opportunities of employing my leisure hours in making experiments upon hydrogen gas; the result of these experiments has been the discovery of the fact above stated, and the consequent formation of a safety lamp, which has been, and is still, used in the Killingworth Colliery, and which my friends consider (with what justice the public must decide) as precisely the same in principle with that subsequently presented to their notice by Sir Humphry Davy."

After setting forth the dates at which Sir Humphry Davy made known to the public the several results of his investigations with respect to the explosive conditions of fire-damp, and of his presentation of his first tube lamp to the Royal Society, (on the 9th Nov. 1815,) Mr. Stephenson goes on to say:

"To the above facts and dates I have now only to request the attention of the public, begging them particularly to observe, that, without adverting to the time when I first embraced the idea, the principle upon which the tube lamp is constructed was published, and a plan of it shown, early in September, and that it was actually burning in the mine on the 21st of October; that Sir Humphry Davy does not announce his discovery of the fact, that explosion will not pass down *tubes*, till the 19th of October in a *private* letter to Mr. Hodgson; that my double-perforated plate lamp was certainly ordered some time before the 24th of November, tried in the mine on the 30th of the same month; and that the earliest notice I had of Sir Humphry Davy having applied wire-gauze for the same purpose, was from the 'Newcastle Chronicle' of the 23d of December.

"Upon the important variation recommended in some cases by Sir Humphry Davy, in his communication of the 9th of September, 1816, which renders his lamp the same as mine, both in construction and principle, it is unnecessary for me to dwell. In the judgment that will be pronounced upon this statement I feel the greatest confidence. This, at least, I trust, I shall have credit for, that in this publication I have been actuated solely by a justifiable attention to my own reputation, and a sincere desire to have the truth investigated, and not by any disgraceful feeling of envy at the rewards and honors which have been bestowed upon a gentleman who has directed his talents to the same object, and whose reputation is too well established to be injured by me, even if I had the baseness to attempt it."

Mr. Stephenson's friends, being fully satisfied of his claims to priority, as the inventor of the safety lamp used in the Killingworth and other collieries, proceeded to hold a public meeting * for the purpose of presenting him with a reward "for the valuable service he had thus rendered to mankind." Charles J. Brandling, Esq., occupied the chair; and a series of resolutions were passed, of which the first and most important was as follows:

"That it is the opinion of this meeting that Mr. George Stephenson, having *discovered the fact* that explosion of hydrogen gas will not pass through tubes and apertures of small dimensions, and having been *the first to apply that principle in the construction of a safety lamp*, is entitled to a public reward."

A subscription was immediately commenced with this object, and a highly influential committee was formed, consisting of the Earl of Strathmore, C. J. Brandling and others.

The subscription list was headed by Lord Ravensworth, one of the partners of the Killingworth Colliery, who showed his appreciation of the merits of Stephenson by giving 100 guineas. C. J. Brandling and partners gave a like sum; and Matthew Bell and partners, and John Brandling and partners, gave fifty guineas each.

When the resolutions of Stephenson's friends appeared in the newspapers, the scientific friends of Sir Humphry Davy in

* Held at Newcastle on the 1st of Nov. 1817.

London met, and passed a series of counter-resolutions, which they published, declaring their opinion that Mr. Stephenson was *not* the author of the discovery of the fact that explosion of hydrogen will not pass through tubes and apertures of small dimensions, and that he was *not* the first to apply that principle to the construction of a safety lamp. To these counter-resolutions were attached the well-known names of Sir Joseph Banks, P. R. S., William Thomas Brande, Charles Hatchett, W. H. Wollaston, and Thomas Young.

Mr. Stephenson's friends then, to make assurance doubly sure, and with a view to set the question at rest, determined to take evidence in detail as to the date of discovery by George Stephenson of the fact in question, and its practical application by him in the formation and actual trial of his safety lamp. The witnesses examined were, George Stephenson himself, Mr. Nicholas Wood, and John Moodie, who had been present at the first trial of the lamp; the several tinmen who made the lamps; the secretary and other members of the Literary and Philosophical Society of Newcastle, who were present at the exhibition of the third lamp; and some of the workmen at Killingworth Colliery, who had been witnesses of Mr. Stephenson's experiments on fire-damp, made with the lamps at various periods, considerably before Sir Humphry Davy's investigations were heard of. This evidence was quite conclusive to the gentlemen who investigated the subject, and they published it in 1817, together with their report, in which they solemnly declared that, "after a careful inquiry into the merits of the case, conducted, as they trust, in a spirit of fairness and moderation, they can perceive no satisfactory reason for changing their opinion." *

After setting forth a comparative table of facts and dates, in proof of their assertion "that Mr. Stephenson was the first to

* Report upon the Claims of George Stephenson relative to the Invention of his Safety Lamp, by the Committee appointed at a meeting holden in Newcastle on the 1st of November, 1817; with an appendix, containing the Evidence. Newcastle: Hodgson, 1817

construct a lamp upon the principle in question," the report proceeds:

"When the friends of Mr. Stephenson remember the humble and laborious station of life which he has occupied; when they consider the scanty means and opportunities which he has had for pursuing the researches of science; and look to the improvements and discoveries which, notwithstanding so many disadvantages, he has been enabled to make by the judicious and unremitting exercise of the energy and acuteness of his natural understanding, they cannot persuade themselves that they have said anything more than every liberal and feeling mind would most readily admit."

The Stephenson subscription, when collected, amounted to about 1000*l.*, which was presented to him, together with a silver tankard, at a public dinner given in the Assembly Rooms at Newcastle, in the month of January (1818) following. Mr. Brandling, on presenting the testimonial, observed: "A great deal of controversy, and, he was sorry to say, of animosity, had prevailed upon the subject of the 'safety lamp;' but this, he trusted, after the example of moderation that had been set by Mr. Stephenson's friends, would subside, and all personalities would cease to be remembered. As to the claim of that individual, to testify their gratitude to whom they were that day assembled, he thought every doubt must have been removed from the minds of unprejudiced persons by a perusal of the evidence recently laid before the public. He begged Mr. Stephenson's acceptance of this token of their esteem, wishing him health long to enjoy it, and to enable him to employ those talents with which Providence had blessed him, for the benefit of his fellow-creatures."

On returning thanks for the honor done him, Mr. Stephenson said: "I shall ever reflect with pride and gratitude that my labors have been honored with the approbation of such a distinguished meeting; and you may rest assured that my time, and any talent I may possess, shall hereafter be employed in such a manner as not to give you, gentlemen, any cause to regret the countenance and support which you have so generously afforded me." That Stephenson amply fulfilled his promise and pledge to his friends, his future career abundantly proved.

But what said Sir Humphry Davy as to this testimonial presented to Stephenson for having invented the safety lamp? In a private letter,* written at the time, he characterized as "infamous" the resolutions adopted by Mr. Stephenson's supporters, alleging that he had only "pirated" his invention. "It will turn out," said he, alluding to the Stephenson testimonial, "a very disgraceful business for the persons who have agitated it;" and in another letter he said, "there never was a more gross imposture than that of Stephenson."

Whilst Sir Humphry Davy spoke thus bitterly in his private letters, it is somewhat remarkable that he never once in his published papers on the subject, alluded to the fact that Mr. Stephenson had constructed and tested a safety lamp in the mine, months before his own was invented, although, as appears from a private letter since published by Dr. Paris, in his "Life of Davy," he was aware of the fact.† Nor did he refer to Humboldt's contrivance of a safety lamp in 1796, on a plan similar to that afterwards adopted by Dr. Clanny.‡ Indeed, the manner in which he alluded to the last named gentleman, who was the first to show Sir H. Davy a safety lamp, imperfect though it might be, was considered very disrespectful by Dr. Clanny and his friends.

Now, that all angry feelings between the contending parties have softened down, it is not perhaps very difficult to get at the truth of this controversy. From what we have stated, we think it must be admitted that the fact that carburetted hydrogen will

* Since published in the *Mechanics' Magazine*, vol. liv, p. 423.

† Paris's Life of Davy, 4to ed., p. 336.

‡ Journal des Mines, tom. viii, p. 839.

not explode down narrow tubes was discovered by Stephenson, and that this fact or principle was applied by him in the invention of three successive lamps constructed under his directions, all perfectly safe. Sir Humphry Davy discovered the same fact about the same time, but most probably at a subsequent date, and afterwards constructed a safety lamp which was preferred to that of Stephenson, on account of its greater cheapness and lightness. Sir H. Davy himself acknowledges that the merit of his lamp rested entirely on the discovery of the principle referred to, which had previously been ascertained and verified by the repeated experiments of Mr. Stephenson.

However great the merits of Mr. Stephenson in connection with the invention of the tube safety lamp, they cannot be regarded as detracting from the distinguished reputation of Sir Humphry Davy. His inquiries into the explosive properties of carburetted hydrogen gas were thoroughly original; and his discovery of the fact that explosion will not pass through tubes of a certain diameter, was doubtless made independently of all that Stephenson had done in verification of the same fact. It even appears that Mr. Smithson Tennant and Dr. Wollaston had observed the same fact several years before,* though neither Stephenson nor Davy knew it while they were prosecuting their experiments. Sir Humphry Davy's subsequent modification of the tube lamp, by which, while diminishing the diameter, he in the same ratio shortened the tubes without danger, and in the form of wire-gauze enveloped the safety lamp by a multiplicity of tubes, was a beautiful application of the true theory which he had formed upon the subject. "The whole theory and operation of the safety lamp," says Davy's biographer, † is nothing more than an apparatus by which the inflammable air, upon exploding in its interior, cannot pass out without being so far *cooled*, as to

* Paris's Life of Davy, 4to ed., p. 316, and note to Davy's Paper read before the Royal Society, November 9th, 1815.

† Paris's Life of Davy, 4to ed., p. 317.

deprive it of the power of communicating inflammation to the surrounding atmosphere. The principle having been once discovered, it was easy to adopt and multiply practical applications of it. From the result of these researches it became evident, that to light mines infested with fire-damp, with perfect security, it was only necessary to use an air-tight lanthorn, supplied with air from tubes of small diameter, through which explosions cannot pass, and with a chimney on a similar principle at the upper part to carry off the foul air. A common lanthorn, to be adapted to the purpose, merely required to be made air-tight in the door and sides, and to be furnished with a chimney, and the system of safety apertures below and above the flame of the lamp. Such, in fact, was Davy's first safety lamp; and having afterwards varied the arrangements of the tubes in different ways, he at length exchanged them for canals, which consisted of close concentric hollow metallic cylinders of different diameters, so placed together as to form circular canals of the diameter of from one twenty-fifth to one fortieth of an inch, and of an inch and seven tenths in length." Carrying out the same principle, the idea occurred to him of constructing the lamp entirely of wire-gauze, with apertures of from one fortieth to one sixtieth of an inch in diameter. A lamp so constructed was exhibited in January, 1816, and shortly after came into general use.

The increased number of accidents which have occurred from explosions in coal mines* since the general introduction of the Davy lamp, have led to considerable doubts as to its safety, and to inquiries as to the means by which it may be further improved; for experience has shown that, under certain circumstances, the Davy lamp is *not* safe. Mr. Stephenson was of opinion that the

* In the eighteen years previous to the introduction of the lamp, 447 persons lost their lives in the counties of Durham and Northumberland, whilst in the eighteen years following, the fatal accidents amounted to 538.—*Report on Accidents in Mines*, 1835, p. iv. The increase in the number of fatal accidents was no doubt in a great measure attributable to the circumstance that, after the invention of the safety lamp, the working was resumed in many dangerous mines, which had formerly been abandoned.

modification of his own and Sir Humphry Davy's lamp, combining the glass cylinder with the wire-gauze, was the most secure lamp; at the same time it must be admitted that the Davy and the Geordy lamps alike failed to stand the severe tests to which they were submitted by Dr. Pereira, when examined before the Committee on Accidents in Mines. Indeed, Dr. Pereira did not hesitate to say, that when exposed to a current of explosive gas, the Davy lamp is "decidedly unsafe," and that the experiments by which its safety had been "demonstrated" in the lecture-room, had proved entirely "fallacious."* The Committee, in their report, make use of these words: "Accidents have occurred when his (Sir H. Davy's) lamp was in general and careful use; no one survived to tell the tale of how these occurrences took place; conjecture supplied the want of positive knowledge most unsatisfactorily; but incidents are recorded which prove what must follow unreasonable testing of the lamp; and your Committee are constrained to believe that ignorance and a false reliance upon its merits, in cases attended with unwarrantable risks, have led to disastrous consequences."

It is worthy of remark, that under circumstances in which the wire-gauze of the Davy lamp becomes red hot from the high explosiveness of the gas, the Geordy lamp is extinguished; and we cannot but think that this fact testifies to the decidedly superior safety of the Geordy. An accident occurred in the Oaks Colliery Pit at Barnsley, on the 20th of August, 1857, which strikingly exemplified the respective qualities of the lamps. A sudden outburst of gas took place from the floor of the mine, along a distance of fifty yards. Fortunately, the men working in the pit at the time were all supplied with safety lamps — the hewers with Stephenson's, and the hurriers with Davy's. Upon this occasion, the whole of the Stephenson lamps, over a space of five hundred yards, were extinguished almost instantaneously; whereas the Davy lamps were filled with fire, and became red

* Report on Accidents in Mines, p. 290. Evidence of Dr. Pereira, F.L.S.

hot — so much so, that several of the men using them had their hands burnt by the gauze. Had a strong current of air been blowing through the gallery at the time, an explosion might thus have taken place—an accident which, it will be observed, could not occur from the use of the Geordy, which is at once extinguished so soon as the air becomes explosive.

The merits of Dr. Clanny of Sunderland, in connection with the invention of his lamp, were considerable; yet a long period elapsed before they were publicly recognized. In 1846, however, a subscription was set on foot by his friends for the purpose of presenting him with a testimonial, and Mr. Stephenson was found amongst the list of subscribers. On sending in his contribution, he said, "I believe Dr. Clanny was the first person who made the attempt to construct a lamp which should burn in an inflammable atmosphere without exploding. Such a lamp was made by Dr. Clanny, although it was not proved practicable to manage in coal mines. Nevertheless, I think great merit is due to him for what he did, and you may therefore put my name down for five pounds towards his testimonial."

CHAPTER XII.

FURTHER IMPROVEMENTS IN THE LOCOMOTIVE.

MR. STEPHENSON'S experiments on fire-damp, and his labors in connection with the invention of the safety lamp, occupied but a small portion of his time, which was mainly devoted to the engineering business of the colliery. He was also giving daily attention to the improvement of his locomotive, which every day's observation and experience satisfied him was still far from being perfect.

At that time, railways were almost exclusively confined to the colliery districts, and attracted the notice of few persons except those immediately connected with the coal trade. Nor were the colliery proprietors generally favorable to locomotive traction. There were great doubts as to its economy. Mr. Blackett's engines at Wylam were still supposed to be working at a loss; the locomotives tried at Coxlodge and Heaton, proving failures, had been abandoned; and the colliery owners, seeing the various locomotive speculations prove abortive, ceased to encourage further experiments.

Stephenson alone remained in the field after all the other improvers and inventors of the locomotive had abandoned it in despair. He continued to entertain confident expectations of its eventual success. He even went so far as to say that it would yet supersede every other tractive power. Many looked upon him as an enthusiast, which no doubt he was, but upon sufficient grounds. As for his traveling engine, it was by most persons regarded as a curious toy; and many, shaking their heads, predicted for it "a terrible blow up some day." Nevertheless, it was daily performing its work with regularity, dragging the coal wagons between the colliery and the staiths, and saving the labor of many men and horses. There was not, however, so marked a saving in the expense of working, when compared with the cost of horse traction, as to induce the northern colliery masters to adopt it as a substitute for horses. How it could be improved and rendered more efficient as well as economical, was never out of Mr. Stephenson's mind. He was quite conscious of the imperfections both of the road and of the engine; and he gave himself no rest until he had brought the efficiency of both up to a higher point. He worked his way step by step, slowly but surely; every step was in advance of the one preceding, and thus inch by inch was gained and made good as a basis for further improvements.

At an early period of his labors, or about the time when he had completed his second locomotive, he began to direct his particular attention to the state of the road; as he perceived that the extended use of the locomotive must necessarily depend in a great measure upon the perfection, solidity, continuity, and smoothness of the way along which the engine traveled. Even at that early period, he was in the habit of regarding the road and the locomotive as one machine, speaking of the rail and the wheel as "man and wife."

All railways were at that time laid in a careless and loose manner, and great inequalities of level were allowed to occur without much attention being paid to repairs; the result was that great loss of power was caused, and also great wear and tear of machinery, by the frequent jolts and blows of the wheels against the rails. His first object, therefore, was to remove the inequalities produced by the imperfect junction between rail and rail. At that time (1816) the rails were made of cast iron, each rail being about three feet long; and sufficient care was not taken to maintain the points of junction on the same level. The chairs, or cast iron pedestals into which the rails were inserted, were flat at the bottom; so that, whenever any disturbance took place in the stone blocks or sleepers supporting them, the flat base of the chair upon which the rails rested, being tilted by unequal subsidence, the end of one rail became depressed, whilst that of the other was elevated. Hence constant jolts and shocks, the reaction of which very often caused the fracture of the rails, and occasionally threw the engine off the road.

To remedy this imperfection, Mr. Stephenson devised a new chair, with an entirely new mode of fixing the rails therein. Instead of adopting the *butt joint*, which had hitherto been used in all cast iron rails, he adopted the *half-lap joint*, by which means the rails extended a certain distance over each other at the ends, somewhat like a scarf joint. These ends, instead of resting upon the flat chair, were made to rest upon the apex of a curve forming the bottom of the chair. The supports were extended from three feet to three feet nine inches or four feet apart. These rails were accordingly substituted for the old cast iron plates on the Killingworth Colliery Railway, and they were found to be a very great improvement upon the previous system, adding both to the efficiency of the horse power (still used on the railway) and to the smooth action of the locomotive engine, but more particularly increasing the efficiency of the latter.

This improved form of the rail and chair was embodied in a patent taken out in the joint names of Mr. Losh, of Newcastle, iron-founder, and of Mr. Stephenson, bearing date the 30th of September, 1816.* Mr. Losh being a wealthy, enterprising

* A grant unto William Losh, of the town and county of Newcastle-upon-Tyne, iron-founder, and George Stephenson, of Killingworth, in the county of Northumberland, engineer, for their invented new method or new methods of facilitating the conveyance of carriages, and all manner of goods and materials along railways and tram-ways, by certain inventions and improvements in the construction of the machine, carriages, car-

iron-manufacturer, and having confidence in George Stephenson and his improvements, found the money for the purpose of taking out the patent, which, in those days, was a very costly as well as troublesome affair.

The specification of the same patent also described various important improvements on all locomotives previously constructed. The wheels of the engine were improved, being altered from cast to malleable iron, in whole or in part, by which they were made lighter as well as more durable and safe. Thus the road was rendered smoother, and the wheels of the locomotive were made stronger. But the most ingenious and original contrivance embodied in this patent was the substitute for springs, which was devised by Mr. Stephenson. He contrived an arrangement by which the steam generated in the boiler was made to perform this important office! The means by which this was effected were so strikingly characteristic of true mechanical genius, that we would particularly call the reader's attention to this ingenious device, which was the more remarkable, as it was contrived long before the possibility of steam locomotion had become an object of parliamentary inquiry, or even of public interest.

It has already been observed that up to, and indeed for some time after, the period of which we speak, there was no such class of skilled mechanics, nor were there any such machinery and tools in use as are now at the disposal of inventors and manufacturers. The same difficulty had been experienced by Watt many years before, in the course of his improvements in the steam-engine; and on the occasion of the construction of his first condensing engine at Soho, Mr. Smeaton, although satisfied of its great superiority over Newcomen's, expressed strong doubts as to the practicability of getting the different parts executed with the requisite precision; and he consequently argued that, in its improved form, this powerful machine would never be generally

riage wheels, railways, and tram-ways employed for that purpose.—30th Sept. 1816, Patent Record Office, No. 4067.

introduced. Such was the low state of the mechanical arts in those days. Although skilled workmen were in course of gradual training in a few of the larger manufacturing towns, they did not, at the date of Stephenson's patent, exist in any considerable numbers, nor was there then any class of mechanics capable of constructing springs of sufficient strength and elasticity to support a locomotive engine ten tons in weight.

The rails then used being extremely light, the road soon became worn down by the traffic, and, from the inequalities of the way, the whole weight of the engine, instead of being uniformly distributed over the four wheels, was occasionally thrown almost diagonally upon two. Hence frequent jerks of the locomotive, and increased stress upon the slender road, which occasioned numerous breakages of the rails and chairs, and consequent interruptions to the safe working of the railway.

In order to avoid the dangers arising from this cause, Mr. Stephenson contrived his steam springs. He so arranged the boiler of his new patent locomotive that it was supported upon the frame of the engine by four cylinders, which opened into the interior of the boiler. These cylinders were occupied by pistons with rods, which passed downwards and pressed upon the upper side of the axles. The cylinders opening into the interior of the boiler, allowed the pressure of steam to be applied to the upper side of the piston; and that pressure being nearly equivalent to one fourth of the weight of the engine, each axle, whatever might be its position, had at all times nearly the same amount of weight to bear, and consequently the entire weight was at all times pretty equally distributed amongst the four wheels of the locomotive. Thus the four floating pistons were ingeniously made to serve the purpose of springs in equalizing the weight, and in softening the jerks of the machine; the weight of which, it must also be observed, had been increased, on a road originally calculated to bear a considerably lighter description of carriage. This mode of supporting the engine remained in use until the progress of spring-making had so far advanced that steel springs could be manufactured of sufficient strength to be used in locomotives.

The result of the actual working of George Stephenson's new locomotive and improved road amply justified the promises held forth in his "specification." The traffic was conducted with greater regularity and economy, and the superiority of the locomotive engine, as compared with horse traction, became more apparent. And it is a fact worthy of notice, that the identical engines constructed by Mr. Stephenson in 1816, are to this day to be seen in regular useful work upon the Killingworth railway, conveying heavy coal trains at the speed of between five and six miles an hour, probably as economically as any of the more perfect locomotives now in use.

Mr. Stephenson's endeavors having been attended with such marked success in the adaptation of locomotive power to railways, his attention was called by many of his friends, about the year 1818, to the application of steam to traveling on common roads. It was from this point, indeed, that the locomotive had been started, Trevethick's first engine having been constructed with this special object. Stephenson's friends having observed how far behind he had left the original projector of the locomotive in its application to railroads, perhaps naturally inferred that he would be equally successful in applying it to the purpose for which Trevethick and Vivian originally intended it.

But the accuracy with which he estimated the resistance to which loads were exposed on railways, arising from friction and gravity, led him at a very early stage to reject the idea of ever successfully applying steam power to common road traveling. In October, 1818, he made a series of careful experiments, in conjunction with Mr. Nicholas Wood, on the resistance to which carriages were exposed on railways, testing the results by means of a dynamometer of his own construction. His readiness at all times with a contrivance to enable him to overcome a difficulty, and his fertility in expedients, were in no respect more strikingly displayed than in the invention of this dynamometer. Though it was found efficient for the purpose for which it was contrived, it will not, of course, bear a comparison with other instruments for a similar purpose that have since been invented. The series of practical observations made by means of this instrument were interesting, as the first systematic attempt to determine the precise amount of resistance to carriages moving along railways.* It was thus for the first time ascertained by experiment that the friction was a constant quantity at all velocities. Although this theory had long before been developed by Vince and Coulomb, and was well known to scientific men as an established truth, yet at the time when Mr. Stephenson made his experiments, the deductions of philosophers on the subject were neither believed in nor acted upon by practical engineers. And notwithstanding that the carefully conducted experiments in question went directly to corroborate the philosophical theories on the subject, it was a considerable time (so great were the prejudices then existing) before the conclusions which they established received the sanction of practical men.

It was maintained by many that the results of these experiments led to the greatest possible mechanical absurdities. For example, it was insisted that, if friction was constant at all velocities upon a level railway, when once a power was applied to a carriage, which exceeded the friction of that carriage by the smallest possible amount, such excess of power, however small, would be able to convey the carriage along a level railway at all conceivable velocities. When this position was taken by those who opposed the conclusions to which Mr. Stephenson had arrived, he felt the greatest hesitation in maintaining his own views; for it appeared to him at first sight really the absurdity which his opponents asserted it to be. Frequent and careful

* The experiments are set forth in detail in "A Practical Treatise on Railroads and Interior Communication in General." By Nicholas Wood, Colliery Viewer, C. E. London: Hurst, Chance & Co., ed. 1831, pp. 197-253.

repetition of his experiments, however, left no doubt upon his mind as to the soundness of his conclusions—that friction was uniform at all velocities. Notwithstanding the ridicule that was thrown upon his views by many persons with whom he associated at the time, he continued to hold to this conclusion as a fact positively established; and he soon afterwards boldly maintained, that that which was an apparent absurdity was indeed an inevitable consequence, and that every increase of speed involved a necessary expenditure of power almost in a direct ratio.

It is unnecessary at this time of day to point out how obvious this consequence is, and how it is limited and controlled by various circumstances; nevertheless it is undoubted, that could you always be applying a power proportionately in excess of the resistance, a constant increase of velocity would follow without any limit. This is so obvious to professional men now, and is indeed so axiomatic, that it is unnecessary further to illustrate the position; and the discussions which took place on the subject, when the results of Mr. Stephenson's experiments were announced, are only here alluded to for the purpose of showing the difficulties he had to contend with and overcome at the time, and how small was the amount of science then blended with engineering practice.*

The other resistances to which carriages are exposed, were at the same time investigated by Mr. Stephenson. He perceived that these resistances were mainly three: the first being upon the axles of the carriage, the second (which may be called the rolling resistance) being between the circumference of the wheel and the surface of the rail, and the third being the resistance of gravity. The amount of friction and gravity was accurately ascertained; but the rolling resistance was a matter of greater difficulty, being subject to great variation. He however satisfied

* Some years afterwards, Mr. Sylvester, of Liverpool, published an able pamphlet on this subject, in which he demonstrated, in a very simple and beautiful manner, the correctness of Mr. Stephenson's conclusions

himself that it was so great when the surface presented to the wheel was of a rough character, that the idea of working steam carriages upon common roads was dismissed by him as entirely out of the question. Even so early as the period alluded to (1818) he brought his theoretical calculations to a practical test: he scattered sand upon the rails when an engine was running, and found that a small quantity was quite sufficient to retard and even to stop the most powerful locomotive that he had at that time made. And he never failed to urge this conclusive experiment upon the attention of those who were at that time wasting their money and ingenuity upon the vain attempt to apply steam power to the purpose of traveling on common roads.

Having ascertained that resistance might be taken as represented by 10 lbs. to a ton weight on a level railway, it became obvious to him that so small a rise as 1 in 100 would diminish the useful effort of a locomotive by upwards of 50 per cent. This was demonstrated by repeated experiments, and the important fact, thus rooted deeply in his mind, was never lost sight of in the course of his future railway career. It was owing in a great measure to these painstaking experiments that he thus early became convinced of the vital importance, in an economical point of view, of reducing the country through which a railway was intended to pass as nearly as possible to a level. Where, as in the first coal railways of Northumberland and Durham, the load was nearly all one way—that is, from the colliery to the shipping-place—it was an advantage to have an inclination in that direction. The strain on the powers of the locomotive was thus diminished, and it was an easy matter for it to haul the empty wagons back to the colliery up even a pretty steep incline. But when the loads were both ways, it appeared obvious to him that the railroad must be constructed as nearly as possible on a level. The strong and sagacious mind of Stephenson early recognized this broad principle; and he had so carefully worked out the important facts as to the resistance offered by adverse gradients, that he never swerved from it. At a much later period, when the days of fast engineering had arrived, while many thought him prejudiced on this point, he himself clung tenaciously to it, and invariably insisted upon the importance of flat gradients. It is true, great and important additions were made to the powers of the locomotive; but no sooner were these effected, than lines of steeper and still steeper gradients were devised, until, as he used to declare, engineers were constantly neutralizing the increased powers of the engine, and in precisely the same degree diminishing the comparative advantages of railways over common roads.

These views, thus early entertained, originated in Mr. Stephenson's mind the peculiar character of railroad works as distinguished from all other roads; for, in railroads, he early contended that large sums would be wisely expended in perforating barriers of hills with long tunnels, and in raising the lower levels with the excess cut down from the adjacent high ground. In proportion as these views forced themselves upon his mind, and were corroborated by his daily experience, he became more and more convinced of the hopelessness of applying steam locomotion to common roads; for every argument in favor of a level railway was, in his view, an argument against the rough and hilly course of a common road. Nor did he cease to urge upon the numerous patrons of road steam carriages, that if, by any amount of ingenuity, an engine could be made, which could by possibility travel on a turnpike road at a speed equal to that obtainable by horse power, and at a less cost, such an engine, if applied to the more perfect surface of a railway, would have its efficiency enormously enhanced.

For instance, he calculated that, if an engine had been constructed, and had been found to travel uniformly between London and Birmingham at an average speed of 10 miles an hour, conveying say 20 or 30 passengers, at a cost of 1*s.* per mile, it was clear that the same engine, if applied to a railway, instead of conveying 20 or 30 persons, would easily convey 200 or 300; and, instead of traveling at a speed of 10 or 12 miles an hour, a speed of at least 30 or 40 miles an hour might be attained.

All this seems trite and common-place enough, now that the thing has been done; but it was not so in those days, before it had been attempted or even thought of, excepting by one man, whom his contemporaries spoke of as a dreamer and enthusiast on the subject of railways. Then, the so-called "practical" men were bent upon a really impracticable thing — the economical application of steam power to turnpike roads; while the "enthusiast" was pursuing the only safe road to practical success. At this day it is difficult to understand how the sagacious and strong common-sense views of Stephenson on this subject, failed to force themselves sooner upon the minds of those who were persisting in their vain though ingenious attempts to apply locomotive power to ordinary roads. For a long time they continued to hold with obstinate perseverance to the belief that, for steam purposes, a soft road was better than a hard one — a road easily crushed better than one incapable of being crushed; and they held to this after it had been demonstrated in all parts of the mining districts, that iron tram-ways were better than paved roads. But the fallacy that iron was incapable of adhesion upon iron, continued to prevail, and the projectors of steam traveling on common roads only shared in the common belief. They still considered that roughness of surface was essential to produce "bite," especially in surmounting acclivities; the truth being, that they confounded roughness of surface with tenacity of surface and contact of parts; not perceiving that a yielding surface which would adapt itself to the tread of the wheel, could never become an unyielding surface to form a fulcrum for its progression. It was the error of reasoning from one circumstance, instead of taking all the circumstances into account.

CHAPTER XIII.

EDUCATION OF HIS SON.

ALTHOUGH men of Mr. Stephenson's scope and frame of mind are in a great measure independent of instruction, none understand better than they do the advantages of scholastic and scientific training. In the course of his progress in life, from the position of an humble colliery brakesman to that of chief engineer of an extensive colliery, every step of which he had gallantly won by dint of constant struggle and persistent industry, he had felt himself almost daily hampered, restrained, and placed at a disadvantage, in consequence of his want of elementary instruction.

Not having been made acquainted with what others before him had done, he had often groped his way, as it were, in the dark, in pursuit of some idea originated by his own independent thinking and observation; and when he had elaborated his views and brought them into a definite shape, lo! he very often found that his supposed original idea was an old one, and that it had long been recorded in scientific works, access to which was not within his reach. "It is a maxim," says Mr. Babbage,* "equally just in all arts, and in every science, that the man who aspires to fortune or to fame by new discoveries, must be content to examine with care the knowledge of his contemporaries, or to exhaust his efforts in inventing what he will most probably find has been

* On "Economy in Machinery and Manufactures."

better executed before." No man was more keenly conscious of this truth than George Stephenson; and he often took occasion to give expression to it in his homely and forcible way, when addressing workmen at the meetings of Mechanics' Institutes, which he took pleasure in attending during the later years of his life.

But these very efforts, fruitless though they were, and leading to no apparent beneficial results—as in the case of his long-continued labors in attempting to invent perpetual motion—yet having originated in his ardent thirst for practical knowledge, really proved of the greatest advantage to him. The very grappling with difficulty was an education of itself, and tended to develop his independent powers of thinking and action, which is indeed the highest object of intellectual discipline. Had he been early provided with those appliances which are considered requisite for the successful prosecution of mechanical and scientific study, it is possible that he might not have acquired that readiness in suggesting expedients, and contriving apparatus for the mastery of difficulties, which so strikingly distinguished him throughout his career. Indeed, in his case, as in that of so many other self-taught men, the old proverb proved true, that Necessity is the mother of Invention.

Over-much dependence upon others' teaching is somewhat to be guarded against; and it is well, even under the most thorough culture, that there should be occasional gaps left for the mind's independent operation. Stephenson's mind was indeed too full of gaps at starting; and all the knowledge with which he filled them up was of his own acquiring. Thrown from the first upon his own resources, he early acquired that habit of self-reliance which formed the backbone of his character. His strength of purpose, energetic will, untiring industry, and vigorous common sense did the rest. He may be said to have learnt his practical science first, and acquired his education afterwards; and although he was a late learner, he nevertheless lived long enough to carve his name deep on the world's records, and to leave works in which future ages will trace the hand of a giant.

Whatever Stephenson learnt, having been acquired by his own laborious efforts, was regarded by him in the light of an actual property. There were many highly educated engineers living in his day, who knew vastly more than he did—trained as they had been in all the science and learning of the schools; but there were none so apt in applying what they knew to practical purposes as the Killingworth "brakesman" and "engine-wright." The great secret of his success, however, was his cheerful perseverance. He was never cast down by obstacles, but seemed to take a pleasure in grappling with them, and he always rose from each encounter a stronger as well as a wiser man. He knew nothing of those sickly phantasies which men, who suppose themselves to be "geniuses," are so apt to indulge in; nor did his poverty or necessities ever impair the elasticity of his character. When he failed in one attempt, he tried again, and again, until eventually he succeeded.

The author well remembers hearing Mr. Stephenson deliver an address to the young men composing a Mechanics' Institute,* at whose soirées he was a frequent and favorite guest, on the subject of his early struggles, and the means by which he had achieved his success in life. "He blushed," he said, "to follow more brilliant speakers," (Dr. Buckland and others had preceded him,) "for he stood amongst them there but as an humble mechanic. He had commenced his career on a lower level than any man present there. He made that remark for the purpose of encouraging young mechanics to do as he had done—TO PERSEVERE. And he would tell them that the humblest amongst them occupied a much more advantageous position than he had done on commencing his life of labor. They had teachers who, going before them, had left their great discoveries as a legacy and a guide; and their works were now accessible to all, in such insti-

* Soiree of the Leeds Mechanics' Institute, 1st December, 1847.

tutions as that which he addressed. But he remembered the time when there was none thus to guide and instruct the young mechanic. With a free access to scientific books, he knew, from his own experience, that they could be saved much unnecessary toil and expenditure of mental capital. Many ingenious young mechanics, if they failed to profit by the teaching of those who had preceded them, might often be induced to believe that they had hit upon some discovery in mechanics; and when they had gone on spending both time and money, they would only arrive at the unpleasant discovery that what they had cherished as an original invention had been known many years before, and was to be found recorded in scientific works."

On another similar occasion, speaking before the same audience,* he observed, that "all his life through he had felt very severely the want of education. He had set out in life without much learning—nay, he might almost say, without any at all. Now, without education of some sort, it was scarcely possible for a man to succeed in any undertaking. But with a sound and comprehensive education, many an humble mechanic might attain to the rank of civil engineer. PERSEVERANCE was one of the principal qualifications requisite on the part of any young man who entered that profession. The civil engineer had many difficulties to contend with; but if a man wished to rise to the higher grades of that, or indeed any other profession, he must never see any difficulties before him. Obstacles might appear to be difficulties; but the engineer must be prepared to throw them overboard, or to conquer them. This was the course which he had himself pursued."

These characteristic sentiments illustrate the man, and show the fibre of which he was made. His views respecting the importance of education were in him firmly-rooted convictions; and when he had an opportunity of speaking to young men, he never

* Soiree of the Leeds Mechanics' Institute, 10th September, 1842; Mr. Charles Dickens in the chair.

failed to urge them. Since the time when, tending the engine at the West Moor Pit during the night shifts, he had employed his spare minutes in cleaning the pitmen's clocks and mending their shoes, that he might save enough money to send his boy to school, experience had only served to strengthen and confirm them.

Mr. Stephenson accordingly steadily carried out these views in the education of his son Robert. For about three years the youth attended Bruce's school, at Newcastle, one of the best seminaries of the district, where he acquired the rudiments of a sound education. It was expensive; but the father did not grudge it, for he held that the best legacy he could leave his son was a well-nurtured mind. He encouraged him to read and study for himself; and he made him, as we have seen, in a measure the instrument of his own better education, by getting the youth to read for him at the library in Newcastle, and bring home the results of his weekly readings, and often a scientific book, which father and son studied together. Many were the discussions in which the two engaged on subjects more immediately bearing upon the business of the colliery, such as the steam-engine, pumping-engine, and, above all, the favorite subject of the locomotive.

On one occasion, they determined to construct a sun-dial for the front of the cottage at West Moor. Robert brought home Ferguson's "Astronomy," and, under his father's directions, he carefully drew out on paper a dial suited to the latitude of Killingworth; then a suitable stone was procured, and, after much hewing and polishing, the stone dial was at length completed, and fixed immediately over the cottage door, greatly to the wonderment of the villagers. It stands there yet; and we trust it will be long before it is removed. The date carved upon it is "August 11th, MDCCCXVI"—a year or two before Robert left school. George Stephenson was very proud of that sun-dial, for it had cost him much thought and labor; and, in its way, it was a success. Many years after, in 1838 when the British Association met at Newcastle, he took over some of his scientific friends to Killingworth, and pointed out his sun-dial with honest exultation, as also the other parts of the cottage which had been his own handiwork. And afterwards, in 1843, when engaged with Mr. John Bourne, engineer, in making the preliminary survey of the Newcastle and Berwick Railway, he drove him round by the cottage in order to point out the sun-dial, and relate to him how and when he had made it.

On leaving school, in 1818, Robert Stephenson was put apprentice to Mr. Nicholas Wood, at Killingworth, to learn the business of the colliery; and he served under him for three years in the capacity of an under viewer in the West Moor Pit. He thus became familiar with all departments of underground work. The occupation was not unattended with peril, as the following incident will show. Though the Geordy lamp was now in general use in the Killingworth pits, and the workmen were bound, under a penalty of half-a-crown, not to use a naked candle, yet it was difficult to enforce the rule, and even the masters themselves occasionally broke it. One day Mr. Nicholas Wood, the head viewer, accompanied by Robert Stephenson and Moodie, the under viewers, was proceeding along one of the galleries, Wood with a naked candle in his hand, and Robert following him with a lamp. They came to a place where a fall of stones from the roof had taken place, and Nicholas Wood, who was first, proceeded to clamber over the stones, holding high the naked candle. He had reached nearly the summit of the heap, when the fire-damp, which had accumulated in the hollow of the roof, exploded, and instantly the whole party were blown down, and the lights extinguished. They were a mile from the shaft, and quite in the dark. There was a rush of the work-people from all quarters towards the shaft, for it was feared that the fire might extend to more dangerous parts of the pit, where, if the gas had exploded, every soul in the mine must inevitably have perished. Robert Stephenson and Moodie, on the first im pulse, ran back at full speed along the dark gallery leading to the shaft, coming in collision, on their way, with the hind quarters of a horse stunned by the explosion. When they had gone halfway, Moodie halted, and bethought him of Nicholas Wood. "Stop, laddie!" said he to Robert, "stop; we maun gang back, and seek the maister." So they retraced their steps. Happily no further explosion had taken place. They found the master lying on the heap of stones, stunned and bruised, with his hands severely burnt. They led him back out of the pit; and he afterwards took care never to venture into the dangerous parts of the mine without the protection of a Geordy lamp.

The time that Robert spent at Killingworth as under viewer was to advantage both to his father and himself. The evenings were generally devoted to reading and study, the two from this time working together as friends and co-laborers. One who used to drop in at the cottage of an evening, well remembers the animated and eager discussions which on some occasions took place, more especially with reference to the then comparatively unknown powers of the locomotive engine, daily at work on the wagon-way. The son was even more enthusiastic than the father on this subject. Robert would suggest alterations and improvements in this, that and the other details of the machine. His father, on the contrary, would offer every possible objection, defending the existing arrangements—proud, nevertheless, of his son's suggestions, and often warmed and excited by his brilliant anticipations of the ultimate triumph of the locomotive.

These discussions, probably, had considerable influence in inducing Mr. Stephenson to take the next important step in the education of his son. Although Robert, who was only nineteen years of age, was doing well, and was certain, at the expiration of his apprenticeship, to rise to a higher position, his father was not satisfied with the amount of instruction which he had as yet given him. Remembering the disadvantages under which he had labored in consequence of his ignorance of practical chemistry during his investigations connected with the safety lamp, more especially with reference to the properties of gas, as well as in the course of his experiments in connection with the improvement of the locomotive engine, he desired to furnish his son with as complete a scientific culture as his means could afford. He was also of opinion that a proper training in technical science was almost indispensable to success in the higher walks of the engineer's profession; and, aware that he himself could not now devote the requisite time and attention to its study, he determined to give to his son that kind and degree of education which he so much desired for himself. He would thus, he knew, secure a hearty and generous co-worker in the elaboration of the great ideas now looming grandly before him, and with their united practical and scientific knowledge he probably felt that they would be equal to any enterprise.

He accordingly took Robert from his labors as under viewer in the West Moor Pit, and, in the year 1820, sent him to the Edinburgh University, there being then no college in England accessible to persons of moderate means, for purposes of scientific culture. He was furnished with some good introductions to men of science in Edinburgh, the reputation of his father in connection with the safety lamp and the locomotive being of some service to him in this respect. Though he studied at Edinburgh College for only one session of six months, he entered upon the work with such zest and interest—his mind was so ripe for the pursuit and reception of knowledge—that it is not too much to say, that in that short period he learnt more than most students do during a three years course. He attended the chemical lectures of Dr. Hope, the lectures on natural philosophy by Sir John Leslie, and the natural history classes of Jameson; and his evenings were sedulously devoted to the study of practical chemistry under Dr. John Murray, himself one of the numerous speculators respecting the safety lamp. This six months study cost his father 80*l.*, a considerable sum with him in those days; but he was amply repaid when his son returned to Killingworth, in the summer of 1821, bringing with him the prize for mathematics, which he had gained at the University.

CHAPTER XIV.

RAILWAY PIONEERS—WILLIAM JAMES, EDWARD PEASE, AND THOMAS GRAY.

It is somewhat remarkable that, although George Stephenson's locomotive engines were in daily use for many years on the Killingworth railway, they excited comparatively little interest. Yet by them he had already solved the great problem of the employment of steam power for the purpose of railway traction. In his hands the locomotive was no longer an experiment; for he had ascertained and proved, by the experience of years, that it worked more steadily, drew heavier loads, and was, on the whole, a more economical power to employ on railways than horses. Nevertheless, eight years passed before another locomotive railway was constructed and opened for the purpose of coal traffic.

It is difficult to account for this early indifference on the part of the public to the merits of the greatest mechanical invention of the age. Steam carriages were exciting great interest; and numerous and repeated experiments were made with them. The improvements effected by M'Adam in the mode of constructing turnpike roads, were the subject of frequent discussions in the legislature; and large sums of money were voted to him by the government for his so-called "discovery." It appears from a discussion which took place in the House of Commons on the 13th of May, 1825, that votes of money had been granted to Mr. M'Adam and his sons, at various times, amounting to not less than 41,000*l.;* and yet at Killingworth, without the aid of a farthing of government money, had a system of road locomotion been in existence since 1814, which was destined, before many years, to revolutionize the internal communications of England and of the world, but of which the English public and the English government as yet knew nothing.

Mr. Stephenson had no means of bringing his important invention prominently under the notice of the public. He himself knew well its importance, and he already anticipated its eventual general adoption; but being an unlettered man, he could not give utterance to the thoughts which brooded within him on the subject. Killingworth Colliery lay far from London, the centre of scientific life in England. It was visited by no savans nor literary men, who might have succeeded in introducing to notice the wonderful machine of Stephenson. Even the local chroniclers seem to have taken no notice of the Killingworth railway. The "Puffing Billy" was doing its daily quota of hard work, and had long ceased to be a curiosity in the neighborhood. Blenkinsop's clumsier and less successful engine—which has long since been disused, while Stephenson's Killingworth engines continue working to this day—excited far more interest, partly, perhaps, because it was close to the large town of Leeds, and used to be visited by strangers as one of the few objects of interest in that place. Blenkinsop was also an educated man, and was in communication with some of the most distinguished personages of his day upon the subject of his locomotive, which thus obtained considerable notoriety. The number of thinkers and observers on the subject of railway locomotion were yet few in number. Amongst these, however, was the late Sir John Sinclair, who had some correspondence with Mr. Blenkinsop on the subject, and also that sagacious observer, Sir Richard Phillips. As early as the year 1813, the latter writer, with clear foresight of the uses to which the railway locomotive might be applied, used the following remarkable words in his "Morning Walk to Kew," for some time a popular book. The reflections occurred to him on witnessing the performances of the horses then employed in working the tramway used for the conveyance of lime from Merstham to Wandsworth in Surrey. The line has long since been abandoned, though the traveler by the Brighton railway can still discern the marks of the old road along the hillside on the south of Croydon.*

"I found delight," said Sir Richard, "in witnessing at Wandsworth the economy of horse labor on the iron railway. Yet a heavy sigh escaped me as I thought of the inconceivable millions of money which had been spent about Malta, four or five of which might have been the means of extending double lines of iron railway from London to Edinburgh, Glasgow, Holyhead, Milford, Falmouth, Yarmouth, Dover and Portsmouth. A reward of a single thousand would have supplied coaches and other vehicles, of various degrees of speed, with the best tackle for readily turning out; and we might, ere this, have witnessed our mail coaches running at the rate of ten miles an hour drawn by a single horse, or impelled fifteen miles an hour by Blenkinsop's

* Charles Knight thus pleasantly describes this old road: "The earliest railway for public traffic in England was one passing from Merstham to Wandsworth, through Croydon; a small single line, on which a miserable team of lean mules or donkeys, some thirty years ago, might be seen crawling at the rate of four miles an hour, with several trucks of stone and lime behind them. It was commenced in 1801, opened in 1803; and the men of science of that day—we cannot say that the respectable name of Stephenson was not among them [Stephenson was then a brakesman at Killingworth]—tested its capabilities, and found that one horse could draw some thirty-five tons at six miles in the hour, and then, with prophetic wisdom, declared that railways could never be worked profitably. The old Croydon Railway is no longer used. The genius loci must look with wonder on the gigantic offspring of the little railway, which has swallowed up its own sire. Lean mules no longer crawl leisurely along the little rails with trucks of stone through Croydon, once perchance during the day, but the whistle and the rush of the locomotive are now heard all day long. Not a few loads of lime, but all London and its contents, by comparison—men, women, children, horses, dogs, oxen, sheep, pigs, carriages, merchandise, food—would seem to be now-a-days passing through Croydon; for day after day, more than 100 journeys are made by the great railroads which pass the place."

steam-engine. Such would have been a legitimate motive for overstepping the income of a nation; and the completion of so great and useful a work would have afforded rational ground for public triumph in general jubilee."

Although Sir Richard Phillips's estimate of the cost of constructing railways was very fallacious, as experience has since proved, his estimate of the admirable uses to which they might be applied—though it was practically impossible for Blenkinsop's engine to have traveled on cogged rails at fifteen miles an hour—was sagacious and far-seeing in a remarkable degree.

There were other speculators, who, about the same time, were urging and predicting the adoption of railways as a mode of rapid transit. For instance, Mr. Edgeworth, in a communication to James Watt, dated the 7th of August, 1813, observed: "I have always thought that steam would become the universal lord, and that we should in time scorn post-horses. An iron railroad would be a cheaper thing than a road on the common construction."* These, however, were merely guesses at what might be done, and were of no assistance towards the practical solution of the problem. Yet they show that many advanced minds were already anticipating the adoption of steam power for purposes of railway traction. At the same time there was at work a more profitable class of laborers—the public-spirited men who were engaged in projecting and actually forming railways to supply the wants of important districts of population. Among the most prominent of these were William James of West Bromwich, and Edward Pease of Darlington.

William James was instrumental in giving a great impetus to the question of railway locomotion; and though he did not discover the locomotive, he did what was the next best thing to it, he discovered George Stephenson. He was a man of considerable fortune, and occupied an influential position in society. Possessed of a good address, and mixing freely with men of the

* Muirhead's Mechanical Inventions of James Watt, vol. i, p. 240.

highest rank, he was enabled to gain a hearing for his speculations where humbler persons had no chance of being listened to. Besides being an extensive land-owner and land-agent, he was engaged as an iron and coal-miner, and at one time occupied the honorable position of chairman of the Staffordshire iron-masters.

Mr. James was a bold, and, as many considered him, a reckless projector. When he had determined upon any scheme, he was quite regardless of the cost at which he carried it out. He did not confine himself to projects connected with his own particular interests, but was constantly engaged in devising things for the public, which the public shook its cautious head at, and would not have at any price. At a very early period of his life he was an advocate of railways. It was not merely a sober conviction of their utility that influenced him; the idea of railway locomotion haunted him like a passion. He went to Camborne, in Cornwall, to see Trevethick upon the subject, in 1803, and witnessed the performances of his engine at Merthyr Tydvil in the following year. In an article which he published in one of the early numbers of the "Railway Magazine," he stated that as early as 1803 he contemplated the projection of a railway between Liverpool and Manchester.* Many years, however, elapsed before he proceeded to enter upon the survey. In the meantime he was occupied with other projects.

In 1806 he contemplated the formation of a tramway from Birmingham towards Wedgebury and the Staffordshire coal districts. We next find him projecting and partly forming a tramway from Clutton Colliery, belonging to the Earl of Warwick—about twelve miles in length—to Bristol. And about the same time he entered into an arrangement with Mr. Protheroe to construct another tramway from the Forest of Dean to Gloucester.

* There were numerous projectors of railways for the accommodation of the large towns, even at that early period. Thus we find in the *Leeds Mercury* of the 16th January, 1802, a letter signed "Mercator," in which the formation of a line of railway from Leeds to Selby was strongly recommended. Thirty years, however, passed, before that railway was formed.

About 1814 he was cutting, at his own expense, a canal between Birmingham and Stratford-on-Avon; and some years after, in conjunction with Lord Redesdale, he constructed a railway from Stratford-on-Avon to Moreton-in-the-Marsh—the first railway in that district laid with wrought iron rails, for the special purpose of being worked by locomotive power.

In the year 1815, we find Mr. James addressing a "Letter to the Prince Regent," in which he showed that he anticipated rapid locomotion by steam and other means. His project was to form a railway between London and Chatham, together with a capacious war-dock at the latter place, the gates of which were to be formed with caissons, after the plan of the docks of the then unknown Russian war-port of Sebastopol. Those caissons were then being manufactured in England; and Mr. James had got his idea of them from Upton, the engineer, with whom he was well acquainted. Nothing, however, came of this Grand Chatham project.

Being a shareholder in the Wandsworth and Merstham Railway, which had thus far proved an abortive project, paying not more than about one per cent. per annum to its proprietors, Mr. James came up to London in 1818, to urge the formation of a line of railway from the neighborhood of the Waterloo Bridge, to join the Merstham line; but the project was abandoned. He next endeavored to have the Merstham tramroad converted into a locomotive railway. The suggestion, however, met with no favor, and his speculations soon turned in another direction.

We have before us an engraved plan, dated 1820, of a "Central Junction Railway" projected by Mr. James, which was extensively circulated by him amongst influential persons, showing a comprehensive scheme of railways connecting London with Oxford, and through his railway at Moreton-in-the-Marsh, with Stratford-on-Avon and Birmingham, a branch line giving accommodation to Cheltenham and Gloucester. But this, too, remained merely a project.

Mr. Edward Pease, of Darlington, was a man of an entirely different stamp. He too, like Mr. James, was connected with coal mines, and interested in improving the internal communications of his neighborhood, chiefly with the object of opening out new markets for the vast stores of coal found in the Bishop Aukland valley above Darlington. But though he was not so ambitious as Mr. James in reference to the extension of railways, the prosperity which attended his one great enterprise did more for their eventual success than all Mr. James's efforts. It would appear that, at first, Mr. Pease contemplated only a horse tram-road between Stockton and Darlington; but as he proceeded with the project, and especially after he had become personally acquainted with George Stephenson, he gradually, but cautiously, became a convert to the locomotive system.

The Stockton and Darlington Railway was an undertaking of great importance, although it was afterwards thrown into the shade by the more brilliant project of the Liverpool and Manchester Railway, which was not commenced for several years after. As the first iron road constructed for the purpose of general traffic, and as the first public highway on which locomotive engines were regularly employed, the Stockton and Darlington project unquestionably exercised very great influence upon the future history of railway locomotion.

Of this railway Edward Pease was the projector. A thoughtful and sagacious man, ready in resources, possessed of indomitable energy and perseverance, he was eminently qualified to undertake what appeared to many the desperate enterprise of obtaining an Act of Parliament to construct a railway through a rather unpromising district. One who knew him in 1818 said, "he was a man who could see a hundred years ahead." When the writer last saw him, in the autumn of 1854, Mr. Pease was in his eighty-eighth year; yet he still possessed the hopefulness and mental vigor of a man in his prime. Hale and hearty, full of interesting reminiscences of the past, he yet entered with interest into the life of the present, and displayed a warm sympathy for all current projects calculated to render the lives of men happier. Still sound in health, his eye had not lost its brilliancy, nor his cheek its color; and there was an elasticity in his step which younger men might have envied. His vigorous judgment and genuine native shrewdness, together with that courageous strength and tenacity of purpose which made him, when once convinced, stand by the railway project upon which he had set his heart, when all the world called him schemer and fool, had not yet departed from him; and he could now afford to crack a lively joke at the prejudiced blindness of those who had so long made him the subject of their ridicule. Pointing to a fine prospect from his drawing-room window, extending to the wooded knolls on the further side of the valley, the numerous full-grown trees within sight, gay in all the gorgeous livery of autumn, Mr. Pease observed:—"What changes happen in a single lifetime! Look at those fine old trees; every one of them has been planted by my own hand. When I was a boy I was fond of planting, and my father indulged me in my pastime. I went about with a spade in my hand, planting trees everywhere as far as you can see: they grew whilst I slept; and now see what a goodly array they make! Ay," continued he, "but RAILWAYS are a far more extraordinary growth even than these. They have grown up not only since I was a boy, but since I became a man. When I started the Stockton and Darlington Railway, some five and thirty years since, I was already fifty years old. Nobody could then have dreamt what railways would have grown to, within one man's lifetime."

In projecting a railway from Witton Colliery, a few miles above Darlington, to Stockton, in the year 1817, Edward Pease at first stood almost alone. Long before this railway was projected—as early as the year 1768—the scheme of a canal had been discussed, and Brindley, the engineer, who had at one period of his life worked in the neighborhood as a laborer, was consulted. The project, however, proceeded no further, probably from want of support. In 1812, Mr. Rennie, the engineer, was employed to make a survey of a tramroad. But the commercial distress which then prevailed in the county of Durham prevented the project from ripening to maturity. The necessity for finding an outlet and new markets for the Bishop Aukland coals continued, however, to be felt. What was at first contemplated by Mr. Pease, was merely the means of effecting land sales of coal at the stations along the proposed railway. The shipment of coal from the Tees was not taken into account as a source of profit. It was not expected that coals could be led there to advantage, or that more than 10,000 tons could be disposed of at Stockton, and those merely for the purpose of ballasting ships disembarking goods at that port. The conveyance of passengers was not even dreamt of.

In getting up a company for the purpose of surveying and forming a railway, Mr. Pease had great difficulties to contend with. The people of the neighborhood spoke of it as a ridiculous undertaking, and predicted that it would be the ruin of all who had to do with it. Even those who were most interested in the opening out of new markets for the vend of their coals, were indifferent, if not actually hostile. The Stockton merchants and ship-owners, whom the formation of a railway was calculated to benefit so greatly, gave the project no support; and not twenty shares were subscribed for in the whole town. Mr. Pease nevertheless persevered with the formation of a company; and he induced many of his friends and relations to subscribe for shares. The Richardsons and Backhouses, members, like himself, of the Society of Friends, influenced by his persuasion, united themselves with him; and so many of the same denomination (having great confidence in these influential Darlington names) followed their example and subscribed for shares, that the railway subsequently obtained the designation, which it still enjoys, of "The Quakers' Line."

The engineer first employed to make a survey of the tramroad, was a Mr. Overton, who had had considerable experience in the formation of similar roads in Wales. The necessary preliminary steps were taken in the year 1818 to apply for an Act to authorize the construction of a tramroad from Witton to Stockton. The measure was, however, strongly opposed by the Duke of Cleveland, because the proposed line passed near to one of his fox covers; and, having considerable parliamentary influence, he succeeded in throwing out the bill by a majority of only thirteen —above one hundred members voting in support of the measure. A nobleman said, when he heard of the division, "Well, if the Quakers in these times, when nobody knows anything about railways, can raise up such a phalanx as they have done on this occasion, I should recommend the county gentlemen to be very wary how they oppose them."

A new survey was then made, avoiding the Duke's fox cover; and in 1819 a renewed application was made to Parliament for an Act. But George III dying in January, 1820, while Parliament was still sitting, there was a dissolution, and the bill was necessarily suspended. The promoters, however, did not lose sight of their project. They had now spent a considerable sum of money in surveys and legal and parliamentary expenses, and were determined to proceed, though they were still unable to enlist the active support of the inhabitants of the districts proposed to be served by the railway.

As an instance of the opposition on the part of the local authorities, which the promoters had to encounter, we may mention that, in 1819, while the bill was before Parliament, the road trustees, perhaps secretly fearing the success of the railway, which openly they denied, got up an alarm, predicting the total and immediate ruin of the turnpike road trusts in event of the bill becoming law. On this Mr. Pease published a notice intimating that if any of the creditors or mortgagees of the road between Darlington and West Aukland were apprehensive that the proposed rail or tramway would be prejudicial to their interests, the promoters would, through their solicitors, (Raisbeck and Mewburn,) purchase their securities at the price originally paid for them. This measure had the salutary effect of quieting the road interests for a season, though they afterwards displayed an active hostility to the railway when it came to be formed.

The energy of Edward Pease, backed by the support of his Quaker friends, enabled him to hold the company together, to raise the requisite preliminary funds from time to time for the purpose of prosecuting the undertaking, and eventually to overcome the opposition raised against the measure in Parliament. The bill at length passed; and the royal assent was given to the first Stockton and Darlington Railway act, on the 19th of April, 1821.

The preamble of this Act recites, that "the making and maintaining of a Railway or Tramroad, for the passage of wagons and other carriages" from Stockton to Witton Park Colliery (by Darlington), "will be of great public utility, by facilitating the conveyance of coal, iron, lime, corn, and other commodities," between the places mentioned. The projectors of the line did not originally contemplate the employment of locomotives; for in the Act they provide for the making and maintaining of the tramroads for the passage upon them "of wagons and other carriages," "*with men and horses* or otherwise," and a further clause made provision as to the damages which might be done in the course of traffic by the "wagoners." The public were to be free "to use, with horses, cattle and carriages," the roads formed by the company, on payment of the authorized rates, "between the hours of seven in the morning and six in the evening," during the winter months; "between six in the morning and eight in the evening," in two of the spring and autumn months each; and "between five in the morning and ten in the evening," in the high summer months of May, June, July and August.

From this it will be obvious that the projectors of this line had themselves at first no very large conceptions as to the scope of their project. A public locomotive railway was as yet a new and untried thing; and the Darlington men merely proposed, by means of their intended road, to provide a more facile mode of transporting their coals and merchandise to market.

Although the locomotive had been working for years successfully at Killingworth, its merits do not seem to have been fairly estimated, even in the locality itself; and it was still regarded rather in the light of a mechanical curiosity, than as the vital force of the railway system.

Thomas Gray, of Nottingham, was a much more sanguine and speculative man. He was not a mechanic nor an inventor, nor a coal owner, but an enthusiastic believer in the wonderful powers of the railroad system. Being a native of Leeds, he had, when a boy, seen Blenkinsop's locomotive at work on the Middleton cogged railroad; and from an early period he seems to have entertained almost as sanguine views on the subject as Sir Richard Phillips himself. It would appear that Gray was residing in Brussels in 1816, when the project of a canal from Charleroi, for the purpose of connecting Holland with the mining districts of Belgium, was the subject of discussion; and, in conversation with Mr. John Cockerill and others, he took the opportunity of advocating the superior advantages of a railway. For some years after, he pondered the subject more carefully, and at length became fully possessed by the grand idea on which other minds were now at work. He occupied himself for some time with the preparation of a pamphlet on the subject. He shut himself up in his room secluded from his wife and relations, declining to give them any information on the subject of his mysterious studies, beyond the assurance that his scheme "would revolutionize the whole face of the material world, and of society." *

* The Railway System and its Author, Thomas Gray, now of Exeter. A Letter to Sir Robert Peel. By Thomas Wilson. 1845. In this very eloquent and generous tribute to

In 1820, Mr. Gray published the result of his studies in his "Observations on a General Iron Railway,"† in which, with great cogency, he urged the superiority of a locomotive railway over common roads and canals, pointing out, at the same time, the advantages of this mode of conveyance for merchandise and persons, to all classes of the community. That Mr. Gray had obtained his idea from Blenkinsop's engine and road, is obvious from the accurate engraving which he gives in his book of the cog-wheeled engine then traveling upon the Middleton cogged railroad.

The treatise seems to have met with a ready sale; for we find that, two years after, it had already passed into a fourth edition. In 1822, Mr. Gray added to the book a diagram, showing a number of suggested lines of railway, connecting the principal towns of England, and another in like manner connecting the principal towns of Ireland. In his first edition, Mr. Gray suggested the propriety of making a railway between Manchester and Liverpool, "which," he observed, "would employ many thousands of the distressed population" of Lancashire.

The publication of this essay must have had the effect of bringing the subject of railway extension more prominently under the notice of the public than it had been brought before. Although little able to afford it, Gray also pressed his favorite project of a general iron road on the attention of public men—

the memory of his friend, Mr. Wilson has endeavored to make it appear that Thomas Gray was the inventor, originator, creator and founder of the Railway Locomotive System, forgetting that railways had been at work before Mr. Gray was born, and that the locomotive had been invented while he was yet a boy. The "true founder of the railway system" certainly was not Thomas Gray, though he wrote a clever and far-seeing treatise about railways. The true founder of the railway system was the man who invented such a locomotive as made railway locomotion practicable and profitable. And this had been done long before Mr. Gray turned his attention to the subject.

† Observations on a General Iron Railway (with Plates and Maps illustrative of the plan), showing its great superiority, by the general introduction of mechanic power, over all the present methods of conveyance by turnpike roads and canals; and claiming the particular attention of merchants, manufacturers, farmers, and indeed every class of society. London: Baldwin, Cradock and Joy, 1820.

mayors, members of Parliament and prime ministers. He sent memorials to Lord Sidmouth in 1820, and to the Lord Mayor and Corporation of London in 1821. In 1822, he addressed the Earl of Liverpool, Sir Robert Peel, and others, urging the great national importance of his system. In the year following, he petitioned the ministers of state to the same effect. He was so pertinacious, that public men pronounced him to be a "bore," and in the town of Nottingham, where he then lived, those who knew him declared him to be "cracked."

William Howitt, who frequently met Gray at that time, has published a lively portraiture* of this indefatigable and enthusiastic projector, who seized all men by the button, and would not let them go until he had unraveled to them his wonderful scheme. With Thomas Gray, "begin where you would, on whatever subject—the weather, the news, the political movement or event of the day—it would not be many minutes before you would be enveloped with steam, and listening to a harangue on the practicability and immense advantages, to the nation and to every man in it, of 'a general iron railway.'"†

While Thomas Gray was thus agitating the general adoption of railways, George Stephenson was doing much more—he was making railways, and building efficient locomotives with which

* People's Journal, August 1st, 1846. Art. "A word for Thomas Gray, the Author of the General Railway System."

† Thomas Gray never got beyond his idea of Blenkinsop's cogged wheel and cogged rail. Probably he was not aware that Blackett and Stephenson had both, as early as 1814, demonstrated the cogs to be not only unnecessary, but positive impediments to the working of the locomotive engine through the jolting and friction which they caused. Notwithstanding the triumphant success of the smooth-wheeled locomotive, and the smooth rail, on the Liverpool and Manchester line, in 1830, we find Thomas Gray in the following year (Mechanics' Magazine, May 14th, 1831), declaring it to be an expensive blunder. He urged the adoption of a greased road, with his favorite device of cog-rails and racks placed outside the smooth rails. Had the advice of this "founder of the railway system," as his friends have styled him, been adopted, the modern railway system would have been simply impracticable. But Thomas Gray himself never claimed to be the inventor or discoverer of railways. He labored under the disadvantage of not being a mechanic. His engraving of a railway train, prefixed to his book, shows that, if once set in motion, it could not have been pulled up without going to pieces.

to work them. Although he had not lost faith in the powers of the locomotive, he had now waited for so many years without observing any prospect of their extended use, that his old idea of removing his skill and small capital to the United States seems for a time to have revived. Before becoming a sleeping partner in a small foundry at Forth Banks in Newcastle, managed by Mr. John Burrell, he had thrown out the suggestion that it would be a good speculation for them to emigrate to North America, and introduce steam-boats upon the great inland lakes. The first steamers were then plying upon the Tyne before his eyes: and he saw in them the germ of a great revolution in navigation. It occurred to him that North America presented the finest field on which to try their wonderful powers. He was an engineer, and Mr. Burrell was an iron-founder; and, between them, he thought they could strike out a path to success in the mighty West. Fortunately, this remained a mere speculation, so far as Mr. Stephenson was concerned; and it was left to others to do what he had dreamt of achieving. After all his patient waiting, his skill, industry, and perseverance were at length about to bear fruit.

In 1819, the owners of the Hetton Colliery, in the county of Durham, determined to have their wagon-way altered into a locomotive railroad. The result of the working of the Killingworth Railway had been so satisfactory that they resolved to adopt the same system. One reason why an experiment so long continued and so successfully as that at Killingworth should have been so slow in producing results, perhaps was, that to lay down a railway and furnish it with locomotives, or fixed engines where necessary, required a very large capital, beyond the means of ordinary coal-owners, whilst the small amount of interest felt in railways by the general public, and the supposed impracticability of working them to a profit, as yet prevented the ordinary capitalists from venturing their money in the promotion of such undertakings. The Hetton Coal Company was, however, possessed of adequate means; and the local reputation of the Killingworth engine-wright pointed him out as the man best calculated to lay out their line and superintend their works. They accordingly invited him to act as the engineer of the proposed railway. Being in the service of the Killingworth Company, Mr. Stephenson felt it necessary to obtain their permission to enter upon this new work. This was at once granted. The best feeling existed between him and his employers; and they regarded it as a compliment that their colliery engineer should be selected for a work so important as the laying down of the Hetton Railway, which was to be the longest locomotive line that had, up to that time, been constructed in the neighborhood. Mr. Stephenson accepted the appointment, his brother Robert acting as resident engineer, and personally superintending the execution of the works.

The Hetton Railway extended from the Hetton Colliery, situated about two miles south of Houghton-le-Spring, in the county of Durham, to the shipping-place on the banks of the Wear, near Sunderland. Its length was about eight miles; and in its course it crossed Warden Law, one of the highest hills in the district. The character of the country forbade the construction of a flat line, or one of comparatively easy gradients, except by the expenditure of a much larger capital than was placed at Mr. Stephenson's command. Heavy works could not be executed: it was, therefore, necessary to form the line with but little deviation from the natural conformation of the district which it traversed, and also to adapt the mechanical methods employed for the working of the railway to the character of the gradients, which in some places were necessarily heavy.

Although Mr. Stephenson had, with every step made towards its increased utility, become more and more identified with the success of the locomotive engine, he did not allow his enthusiasm to carry him away into costly mistakes. He carefully drew the line between the cases in which the locomotive could be usefully employed, and those in which stationary engines were calculated to be more economical. This led him, as in the instance of the Hetton Railway, to execute lines through and over rough countries, where gradients within the powers of the locomotive engine of that day could not be secured, employing in their stead stationary engines where locomotives were not practicable. In the present case, this course was adopted by him most successfully. On the original Hetton line, there were five self-acting inclines—the full wagons drawing the empty ones up—and two inclines worked by fixed reciprocating engines of sixty-horse power each. The locomotive traveling engine, or "the iron-horse," as the people of the neighborhood then styled it, did the rest. On the day of the opening of the Hetton Railway, the 18th of November, 1822, crowds of spectators assembled from all parts to witness the first operations of this ingenious and powerful machinery, which was entirely successful. On that day, five of Stephenson's locomotives were at work upon the railway, under the direction of his brother Robert; and the first shipment of coal was then made by the Hetton Company, at their new staiths on the Wear. The speed at which the locomotives traveled was about four miles an hour, and each engine dragged after it a train of seventeen wagons, weighing about sixty-four tons.

Thus another important practical step was effected towards the more general adoption of the railway system.

CHAPTER XV.

FIRST SURVEY OF THE LIVERPOOL AND MANCHESTER RAILWAY.

MR. JAMES's business as a land-agent led him into the neighborhood of Liverpool in the year 1821. The formation of a tramroad between Liverpool and Manchester was at that time the subject of some speculation in both towns, but especially at Liverpool. Mr. James, who was quick to hear of all such projects, went over to Liverpool to have an interview with the promoters. Day by day the necessity was becoming more urgent for some improved mode of transporting goods inland to the manufacturing districts. The rapidity of increase in the trade, between Liverpool and Manchester especially, was something marvelous. In nine years, the quantity of raw cotton sent from one town to the other had increased by 50,000,000 pounds weight; and all other raw materials had increased in proportion. Around Manchester, hamlets had expanded into towns, and towns had assumed the dimensions of cities, the inhabitants of which were for the most part dependent for their means of subsistence upon the regularity of the supply of cotton from Liverpool. Up to this time the Duke of Bridgewater's Canal and the Irwell and Mersey navigation had principally supplied the means of transport; but the enormously increasing demands of the trade outstripped their tardy efforts. Possessing a monopoly of the traffic, and having no rivals to fear, the canal managers were most dictatorial in the treatment of their customers. Perhaps, however, the canal companies did all that could be done under the circumstances, and had already fully taxed the resources of the navigation. The immense mass of goods to be conveyed had simply outgrown all their appliances of wharves, boats and horses. Cotton lay at Liverpool for weeks together, waiting to be removed; and it occupied a longer time to transport the cargoes from Liverpool to Manchester than it had done to bring them across the Atlantic from the United States to England. Carts and wagons were tried; but these proved altogether insufficient. Sometimes manufacturing operations had to be suspended altogether; and during a frost, when the canals were frozen up, the communication was entirely stopped. The consequences were often disastrous, alike to operatives, merchants and manufacturers. The same difficulty was experienced in the conveyance of manufactured goods from Manchester to Liverpool for export. Mr. Huskisson, in the House of Commons, referring to these ruinous delays, truly observed that "cotton was detained a fortnight at Liverpool, while the Manchester manufacturers were obliged to suspend their labors, and goods manufactured at Manchester, for foreign markets, could not be transmitted in time, in consequence of the tardy conveyance."

The Liverpool merchants and the Manchester manufacturers were therefore prepared to welcome any new mode of transit which would relieve them of the losses arising from these constant interruptions to their commercial operations. The scheme of a tramroad was, however, so new to them, that it is not surprising they should have hesitated before committing themselves fully to it. Mr. Sandars, an influential Liverpool merchant, was amongst the first to broach the subject of a tramroad or railway. He himself had suffered in his business, in common with many other merchants, from the insufficiency of the existing modes of communication, and was ready to give due consideration to any plan presenting elements of practical efficiency, which proposed a remedy for the generally admitted grievance. The first idea was a tramroad, to be worked by horses, though this gradually gave way to a larger and more efficient plan. Mr. James met Mr. Sandars frequently to discuss the subject; and about the month of June, 1821, a party, consisting of Mr. Sandars, Mr. James, Mr. Francis Giles and Mr. Padley, (Mr. James's brother-in-law, a surveyor,) went out and inspected the ground in the neighborhood of Liverpool, in order to ascertain at what point a tramroad could be best brought into the town. They first examined the land about Easton Hill with this object. Mr. James then intrusted his brother-in-law (Padley) to proceed with a trial survey. Robert Stephenson came over from Newcastle to assist him, and at the same time to obtain some experience in railway leveling.

The people in the neighborhood of Easton Hill observing the extraordinary proceedings going on with chains and theodolite, having also heard the rumor which was now abroad, and fearing that their farms and gardens would be damaged by the intended tramroad, rose against the surveyors, and compelled them to desist. Mr. Padley's assistant was apprehended, forcibly dragged off the ground, and was only liberated on giving his solemn promise never to return there on a similar business. Finding it impossible to proceed with any survey in the neighborhood of Liverpool, in consequence of this opposition on the part of the inhabitants, Mr. Sandars suggested that the party should proceed to Prescot, and make a trial survey there. He was under the impression that the Mersey might be connected by tramway with Manchester without at all touching the town of Liverpool; and the surveyors were directed to ascertain by the levels whether this could be done. In order to carry out this survey in a proper manner, he and Mr. Moss guaranteed to pay Mr. James, who was to superintend it, at the rate of 10*l.* a mile, or about 300*l.* for the entire survey between the Mersey and Manchester. They proceeded accordingly with the survey near Prescot, meeting with great opposition from the land-owners and farmers along the proposed line of road, who drove them off their grounds, and subjected them to all manner of insults.

The next surveying station was at Newton-in-the-Willows, where the surveyors took a temporary office in the Horse and Jockey public-house. While they were proceeding with their survey at this place, Mr. Legh, of Legh Park, a large land-owner, made himself acquainted with their proceedings. He was the first land-owner of the neighborhood who declared himself favorable to the promotion of a tramroad, or who gave the projectors the slightest encouragement to proceed. All the rest were indifferent or hostile. Justice Bourne ordered his men to be constantly on the watch to turn back the surveyors wherever met with in the fields. The farmers and laborers were only too ready to follow up his instructions. Men were stationed at the field gates with pitchforks, and sometimes with guns, to drive them back. At St. Helen's, one of the chainmen was laid hold of by a mob of colliers, and threatened to be hurled down a coal-pit. A number of men, women and children, collected and ran after the surveyors wherever they made their appearance, bawling nicknames and throwing stones at them. As one of the chainmen was climbing over a gate one day, a laborer made at him with a pitchfork, and ran it through his clothes into his back; other watchers running up, the chainman, who was more stunned than hurt, took to his heels and fled. But the theodolite most excited the fury of the natives, who concentrated on the man who carried it, their fiercest execrations and their most offensive nicknames.

A powerful fellow, a noted bruiser, was hired by the surveyors to carry the instrument, with a view to its protection against all assailants; but one day an equally powerful fellow, a St. Helen's collier, who was the cock of the walk in his neighborhood, made up to the theodolite carrier to wrest it from him by sheer force. A battle took place, the collier was soundly pummeled, the natives poured in volleys of stones upon the surveyors and their instruments, and the theodolite was smashed to pieces.

It may readily be conceived that a survey made in the face of such opposition would necessarily be very incomplete; but the surveyors did their best, and when they found they could proceed no further at St. Helen's, they proceeded round Chat Moss to Hiliffe to try the ground there. Their proceedings at that place excited the same degree of surprise amongst the villagers, who turned out in a body to watch them, and appeared perfectly bewildered. The Moss was so soft, in consequence of the wetness of the season, that it was impossible to enter upon it; and the party very shortly retraced their steps, and stationed themselves for a short time at the Three Swans, at Eardley. There they began an intermediate survey of a branch tramroad between St. Helen's and the Mersey; and after about a month's labor, when the wet weather set in, the survey was suspended until the following spring.

In the meantime public meetings had been got up by Mr. Sandars in several of the principal towns of the district, on the subject of the proposed tramway. One was held in the Exchange at Liverpool, and another in the George Hotel, Warrington, at which Mr. Sandars, Mr. Moss and Mr. James appeared as the advocates of the measure, which, however, did not as yet meet with any degree of general support. But the subject was thus brought prominently under notice, and only wanted time to enable it to work its way into public estimation.

About the middle of the year 1821, Mr. James, having heard of Stephenson's engines, which were reported to him as being more efficient than any locomotives that had yet been constructed, determined to go down to Killingworth to inspect them in person. He was not so fortunate as to meet Mr. Stephenson on that occasion; but he examined his locomotive at work, and was very much struck by its power and efficiency. He saw at a glance the magnificent uses to which it might be applied. "Here," said he, "is an engine that will, before long, effect a complete revolution in society." Returning to Moreton-in-the-Marsh, he wrote to Mr. Losh, (Stephenson's partner in the patent,) expressing his admiration of the Killingworth engine. "It is," said he, "the greatest wonder of the age, and the forerunner, as I firmly believe, of the most important changes in the internal communications of the kingdom." Mr. Losh invited him again to visit Killingworth, for the purpose of having an interview with Mr. Stephenson on the subject of the locomotive. Accordingly, in September of the same year, accompanied by his two sons, he met Mr. Losh at Newcastle; they proceeded together to Killingworth, where Mr. Stephenson met them; and taking them to where the locomotive was working, he invited them to mount. The uncouth and extraordinary appearance of the machine, as it came snorting along, was somewhat alarming to the youths, who expressed their fears lest it should burst; and they were with some difficulty induced to mount.

The locomotive went through its usual performances, dragging a heavy load of coal wagons at about six miles an hour with apparent ease, at which Mr. James expressed his extreme satisfaction, and declared to Mr. Losh his opinion that Stephenson "was the greatest practical genius of the age," and that "if he developed the full powers of that engine, (the locomotive,) his fame in the world would rank equal to that of Watt." Mr. James, who had long been an advocate of the locomotive system, was confirmed in his views by the performances of the Killingworth engine; and informing Stephenson and Losh of the survey of the proposed tramroad between Liverpool and Manchester, upon which he had been engaged, he did not hesitate to state that he would henceforward advocate the adoption of a locomotive railroad instead of the tramroad which had originally been proposed.

As Mr. James's influence amongst persons of influence was considerable, and he was particularly identified with the more important railway projects of the day, Stephenson and Losh were naturally desirous of enlisting his good services on behalf of their patent locomotive. As yet it had proved comparatively unproductive. The Hetton Railway was the only line, in addition to the Killingworth, on which they had then a prospect of getting their engines introduced. Although Stephenson had virtually solved the problem of the locomotive, and demonstrated its profitable employment as a tractive power on railroads, neither he nor Mr. Losh were able to write up and advocate the invention so as to insure its more extensive adoption. This they believed Mr. James might be able effectually to do for them. With this object they proposed to give him an interest in their patent, in exchange for his services in this way; and accordingly, by a deed, dated 1st September, 1821, they assigned to Mr. James one fourth of the profits which might be derived from the use of their patent locomotive for railroads on any line which might be constructed south of a line drawn across England from Liverpool to Hull, the deed setting forth that this assignment of profits was made in consideration of Mr. James giving "his recommendation and best assistance" towards the use of the patent locomotive on all such railways.

Mr. James's first recommendation did not prove successful. He endeavored to introduce the locomotive upon the Moreton-on-Marsh Railway; but Mr. Rastrick, who was the engineer of the line, was so much opposed to its use that Mr. James failed in carrying his point, and he consequently gave up all further connection with that company. In the following year (1822) he wrote to Mr. Losh from Boswell Court, as to a locomotive which he wished to get from Mr. Stephenson for the working of the Croydon and Merstham Railroad, but against which Mr. Stephenson had dissuaded him, as the cast-iron plates were not calculated to bear the weight of the engine, and the result could only bring the locomotive into disrepute. Mr. James was, however, very anxious to have the engine introduced on some railway in the south of England. "I can appreciate," he said, "Mr. Stephenson's objections to use his engine on this defective road; but years will elapse, and the patent may expire, before we can get a new road in the south for his engine if this plan is not embraced." Mr. James at the same time intimated that he was busy with the plans and sections of the Liverpool line, which would furnish a proper opportunity for the introduction of the engine "for the conveyance of passengers and light goods with the utmost dispatch" between that town and Manchester. By the following year, he added, he hoped to have four bills before Parliament for railroads 150 miles in length, the surveys of which were completed.

The survey of the Liverpool and Manchester line was proceeded with early in 1822, Mr. Padley conducting the work under the superintendence of Mr. Francis Giles. The people of the locality still offered every possible resistance to their proceedings; and the surveyors were, on several occasions, driven off the ground by force. They were under the necessity of proceeding with their work in the early dawn, before the inhabitants were astir. Chat Moss was surveyed by placing hurdles on the bog; and thus, with great difficulty, a very imperfect survey of the proposed line was at length effected.

Mr. James, however, failed to produce the plans and estimates for the session of 1823; but he sent in to the promoters of the line his preliminary report on the survey of investigation, in which he stated "that from their commencement the works may be completed in eighteen months, on a capital not exceeding 100,000*l.*, but the parliamentary survey and estimates will state the sums at which contractors will be found to execute the work." Mr. James was repeatedly pressed to supply the necessary plans and estimates; but though he made many promises, he failed to perform any of them. And thus the parliamentary session of 1824 was also lost.

Indeed, the time seems to have been not yet fully come for

the adoption of the railway. The projectors found that the line, as laid out, would provoke a powerful opposition in Parliament; and the local support which they had received was not such as to justify them in proceeding in the face of such opposition. The project therefore slept for a time, but it was not lost sight of. Mr. Sandars continued to agitate the question, and he shortly found the number of his supporters was such as to enable him again to take the field with a better prospect of success.

CHAPTER XVI.

MR. STEPHENSON APPOINTED ENGINEER OF THE STOCKTON AND DARLINGTON RAILWAY.

SOME time elapsed after the passing of the Act authorizing the construction of the Stockton and Darlington Railway, before any active steps were taken to carry it into effect. Doubts had been raised whether the line was the best that could be adopted for the district; and the subscribers generally were not so sanguine about their undertaking as to induce them to press on the formation of the railway.

One day, about the end of the year 1821, two strangers knocked at the door of Mr. Pease's house in Darlington; and the message was brought to him that some persons from Killingworth wanted to speak with him. They were invited in, on which one of the visitors introduced himself as Nicholas Wood, viewer at Killingworth, and then, turning to his companion, he introduced him to Mr. Pease as George Stephenson, of the same place. Mr. Stephenson came forward and handed to Mr. Pease a letter from Mr. Lambert, the manager at Killingworth, in which it was stated that the bearer was the engine-wright at the pits, that he had had experience in the laying out of railways and had given satisfaction to his employers, and that he would therefore recommend him to the notice of Mr. Pease if he stood in need of the services of such a person.

Mr. Pease entered into conversation with his visitors, and soon ascertained the object of their errand. Stephenson had heard of the passing of the Stockton and Darlington Act, and desiring to increase his railway experience, and also to employ in some larger field the practical knowledge he had already gained, he determined to visit Mr. Pease, the known projector of the undertaking, with the view of being employed to carry it out. He had brought with him his friend Nicholas Wood, for the purpose at the same time of relieving his diffidence and supporting his application.

Mr. Pease liked the appearance of his visitors. "There was," as he afterwards remarked in speaking of Stephenson, "such an honest, sensible look about him, and he seemed so modest and unpretending. He spoke in the strong Northumbrian dialect of his district, and described himself as 'only the engine-wright at Killingworth; that's what he was.'"

Mr. Pease very soon saw that his visitor was the man for his purpose. The whole plans of the railway being still in an undetermined state, Mr. Pease was glad to have the opportunity of gathering from Mr. Stephenson the results of his experience. The latter strongly recommended a *railway* in preference to a tramroad, in which Mr. Pease was disposed to concur with him. The conversation next turned on the tractive power which the company intended to employ, and Mr. Pease said that they had based their whole calculations on the employment of *horse* power. "I was so satisfied," said he afterwards, "that a horse upon an iron road would draw ten tons for one ton on a common road, that I felt sure that before long the railway would become the King's Highway."

But Mr. Pease was scarcely prepared for the bold assertion made by his visitor, that the locomotive engine with which he had been working the Killingworth Railway for many years past, was worth fifty horses, and that engines made after a similar plan would yet entirely supersede all horse power upon railroads. Mr. Stephenson was daily becoming more positive as to the superiority of his locomotive; and on this, as on all subsequent occasions, he strongly urged Mr. Pease to adopt it. "Come over to Killingworth," said he, "and see what my Blutcher can do; seeing is believing, sir." And Mr. Pease promised that on some early day he would go over to Killingworth with his friend Thomas Richardson, and take a look at this wonderful machine that was to supersede horses.

On Mr. Pease referring to the difficulties and the opposition which the projectors of the railway had had to encounter, and the obstacles which still lay in their way, Stephenson said to him, "I think, sir, I have some knowledge of craniology, and from what I see of your head, I feel sure that if you will fairly *buckle* to this railway, you are the man successfully to carry it through." "I think so too," rejoined Mr. Pease; "and I may observe to thee, that if thou succeed in making this a good railway, thou may consider thy fortune as good as made." He added that all they would require at present was an estimate of the cost of resurveying the line, with the direction of which the company was not quite satisfied; and as they had already paid away several hundred pounds, and found themselves very little advanced, Mr. Pease asked that this new survey should be done at as little expense as possible. This Stephenson readily assented to; and after Mr. Pease had pledged himself to bring his application for the appointment of engineer before the Directors on an early day, and to support it with his influence, the two visitors prepared to take their leave, informing Mr. Pease that they intended to return as they had come, "by nip;" that is, they would obtain a sort of smuggled lift on the stage coach, by tipping Jehu —for in those days the stage coachmen were wont to regard all casual roadside passengers as their special perquisite. And thus the two contrived to make a cheap journey of it between Darlington and Killingworth.

Mr. Pease having made further inquiries respecting the character and qualifications of George Stephenson, and having received, from John Grimshaw—also a Friend, the inventor of endless spinning—a very strong recommendation of him as the right man for the intended work, he brought the subject of his application before the directors of the Stockton and Darlington Company. They resolved to adopt his recommendation that a railway be formed instead of a tramroad; and they further requested Mr. Pease to write to Mr. Stephenson, which he accordingly did, requesting him to report as to the practicability, or otherwise, of the line as laid out by Mr. Overton, and to state his recommendations as to any deviations or improvements in its course, together with estimates of comparative expenses. "In short," said Mr. Pease, "we wish thee to proceed in all thy levels, estimates and calculations, with that care and economy which would influence thee if the whole of the work were thy own."

Mr. Stephenson replied (August 2d, 1821) that the resurvey of the line would occupy at least four weeks, and that his charge would include all necessary assistance for the accomplishment of the survey, estimates of the expense of cuts and batteries (since called cuttings and embankments) on the different projected lines, together with all remarks, reports, etc., on the same; also the comparative cost of malleable and cast-iron rails, laying the same, winning and preparing the blocks of stone, and all other materials wanted to complete the line. "I could not do this," said he, "for less than 140*l.*, allowing me to be moderately paid. Such a survey would of course have to be made before the work could be begun, as it is impossible to form any idea of contracting for the cuts and batteries by the former one; and I assure you I shall, in completing the undertaking, act with that economy which would influence me if the whole of the work was my own."

About the end of September Mr. Stephenson went over the line of the proposed railway, for the purpose of suggesting such improvements and deviations as he might consider desirable. He went over every foot of the ground himself, accompanied by an assistant and a chainman—his son Robert, who had recently returned from college, entering the figures while his father took the sights. After being engaged in the work at intervals for about six weeks, Mr. Stephenson reported the result of his survey to the Board of Directors, and showed that by certain deviations, a line shorter by about three miles might be constructed at a considerable saving in expense, while at the same time more favorable gradients—an important consideration—would be secured.

The directors of the company, being satisfied that the improvements suggested in the line, and the saving which would thus be effected in mileage and in money, fully warranted them in incurring the trouble, delay and expense of making a further application to Parliament for an amended Act, took the requisite steps with this object. And in the meantime they directed Mr. Stephenson to prepare the specifications for the rails and chairs, and make arrangements to enter into contracts for the supply of the stone and wooden blocks on which the rails and chairs were to be laid. It was determined in the first place to proceed with the works at those parts of the line where no deviation was proposed; and the first rail of the Stockton and Darlington Railway was laid with considerable ceremony, by Thomas Meynell, Esq., of Yarm, at a point near St. John's Well, Stockton, on the 23d of May, 1822.

It is worthy of note, that Mr. Stephenson, in making his first estimate of the cost of forming the railway, according to the instructions of the directors, set down, as part of the cost, 6,200*l.*, for stationary engines, not mentioning locomotives at all. The directors as yet confined their views to the employment only of horses for the haulage of the coals, and of fixed engines and ropes where horse power was not applicable. The whole question of steam locomotive power was, in the estimation of the public, as well as of practical and scientific men, as yet in doubt. The confident anticipations of Mr. Stephenson, as to the eventual success of locomotive engines, were regarded as mere speculations; and when he gave utterance to his views, as he frequently took the opportunity of doing, it had the effect of shaking the confidence of some of his friends in the solidity of his judgment and his practical qualities as an engineer.

When Mr. Pease discussed the question with Stephenson, his remark was, "Come over and see my engines at Killingworth, and satisfy yourself as to the efficiency of the locomotive. I will show you the colliery books, that you may ascertain for yourself the actual cost of working. And I must tell you that the economy of the locomotive engine is no longer a matter of theory, but a matter of fact." So confident was the tone in which Stephenson spoke of the success of his engines, and so important were the consequences involved in arriving at a correct conclusion on the subject, that Mr. Pease at length resolved upon paying a visit to Killingworth; and accordingly he proceeded thither, in company with his friend Mr. Thomas Richardson,* a considerable subscriber to the Stockton and Darlington project, in the summer of 1822.

When Mr. Pease arrived at Killingworth village, he inquired for George Stephenson, and was told that he must go over to the West Moor, and seek for a cottage by the roadside, with a dial over the door—that was where George Stephenson lived. They soon found the house with the dial; and on knocking, the door was opened by Mrs. Stephenson—his second wife, (Elizabeth Hindmarsh,) the daughter of a farmer at Black Callerton, whom he had married in 1819. Her husband, she said, was not in the house at present, but she would send for him to the colliery. And in a short time Stephenson appeared before them in his working dress, just out of the pit.

He very soon had his locomotive brought up to the crossing close by the end of the cottage—made the gentlemen mount it,

* Mr. Richardson was the founder of the celebrated discount house of Richardson, Overend and Gourney, in Lombard Street

and showed them its paces. Harnessing it to a train of loaded wagons, he ran it along the railroad, and so thoroughly satisfied his visitors of its powers and capabilities, that from that day Edward Pease was a declared supporter of the locomotive engine. In preparing, in 1823, the Amended Stockton and Darlington Act, at Mr. Stephenson's urgent request, Mr. Pease had a clause inserted, taking power to work the railway by means of locomotive engines, and to employ them for the haulage of passengers as well as of merchandise;* and Mr. Pease gave a further and still stronger proof of his conviction as to the practical value of the locomotive, by entering into a partnership with Mr. Stephenson, in the following year, for the establishment of a locomotive foundry and manufactory in the town of Newcastle—the northern centre of the English railroad system.

The second Stockton and Darlington Act was obtained in the session of 1823, not, however, without opposition, the Duke of Cleveland and the road trustees still appearing as the determined opponents of the bill. Nevertheless, the measure passed into law, and the works were now vigorously proceeded with, Mr. Stephenson having been appointed the company's engineer, at a salary of 300*l.* per annum.

* The first clause in any railway act, empowering the employment of locomotive engines for the working of passenger traffic.

CHAPTER XVII.

COMPLETION AND OPENING OF THE STOCKTON AND DARLINGTON RAILWAY.

Mr. Stephenson now proceeded with the working survey of the improved line of the Stockton and Darlington Railway, laying out every foot of the ground himself, accompanied by his assistants. Railway surveying was as yet in its infancy, and was very slow and deliberate work. Afterwards it became a separate branch of railway business, and was left to a special staff of surveyors. Indeed on no subsequent line did Mr. Stephenson take the sights through the spirit level with his own hands and eyes, as he did on this railway. He would start very early in the morning, and survey until dusk. Mr. John Dixon, who assisted in the survey, mentions that he remembers on one occasion, after a long day's work near Aycliffe, when the light had completely failed them, the party separated—some to walk to Darlington, four miles off, Mr. Stephenson himself to the Simpasture farmhouse, where he had arranged to stay for the night; and his last stringent injunction was, that they must all be on the ground to resume leveling as soon as there was light enough for the purpose. "You must not," said he, "set off from Darlington by daybreak, for then we shall lose an hour; but you must be *here*, ready to begin work as soon as it is daylight."

Mr. Stephenson performed the survey in top boots and breeches —a usual dress at the time. He was not at any time particular as to his living; and during the survey, he took his chance of getting a drink of milk and a bit of bread at some cottager's house along the line, or occasionally joined in a homely dinner at some neighboring farmhouse. The country people were accustomed to give him a hearty welcome when he appeared at their door; for he was always full of cheery and homely talk, and, when there were children about the house, he had plenty of surplus humor for them as well as for their seniors.

After the day's work was over, Mr. Stephenson would drop in at Mr. Pease's, to talk over with him the progress of the survey, and discuss various matters connected with the railway. Mr. Pease's daughters were usually present; and on one occasion, finding the young ladies learning the art of embroidery, he volunteered to instruct them. "I know all about it," said he; "and you will wonder how I learnt it. I will tell you. When I was a brakesman at Killingworth, I learnt the art of embroidery while working the pitman's button-holes by the engine fire at nights." He was never ashamed, but on the contrary rather proud, of reminding his friends of these humble pursuits of his early life. Mr. Pease's family were greatly pleased with his conversation, which was always amusing and instructive; full of all sorts of experience, gathered sometimes in the oddest and most out-of-the-way places. Even at that early period, before he had mixed in the society of educated persons, there was a dash of speculativeness in his remarks, which gave a high degree of originality to his conversation; and sometimes he would, in a casual remark, throw a flash of light upon a subject, which called up a whole train of pregnant suggestions.

One of the most important subjects of discussion at these meetings with Mr. Pease, was the establishment of a manufactory at Newcastle for the building of locomotive engines. Up to this time all the locomotives constructed after Mr. Stephenson's designs, had been made by ordinary mechanics working amongst the collieries in the north of England. But he had long felt that the accuracy and style of their workmanship admitted of great improvement, and that upon this the more perfect action of the locomotive engine, and its general adoption as the tractive power on railways, in a great measure depended. One great object that he had in view in establishing the proposed factory was, to concentrate a number of good workmen for the purpose of carrying out the improvements in detail which he was constantly making in his engine. He felt hampered by the want of efficient helpers in the shape of skilled mechanics, who could work out in a practical form the ideas of which his busy mind was always so prolific. Doubtless, too, he believed that the locomotive manufactory would prove a remunerative investment, and that, on the general adoption of the railway system, which he now anticipated, he would derive solid advantages from the fact of his manufactory being the only establishment of the kind for the special construction of railway locomotives.

He still believed in the eventual success of railways, though it might be slow. Much, he believed, would depend upon the issue of this great experiment at Darlington; and as Mr. Pease was a man on whose sound judgment he could rely, he determined upon consulting him about his proposed locomotive factory. Mr. Pease approved of his design, and strongly recommended him to carry it into effect. But there was the question of means; and he did not think he had capital enough for the purpose. He told Mr. Pease that he could advance a thousand pounds—the amount of the testimonial presented by the coal-owners for his safety-lamp invention, and which he had still left untouched; but he did not think this sufficient for the purpose, and that he should at least require another thousand pounds. Mr. Pease had been very favorably struck by the successful performances of the Killingworth engine; and being an accurate judge of character, he was not slow to perceive that he could not go far wrong in linking a portion of his fortune with the energy and industry of George Stephenson. He consulted his friend Thomas Richardson in the matter; and the two consented to advance 500*l.* each for the purpose of establishing the engine factory at Newcastle. A piece of land was accordingly purchased in Forth Street, in August, 1823, on which a small building was erected—the nucleus of the gigantic establishment which was afterwards formed around it; and active operations commenced early in 1824.

While the Stockton and Darlington Railway works were in progress, Mr. Stephenson held many interesting discussions with Mr. Pease, on points connected with its construction and working, the determination of which in a great measure affected the formation and working of all future railways. The most important points were these: 1. The comparative merits of cast and wrought-iron rail. 2. The gauge of the railway. 3. The employment of horse or engine power in working it when ready for traffic.

The kind of rails to be laid down to form the permanent road, was a matter of considerable importance. A wooden tramroad had been contemplated when the first Act was applied for; but Stephenson having advised that an iron road should be laid down, he was instructed to draw up a specification of the rails. He went before the directors to discuss with them the kind of rails which were to be specified. He was himself interested in the patent for cast-iron rails, which he had taken out in conjunction with Mr. Losh in 1816; and, of course, it was to his interest that his articles should be adopted. But when requested to give his opinion on the subject, he frankly said to the directors, "Well, gentlemen, to tell you the truth, although it would put 500*l.* in my pocket to specify my own patent rails, I cannot do so after the experience I have had. If you take my advice, you will not lay down a single cast-iron rail." "Why?" asked the directors. "Because they will not stand the weight; there is no wear in them, and you will be at no end of expense for repairs and relays." "What kind of road, then," he was asked, "would you recommend?" "Malleable rails, certainly," said he; "and

I can recommend them with the more confidence from the fact that at Killingworth we have had some Swedish bars laid down —nailed to wooden sleepers—for a period of fourteen years, the wagons passing over them daily; and there they are, in use yet, whereas the cast rails are constantly giving way.

The price of malleable rails was, however, so high—being then worth about 12*l.* per ton—as compared with cast-iron rails at about 5*l.* 10*s.*, and the saving of expense was so important a consideration with the subscribers to the railway, that Mr. Stephenson was directed to provide, in the specification drawn by him, that only one half of the quantity of the rails required—or 800 tons—should be of malleable iron, the remainder being of cast-iron. The malleable rails were required by the specification to be "made from scraps or good English bars remanufactured." They were also of the kind called "fish-bellied," after Birkenshaw's patent, and weighed only 28lbs. to the yard, being 2¼ inches broad at the top, with the upper flange ¾ inch thick. They were only 2 inches in depth at the points at which they rested on the rails, and 3¼ inches in the middle or bellied part.

When forming the road, the proper gauge had also to be determined. What width was this to be? The gauge of the first tramroad laid down had virtually settled the point. The gauge of wheels of the common vehicles of the country—of the carts and wagons employed on common roads, which were first used on the tramroads—was 4 feet 8½ inches. And so the first tramroads were laid down of this gauge. The tools and machinery for constructing coal-wagons and locomotives were formed with this gauge in view. The Wylam wagon-way, afterwards the Wylam plateway, the Killingworth railroad, and the Hetton railroad, were all laid down on this gauge. Some of the earth-wagons used to form the Stockton and Darlington road were brought from the Hetton Railway; and others which were specially constructed were formed of the same dimensions, these being intended afterwards to be employed in the working of the traffic.

As the time for the opening of the line approached, the question of the Tractive Power to be employed was warmly discussed. At the Brusselton incline, fixed engines must necessarily be made use of; and the designs for these were completed by Robert Stephenson in 1824, previous to his departure for Columbia, in South America. With respect to the mode of working the railway generally, it was decided that horses were to be largely employed, and arrangements were made for their purchase. The influence of Mr. Pease also secured that a fair trial should be given to the experiment of working the traffic by locomotive power; and three engines were ordered from the firm of George Stephenson and Company, at Newcastle, and were accordingly put in hand forthwith, in anticipation of the opening of the railway. These were constructed after Mr. Stephenson's most matured designs, and embodied all the improvements in the locomotive which he had contrived up to that time. No. 1 engine, the "Active," which was first delivered upon the line, weighed about eight tons. It had one large flue or tube through the boiler, through which the heated air passed direct from the furnace at one end, lined with fire-bricks, to the chimney at the other. The combustion in the furnace was quickened by the adoption of the steam-blast into the chimney. The heat raised was sometimes so great, and was so imperfectly abstracted by the surrounding water, that the chimney became almost red-hot. These engines, when put to the top of their speed, were found capable of running at the rate of from twelve to sixteen miles an hour; but they were better adapted for the heavy work of hauling coal trains at low speeds—for which, indeed, they were specially constructed—than for running at the higher speeds afterwards adopted. Nor was it contemplated by the directors as possible, at the time when they were ordered, that locomotives could be made available for the purpose of passenger traveling.

Besides, the Stockton and Darlington Railway did not run through a district in which passengers were very likely to constitute any considerable portion of the traffic.

We may easily imagine the anxiety felt by Mr. Stephenson during the progress of the works towards completion, and his mingled hopes and doubts (though his doubts were but few) as to the issue of this great experiment. When the formation of the line near Stockton was well advanced, Mr. Stephenson one day, accompanied by his son Robert and John Dixon, made a journey of inspection of the works. His son, as we have said, was about to set out for South America, having received an appointment to superintend some mining operations in Columbia, respecting which there was then a large amount of speculation on foot. His health also had recently suffered through the closeness of his application to work and study; and his father, hoping that he might derive benefit from the change of climate, encouraged him to undertake the charge which was offered him. On the day in question the party reached Stockton, and proceeded to dine at one of the inns there. After dinner, Mr. Stephenson ventured on the very unusual measure of ordering in a bottle of wine, to drink success to the railway. John Dixon remembers and relates with pride the utterance of the master on the occasion. "Now lads," said he to the two young men, "I will tell you that I think you will live to see the day, though I may not live so long, when railways will come to supersede almost all other methods of conveyance in this country—when mail coaches will go by railway, and railroads will become the Great Highway for the king and all his subjects. The time is coming when it will be cheaper for a working man to travel on railway than to walk on foot. I know there are great and almost insurmountable difficulties that will have to be encountered; but what I have said will come to pass as sure as we live. I only wish I may live to see the day, though that I can scarcely hope for, as I know how slow all human progress is, and with what difficulty I have been able to get the locomotive adopted, notwithstanding my more than ten years successful experiment at Killingworth." The result, however, outstripped even the most sanguine anticipations of Stephenson; and his son Robert, shortly after his return from America in 1827, saw his father's locomotive generally adopted as the tractive power on railways.

The Stockton and Darlington line was opened for traffic on the 27th of September, 1825. An immense concourse of people assembled from all parts to witness the ceremony of opening this first public railway. The powerful opposition which the project had encountered, the threats which were still uttered against the railway by the road trustees and others, who declared that they would yet prevent its being worked, and perhaps the general unbelief as to its success which still prevailed, tended greatly to excite the curiosity of the public as to the result. Some went to rejoice at the opening, some to see "the bubble burst;" and there were many prophets of evil who would not miss the blowing up of the boasted Traveling Engine. The opening was, however, auspicious. The proceedings commenced at Brusselton Incline, about nine miles above Darlington, when the fixed engine drew a train of loaded wagons up the incline from the west, and lowered them on the east side. At the foot of the incline, a locomotive was in readiness to receive them, Mr. Stephenson himself driving the engine. The train consisted of six wagons, loaded with coals and flour; after these was the passenger coach, filled with the Directors and their friends, and then twenty-one wagons fitted up with temporary seats for passengers; and lastly came six wagon-loads of coals, making in all a train of thirty-eight vehicles. The local chronicler of the day went almost out of breath in describing the extraordinary event:—"The signal being given," he says, "the engine started off with this immense train of carriages; and such was its velocity, that in some parts the speed was frequently 12 miles an hour; and at that time the number of passengers was counted to be 450, which, together with the coals, merchandise and carriages, would amount to near 90 tons. The engine, with its load, arrived at Darlington, a distance of 8¾ miles, in 65 minutes. The six wagons loaded with coals, intended for Darlington, were then left behind; and, obtaining a fresh supply of water and arranging the procession to accommodate a band of music, and numerous passengers from Darlington, the engine set off again, and arrived at Stockton in 3 hours and 7 minutes, including stoppages, the distance being nearly 12 miles." By the time the train reached Stockton, there were about 600 persons in the train or hanging on to the wagons, which must have gone at a safe and steady pace of from 4 to 6 miles an hour from Darlington. "The arrival at Stockton," it is added, "excited a deep interest and admiration."

The working of the line then commenced, and the results were such as to surprise even the most sanguine of its projectors. The traffic upon which they had formed their estimates of profit, proved to be small in comparison with the traffic which flowed in upon them that had never been taken into account. Thus, what the company had principally relied upon for their profit, was the carriage of coals for land sale at the stations along the line, whereas the haulage of coals to the seaports for exportation to the London market, was not contemplated as possible. When the bill was before Parliament, Mr. Lambton (afterwards Earl of Durham) succeeded in getting a clause inserted, limiting the charge for the haulage of all coal to Stockton-on-Tees for the purpose of shipment, to one halfpenny per ton per mile; whereas a rate of fourpence per ton was allowed to be taken for all coals led upon the railway for land sale. Mr. Lambton's object in enforcing the low rate of one halfpenny was to protect his own trade in coal exported from Sunderland and the northern ports. He believed, in common with everybody else, that the halfpenny rate would effectually secure him against any competition on the part of the Stockton and Darlington Company; for it was not considered possible for coals to be led at that low price, and the proprietors of the railway themselves considered that to carry coals at such a rate would be utterly ruinous. The projectors never contemplated sending more than ten thousand tons a year to Stockton, and those only for shipment as ballast; they looked for their profits almost exclusively to the land sale. The result, however, was as surprising to them as it must have been to Mr. Lambton. The halfpenny rate which was forced upon them, instead of being ruinous, proved the vital element in the success of the railway. In the course of a few years, the annual shipment of coal, led by the Stockton and Darlington Railway to Stockton and Middlesborough, exceeded five hundred thousand tons; and it has since far exceeded this amount. Instead of being, as anticipated, a subordinate branch of traffic, it proved, in fact, the main traffic, while the land sale was merely subsidiary.

The anticipations of the company as to passenger traffic were in like manner more than realized. At first, passengers were not thought of; and it was only while the works were in progress that the starting of a passenger coach was seriously contemplated. The number of persons traveling between the two towns was very small; and it was not known whether these would risk their persons upon the iron road. It was determined, however, to make the trial of a railway coach; and Mr. Stephenson was authorized by the Directors to have one built to his order at Newcastle, at the cost of the company. This was done accordingly; and the first railway passenger carriage was built after our engineer's plans. It was, however, a very modest, and indeed a somewhat uncouth machine, more resembling a caravan such as is still to be seen at county fairs, containing the "Giant and the Dwarf" and other wonders of the world, than a passenger coach of any extant form. A row of seats ran along each side of the interior, and a long deal table was fixed in the centre; the access being by means of a door at the end, in the manner of an omnibus. This coach arrived from Newcastle the day before the opening, and formed part of the railway procession above described. Mr. Stephenson was consulted as to the name of the coach, and he at once suggested the "Experiment;" and by this name it was called. The company's arms were afterwards painted on her panels, with the motto of "Periculum privatum utilitas publica." Such was the sole passenger-carrying stock of the Stockton and Darlington Company in the year 1825. But the "Experiment" proved the forerunner of a mighty traffic; and long time did not elapse before it was displaced, not only by improved coaches (still drawn by horses), but afterwards by long trains of passenger carriages drawn by locomotive engines.

No sooner did the coal and merchandise trains begin to run regularly upon the line, than new business relations sprang up between Stockton and Darlington, and there were many more persons who found occasion to travel between the two towns — merchandise and mineral traffic invariably stimulating, if not calling into existence an entirely new traffic in passengers. Before the construction of the line, the attempt had been made to run a coach between Stockton, Darlington and Barnard Castle three times a week; but it was starved off the road for want of support. Now, however, that there were numbers of people desiring to travel, the stage-coach by the common road was revived, and prospered, and many other persons connected with the new traffic got a "lift" by the railway wagons, which were even more popular than the stage-coach.

The "Experiment" was fairly started as a passenger-coach on the 10th of October, 1825, a fortnight after the opening of the line. It was drawn by one horse, and performed a journey daily each way between the two towns, accomplishing the distance of twelve miles in about two hours. The fare charged was a shilling, without distinction of class; and each passenger was allowed fourteen pounds of luggage free. The "Experiment" was not, however, worked by the company, but was let to

Messrs. Pickersgill and Harland, carriers on the railway, under an arrangement with them as to the payment of tolls for the use of the line, rent of booking cabins, etc.

The speculation answered so well, that several coaching companies were shortly got up by innkeepers at Darlington and Stockton, for the purpose of running other coaches upon the railroad—and an active competition for passenger traffic now sprang up. The "Experiment" being found too heavy for one horse to draw between Stockton and Darlington, besides being found an uncomfortable machine, was banished to the coal district, and ran for a time between Darlington and Shildon. Its place on the line between Stockton and Darlington was supplied by other and better vehicles—though they were no other than old stage-coach bodies, which were purchased by the company, each mounted upon an underframe with flange wheels, and let out to the coaching companies, who horsed and managed them under an arrangement as to tolls, in like manner as the "Experiment" had been worked. Now began the distinction of inside and outside passengers, equivalent to first and second class, paying different fares. The competition with each other upon the railway, and with the ordinary stage-coaches upon the road, soon brought up the speed, which was increased to ten miles an hour—the mail coach rate of traveling in those days, and considered very fast. The coaches filled almost daily. "In fact," says a writer of the time, "the passengers do not seem to be at all particular, for, in cases of urgency, they are seen crowding the coach on the top, sides, or any part where they can get a footing; and they are frequently so numerous, that when they descend from the coach and begin to separate, it looks like the dismissal of a small congregation!"

Mr. Clephan, a native of the district, thus piquantly describes some of the more prominent features of the competition between the rival coach companies: "There were two separate coach companies in Stockton, and amusing collisions sometimes occurred between the drivers—who found on the rail a novel element for contention. Coaches cannot pass each other on the rail as on the road; and at the more westward public-house in Stockton (the Bay Horse, kept by Joe Buckton,) the coach was always on the line betimes, reducing its eastward rival to the necessity of waiting patiently (or impatiently) in the rear. Difficulties, too, occurred along the road. The line was single, with four sidings in the mile; and when two coaches met, or two trains, or coach and train, the question arose which of the drivers must go back? This was not always settled in silence. As to trains, it came to be a sort of understanding that light wagons should give way to loaded; and as to trains and coaches, that the passenger should have preference over coals; while coaches, when they met, must quarrel it out. At length, midway between sidings, a post was erected; and a rule was laid down that he who had passed the pillar must go on, and the 'coming man' go back. At the Goose Pool and Early Nook, it was common for these coaches to stop; and there, as Jonathan would say, passengers and coachmen 'liquored.' One coach, introduced by an innkeeper, was a compound of two mourning-coaches—an approximation to the real railway coach, which still adheres, with multiplying exceptions, to the stage-coach type. One Dixon, who drove the 'Experiment' between Darlington and Childon, is the inventor of carriage lighting on the rail. On a dark winter night, having compassion on his passengers, he would buy a penny candle, and place it, lighted, amongst them, on the table of the 'Experiment' —the first railway coach, (which, by the way, ended its days at Shildon, as a railway cabin,) being also the first coach on the rail (first, second and third class jammed all into one) that in dulged its customers with light in darkness." *

The traffic of all sorts increased so steadily and so rapidly that

* Mr. Clephan has introduced these particulars in his interesting review of the first edition of this book, published in the *Gateshead Observer;* and I gladly avail myself of his excellent local knowledge on the subject.

the Directors of the company shortly found it necessary to take into their own hands the entire working—of minerals, merchandise and passengers. It had been provided by the first Stockton and Darlington Act that the line should be free to all parties who chose to use it at certain prescribed rates, and that any person might put horses and wagons on the railway, and carry for himself. But this arrangement led to increasing confusion and difficulty, and could not continue in the face of a large and rapidly increasing traffic. The goods trains got so long, that the carriers found it necessary to call in the aid of the locomotive engine to help them on their way. Then mixed trains began to be seen of passengers and merchandise—the final result being the assumption of the entire charge of the traffic by the railway company. In course of time new passenger carriages were specially built for the better accommodation of the public, until at length regular passenger trains were run, drawn by the locomotive engine—though this was not until after the Liverpool and Manchester Company had established passenger trains as a distinct branch of their traffic.

Three of Stephenson's locomotives were from the first regularly employed to work the coal trains; and their proved efficiency for this purpose led to the gradual increase of the locomotive power. The speed of the engines—slow though it was in those days—was regarded as something marvelous; and a race actually came off between No. 1 engine, the "Active," and one of the stage-coaches traveling from Darlington to Stockton by the ordinary road; and it was regarded as a great triumph of mechanical skill that the locomotive reached Stockton first, beating the stage-coach by about a hundred yards! *

* The same engine continued in good working order in the year 1846, when it headed the railway procession on the opening of the Middlesborough and Redcar Railway, traveling at the rate of about fourteen miles an hour. This engine, the first that traveled upon the first public railway, has quite recently been placed upon a pedestal in front of the railway station at Darlington.

For some years, however, the principal haulage of the line was performed by horses. The inclination of the gradients being towards the sea, this was perhaps the cheapest mode of traction, so long as the traffic was not very large. The horse drew the train along the level road until, on reaching a descending gradient, down which the train ran by its own weight, the horse was unharnessed, and, when loose, he wheeled round to the other end of the wagons, to which a "dandy-cart" was attached, its bottom being only a few inches from the rail. Bringing his step into unison with the speed of the train, the horse leapt nimbly into his place in this wagon, which was usually fitted with a well-filled hay-rack. Mr. Clephan relates the story of a sagacious gray horse, which was fertile in expedients when emergencies arose: "On one occasion perceiving that a train, which had run amain, must rush into his dandy-cart, he took a leap for life over the side, and escaped. In a similar peril, a leap over the side being impracticable, he sprung on to the coal-wagon in front, and stood like an equestrian statue on a pedestal. But the time came, at last, when there was no escape; and the poor old gray was destroyed."

The details of the working were gradually perfected by experience, the projectors of the line being at first scarcely conscious of the importance and significance of the work which they had taken in hand, and little thinking that they were laying the foundation of a system which was yet to revolutionize the internal communications of the world, and confer the greatest blessings on mankind. It is important to note that the commercial results of the enterprise were considered satisfactory from the opening of the railway. Besides conferring a great public benefit upon the inhabitants of the district, and throwing open entirely new markets for the almost boundless stores of coal found in the Bishop Aukland district, the profits derived from the traffic created by the railway, enabled increasing dividends to be paid to those who had risked their capital in the undertaking, and thus held forth an encouragement to the projectors of railways generally, which was not without an important effect in stimulating the projection of similar enterprises in other districts.*

Before leaving the subject of the Stockton and Darlington Railway, we cannot avoid alluding to one of its most remarkable and direct results—the creation of the town of Middlesborough-on-Tees. When the railway was opened in 1825, the site of this future metropolis of Cleveland was occupied by one solitary farmhouse and its outbuildings. All round was pasture land or mud banks; scarcely another house was within sight. But when the coal export trade, fostered by the halfpenny maximum rate imposed by the legislature, seemed likely to attain a gigantic growth, and it was found that the accommodation furnished at Stockton was insufficient, Mr. Edward Pease, joined by a few of his Quaker friends, bought about 500 or 600 acres of land, five miles lower down the river—the site of the modern Middlesborough—for the purpose of there forming a new seaport for the shipment of coals brought to the Tees by the railway. The line was accordingly shortly extended thither; docks were excavated;

* From the minute books of the Stockton and Darlington Company, it appears that a dividend of 2½ per cent. was paid to the shareholders for the first nine months after the line was opened, during which period the traffic arrangements must necessarily have been in a very incomplete state. The Company had all their experience to gather, having none to fall back upon. Everything was to organize from the very beginning. Under these circumstances, it was matter of congratulation to the proprietors that *any* profits should have been made during those first nine months. But in the next year ending June, 1827, a dividend of 5 per cent. was paid; and the same rate was maintained until 1831, when it was increased to 6 per cent., and in 1832 to 8 per cent. It was matter of notoriety that 10 per cent. was afterwards paid during many years, which arose in some measure from the circumstance that the Company were enabled to borrow a large proportion of their capital at a low rate of interest, whilst the share capital upon which dividend was paid, remained comparatively small. These arrangements, however, proved the shrewd business qualities of the men who originally conducted the undertaking. The results, as displayed in the annual dividends, must have been eminently encouraging to the astute commercial men of Liverpool and Manchester, who were then engaged in the prosecution of their railway. Indeed, the commercial success of the Stockton and Darlington Company may be justly characterized as the turning-point of the railway system. With that practical illustration daily in sight of the public it was no longer possible for Parliament to have prevented its eventual extension.

a town sprang up; churches, chapels and schools were built, with a custom-house, mechanics' institute, banks, ship-building yards and iron factories; and in a few years the port of Middlesborough became one of the most important on the north-east coast of England. In the year 1845, 505,486 tons of coals were shipped in the nine-acre dock, by means of the ten coal-drops abutting thereupon. In about ten years a busy population of about 6,000 persons (since swelled into 15,000) occupied the site of the original farmhouse. More recently, the discovery of vast stores of ironstone in the Cleveland Hills, close adjoining Middlesborough, has tended still more rapidly to augment the population and increase the commercial importance of the place. Iron furnaces are now blazing along the vale of Cleveland: and new smelting works are rising up in all directions, fed by the railway, which brings to them their supplies of fuel from the Durham coal-fields.

It is pleasing to relate, in connection with this great work—the Stockton and Darlington Railway, projected by Edward Pease and executed by George Stephenson—that afterwards, when Mr. Stephenson became a prosperous and celebrated man, he did not forget the friend who had taken him by the hand, and helped him on in his early days. He always remembered Mr. Pease with gratitude and affection; and that gentleman is still proud to exhibit a handsome gold watch, received as a gift from his celebrated *protégé,* bearing these words: "Esteem and gratitude: from George Stephenson to Edward Pease."

CHAPTER XVIII.

MR. STEPHENSON APPOINTED TO SURVEY A RAILWAY FROM LIVERPOOL TO MANCHESTER.

THE project of a line of railway from Liverpool to Manchester was revived in the speculative year 1824. It had not, indeed, been lost sight of by its advocates, who had merely waited for a time in the hope of mitigating the opposition of the powerful canal companies and land-owners. But the interruptions to the conveyance of goods between the two towns had at length become intolerable; and it was a matter of absolute necessity that some mode should be adopted for remedying the evil.

Mr. Sandars continued to hold by his project of a railway; and his first idea, of a solidly constructed tramway, to be worked by horse power, gradually assumed a more comprehensive form. He continued to propagate his ideas upon 'Change, and gradually succeeded in enlisting on his side an increasing number of influential merchants and manufacturers, both at Liverpool and Manchester. In 1824 he published a pamphlet, in which he strongly urged the great losses and interruptions to the trade of the district by the delays in the transport of goods; and in the same year a Public Declaration was drawn up, and signed by upwards of 150 of the principal merchants of Liverpool, setting forth that they considered "the present establishments for the transport of goods quite inadequate, and that a new line of conveyance has become absolutely necessary to conduct the increasing trade of the country with speed, certainty and economy."

The formation of a *third* line of water conveyance, in addition to the Mersey and Irwell Canals, was also considered; but it was almost immediately dismissed as impracticable, as the two existing establishments had already possession of all the water. There was no choice left but a tram or railroad, and the very necessities of the case forced on the adoption of the measure. Even though worked by horses, the proposed tramroad would be a valuable auxiliary to the existing means of conveyance. A public meeting was held at Liverpool to consider the best plan to be adopted, and a railway was determined on. A committee was appointed to take the necessary measures; but, as if reluctant to enter upon their arduous struggle with "vested interests," they first waited on Mr. Bradshaw, the Duke of Bridgewater's canal agent, in the hope of persuading him to increase the means of conveyance, as well as to reduce the charges; but they were only met by an unqualified refusal. They suggested the expediency of a railway, and even invited Mr. Bradshaw to become a large proprietor of shares. But his reply was: "All or none!" The canal proprietors were confident in their imagined security. They reveled in the prospect of enjoying in perpetuity their enormous dividends, which were so great that one of their undertakings (the Old Quay) had paid to its thirty-nine proprietors, every other year for half a century, the total amount of their original investment; and the income derived from the Duke of Bridgewater's canal amounted to not less than 100,000*l.* a year. Mr. Bradshaw knew that no third canal could be made, because all the available water was already absorbed by the two existing ones. As for the proposed railway, the canal proprietors ridiculed it as a chimera. It had been spoken about years before, when Mr. James made his survey, and nothing had come of it then. It would be the same now. The thing, they said, was got up merely to frighten them; but they were not so to be intimidated. The old system must therefore continue; and there was no alternative for the merchants of Liverpool and the manufacturers of Manchester but to submit with the best grace possible to the obstructions and extortions of the canal-companies.

In order to form an opinion of the practicability of a railroad, a deputation consisting of Mr. Sandars, Mr. Lister Ellis, Mr. Henry Booth of Liverpool, and Mr. Kennedy of Manchester, proceeded to Killingworth, to inspect the engines which had been so long in use there. They first went to Darlington, where they found the works of the Stockton line in full progress, though still unfinished. Proceeding next to Killingworth with Mr. Stephenson, they there witnessed the performances of his locomotive engines. The result of their visit was, on the whole, so satisfactory, that on their report being delivered to the committee at Liverpool, it was finally determined to form a company of proprietors for the construction of a double line of railway between Liverpool and Manchester.

The first prospectus of the scheme was dated the 29th of October, 1824, and had attached to it the names of the leading merchants of Liverpool—amongst them those of Gladstone, Lawrence, Ewart, Ellis, Moss, Cropper, and other well known men, representatives of the wealth, the enterprise and the energy of that great seaport. Nor were the manufacturers of Manchester behind the merchants and bankers of Liverpool in signifying their adhesion to the measure; for amongst the first subscribers we find the influential names of Birley, Potter, Sharpe and Garnett, of that town. Mr. Charles Lawrence, mayor of Liverpool, was appointed chairman of the provisional committee.

The prospectus was a carefully prepared document, very unlike the inflated balloons which were sent up by railway speculators in succeeding years. It set forth as its main object the establishment of a safe and cheap mode of transit for merchandise, by which the conveyance of goods between the two towns would be effected in four or five hours (instead of thirty-six hours as by the canal), whilst the charges would be reduced one third. On looking at the prospectus now, it is curious to note that, while the advantages anticipated from the carriage of merchandise were strongly insisted upon, the conveyance of passengers—which proved to be the chief source of profit—was only very cautiously referred to. "As a cheap and expeditious means of conveyance for travelers," says the prospectus in conclusion, "the railway holds out the fair prospect of a public accommodation, the magnitude and importance of which cannot be immediately ascertained."

The estimated expense of forming the line was set down at 400,000*l.*—a sum which was eventually found to be quite inadequate. A subscription list was opened, and speedily filled up. Four thousand shares of 100*l.* each were created; and it was a condition of the subscription that no one person was to hold more than ten shares. This secured a large and influential proprietary; and such was the interest felt in the measure at Liverpool and Manchester—so strongly convinced were the merchants, manufacturers and tradesmen, of the necessity of the undertaking, and so determined that it should now be carried out—that if the amount of capital had been ten times as great, it would immediately have been subscribed for.

While the project was still under discussion in its earlier stages, its promoters, desirous of removing the doubts which existed as to the employment of steam-carriages on the proposed railway, sent a second deputation to Killingworth for the purpose of again observing the action of Mr. Stephenson's engines. The deputation was on this occasion accompanied by Mr. Sylvester, an ingenious mechanic and engineer, who afterwards presented an able report on the subject to the committee.* Mr. Sylvester showed that the high-pressure engines employed by Mr. Stephen-

* Report of Railroads and Locomotive Engines, addressed to the Chairman and Committee of the Liverpool and Manchester projected Railroad. By Charles Sylvester, Civil Engineer. Liverpool: 1825.

son were both safe and economical in their working. With respect to the speed of the engines, he says: "Although it would be practicable to go at any speed, limited by the means of creating steam, the size of the wheels, and the number of strokes in the engine, it would not be safe to go at a greater rate than nine or ten miles an hour." This was considered a very high rate of speed in those days; and speculators were considered reckless who ventured to express themselves in favor of any more accelerated pace.

Satisfactory though the calculations and statements of Mr. Sylvester were, the cautious projectors of the railway were not yet quite satisfied; and a third journey was made to Killingworth, in January, 1825, by several gentlemen of the committee, for the purpose of being personal eye-witnesses of what steam-carriages were able to perform upon a railway. There they saw a train, consisting of a locomotive and loaded wagons, weighing in all fifty-four tons, traveling at the average rate of about seven miles an hour, the greatest speed being about nine and a half miles an hour. But when the engine was run by itself, with only one wagon attached, containing twenty gentlemen, five of whom were engineers, the speed attained was from ten to twelve miles an hour. "When it is considered," said the *Quarterly Review*,* "that neither the road nor the engines are to be compared with those that are now made, and that some parts of the rails were loose and irregular, these experiments may be regarded as quite decisive as to the power and the speed that may with safety be exerted on railroads."

When the promoters of the measure had finally determined to proceed to Parliament for the requisite powers to form the railway, they invited Mr. Stephenson to undertake the survey. Mr. James's dilatoriness in providing the plans and sections had by this time thoroughly provoked the promoters of the undertaking.

* March, 1825; published before the Liverpool and Manchester Bill was in Committee of the House of Commons.

Besides, he was now involved in pecuniary difficulties, in consequence of the failure of several of his extensive speculations; and he was under the necessity of removing to France, where he resided for some years. Before leaving England, however, he placed the imperfect plans of his first survey in the hands of the promoters, and he also made over to them his surveying apparatus; at the same time pointing to George Stephenson as the only man in England fitted by his practical knowledge and experience of railways to carry out the undertaking to a successful issue. The frequent interviews which the deputations from Liverpool had held with him on the subject, as well as on the best mode of working the line when made, had already convinced them that he was, of all others, the man best calculated to help them at this juncture. The successful working of his Killingworth locomotives; the energy which he had displayed in carrying on the works of the Stockton and Darlington Railway, now approaching completion; his readiness to face difficulties, and his practical ability in overcoming them; the enthusiasm which he displayed on the subject of railways and railway locomotion—had indeed directed their attention to him from the first as the most fitting man for the office of engineer of their great undertaking; and his appointment was unanimously confirmed.

The survey was proceeded with, in the face of great opposition on the part of the proprietors of the lands through which the railway was intended to pass. The prejudices of the farming and laboring classes were strongly excited against the persons employed upon the ground, and it was with the greatest difficulty that the levels could be taken. This opposition was especially manifested when the attempt was made to survey the line through the property of Lord Derby and that of Lord Sefton, and also where it crossed the Duke of Bridgewater's canal. At Knowsley, Mr. Stephenson was driven off the ground by the keepers, and threatened with rough handling if found there again. Lord Derby's farmers also turned out their men to watch the surveying party, and prevent them entering upon any lands where they had the power of driving them off. Afterwards, Mr. Stephenson suddenly and unexpectedly went upon the ground with a body of surveyors and their assistants who outnumbered Lord Derby's keepers and farmers, hastily collected to resist them; and this time they were only threatened with the legal consequences of their trespass. The engineer's excuse for taking so many people with him was, that he "did not like the instruments to be broken, as they had cost a great deal of money;" and his reason for making the survey in spite of Lord Derby's refusal to permit him to enter on his lands was, that he "had received the orders of the committee to make the survey." * The same sort of resistance was offered by Lord Sefton's keepers and farm-laborers, so that only a very imperfect survey could be made of the line where it passed through those two noblemen's domains. The obstructions placed in the way by these means prevented borings being made of the soil at Knowsley Moss, which was afterwards made a ground of objection to Mr. Stephenson's estimate when the bill came before Parliament. Great indignation was also expressed at the forcible entries made by his surveyors on the lands along the projected line, by which the strawberry beds of gardeners had been damaged and the cornfields of widows had been trampled under foot. In all such instances of even alleged damage, Mr. Stephenson paid compensation, though in most of the cases he was of opinion that not the slightest damage had been done.

The principal opposition, however, was experienced from Mr. Bradshaw, the manager of the Duke of Bridgewater's canal property, who offered a vigorous and protracted resistance to the railway in all its stages. The Duke of Bridgewater's farmers obstinately refused permission to enter upon their fields, although Mr. Stephenson offered to pay for any damage that might be

* Evidence before the Committee of the House of Commons on the Liverpool and Manchester Railroad Bill. Session 1825, pp. 272, 273.

done. Mr. Bradshaw positively refused permission in any case. The survey through the Duke of Bridgewater's property was consequently made entirely by stealth. Mr. Stephenson, afterwards describing the difficulties which he had thus encountered, said:—"I was threatened to be ducked in the pond if I proceeded, and, of course, we had a great deal of the survey to take by stealth, at the time when the people were at dinner. We could not get it done by night: indeed, we were watched day and night, and guns were discharged over the grounds belonging to Captain Bradshaw to prevent us. I can state further, that I was myself twice turned off Mr. Bradshaw's grounds by his men; and they said if I did not go instantly, they would take me up and carry me off to Worsley." *

The levels of the line were taken by Mr. Steel and Mr. Gillever, and the surveys were made by numerous assistants, not then so expert or so correct in railway surveying as they afterwards became. Mr. Stephenson was under the necessity of relying upon these imperfect surveys in the preparation of his estimates; and it is not at all a matter of surprise that, when the first engineers of the country were afterwards set in array against them by the wealthy canal and landed interests, they should have been able to pick so many holes in them, and thus for a brief period to defeat the designs of the promoters of the measure.

When the canal companies found that the Liverpool merchants were determined to proceed with their scheme—that they had completed their survey, and were ready to apply to Parliament for an act to enable them to form the railway, they at last reluctantly, and with a bad grace, made overtures of conciliation. They promised to employ steam-vessels both on the Mersey and on the canals. One of the companies offered to reduce its length by three miles at a considerable expenditure. At the same time they made a show of lowering their rates. But it was all too

* Proceedings of the Committee on the Liverpool and Manchester Railroad Bill. Evidence, p. 261.

late; for the project of the railway had now gone so far that the promoters (who might have been conciliated by such overtures at an earlier period) felt they were fully committed to the scheme, and that now they could not well draw back. Besides, the remedies offered by the canal companies could only have had the effect of staving off the difficulty for a brief season—the absolute necessity of forming a new line of communication between Liverpool and Manchester becoming more urgent from year to year. Arrangements were therefore made for proceeding with the bill in the parliamentary session of 1825. On this becoming known, the canal companies prepared to resist the measure tooth and nail. The public were appealed to on the subject; pamphlets were written and newspapers were hired to revile the railway. It was declared that its formation would prevent cows grazing and hens laying. The poisoned air from the locomotives would kill birds as they flew over them, and render the preservation of pheasants and foxes no longer possible. Householders adjoining the projected line were told that their houses would be burnt up by the fire thrown from the engine-chimneys, while the air around would be polluted by clouds of smoke. There would no longer be any use for horses; and if railways extended, the species would become extinguished, and oats and hay unsalable commodities. Traveling by road would be rendered highly dangerous, and country inns would be ruined. Boilers would burst and blow passengers to atoms. But there was always this consolation to wind up with—that the weight of the locomotive would completely prevent its moving, and that railways, even if made, could *never* be worked by steam-power!

Nevertheless, the canal companies of Leeds, Liverpool, and Birmingham, called upon every navigation company in the kingdom to oppose railways wherever they were projected, but more especially the projected Liverpool and Manchester line, the battle with which they evidently regarded as their Armageddon. A Birmingham newspaper invited opposition to the measure, and a public subscription was entered into for the purpose of making it effectual. The newspapers generally spoke of the project as a mere speculation; some wishing it success, although greatly doubting; others ridiculing it as a delusion, similar to the many other absurd projects of that madly-speculative period. It was a time when balloon companies proposed to work passenger traffic through the air at forty miles an hour, and when road companies projected carriages to run on turnpikes at twelve miles an hour, with relays of bottled gas instead of horses. There were companies for the working of American gold and silver mines—companies for cutting ship canals through Panama and Nicaragua—milk companies, burying companies, fish companies and steam companies of all sorts; and many less speculatively disposed than their neighbors, were ready to set down the projected railways of 1825 as mere bubbles of a similarly delusive character.

Among the most remarkable newspaper articles of the day calling attention to the application of the locomotive engine to the purposes of rapid steam traveling on railroads, was a series which appeared in 1824, in the *Scotsman* newspaper,* then edited by Charles Maclaren. In those publications the wonderful powers of the locomotive were logically demonstrated, and the writer, arguing from the experiments on friction, made more than half a century before, by Vince and Colomb, which scientific men seemed to have altogether lost sight of, clearly showed that, by the use of steam-power on railroads, the more rapid, as well as cheaper transit of persons and merchandise might be confidently anticipated. The important experiments referred to had demonstrated that friction upon roads is the same at all velocities. Dr. Young had, indeed, in referring to these experiments, as early

* The able articles referred to were published in December, 1824, and were republished, or extensively quoted, in most of the English newspapers. They were also translated into French and German, and reprinted in the United States.

as 1807,* made use of the following prophetic words: "It is possible that roads paved with iron may be hereafter employed for the purpose of expeditious traveling, since there is scarcely any resistance to be overcome except that of the air; and such roads will allow the velocity to be increased almost without limit."

Mr. Maclaren, after going carefully into the questions of gravity, resistance, friction and other impediments to motion upon a road, proceeded to prove by fair inferences, clearly argued out, "that were railways to come into general use, two-thirds or more of the expense of transporting commodities would be saved. After anticipating that an average velocity of twenty miles an hour would be secured on railways at very little more cost than a velocity of one mile, and that it must be left to the engineer to find out the best means of giving effect to the truths thus demonstrated, the writer went on to say—"We are afraid that some practical men will be disposed to treat these propositions as matter of idle and profitless speculation. But we confess that this does not abate our confidence in their truth. . . . . The application of the laws of friction to the motion of carriages on railways has scarcely ever been investigated. Yet the subject is of vast importance, and the results are extraordinary. Among all the new projects and inventions with which this age teems, there is certainly not one which opens up such a boundless prospect of improvement, as the general introduction of railways for the purpose of commercial communication. We have spoken of vehicles traveling at 20 miles an hour; but we see no reason for thinking that, in the progress of improvement, a much higher velocity might not be found practicable. Tiberius traveled 200 miles in two days, and this was reckoned an extraordinary effort; but in twenty years hence, a shopkeeper or mechanic, on the most ordinary occasion, may probably travel with a speed that would leave the fleetest courser behind."

* Dr. Young's Lectures on Natural Philosophy.

Little more than five years passed before these anticipations, sanguine and speculative though they were regarded at the time, were amply realized. And yet even Mr. Nicholas Wood,* in 1825, speaking of the powers of the locomotive, and referring doubtless to the speculations of the *Scotsman* as well as of his equally sanguine friend Stephenson, observed: "It is far from my wish to promulgate to the world that the ridiculous expectations, or rather professions, of the enthusiastic speculator will be realized, and that we shall see engines traveling at the rate of twelve, sixteen, eighteen, or twenty miles an hour. Nothing could do more harm towards their general adoption and improvement than the promulgation of such nonsense."

Indeed, when Mr. Stephenson, at the consultation of counsel previous to the Liverpool and Manchester bill going into Committee of the House of Commons, confidently stated his expectation of being able to impel his locomotive at the rate of twenty miles an hour, Mr. William Brougham, who was retained by the promoters to conduct their case, frankly told him, that if he did not moderate his views, and bring his engine within a *reasonable* speed, he would "inevitably damn the whole thing, and be himself regarded as a maniac fit for Bedlam." †

The idea of traveling at a rate of speed double that of the fastest mail-coach, appeared at that time so preposterous that Mr. Stephenson was unable to find any engineer who would risk his reputation in supporting his "absurd views." Speaking of his isolation at this time, he subsequently observed, at a public meeting of railway men in Manchester: "He remembered the time when he had very few supporters in bringing out the railway system — when he sought England over for an engineer to support him in his evidence before Parliament, and could find

* A Practical Treatise on Railroads. By Nicholas Wood, Collier Viewer, C. E. London: Hurst, Chance & Co.

† Mr. John Dixon, engineer of the Stockton and Darlington Railway, then Mr. Stephenson's assistant, relates the above circumstance.

only one man, James Walker, but was afraid to call that gentleman, because he knew nothing about railways. He had then no one to tell his tale to but Mr. Sandars of Liverpool, who did listen to him, and kept his spirits up; and his schemes had at length been carried out only by dint of sheer perseverance." *

George Stephenson's idea was indeed at that time regarded as but the dream of a chimerical projector. It stood before the public friendless, struggling hard to gain a footing, but scarcely daring to lift itself into notice for fear of ridicule. The civil engineers generally rejected the notion of a Locomotive Railway; and when no leading man of the day could be found to stand forward in support of the Killingworth mechanic, its chances of success must have been pronounced small. But, like all great truths, the time was surely to come when it was to prevail.

When such was the hostility of the civil engineers, no wonder the reviewers were puzzled. The *Quarterly*,† in an able article in support of the projected Liverpool and Manchester Railway—while admitting its *absolute necessity*, and insisting that there was no choice left but a railroad, on which the journey between Liverpool and Manchester, whether performed by horses or engines, would always be accomplished "within the day"—nevertheless scouted the idea of traveling at a greater speed than eight or nine

* Speech of Mr. Stephenson at a meeting held in Manchester on the 15th of June, 1847, to present a service of plate to J. P. Westhead, Esq., chairman of the Manchester and Birmingham Railway Co.

Mr. Stephenson did not hesitate to speak freely to his intimate friends of the high speeds which he anticipated securing on railways by means of his improved engines. At a dinner given to his son, Mr. Robert Stephenson, on the presentation of a testimonial from the contractors on the London and Birmingham Railway, on the 16th November, 1839, Mr. Biddulph related the following circumstance: "He could well recollect the time when railroads, and, indeed, all plans for speedy communication, were treated as chimerical; and he recollected a conversation he had had with Mr. George Stephenson, which, although perhaps that gentleman had forgotten it, he (Mr. Biddulph) had not. Mr. Stephenson on that occasion observed, 'Whatever may be said of horses or dogs racing, what comparison could there be between that and seeing an engine flying across the country with more than a hundred people in its train, at a far greater speed than either the fleetest horses or dogs could run?'"

† Quarterly Review, for March, 1825.

miles an hour. "We are not the advocates," said the reviewer, "for visionary projects that interfere with useful establishments; we scout the idea of a *general* railroad as altogether impracticable, or as one, at least, which will be rendered nugatory in lines where the traffic is so small that the receipts would scarcely pay for the consumption of coals. . . . The gross exaggerations of the powers of the locomotive engine, or, to speak in plain English, the *steam-carriage*, may delude for a time, but must end in the mortification of those concerned." Adverting to a project for forming a railway to Woolwich, by which passengers were to be drawn by locomotive engines, moving with twice the velocity and with greater safety than ordinary coaches, the reviewer proceeded:—"What can be more palpably absurd and ridiculous than the prospect held out of locomotives traveling *twice as fast* as stage-coaches! We should as soon expect the people of Woolwich to suffer themselves to be fired off upon one of Congreve's ricochet rockets, as trust themselves to the mercy of such a machine going at such a rate. We will back old Father Thames against the Woolwich Railway for any sum. We trust that Parliament will, in all railways it may sanction, limit the speed to *eight or nine miles an hour*, which we entirely agree with Mr. Sylvester is as great as can be ventured on with safety."

The article in the *Quarterly*, in which these passages occur, was nevertheless an able argument in favor of the formation of the proposed railway from Liverpool to Manchester. It denounced the monopoly of the carriage of merchandise between the two towns, attempted to be upheld by the canal companies—argued against their so-called "vested rights," which, it averred, could not stand for a moment against the rights of the million, if it could be shown that by an improved application of steam the transport of goods can be effected in a more safe, certain, expeditious, and economical manner—and it also combated the fears of the landlords lest their property should be injured by the proposed new line of communication. "It has been said," observed the writer, "that an opposition to railroads will be made on the part of the landed proprietors; but the absurdity of this is so glaring, that it must defeat itself. Country gentlemen may not at first see their own interest, but their tenants will find it out for them; they will discern immediately the advantage which a railroad will confer along the whole line of country through which it passes, by the increased facility of sending their produce to market, and of receiving the objects of their wants in return."

The article was so strongly favorable to the proposed railway, that allegations were even made by the opponents of the bill, when in committee, that the writer had been bought by the Liverpool and Manchester party; which was, of course, a mere license of counsel. The objections urged by the reviewer against the high speed attainable on railways — then a mere matter of speculation — were also entertained by nearly all the practical and scientific men* of the kingdom, and by the public generally. Taken as a whole, the article was most admirable and salutary.

* For instance, Dr. Lardner affirmed that "carriages could not go at any thing like the contemplated speed; if driven to it, the wheels would merely spin on their axles, and the carriages would stand stock-still."

CHAPTER XIX.

MR. STEPHENSON EXAMINED BEFORE THE PARLIAMENTARY COMMITTEE ON THE LIVERPOOL AND MANCHESTER BILL.

THE Liverpool and Manchester Bill went into Committee of the House of Commons on the 21st of March, 1825. There was an extraordinary array of legal talent on the occasion, but especially on the side of the opponents to the measure. Their wealth and influence enabled them to retain the ablest counsel at the bar. Mr. (since Baron) Alderson and Mr. Stephenson appeared on behalf of Mrs. Atherton, Miss Byrom, and the Rev. John Clowes; Mr. (afterwards Baron) Parke appeared for Charles Orell, Esq., and Sir W. Gerrard, Bart.; Mr. Rose for the Barton Road Trustees; Mr. Macdonnell and Mr. Harrison for the Duke of Bridgewater's Trustees; Mr. (afterwards Baron) Erle for the Mersey and Irwell Navigation Company; and Mr. Cullen for the Leeds and Liverpool Canal Company. These gentlemen made common cause with each other in their opposition to the bill, the case for which was conducted by Mr. Adam, Mr. Sergeant Spankie, Mr. William Brougham, and Mr. Joy.

Evidence was taken at great length as to the difficulties and delays in forwarding raw goods of all kinds from Liverpool to Manchester, as also in the conveyance of manufactured articles from Manchester to Liverpool. The evidence adduced in support of the bill on these grounds was overwhelming. The utter inadequacy of the existing modes of conveyance to carry on satisfactorily the large and rapidly-growing trade between the two towns was fully proved. But then came the gist of the promoters' case—the evidence to prove the practicability of a railroad to be worked by locomotive power. Mr. Adam, in his opening speech, referred to the cases of the Hetton and the Killingworth railroads, where heavy goods were safely and economically transported by means of locomotive engines. "None of the tremendous consequences," he observed, "have ensued from the use of steam in land carriage that have been stated. The horses have not started, nor the cows ceased to give their milk, nor have ladies miscarried at the sight of these things going forward at the rate of four miles and a half an hour." Notwithstanding the petition of two ladies, alleging the great danger to be apprehended from the bursting of the boilers of such engines, he urged the safety of the high-pressure engine when the boilers were constructed of wrought-iron; and as to the rate at which they could travel, he expressed his full conviction that such engines "could supply force to drive a carriage at the rate of five or six miles an hour."

The taking of the evidence on the impediments thrown in the way of trade and commerce by the existing system extended over a month, and it was the 21st of April before the Committee went into the engineering evidence, which was the vital part of the question. Mr. Rastrick, then a manufacturer of steam-engines at Stourbridge, near Birmingham, was examined as to the safety of high-pressure engines. He had made a traveling engine of this sort for Mr. Trevethick about twelve years before (in 1813), which was exhibited in London, when a circular railroad was laid down, and the engine was run against a horse for a wager. He had also seen the locomotive engines of Mr. Stephenson at work on the Killingworth and Hetton railroads. He had examined them together with Mr. Cubitt, Mr. James Walker, Mr. Sylvester, and others, and was satisfied of their applicability to the purposes of railway traction. He described to the Committee the proper form of the boiler, and the arrangement of the valves, so as to secure complete safety in the working of the locomotive. He was of opinion that such an engine might be constructed as would take forty tons' weight, at the rate of six miles an hour, with perfect ease and safety.

On the 25th of April, Mr. George Stephenson was called into the witness-box. It was his first appearance before a Committee of the House of Commons, and he well knew what he had to expect. He was aware that the whole force of the opposition was to be directed against him; and if they could break down his evidence, the canal monopoly might yet be upheld for a time. Many years afterwards, when looking back at his position on this trying occasion, he said:—"When I went to Liverpool to plan a line from thence to Manchester, I pledged myself to the directors to attain a speed of ten miles an hour. I said I had no doubt the locomotive might be made to go much faster, but that we had better be moderate at the beginning. The directors said I was quite right; for that if, when they went to Parliament, I talked of going at a greater rate than ten miles an hour, I should put a cross upon the concern. It was not an easy task for me to keep the engine down to ten miles an hour, but it must be done, and I did my best. I had to place myself in that most unpleasant of all positions—the witness-box of a Parliamentary Committee. I was not long in it, before I began to wish for a hole to creep out at! I could not find words to satisfy either the Committee or myself. I was subjected to the cross-examination of eight or ten barristers, purposely, as far as possible, to bewilder me. Some member of the Committee asked if I was a foreigner, and another hinted that I was mad. But I put up with every rebuff, and went on with my plans, determined not to be put down." *

Mr. Stephenson stood before the Committee to prove what the public opinion of that day held to be impossible. The self-taught mechanic had to demonstrate the practicability of accomplishing that which the most distinguished engineers of the time regarded

* Speech at Newcastle on the opening of the Newcastle and Darlington Railway.

as impracticable. Clear though the subject was to himself, and familiar as he was with the powers of the locomotive, it was no easy task for him to bring home his convictions, or even to convey his meaning, to the less informed minds of his hearers. In his strong Northumbrian dialect, he struggled for an utterance, in the face of the sneers, interruptions, and ridicule of the opponents of the measure, and even of the Committee, some of whom shook their heads and whispered doubts as to his sanity, when he energetically avowed that he could make the locomotive go at the rate of twelve miles an hour! It was so grossly in the teeth of all the experience of honorable members, that the man must certainly be laboring under a delusion!

And yet his large experience of railways and locomotives, as described by himself to the Committee, entitled this "untaught, inarticulate genius," as he has so well been styled, to speak with confidence on such a subject. Beginning with his experience as brakesman at Killingworth in 1803, he went on to state that he had been appointed to take the entire charge of the steam-engines in 1813, and superintended the railroads connected with the numerous collieries of the Grand Allies from that time downwards. He had laid down or superintended the railways at Borrertown, Mount Moor, Spring Darlington, Bedington, Hetton and Darlington, besides improving those of Killingworth, South Moor and Derwent Brook. He had constructed fifty-five steam-engines, of which sixteen were locomotives. Some of these had been sent to France. The only accident that had occurred to any of these engines was on the occasion of the tubes in one of them wearing out, by which a man and boy were slightly scalded. The engines constructed by him for the working of the Killingworth Railroad, eleven years before, had continued steadily at work ever since, and fulfilled his most sanguine expectations. He was prepared to prove the safety of working high-pressure locomotives on a railroad, and the superiority of this mode of transporting goods over all others. As to speed, he said he had recommended eight miles an hour with twenty tons, and four miles an hour with forty tons; but he was quite confident that much more might be done. Indeed, he had no doubt they might go at the rate of twelve miles.

As to the charge that locomotives on a railroad would so terrify the horses in the neighborhood, that to travel on horseback or to plow the adjoining fields would be rendered highly dangerous, the witness said that horses learnt to take no notice of them, though there *were* horses that would shy at a wheelbarrow. A mail-coach was likely to be more shied at by horses than a locomotive. In the neighborhood of Killingworth, the cattle in the fields went on grazing while the engines passed them, and the farmers made no complaints.

Mr. Alderson, who had carefully studied the subject, and was well skilled in practical science, subjected the witness to a protracted and severe cross-examination as to the speed and power of the locomotive, the strokes of the engine, the slipping of the wheels upon the rails, and various other points of detail. Mr. Stephenson insisted that no slipping took place, as attempted to be extorted from him by the counsel. He said: "It is impossible for slipping to take place so long as the adhesive weight of the wheel upon the rail is greater than the weight to be dragged after it." There was a good deal of interruption to the witness's answers by Mr. Alderson, to which Mr. Joy more than once objected. As to accidents, Mr. Stephenson knew of none that had occurred with his engines. There had been one, he was told, at the Middleton Colliery, near Leeds, with a Blenkinsop engine. The driver had been in liquor, and had put a considerable load on the safety valve, so that upon going forward the engine blew up, and the man was killed. But he added, that if proper precautions had been used with that boiler the accident could not have happened. The following cross-examination occurred in reference to the question of speed:

"Of course" (he was asked), "when a body is moving upon a

road, the greater the velocity the greater the momentum that is generated?" "Certainly."—"What would be the momentum of forty tons moving at the rate of twelve miles an hour?" "It would be very great."—"Have you seen a railroad that would stand that?" "Yes."—"Where?" "Any railroad that would bear going four miles an hour: I mean to say, that if it would bear the weight at four miles an hour, it would bear it at twelve."—"Taking it at four miles an hour, do you mean to say that it would not require a stronger railway to carry the same weight twelve miles an hour?" "I will give an answer to that. I dare say every person has been over ice when skating, or seen persons go over, and they know that it would bear them at a greater velocity than it would if they went slower; when it goes quick, the weight in a measure ceases."—"Is not that upon the hypothesis that the railroad is perfect?" "It is; and *I mean to make it perfect*."*

Mr. Alderson next cross-examined the witness on the dangers of curves. "Do not wrought-iron rails bend; take Hetton Colliery for instance?" "They are wrought-iron, but they are weak rails."—"Do you not know that those bend?" "Perhaps they may bend, not being made sufficiently strong."—"And if they are made sufficiently strong, that will involve an additional expense?" "It will."—"Then if you were to make them of adamant, that would be very expensive?" "It does not require a very great expense to make them strong enough for heavier work; I mean the difference between making them for easy work and heavy work is not great."—"You say that the machine can go at the rate of twelve miles an hour; suppose there is a turn on the road—what will become of the machine?" "It would go round the turn."—"Would it not go straight forward?" "No."—"What is to be the plan of the road, and the height of the rail?" "That has nothing to do with it."—"I ask you, what is to be the height of the flanch of the wheel?" "One and a quarter

* Evidence, p. 203.

inch."—"Then if the rail bends to the extent of an inch and a quarter, it will go off the rail?" "It cannot bend; I know it is so in practice."—"Did you ever see forty tons going at the rate of twelve miles an hour?" "No, I have not seen it; but I have seen the engine running from eight to ten miles round a curve." —"What was the weight moved?" "I think little, except the engine—the weight of the engine itself."—"Do you mean to tell us that no difference is to be made between those forty tons after the engine, and the engine itself?" "It is scarcely worth notice." —"Then, though the engine might run round, and follow the turn, do you mean to say that the weight after it would not pass off?" "I have stated that I never saw such a weight move at that velocity; but I could see at Killingworth that the weight was following the engines, and it is a very sharp curve; I believe they came down very frequently at the velocity of fully ten miles an hour; it is a sharper curve there than I should ever recommend to be put on any railroad."—"Have you known a stage-coach overturn when making not a very sharp curve, when going very fast?" "That is a different thing; it is top-heavy."—"Do you mean to say, none of your wagons will be top-heavy?" "They will not; perhaps they may get a good deal of cotton upon them; but I should construct the carriages so that they should not be top-heavy.*

Mr. Alderson had so pressed the point of "twelve miles an hour," and the promoters were so alarmed lest it should appear in evidence that they contemplated any such extravagant rate of speed, that immediately on Mr. Alderson sitting down, Mr. Joy proceeded to reëxamine Mr. Stephenson, with the view of removing from the minds of the Committee an impression so unfavorable, and, as they supposed, so damaging to their case. "With regard," asked Mr. Joy, "to all those hypothetical questions of my learned friend, they have been all put on the supposition of going twelve miles an hour: now that is not the rate at

* Evidence, pp. 205–6.

which, I believe, any of the engines of which you have spoken have traveled?" "No," replied Mr. Stephenson, "except as an experiment for a short distance."—"But what they have gone has been three, five, or six miles an hour?" "Yes."—"So that those hypothetical cases of twelve miles an hour do not fall within your general experience?" "They do not."*

The Committee also seem to have entertained some alarm as to the high rate of speed which had been spoken of, and proceeded to examine the witness further on the subject. They supposed the case of the engine being upset when going at nine miles an hour, and asked what, in such a case, would become of the cargo astern. To which the witness replied, that it would not be upset. One of the members of the Committee pressed the witness a little further. He put the following case: "Suppose, now, one of these engines to be going along a railroad at the rate of nine or ten miles an hour, and that a cow were to stray upon the line and get in the way of the engine; would not that, think you, be a very awkward circumstance?" "Yes," replied the witness, with a twinkle in his eye, "very awkward indeed—*for the coo!*" The honorable member did not proceed further with his cross-examination: to use a railway phrase, he was "shunted."

On the following day (the 26th April), Mr. Stephenson was subjected to a most severe examination. On that part of the scheme with which he was most practically conversant, his evidence was clear and conclusive. Now, he had to give evidence on the plans made by his surveyors, and the estimates which had been founded on such plans. So long as he was confined to locomotive engines and iron railroads, with the minutest details of which he was more familiar than any man living, he felt at home, and in his element. But when the designs of bridges and the cost of constructing them, the geological formation of the country and the borings of the strata through which the line passed, the levels and surveys made in detail by the surveyors

* Evidence, p. 207.

appointed by the Company, had to be gone into, it may well be imagined that Mr. Stephenson, whose special attention had been little directed to such subjects, felt embarrassed and confused in the face of the array of distinguished counsel and engineers who were now bent on upsetting his evidence.

Mr. Alderson cross-examined him at great length on the plans of the bridges, the tunnels, the crossings of the roads and streets, and the details of the survey, which, it soon clearly appeared, were seriously at fault. At one part of the line, the survey was so far wrong that it would be necessary, in crossing a road, to work the railway, if made, by means of an inclined plane. It also appeared that, after the plans had been deposited, Mr. Stephenson found that a much more favorable line might be made; and he thus explained certain discrepancies which appeared in his estimates: — "The plan being made before I commenced my estimates, I could not alter the line then, but I made my estimates upon different data from those on which the plan was laid down, when I found a more favorable line to go upon, and made such alterations as would not inconvenience the plan. I made my estimates accordingly, supposing that Parliament would not confine the Company to the precise estimate." * The proposed formation of the line of railway over Chat Moss was also the subject of much cross-examination — the witness stating that it was quite practicable, although it would require time to become consolidated.

For three entire days was Mr. Stephenson subjected to this cross-examination by Mr. Alderson, Mr. Cullen, and the other leading counsel for the opposition. He held his ground bravely, and defended the plans and estimates with consummate ability and skill; but it was clear they were very imperfect, and the result was on the whole damaging to the bill. Mr. (afterwards Sir William) Cubitt was called by the promoters — Mr. Adam stating that he proposed by this witness to correct some of the

* Evidence, p. 241.

levels as given by Mr. Stephenson. It seems a singular course to have been taken by the promoters of the measure; for Mr. Cubitt's evidence went to upset the statements made by Mr. Stephenson as to the survey. This adverse evidence was, of course, made the most of by the opponents of the bill.

Mr. Sergeant Spankie then summed up for the bill, on the 2d of May, in a speech of great length. Referring to the error in the levels, he said: "Mr. Stephenson, by relying upon the information of those who surveyed the levels, estimated the whole excavations and embankments at the sum of 87,000*l.*, upon that unfavorable supposition. It will be said on the other side that, Mr. Stephenson having been guilty of one error, the whole credit of his estimate is shaken; but the truth is, that Mr. Stephenson, on a datum given by other persons, calculated it would cost so much to make the railway. Mr. Stephenson did not commit his general judgment: it is not an error as a matter of truth, but a mere mistake of other persons; and there is no other part of the estimate to which a similar observation applies; for Mr. Stephenson's estimate, in other respects, is founded upon what he saw. Of all the men who could be examined in this kingdom, they would not have found any man who had better means to make a correct estimate than Mr. Stephenson; the error had been wholly occasioned by the calculations of others." * With reference to the evidence given as to the practicability of working the railroad by the locomotive engine, Sergeant Spankie said: "Another part of the scheme is — the locomotive engine. It appears, by the most labored, and ingenious, and clever cross-examination of Mr. Rastrick and Mr. Stephenson, in such a way that the Committee must be satisfied that there are no objections to this instrument. It went through its probation with wonderful success, for one has been taught to consider those high-pressure engines as a sort of bugbear; that they would go off by themselves and blow us into the air. It was clearly proved that the

* Report and Evidence, p. 322.

machine went along at the rate of seven miles an hour, and that there is no difficulty in increasing the speed."

The case of the opponents to the bill was then gone into, and Mr. Harrison opened with an eloquent speech on behalf of his clients, Mrs. Atherton and others. He indulged in the severest vituperation against the witnesses for the bill, and especially dwelt upon the manner in which Mr. Cubitt, for the promoters, had proved that Mr. Stephenson's levels were wrong. "They got a person," said he, "whose character and skill I do not dispute, though I do not exactly know that I should have gone to the inventor of the treadmill as the fittest man to take the levels of Knowsley Moss and Chat Moss, which shook almost as much as a treadmill, as you recollect, for he (Mr. Cubitt) said Chat Moss trembled so much under his feet that he could not take his observations accurately. . . . In fact, Mr. Cubitt did not go to the Chatt Moss, because he knew that it was an immense mass of pulp, and nothing else. It actually rises in height, from the rain swelling it like a sponge, and sinks again in dry weather: and if a boring instrument is put into it, it sinks immediately by its own weight. The making of an embankment out of this pulpy, wet moss, is no very easy task. Who but Mr. Stephenson would have thought of entering into Chat Moss, carrying it out almost like wet dung? It is ignorance almost inconceivable. It is perfect madness, in a person called upon to speak on a scientific subject, to propose such a plan. . . . Every part of the scheme shows that this man has applied himself to a subject of which he has no knowledge, and to which he has no science to apply." * Then adverting to the proposal to work the proposed line by means of locomotives, the learned gentleman proceeded: "When we set out with the original prospectus, we were to gallop, I know not at what rate—I believe it was at the rate of twelve miles an hour. My learned friend, Mr. Adam, contemplated—possibly alluding to Ireland—that some of the Irish

* Report and Evidence, pp. 346, 349, 351, 353.

members would arrive in the wagons to a division. My learned friend says that they would go at the rate of twelve miles an hour with the aid of the devil in the form of a locomotive, sitting as postilion on the fore horse, and an honorable member sitting behind him to stir up the fire, and keep it at full speed. But the speed at which these locomotive engines are to go has slackened: Mr. Adam does not go faster now than five miles an hour. The learned sergeant (Spankie) says he should like to have seven, but he would be content to go six. I will show he cannot go six; and probably, for any practical purposes, I may be able to show that I can keep up with him *by the canal.* . . . Locomotive engines are liable to be operated upon by the weather. You are told they are effected by rain, and an attempt has been made to cover them; but the wind will affect them; and any gale of wind which would affect the traffic on the Mersey would render it *impossible* to set off a locomotive engine, either by poking of the fire, or keeping up the pressure of the steam till the boiler is ready to burst." * How amusing it now is to read these extraordinary views as to the formation of a railway over Chat Moss, and the impossibility of starting a locomotive engine in the face of a gale of wind! The men who then laughed at Stephenson's "mad projects" had but to live a few years longer to find that the laugh was all on the other side.

Evidence was called to show that the house property passed by the proposed railway would be greatly deteriorated—in some places almost destroyed; that the locomotive engines would be terrible nuisances, in consequence of the fire and smoke vomited forth by them; and that the value of land in the neighborhood of Manchester alone would be deteriorated by no less than 20,000*l.*! † But the opposition mainly relied upon the evidence of the leading engineers—not, like Mr. Stephenson, self-taught men, but regular professionals. Mr. Francis Giles, C. E., was their great card. He had been twenty-two years an engineer,

* Report and Evidence, p. 354. † Evidence, p. 379.

and could speak with some authority. His testimony was mainly directed to the utter impossibility of forming a railway over Chat Moss. "*No engineer in his senses,*" said he, "would go through Chat Moss if he wanted to make a railroad from Liverpool to Manchester." * Mr. Giles thus described this bottomless pit: "The surface of the Moss is a sort of long, coarse, sedgy grass, tough enough to enable you to walk upon it, about half-leg deep; underneath that, on putting an iron into the soil (a boring-rod), it will, with its own weight, sink down. In the centre, where this railroad is to cross, it is all pulp from the top to the depth of 34 feet; at 34 feet there is a vein of 4 or 6 inches of clay; below that there are 2 or 3 feet of quicksand; and the bottom of that is hard clay, which keeps all the water in. The boring-rod will get down to the first vein of clay by its own weight; a slight pressure of the hand will carry it to the next vein of clay; a very little pressure indeed will get it to the additional depth of 2 or 3 feet, beyond which you must use more pressure to get it down to the foundation. If this sort of material were to be carried, it would greatly increase the expense; and it would be necessary to lay it aside, for the purpose of draining and drying, before any man in his senses would convey it along the railroad for the purpose I have been speaking of. . . . In my judgment," (the judgment of Mr. F. Giles, C. E., against that of the unprofessional person "not in his senses," who proposed to form the railroad,)—"in my judgment a railroad certainly cannot be safely made over Chat Moss without going to the bottom of the Moss. The soil ought all to be taken out, undoubtedly; in doing which it will not be practicable to approach each end of the cutting as you make it, with the carriages. No carriage would stand upon the Moss short of the bottom. My estimate for the whole cutting and embankment over Chat Moss is 270,000*l.* nearly, at those quantities and those prices which are

* Evidence, p. 386

decidedly correct. . . . It will be necessary to take this Moss completely out at the bottom, in order to make a solid road." *

Mr. Henry Robinson Palmer, C. E., gave his evidence to prove that resistance to a moving body going under four and a quarter miles an hour was *less* upon a canal than upon a railroad; and that, when going against a strong wind, the progress of a locomotive was retarded "very much." Mr. George Leather, C. E., the engineer of the Croydon and Wandsworth Railway, on which he said the wagons went at from two and a half to three miles an hour, also gave his evidence against the practicability of Mr. Stephenson's plan. He considered his estimate a "very wild" one. He had no confidence in locomotive power. The Weardale Railway, of which he was engineer, had given up the use of locomotive engines. He supposed that, when used, they traveled at three and a half to four miles on hour, because they were considered to be then more effective than at a higher speed.†

When these distinguished engineers had given their evidence, Mr. Alderson summed up in a speech which extended over two days. He declared Mr. Stephenson's plan to be "the most absurd scheme that ever entered into the head of man to conceive. My learned friends," said he, "almost endeavored to stop my examination; they wished me to put in the plan, but I had rather have the exhibition of Mr. Stephenson in that box. I say he never had a plan—I believe he never had one—I do not believe he is capable of making one. His is a mind perpetually fluctuating between opposite difficulties: he neither knows whether he is to make bridges over roads or rivers, of one size or of another; or to make embankments, or cuttings, or inclined planes, or in what way the thing is to be carried into effect. Whenever a difficulty is pressed, as in the case of a tunnel, he gets out of it at one end, and when you try to catch him at that, he gets out at the other." Mr. Alderson proceeded to declaim against the gross ignorance of this so-called engineer, who pro-

* Evidence, pp. 383-386. † Ibid p. 436.

posed to make "impossible ditches by the side of an impossible railway" through Chat Moss, and he contrasted with his evidence that given "by that most respectable gentleman we have called before you, I mean Mr. Giles, who has executed a vast number of works," etc. Then Mr. Giles's evidence as to the impossibility of making any railway over the Moss that would stand short of the bottom, was emphatically dwelt upon; and Mr. Alderson proceeded to say: "Having now, sir, gone through Chat Moss, and having shown that Mr. Giles is right in his principle when he adopts a solid railway—and I care not whether Mr. Giles is right or wrong in his estimate, for whether it be effected by means of piers raised up all the way for four miles through Chat Moss, whether they are to support it on beams of wood or by erecting masonry, or whether Mr. Giles shall put a solid bank of earth through it—in all these schemes there is not one found like that of Mr. Stephenson's, namely, to cut impossible drains on the side of this road; and it is sufficient for me to suggest and to show, that this scheme of Mr. Stephenson's is impossible or impracticable, and that no other scheme, if they proceed upon this line, can be suggested which will not produce enormous expense. I think that has been irrefragably made out. Every one knows Chat Moss—every one knows that Mr. Giles speaks correctly when he says the iron sinks immediately on its being put upon the surface. I have heard of culverts, which have been put upon the Moss, which, after having been surveyed the day before, have the next morning disappeared; and that a house, (a poet's house, who may be supposed in the habit of building castles even in the air,) story after story, as fast as one is added, the lower one sinks! There is nothing, it appears, except long sedgy grass, and a little soil, to prevent its sinking into the shades of eternal night. I have now done, sir, with Chat Moss, and there I leave this railroad."* Mr. Alderson, of course, called upon the Committee to reject the bill; and he protested "against the

* Report and Evidence, p. 478.

despotism of the Exchange at Liverpool striding across the land of this country. I do protest," he concluded, "against a measure like this, supported as it is by such evidence, and founded upon such calculations." *

The case, however, was not yet concluded. Mr. Stephenson (another of the counsel on the same side) declined addressing the Committee, after the speech of Mr. Alderson, "in which he had so clearly, so ably, and so fully shown the utter impracticability of the scheme;" but the case of the other numerous petitioners against the bill still remained to be gone into. Witnesses were called to prove the residential injury which would be caused by the "intolerable nuisance" of the smoke and fire from the locomotives; and others to prove that the price of coals and iron would "infallibly" be greatly raised throughout the country. This was part of the case of the Duke of Bridgewater's trustees, whose witnesses "proved" many very extraordinary things. The Leeds and Liverpool Coal Company were so fortunate as to pick up a witness from Hetton, who was ready to furnish some damaging evidence as to the use of Mr. Stephenson's locomotives on that railway. This was Mr. Thomas Wood, one of the Hetton company's clerks, whose evidence was to the effect that the locomotives, having been found ineffective, were about to be discontinued in favor of fixed engines. The locomotives, he said, were greatly affected by the weather, and the wagons had then to be drawn on by horses. The engines were also frequently getting off the road, and were liable to accident. The evidence of this witness, incompetent though he was to give an opinion on the subject, and exaggerated as his statements were afterwards proved to be, was made the most of by Mr. Harrison, when summing up the case of the canal companies. "At length," he said, "we have come to this—having first set out at twelve miles an hour, the speed of these locomotives is reduced to six, and now comes down to two or two and a-half. They must be content to

* Report and Evidence, p. 485.

be pulled along by horses and donkeys; and all those fine promises of galloping along at the rate of twelve miles an hour are melted down to a total failure—the foundation on which their case stood is cut from under them completely; for the Act of Parliament, the Committee will recollect, prohibits any person using any animal power, of any sort, kind or description, except the projectors of the railway themselves; therefore, I say, that the whole foundation on which this project exists is gone." After further personal abuse of Mr. Stephenson, whose evidence he spoke of as "trash and confusion," he closed the case of the canal companies on the 30th of May. Afterwards Mr. Adam replied for the promoters, recapitulating the principal points of their case, and vindicating Mr. Stephenson and the evidence which he had given before the Committee. Even Mr. Adam himself, however, seemed to have fears of the railway formation across Chat Moss, after the positive evidence given by Mr. Giles. "Supposing that Mr. Stephenson is rash," said he, "and I do not deny it, I say his error is an error from want of caution, and not from want of knowledge; and he ought not to be reproached with his want of knowledge of railways, being a man of great practical experience"—which Mr. Giles was not, as respected railways. "Will you now," he said to the Committee, in winding up his speech, "will you now—when this experiment is brought before you and discussed so fully for the first time, while we are in the infancy of the application of this most powerful agent for the purpose of forming a communication for goods throughout the country—will you reject it because my learned friend, by some ingenious objections, has endeavored to throw discredit upon it? All I ask you is, not to crush it in its infancy. Let not this country have the disgrace of putting a stop to that which, if cherished, may ultimately prove of the greatest advantage to our trade and commerce, and which, if we do not adopt it, will be adopted by our rivals. . . . My learned friends appeal to the Committee on the ground of private rights, all of which will be recognized. I appeal to you in the name of the two largest towns in England, the one as a commercial port and the other as a commercial town; I appeal to you in the name of the country at large; and I implore you not to blast the hopes that this powerful agent—steam—may be called in aid for the purpose of land communication; only let it have a fair trial, and these little objections and private prejudices will, I am quite sure, be instantly dispelled."

The Committee then divided on the preamble, which was carried by a majority of only *one*—thirty-seven voting for it, and thirty-six against it. The clauses were next considered; and on a division, the first clause, empowering the company to make the railway, was lost by a majority of nineteen to thirteen. In like manner the next clause, empowering the company to take land, was lost; on which Mr. Adam, on the part of the promoters, withdrew the bill.

Thus ended this memorable contest, which had extended over two months—carried on throughout with great pertinacity and skill, especially on the part of the opposition, who left no stone unturned to defeat the measure. The want of a third line of communication between Liverpool and Manchester had been clearly proved; but the engineering evidence in support of the proposed railway, having been thrown almost entirely upon Mr. Stephenson, who fought this, the most important part of the battle, single-handed, was not brought out so clearly as it would have been had he secured more efficient engineering assistance—which he was not able to do, as all the engineers of eminence of that day were against the locomotive railway. The obstacles thrown in the way of the survey by the land-owners and canal companies also in a great measure tended to defeat the bill. From this temporary failure, however, the projectors drew a valuable lesson for the future; and when they next appeared before Parliament, they were better prepared to meet the obstinate opposition both of the canal companies and the land-owners.

CHAPTER XX.

THE LIVERPOOL AND MANCHESTER RAILWAY BILL CARRIED, AND MR. STEPHENSON APPOINTED ENGINEER.

THE result of this first application to Parliament was so far discouraging. Mr. Stephenson had been so terribly abused by the leading counsel for the opposition in the course of the proceedings before the Committee — stigmatized by them as an ignoramus, a fool, and a maniac—that even his friends seem for a time to have lost faith in him and in the locomotive system, whose efficiency he continued to uphold. Things never looked blacker for the success of the railway system than at the close of this great parliamentary struggle. And yet it was on the very eve of its triumph. The absolute necessity for a new line of communication between Liverpool and Manchester had been proved beyond all doubt; and the Committee of Directors appointed to watch the measure in Parliament were so determined to press on the project of a railway, even though it should have to be worked merely by horse power, that the bill had scarcely been defeated, ere they met, in London, to consider their next step.

They called their parliamentary friends together to consult as to their future proceedings. Among those who attended the meeting of gentlemen with this object, in the Royal Hotel, St. James Street, on the 4th of June, were Mr. Huskisson, Mr. Spring Rice, and General Gascoyne. Mr. Huskisson urged the promoters to renew their application to Parliament. They had secured the first step by the passing of their preamble; the measure was of great public importance; and whatever temporary opposition it might meet with, he conceived that Parliament must ultimately give its sanction to the undertaking. Similar views were expressed by other speakers; and the deputation went back to Liverpool determined to renew their application to Parliament in the ensuing session.

It was not considered desirable to employ Mr. Stephenson in making the new survey. He had not as yet established his reputation as an engineer beyond the boundaries of his own county; and the promoters of the bill had doubtless felt the disadvantages of this in the course of their parliamentary struggle. They therefore resolved now to employ engineers of the highest established reputation, as well as the best surveyors that could be obtained. In accordance with these views, they engaged Messrs. George and John Rennie to be the engineers of the railway; and Mr. Charles Vignolles, on their behalf, was appointed to prepare the plans and sections. The line which was eventually adopted differed somewhat from that surveyed by Mr. James and Mr. Stephenson — entirely avoiding Lord Sefton's property, and passing through only a few detached fields of Lord Derby's at a considerable distance from the Knowsley domain. The principal game preserves of the district were carefully avoided. The promoters thus hoped to get rid of the opposition of the most influential of the resident land-owners. The crossing of certain of the streets of Liverpool was also avoided, and the entrance contrived by means of a tunnel and inclined plane. The new line stopped short of the river Irwell at the Manchester end, and thus in some measure removed the objections grounded on an illegal interruption to the canal or river traffic. With reference to the use of the locomotive engine, the promoters, remembering with what effect the objections to it had been urged by the opponents of the measure, intimated, in their second prospectus, that "as a guarantee of their good faith towards the public they will not require any clause empowering them to use it; or they will submit to such restrictions in the employment of it as Parliament may impose, for the satisfaction and ample protection both of proprietors on the line of road and of the public at large." *

It was found that the capital required to form the line of railway, as laid out by the Messrs. Rennie, was considerably beyond the amount of Mr. Stephenson's estimate; and it became a question with the Committee in what way the new capital should be raised. A proposal was made to the Marquis of Stafford, who was principally interested in the Duke of Bridgewater's Canal, to become a shareholder in the railway. A similar proposal, it will be remembered, had at an earlier period been made to Mr. Bradshaw, the trustee for the property; but his answer was "all or none," and the negotiation was broken off. The Marquis of Stafford, however, now met the projectors of the railway in a more conciliatory spirit; and it was ultimately agreed that he should become a subscriber to the extent of 1000 shares.

The survey of the new line having been completed, the plans were deposited, the standing orders duly complied with, and the bill went into Committee. The same counsel appeared for the promoters; but the examination of witnesses was not nearly so protracted as on the previous occasion. Mr. Erle and Mr. Harrison led the case of the opposition. The bill went into Committee on the 6th of March; and on the 16th the preamble was declared proved by a majority of forty-three to eighteen. On the third reading in the House of Commons, an animated, and what now appears a very amusing, discussion took place. The Hon. Edward Stanley moved that the bill be read that day six months; and in the course of his speech he undertook to prove that the railway trains would take *ten hours* on the journey, and that they could only be worked by horses. Sir Isaac Coffin

* An Account of the Liverpool and Manchester Railway. By Henry Booth, Treasurer to the Company. Liverpool: Wales and Baines.

seconded the motion, and in doing so denounced the project as a most flagrant imposition. He would not consent to see widows' premises invaded; and "how," he asked, in the most dignified senatorial manner, "how would any person like to have a rail-road under his parlor window? . . . What, he would like to know, was to be done with all those who had advanced money in making and repairing turnpike-roads? What with those who may still wish to travel in their own or hired carriages, after the fashion of their forefathers? What was to become of coach-makers and harness-makers, coach-masters and coachmen, inn-keepers, horse-breeders, and horse-dealers? Was the House aware of the smoke and the noise, the hiss and the whirl, which locomotive engines, passing at the rate of ten or twelve miles an hour, would occasion? Neither the cattle plowing in the fields or grazing in the meadows could behold them without dismay. . . . Iron would be raised in price 100 per cent., or, more probably, exhausted altogether! It would be the greatest nuisance, the most complete disturbance of quiet and comfort in all parts of the kingdom, that the ingenuity of man could invent!"

Mr. Huskisson and other speakers, though unable to reply to such arguments as these, strongly supported the bill; and it passed the third reading by a majority of eighty-eight to forty-one.

The bill passed the House of Lords almost unanimously, the only opponents being the Earl of Derby and his relative the Earl of Wilton. "The evidence on both sides," says Mr. Booth, "was similar in effect to that offered in the House of Commons. On the subject of the locomotive engine, however—a machine which had been represented to the House of Commons in so formidable a light—evidence was brought forward by the opponents of the bill; but so poor a case was made, and so little objectionable did the engine appear to be, even from the testimony of the opponents, that the Lords did not think it necessary to have any evidence on the other side, although it was tendered by the counsel for the bill."* The cost of obtaining the Act amounted to the enormous sum of 27,000*l.*

At the first meeting of the directors of the Company at Liverpool, the selection of a principal engineer was taken into consideration. The magnitude of the proposed works, and the vast consequences involved in the experiment, were deeply impressed upon their minds; and they resolved to secure the services of a resident engineer of proved experience and ability. Their attention was naturally directed to Mr. Stephenson as the best man to carry out the undertaking; at the same time they desired to have the benefit of the Messrs. Rennie's professional assistance in superintending the works. Mr. George Rennie had an interview with the directors on the subject, and proposed to undertake the chief superintendence, making six visits in each year, and stipulating that he should have the appointment of the resident engineer. But the responsibility attaching to the direction, in the matter of the efficient carrying on of the works, would not admit of their being influenced by ordinary punctilios on the occasion; and they accordingly declined Mr. Rennie's proposal, and proceeded to appoint Mr. George Stephenson their principal engineer at a salary of 1000*l.* per annum.

The appointment of Mr. Stephenson was alleged as a grievance by the Messrs. Rennie; but we cannot see that the directors could have acted differently on the occasion. His practical experience and ability were undoubted; his fertility in expedients had been tried and proved in the course of a long life, twenty years of which had now been directed to railway working and construction; he had nearly completed the works of the Stockton and Darlington Railway, which were the admiration of all who had seen them. There was, indeed, no other man in England to compare with him in point of practical railway knowledge and experience; and the Liverpool and Manchester directors would have neglected the duty which they owed to their proprietors,

* Mr. Booth's Account, etc., p. 33.

had they, out of personal regard or predilection for Mr. Rennie, selected him in preference to George Stephenson. In the course of his six visits in the year, he could have given but an intermittent attention to the works connected with the undertaking, the magnitude of which required the constant personal supervision of an engineer of practical ability. The result amply justified the wisdom of the selection which the directors made.

Mr. Stephenson was no sooner appointed engineer, than he removed his residence to Liverpool, and made arrangements to commence the works. He began with the "impossible"—to do that which the most distinguished engineers of the day had declared that "no man in his senses would undertake to do"—namely, to make the road over Chat Moss! The drainage of the Moss was commenced in June, 1826. It was, indeed, a most formidable undertaking; and it has been well observed that to carry a railway along, under or over such a material as the Moss presented, could never have been contemplated by an ordinary mind. Michael Drayton supposed Chat Moss to have had its origin at the deluge. Nothing more impassable could have been imagined than that dreary waste; and Mr. Giles only spoke the popular feeling of the day when he declared that no carriage could stand on it "short of the bottom." In this bog, singular to say, Mr. Roscoe, the accomplished historian of the Medicis, buried his fortune in the hopeless attempt to cultivate it. Nevertheless, farming operations had for some time been going on and were extending along the verge of the Moss; but the tilled ground, underneath which the bog extended, was so soft that the horses, when plowing, were provided with flat-soled boots, to prevent their hoofs sinking deep into the soil.

Mr. Stephenson proceeded to form the line over Chat Moss in the following manner: He had deep drains cut about five yards apart, and when the Moss between those drains had become perfectly dry, it was used to form the embankment, where necessary; and so well did it succeed, that only about four times the quantity was required that would have been necessary on hard ground. Where the road was to be on a level, drains were cut on each side of the intended line, by which, intersected with occasional cross drains, the upper part of the Moss became dry and tolerably firm; and on this hurdles were placed, either in double or single layers, as the case required, four feet broad and nine feet long, covered with heath. The ballast was then placed on these floating hurdles; longitudinal bearings, as well as cross sleepers, were used to support the rails where necessary; and the whole was thoroughly drained. In the cutting, the work had to be accomplished by drainage alone. The only advantage in favor of these operations was, that the surface of the Moss was somewhat higher than the surrounding country, which circumstance partially assisted the drainage. In proceeding with these operations, however, difficulties from time to time presented themselves, which were overcome with singular sagacity by the engineer. Thus, when the longitudinal drains were first cut along either side of the intended railway, the oozy fluid of the bog poured in, threatening in many places to fill it up entirely, and bring it back to the original level. Mr. Stephenson then hit upon the following expedient. He sent to Liverpool and Manchester, and bought up all the old tallow casks that could be found; and, digging out the trench anew, he had the casks inserted along the bottom, with their ends thrust into each other—thus keeping up the continuity of the drain. The pressure of the bog, however, on both sides of the casks, as well as from beneath, forced them out of position, and the line of casks lay unequally along the surface. They were then weighted with clay for the purpose of keeping them down. This expedient proved successful; and the drainage proceeded. Then the Moss between the two lines of drains was spread over with hurdles, sand and earth, for the purpose of forming the road. But it was soon apparent that this weight was squeezing down the Moss and making it rise up on either side of the line, so that the railway lay as it were in a valley, and formed one huge drain running across the bog. To correct this defect, the Moss was weighted with hurdles and earth, to the extent of about thirty feet outside the line on either side, by which means the adjacent bog was forced down, and the line of railway in the centre was again raised to its proper position. By these expedients, the necessity for devising which was constantly occurring, and as constantly met with remarkable success, the work went forward, and the rails were laid down.

Mr. Stephenson himself thus described the general outline of this formidable work, in an account which he furnished to Mr. Charles Knight, dated the 1st November, 1828:*

"Chat Moss extends four miles along the line of road. On each side of the Moss the land lies low. On the western side an embankment is formed of moss nearly a mile in length and varying from ten to twelve feet in height, which stands extremely well. The slopes of this embankment are a little more upright than an angle of 45°, which, from my experience, stands better than if more inclined. It is now covered with a material from two to three feet thick, consisting of sand and gravel. The permanent road is laid upon this covering, and remains very firm. The quantity of excavations made in the Moss, to form the embankments adjoining, amount to 520,000 cubic yards. That portion of the Moss, about three-quarters of a mile from the western edge, called 'Flow Moss,' from its extreme softness, is also covered with sand and gravel; underneath I have laid hurdles thickly interwoven with twisted heath, which forms a platform for the covering. Two years ago a person was not able to walk over this portion of the Moss, except in the dryest weather; at present we have horses traveling with loads of from six to twelve tons.

"A considerable embankment is completed near the centre of the Moss, and resists pressure remarkably well. From the termination of the last work, for a mile there is little required

* Companion to the Almanac and Year Book of General Information for 1829.

except drainage, the surface being uniform, and nearly at the desired level. Thenceforward the surface descends, consequently an embankment is required, which gradually increases until it attains the height of twenty feet or more. The foundation in this part being exceedingly soft, we have experienced some difficulty during its formation, where the height is great, from the shrinking. Notwithstanding this, in the course of next summer we shall have a good road over this part. Much advantage has been derived from removing the heathy surface with a spade depth of the Moss on each side of this embankment. This expedient accelerates the drying of the substratum of the Moss, by presenting a surface to the atmosphere much more favorable for evaporation than the heath. Indeed, the latter being a bad conductor of heat, tends much to keep the temperature of the Moss below that of the air. The covering of the Moss, from the nature of the surface which it presents to the atmosphere, also materially assists in reducing the temperature of the subjacent fluid, by the rapid radiation of caloric."

The formation of the heavy embankment above referred to, on the verge of the bog, presented considerable difficulties. The weight of the earth pressed it down through the fluid: and thousands of cubic yards were engulfed before the road made any approach to the required level. For weeks the stuff was poured in, and little or no progress seemed to have been made. The directors of the railway became alarmed, and they feared that the evil prognostications of the eminent civil engineers were now about to be realized. Mr. Stephenson was asked for his opinion; and his invariable answer was—"We must persevere." And so he went on; but still the insatiable bog gaped for more material, which was emptied in truck-load after truck-load without any apparent effect. Then a special meeting of the board was summoned, and it was held upon the spot, to determine whether the work should be proceeded with, or *abandoned.* Mr. Stephenson himself afterwards described the transaction at a public dinner given at Birmingham, on the 23d of December, 1837, on the occasion of a piece of plate being presented to his son, the engineer of the London and Birmingham Railway. He related the anecdote, he said, for the purpose of impressing upon the minds of those who heard him the necessity of perseverance.

"After working for weeks and weeks," said he, "in filling in materials to form the road, there did not yet appear to be the least sign of our being able to raise the solid embankment one single inch; in short we went on filling in without the slightest apparent effect. Even my assistants began to feel uneasy, and to doubt of the success of the scheme. The directors, too, spoke of it as a hopeless task; and at length they became seriously alarmed, so much so, indeed, that a board meeting was held on Chat Moss to decide whether I should proceed any further. They had previously taken the opinion of other engineers, who reported unfavorably. There was no help for it, however, but to go on. An immense outlay had been incurred; and great loss would have been occasioned had the scheme been then abandoned and the line taken by another route. So the directors were *compelled* to allow me to go on with my plans, of the ultimate success of which I myself never for one moment doubted. Determined, therefore, to persevere as before, I ordered the work to be carried on vigorously; and, to the surprise of every one connected with the undertaking, in six months from the day on which the board had held its special meeting on the Moss, a locomotive engine and carriage passed over the very spot with a party of the directors' friends on their way to dine at Manchester."

The idea which bore him up, in the face of so many adverse opinions, in assuming that a safe road could be formed across the floating bog was this: That a ship floated in water, and the Moss was certainly more capable of supporting such a weight than water was; and he knew that if he could once get the material to float he would succeed. That his idea was correct is proved by the fact that Chat Moss now forms the very best part of the line of railroad between Liverpool and Manchester. Nor was the cost of construction of this part of the line excessive. The formation of the road across Chat Moss amounted to about 28,000*l.*, Mr. Giles's estimate having been 270,000*l.*!

During the progress of these works the most ridiculous rumors were set afloat. The drivers of the stage-coaches, who feared for their calling, brought the alarming intelligence into Manchester from time to time, that "Chat Moss was blown up!" "Hundreds of men and horses had sunk in the bog; and the works were completely abandoned!" The engineer himself was declared to have been swallowed up in the Serbonian bog; and "railways were at an end forever!" With the originators of these alarming reports, the wish was father to the thought. The majority of people knew nothing about railways—they were yet a deep mystery; and they were not disposed to believe in them till they had seen them put to the proof. The rumors were therefore credited for the time, until supplanted by others.

Although the works of the Liverpool and Manchester Railway are of a much less formidable character than those of many lines which have since been constructed, they were then regarded as of the most stupendous description. Indeed, the like of them had not before been executed in England. There were sixty-three bridges over and under the line at different points. The great Sankey viaduct, consisting of nine arches of fifty feet span, was a noble structure, rising to a height of nearly seventy feet above the level of the Sankey canal. The skew bridge at Rainhill, the bridge at Newton, and the bridge over the Irwell at Manchester, are still looked upon as good specimens of railway work, and at the time of their formation were regarded with high admiration by engineers. The tunnel under part of the town of Liverpool, and the Olive Mount excavation—a deep cutting through solid sandstone rock, extending for upwards of two miles—were formidable works, occupying much time in the quarrying and removal of the stone. Some idea of the extensive character of the cuttings may be formed from the fact that upwards of three millions of cubic yards of stone, clay and soil, were removed and formed into embankments at various parts of the line.

In the construction of the railway, Mr. Stephenson's capacity for organizing and directing the labors of a large number of workmen of all kinds eminently displayed itself. A vast quantity of ballast-wagons had to be constructed for the purposes of the work, and implements and materials had to be collected, before the mass of labor to be employed could be efficiently set in motion at the various points of the line. There were not at that time, as there are now, large contractors possessed of railway plant, capable of executing earthworks on a large scale. There was no division of labor between the engineer and contractor, such as now exists. The engineer had then not only to contrive the plant, but to organize the labor, and direct it in person. The very laborers themselves had to be trained to their work by the engineer; and it was on the Liverpool and Manchester Railway that Mr. Stephenson first called into existence that formidable band of navvies, whose handiworks will be the wonder and admiration of succeeding generations. Looking at their gigantic traces, the men of some future age may be found ready to declare, of the engineer and of his workmen, that "there were giants in those days."

These navvies were men drawn by the attraction of good wages from all parts of the kingdom; and they were ready for any sort of rough work. Many of the laborers employed on the Liverpool line were Irish; others were from the Northumberland and Durham railways, where they had been accustomed to similar work; the best and most powerful came from the hilly districts of Lancashire and Yorkshire, where men of the finest physical development in England are to be found; and some were drawn from the loose and unemployed population of the surrounding counties. Working together, eating, drinking, and sleeping together, and daily exposed to the same influences, they soon began to assume a distinct and well-defined character, strongly marking them from the population of the districts in which they labored. Reckless alike of his life as of his earnings, the navvy worked hard and lived hard. For his lodging, a hut of turf would content him; but he required large quantities of flesh meat, and what remained of his wages was often spent in drink. With few or no domestic ties to bind him, or family affections to soften his nature—wanting in moral and religious training, and placed suddenly in the receipt of high wages, paid at unusually long intervals—the navvy shortly became distinguished by a sort of savage manners, which contrasted strangely with those of the surrounding population. His pay-night was often a saturnalia of riot and disorder, dreaded by the inhabitants of the quiet villages along the line of works. Yet these brawny laborers, with their powerful bones and muscles, ignorant and violent though they might be, were usually good-hearted fellows in the main—frank and open-handed with their comrades, and ready to share their last penny with those in distress. As for their powers of endurance, probably no class of laborers in the world can compete with them: they have been toiled after in vain by French and German workmen, who have failed to justify the claim to be paid a similarly high rate of wages. Their pluck is wonderful, and their contempt for danger almost proverbial. Indeed, the most dangerous sort of labor — such as working horse-barrow runs, in which accidents are of constant occurrence — has always been most in request amongst them, the danger seeming to be one of its chief recommendations.

It was some time, however, before Mr. Stephenson could, out of the raw material of laborers attracted to the Liverpool and Manchester line, form an efficient body of workmen of this sort. The principal difficulty was experienced in pushing on the works connected with the formation of the tunnel under Liverpool, 2200 yards in length. The blasting and hewing of the rock was vigorously carried on night and day; and the engineer's practical experience in the collieries here proved of great use to him. Many obstacles had to be encountered and overcome in the formation of the tunnel, the rock varying in hardness and texture at different parts. In some places the miners were deluged by water, which surged from the soft blue shale found at the lowest level of the tunnel. In other places, beds of wet sand were cut through; and there careful propping and pinning were necessary to prevent the roof from tumbling in, until the masonry to support it could be erected. On one occasion, while Mr. Stephenson was absent from Liverpool, a mass of loose moss-earth and sand fell from the roof, which had been insufficiently propped. The miners withdrew from the work; and on Mr. Stephenson's return, he found them in a refractory state, refusing to reënter the tunnel. He induced them, however, by his example, to return to their labors; and when the roof had been secured, the work went on again as before. When there was danger, he was always ready to share it with the men; and gathering confidence from his fearlessness, they proceeded vigorously with the undertaking, boring and mining their way towards the light.

By the end of 1828, the directors found they had expended 460,000*l.* on the works, and that they were still far from completion. They looked at the loss of interest on this large investment, and began to grumble at the delay. They desired to see their capital becoming productive; and in the spring of 1829, they urged the engineer to push on the works with increased vigor. Mr. Cropper, one of the directors, who took an active interest in their progress, said to him one day, "Now, George, thou must get on with the railway, and have it finished without further delay: thou must really have it ready for opening by the first day of January next." "Consider the heavy character of the works, sir, and how much we have been delayed by the want of money, not to speak of the wetness of the weather: it is impossible." "Impossible!" rejoined Cropper; "I wish I could get Napoleon to thee—he would tell thee there is no such word as 'impossible' in the vocabulary." "Tush!" exclaimed Stephenson, with warmth; "don't speak to me about Napoleon! Give me men, money, and materials, and I will do what Napoleon couldn't do—drive a railroad from Liverpool to Manchester over Chat Moss!" And truly, the formation of a high road over that bottomless bog was, apparently, a far more difficult task than the hewing even of Napoleon's far-famed road across the Simplon.

The directors had more than once been pressed by want c funds to meet the heavy expenditure. The country had scarcely yet recovered from the general panic and crash of 1825; and it was with difficulty that the calls could be raised from the shareholders. A loan of 100,000*l.* was obtained from the Exchequer Loan Commissioners in 1826; and in 1829 an Act was obtained enabling the company to raise further capital, to provide working plant for the railway. Two acts were also obtained during the progress of the works, enabling deviations and alterations to be made, one to improve the curves and shorten the line near Rainhill, and the other to carry the line across the Irwell into the town of Manchester. Thanks to the energy of the engineer, the industry of his laborers, and the improved supply of money by the directors, the railway made rapid progress in the course of the year 1829. Double sets of laborers were employed on Chat Moss and other points, in carrying on the works by night and day, the night shifts working by torch and fire-light; and at length, the work advancing at all points, the directors saw their way to the satisfactory completion of the undertaking.

It may well be supposed that Mr. Stephenson's time was fully occupied in superintending the extensive, and, for the most part, novel works connected with the railway, and that even his extraordinary powers of labor and endurance were taxed to the utmost during the four years that they were in progress. Although he had able helpers in the young engineers whom he had selected to take charge of the different "lengths" of the line, every detail in the plans was directed and arranged by himself. Every bridge, from the simplest to the most complicated, including the then novel structure of the "skew bridge," iron girders, siphons, fixed engines, the machinery for working the tunnel at the Liverpool end, had all to be thought out by his own head, and reduced to definite plans by his own hands. Besides all this, he had to design the working plant in anticipation of the opening of the railway. He planned the wagons, trucks, and carriages; and himself superintended their manufacture. The turntables, switches, crossings, and signals — in short, the entire structure and machinery of the line, from the turning of the first sod to the running of the first train of carriages upon the railway — went on under his immediate supervision.

He had no staff of experienced assistants—not even a staff of draughtsmen in his office—but only a few young pupils learning their business; and frequently he was without even their help. The time of his engineering inspectors was fully occupied in the actual superintendence of the works at different parts of the line; and he directed all their more important operations in person. Mr. Locke, formerly in his employment as a clerk at Newcastle, had charge of the important works between Liverpool and Rainhill; Mr. John Dixon superintended the formation of the road over Chat Moss; and Mr. T. L. Gooch and Mr. Allcard were stationed at other points. It was in the midst of this vast accumulation of work and responsibility that the battle of the locomotive engine had to be fought—a battle not merely against material difficulties, but against the still more trying obstructions of deeply-rooted mistrust and prejudice on the part of a considerable minority of the directors.

The usual routine of his life at this time—if routine it might be called—was, to rise early, by sunrise in summer and before it in winter, and thus "break the back of the day's work" by mid-day. Before breakfast he would visit the extensive workshops at Edgehill, where most of the "plant" for the line was manufactured. Then, returning home, after a hurried breakfast, he would ride along the works to inspect their progress, and push them on with greater energy where needful. On other days he would prepare for the much less congenial engagement of meeting the board, which was often a cause of great anxiety and pain to him; for it was difficult to satisfy men of all tempers, and some of these not of the most generous sort. On such occasions he might be seen with his right-hand thumb thrust through the top-most button-hole of his coat breast, vehemently hitching his right shoulder, as was his habit when laboring under any considerable excitement. On other days he would take an early ride before breakfast, to inspect the progress of the Sankey viaduct. He had a favorite horse, brought by him from Newcastle, called "Bobby," so tractable that, with his rider on his back, he would walk up to a locomotive with the steam blowing off, and put his nose against it without shying. "Bobby," saddled and bridled, was brought to Mr. Stephenson's door betimes in the morning; and mounting him, he would ride the fifteen miles to Sankey, putting up at a little public house which then stood upon the banks of the canal. There he had his breakfast of "crowdie," which he made with his own hands. It consisted of oatmeal stirred into a basin of hot water—a sort of porridge—which was supped with cold sweet milk. After this frugal breakfast, he would go upon the works, and remain there, riding from point to point, for the greater part of the day. If he returned home before mid-day, it would be to examine the pay-sheets in the different departments, sent in by the assistant engineers, or by the foremen of the workshops; all this he did himself, with the greatest care, requiring a full explanation of every item.

After a late dinner, which occupied very short time and was always of a plain and frugal description, he would proceed to dispose of his correspondence, or prepare sketches of drawings, and give instructions as to their completion. He would occasionally refresh himself for this evening work by a short doze, which however, he would never admit had exceeded the limits of "winking," to use his own term. Mr. Frederick Swanwick, one of his most rising pupils, officiated as his amanuensis; and he then remarked—what in after years he could better appreciate—the clear, terse, and vigorous style of his dictation: there was nothing superfluous in it; but it was close, direct, and to the point—in short, thoroughly business-like. And if, in passing through the pen of the amanuensis, his meaning happened in any way to be distorted or modified, it did not fail to escape his detection, though he was always tolerant of any liberties taken with his own form of expression, so long as the words written down conveyed his real meaning. His strong natural acumen showed itself even in such matters as grammar and composition—a department of knowledge in which, it might be supposed, he could scarcely have had either time or opportunity to acquire much information. But here, as in all other things, his shrewd common sense came to his help; and his simple, vigorous English might almost be cited as a model of composition.

His letters and reports written, and his sketches of drawings made and explained, the remainder of the evening was usually devoted to conversation with his wife and those of his pupils who lived under his roof, and constituted, as it were, part of the family. He delighted to test the knowledge of his young companions, and to question them upon the principles of mechanics. If they were not quite "up to the mark" on every point, there was no escaping detection by any evasive or specious explanations on their part. These always met with the verdict of, "Ah! you know naught about it now; but think it over again, and tell me the answer when you understand it." If there was even partial success in the reply, it would at once be acknowledged, and a full explanation was given, to which the master would add illustrative examples for the purpose of impressing the principle more deeply upon the pupil's mind.

It was not so much his object and purpose to "cram" the minds of the young men committed to his charge, with the *results* of knowledge, as to stimulate them to educate themselves—to induce them to develop their mental and moral powers by the exercise of their own free energies, and thus acquire that habit of self-thinking and self-reliance which is the spring of all true manly action. In a word, he sought to bring out and invigorate the *character* of his pupils. He felt that he himself had been made stronger and better through his encounters with difficulty; and he would not have the road of knowledge made too smooth and easy for them. "Learn for yourselves—think for yourselves," he would say—"make yourselves masters of principles—persevere—be industrious—and there is then no fear of you." And not the least emphatic proof of the soundness of this system of education, as conducted by Mr. Stephenson, was afforded by the after history of these pupils themselves. There was not one of those trained under his eye who did not rise to eminent usefulness and distinction as engineers. He sent them forth into the world braced with the spirit of manly self-help—inspired by his own noble example; and they repeated in their after career the lessons of earnest effort and persistent industry which his own daily life had taught them.

Mr. Stephenson's evenings at home were not, however, exclusively devoted either to business or to the graver exercises above referred to. He would often indulge in cheerful conversation and anecdote, falling back from time to time upon the struggles and difficulties of his early life. The not unfrequent winding up of his story, addressed to the pupils about him, was—"Ah! ye young fellows don't know what wark is in these days!" Mr. Swanwick delights recalling to mind how seldom, if ever, an angry or captious word, or an angry look, marred the enjoyment of those evenings. The presence of Mrs. Stephenson conferred upon them an additional charm: amiable, kind-hearted and intelligent, she shared quietly in the pleasure; and the atmosphere of comfort which always pervaded her home, contributed in no small degree to render it a centre of cheerful, hopeful intercourse, and of earnest, honest industry. She was a wife who well deserved, what she through life retained, the strong and unremitting affection of her husband.

When Mr. Stephenson retired for the night, it was not always that he permitted himself to sink into slumber. Like Brindley, he worked out many a difficult problem in bed; and for hours he would turn over in his mind and study how to overcome some obstacle, or to mature some project, on which his thoughts were bent. Some remark inadvertently dropped by him at the breakfast table in the morning, served to show that he had been stealing some hours from the past night in reflection and study. Yet he would rise at his accustomed early hour, and there was no abatement of his usual energy in carrying on the business of the day.

Such is a brief sketch of Mr. Stephenson's private life and habits while carrying on the works of the Liverpool and Manchester Railway.

CHAPTER XXI.

A PRIZE OFFERED FOR THE BEST LOCOMOTIVE ENGINE.

THE works were far advanced towards completion before the directors had determined as to the kind of tractive power to be employed in working the railway when opened for traffic. It was necessary that they should now come to a decision, and many board meetings were held for the purpose of discussing the subject. The old-fashioned and well-tried system of horse haulage was not without its advocates; but, looking at the large amount of traffic which there was to be conveyed, and at the probable delay in the transit from station to station, if this method were adopted, the directors, after a visit made by them to the Northumberland and Durham railways in 1828, came to the conclusion that the employment of horse power was inadmissible.

The tunnel at Liverpool had been finished, a firm road had been formed over Chat Moss, and yet the directors had got no further than this decision against the employment of horse power. It was felt that some mechanical agency must be adopted; but whether fixed or locomotive power, was still a moot point. Fixed engines had many advocates, the locomotive very few: it stood as yet almost in a minority of one—George Stephenson. The prejudice against the employment of the latter power had even increased since the Liverpool and Manchester Bill underwent its first ordeal in the House of Commons. In proof of this, we may mention that the Newcastle and Carlisle Railway Act was conceded in 1829, on the express condition that it should *not* be worked by locomotives, but by horses only.

Grave doubts existed as to the practicability of working a large traffic by means of traveling engines. Thus, Sir William Cowling, who was appointed by the Emperor Alexander of Russia to examine the internal communications of England, and who visited the Stockton and Darlington Railway after it was opened for traffic, declared that it could never answer as a route for passengers, in comparison with stage-coaches. He expressed his decided preference for the Atmospheric Railway, then proposed by Mr. Vallance between Brighton and Shoreham, which he considered "very far superior" to the locomotive system. Mr. Palmer, in his "Description of a Railway," declared that "there is no instance of any locomotive engine having (regularly and as a constant rate) traveled faster than, if so fast as, six miles an hour." Vallance, in his letter to Ricardo, pronounced that "locomotive engines cannot, on an open railway, ever be driven so fast as horses will draw us;" and that railways as an investment would be unproductive, and as an effective means of transit a failure. Tredgold, in his "Practical Treatise on Railroads and Carriages," dismissed the locomotive in favor of the fixed-engine system, which he pronounced to be cheaper as well as safer. "Locomotives," he said, "must always be objectionable on a railroad for general use, where it is attempted to give them a considerable degree of speed." As to the speed of railway traveling being equal to that of horses on common roads, Mr. Tredgold entertained great doubts. "That any general system of carrying passengers would answer, to go at a velocity exceeding ten miles an hour, or thereabouts, is extremely improbable." *

The most celebrated engineers offered no opinion on the subject. They did not believe in the locomotive, and would not even give themselves the trouble to examine it. The ridicule

* Tredgold on Railways, 2d ed., p. 119.

with which George Stephenson had been assailed by the barristers before the Parliamentary Committee had pleased them greatly. They did not relish the idea of a man who had picked up his experience at Newcastle coal-pits appearing in the capacity of a leading engineer before Parliament, and attempting to establish a new system of internal communication in the country.

Telford and the Rennies were then the great lights of the engineering world. The former was consulted by the Government on the subject of the power to be employed to work the Liverpool line, on the occasion of the directors applying to the Exchequer Loan Commissioners to forego their security of 30 per cent. of the calls, which the directors wished to raise to enable them to proceed more expeditiously with the works. Mr. Telford's report was, however, so unsatisfactory that the Commissioners would not release any part of the calls. All that Mr. Telford would say on the subject of the power to be employed was, that the use of horses* had been done away with by introducing two sets of inclined planes, and he considered this an evil, inasmuch as the planes must be worked either by locomotive or fixed engines; "but," he said, "which of the two latter modes

* The engineers who were examined before Parliament in support of the second Liverpool and Manchester Bill, were opposed to the locomotive, in their entire ignorance of its construction and properties; indeed, they would not give themselves the trouble to understand it. Their intention was so to lay out the line that it should be worked by horses. One of the gradients at Rainhill, as originally planned by them, was very steep, about one in fifty, and the counsel for the opposition, in cross-examining one of the eminent engineers employed for the promoters, asked him if he knew "how much additional power would be required to surmount a gradient of one in fifty." "Not very much," replied the engineer; "a little more whipcord will do it." The counsel for the opposition, in the course of his reply, alluded to this evidence. "Mr. ——," said he, "has told you, that by means of a little whipcord, a rising gradient, so steep as one foot in fifty, is to be overcome. *I* know where the whipcord, and not a little whipcord, ought to have been applied, before that witness left school." Some years after, when the Brighton Railway Bill was before Parliament, the same eminent engineer was asked by counsel "whether the wheels of the locomotive revolved on the axle or were fixed to it?" The engineer was rather taken aback, for he did not know; but he adroitly got out of the difficulty by saying, "Really, that is a matter entirely of detail, to be settled by mechanics!"

shall be adopted, I understand has not yet been finally determined; and both being recent projects, in which I have had no experience, I cannot take upon me to say whether either will fully answer in practice." And yet the locomotive engine had been in regular use on the Killingworth Railway for fifteen years at the time when Mr. Telford made this report in 1829. He himself had laid out railways, and it was part of his business to make himself familiar with the best mode of working them. But the only successful engines were those of George Stephenson; and Mr. Telford, in common with the leading professional men of his day, studiously kept aloof from him. Indeed, had the establishment of the locomotive system depended upon the leading engineers, it would have been swamped at the beginning. In the meantime it was absolutely necessary that the directors of the Liverpool Railway should come to a decision whether fixed or locomotive engines were to be employed. Mr. Stephenson urged, as usual, the superiority of the latter, in point of efficiency, convenience and economy, over any other mode of traction. The directors, who were no engineers, could not disregard the adverse opinions of professional men, and they declined to indorse his recommendation. But Mr. Stephenson had so repeatedly and earnestly urged upon them the propriety of making a trial of the locomotive before coming to any decision against it, that they at length authorized him to proceed with the construction of one of his engines by way of experiment. In their report to the proprietors at their annual meeting on the 27th March, 1828, they state that they had, after due consideration, authorized the engineer "to prepare a locomotive engine, which, from the nature of its construction and from the experiments already made, he is of opinion will be effective for the purposes of the company, without proving an annoyance to the public." In the same report the directors express their confidence in Mr. Stephenson, whose ability and unwearied activity they are glad to take the opportunity of acknowledging. The locomotive thus ordered, was placed upon the line in 1829, and was found of great service in drawing the wagons full of marl from the two great cuttings.

In the meantime the discussion proceeded as to the kind of power to be permanently employed for the working of the railway. The directors were innundated with schemes of all sorts for facilitating locomotion. The projectors of England, France and America, seemed to be let loose upon them. There were plans for working the wagons along the line by water power. Some proposed hydrogen, and others carbonic acid gas. Atmospheric pressure had its eager advocates. And various kinds of fixed and locomotive steam power were suggested. Thomas Gray urged his plan of a greased road with cog rails; and Messrs. Vignolles and Ericsson recommended the adoption of a central friction rail, against which two horizontal rollers under the locomotive, pressing upon the sides of this rail, were to afford the means of ascending the inclined planes. The directors felt themselves quite unable to choose from amidst this multitude of projects. Their engineer expressed himself as decided as heretofore in favor of smooth rails and locomotive engines, which he was confident would be found the most economical and by far the most convenient moving power that could be employed.* The Stockton and Darlington Railway being now at work, another deputation went down personally to inspect the fixed and locomotive engines on that line, as well as at Hetton and Killingworth. They returned to Liverpool with much information; but their testimony as to the relative merits of the two kinds of engines was so contradictory, that the directors were as far from a decision as ever.

They then resolved to call to their aid two professional engineers of high standing, who should visit the Darlington and Newcastle railways, carefully examine both modes of working—the fixed and locomotive—and report to them fully on the subject. The gentlemen selected were Mr. Walker of Limehouse, and

* Booth's Account, p. 71.

Mr. Rastrick of Stourbridge. After carefully examining the modes of working the northern railways, they made their report to the directors in the spring of 1829. These engineers concurred in recommending the employment of fixed engines in preference to locomotive power! Mr. Walker considered stationary engines, working on the low-pressure system, to be safer than high pressure locomotive engines which accompanied the passengers and goods on their way. Even Mr. Stephenson's early friend, Nicholas Wood, seems to have agreed with the other engineers in their report against the use of locomotives. Mr. Wood's evidence before the Committee on the Liverpool and Manchester Bill was by no means cordial in support of the locomotive. He did not seem to have any faith in the efficiency of Stephenson's favorite steam blast. Speaking of the Killingworth engines, he then said: "Those engines puff very much, and the cause is to get an increased draught in the chimney; now we have got a sufficiency of steam without it. I have no doubt that by allowing the steam to exhaust itself in a reservoir, it would pass quietly into the chimney without that noise." * And now, it seems, he had been depreciating the power and speed of the locomotive engine to the reporting engineers. Mr. Rastrick said, "It was the decided opinion of Mr. Nicholas Wood, when he saw him at Killingworth, that no locomotive engine could travel more than eight miles an hour." † He quoted Mr. Wood's opinion against Stephenson's locomotive, the "Lancashire Witch," then working on the Bolton and Leigh Railway, which he held to be an experiment of no value. Mr. Wood had even gone so far as hint to him that Chat Moss must sink under the weight of the locomotive.

Although admitting with apparent candor that improvements were to be anticipated in the locomotive engine, the reporting engineers clearly had no faith in its power, nor belief in its eventual success; and the united conclusion of the two was, that

* Evidence, p. 216.

† Mr. Rastrick's Report, p. 49.

"considering the question in every point of view—taking the two lines of road as now forming—and having reference to economy, dispatch, safety, and convenience—our opinion is, that, if it be resolved to make the Liverpool and Manchester Railway complete at once, so as to accommodate the traffic, or a quantity approaching to it, *the stationary reciprocating system is the best.*"* And in order to carry the system recommended by them into effect, they proposed to divide the railroad between Liverpool and Manchester into nineteen stages of about a mile and a half each, with twenty-one engines fixed at the different points to work the trains forward.

Here was the result of all George Stephenson's labors! The two best practical engineers of the day concurred in reporting against the employment of his locomotive! Not a single professional man of eminence could be found to coincide with him in his preference for locomotive over fixed engine power. He had scarcely a supporter; and the locomotive system seemed on the eve of being abandoned. Still he did not despair. With the profession against him, and public opinion against him—for the most frightful stories were abroad respecting the dangers, the unsightliness, and the nuisance which the locomotive would create—Mr. Stephenson held to his purpose. Even in this, apparently the darkest hour of the locomotive, he did not hesitate to declare that locomotive railroads would, before many years had passed, be "the great highways of the world."

At the meetings of the directors, and in his numerous reports, he combated in detail the reports of the consulting engineers—urged that the simplicity of the locomotive engine power, and its application to any quantity of trade, would best answer the purpose of the railway—pointed out that the Messrs. Walker and Rastrick had under-estimated the working expense of fixed en-

* Report to the Directors of the Liverpool and Manchester Railway, on the comparative Merits of Locomotive and Fixed Engines. By James Walker and J. U. Rastrick, Civil Engineers. 1829.

gines, while they had overstated that of locomotives; but, above all, he insisted that the adoption of fixed engines and ropes—an accident to any of which would involve the stoppage of the entire arrangements—would render the Liverpool and Manchester line altogether unfitted for the purposes of a public railway. The convenience of locomotives, which could be increased in power and number according to the requirements of the traffic, appeared to him one of their chief advantages; they would form a series of short unconnected chains, any one of which could be removed and another at once substituted, in event of an accident, without interruption to the traffic; whereas, according to the admission of Mr. Walker himself, the fixed engine system would constitute a continuous chain, extending from Liverpool to Manchester, "the failure of one link of which would derange the whole." This, in Mr. Stephenson's view, constituted a capital objection to the adoption of the latter plan. Besides, he did not hesitate to express his decided conviction that, in reporting against the locomotive, the consulting engineers had not made themselves fully acquainted with its powers, and especially that they had not taken into account the value of the steam blast. They had obviously overlooked the most important property of this beautiful contrivance, by which it increases the production of steam exactly in proportion to the velocity of the engine. The quicker the strokes of the piston, the stronger the draught in the chimney, the more intense the combustion of fuel in the furnace, and the more rapid the production of steam, on which the power of the engine depends. Mr. Walker, in his report, assumed that the power of the engine was in an inverse ratio to its velocity; but Mr. Stephenson held, what has since been clearly established, that, instead of the steam becoming exhausted, and the working power of the locomotive lessened, in proportion to its speed, the result was the very reverse, and that the expenditure of steam was, by means of the important contrivance of the blast, made subservient, through the more intense combustion of fuel which it excited, to the increased production of power in the engine.*

The directors could not fail to have been influenced by these arguments. But the fixed-engine party was very strong at the board, and, led by Mr. James Cropper, they urged the propriety of forthwith adopting the report of Messrs. Walker and Rastrick. Mr. Sandars and Mr. William Rathbone, on the other hand, desired that a fair trial should be given to the locomotive; and they with reason objected to the expenditure of the large capital necessary to construct the proposed engine-houses, with their

* This principle was afterwards clearly illustrated by Mr. Robert Stephenson, in the joint essay entitled "Observations on the Comparative Merits of Locomotive and Fixed Engines," published by himself and Mr. Locke (as compiled from the Reports of Mr. George Stephenson), in reply to the Report of Mr. James Walker, C. E. The pamphlet was published in February, 1830.

Mr. Robert Stephenson there observes:

"In locomotive engines hitherto constructed, the area of the surface in the boiler acted upon by the fire is much less than that generally employed in stationary engines; and hence it is that the consumption has been much greater to produce equal effects. This inconvenience has been submitted to, in order that simplicity and compactness might be achieved.

"To compensate for the loss of heating surface, it was necessary to augment the temperature of the fire. This was effected, shortly after the first locomotive engine was tried on the Killingworth Colliery Railway, by conveying the steam into the chimney, where it escaped in a perpendicular direction up the centre, after it had performed its office in the cylinders. The velocity of the steam on entering the chimney being much greater than that due to the ascending current of air from the natural draft of the furnace, the effect was to increase the draught, and consequently the temperature of the fire. . . . . Since it has been shown that the power of these engines, under similar circumstances, is chiefly dependent on the quantity of fuel consumed, it is evident that, by this application ot the waste steam to accelerate combustion, the power of the engine actually varies under different velocities. This curious fact, connected with the construction of locomotive engines on the principle of the 'Rocket,' has not hitherto, we believe, been represented in this manner; and it is so important, that any calculation neglecting its consideration, at high velocities, must be regarded as futile and absolutely false.

"Mr. Walker takes the power of a locomotive engine, of the size and construction of those used upon the Darlington Railway, equal to 10 horses, at 2½ miles an hour. Presuming that the effect is inversely as the velocities, he reduces the power of the engine at 10 miles an hour to 2½ horses' power, or = 375 lbs. This conclusion would have been perfectly correct if the quantity of steam generated in the boiler in equal times were the same at all velocities; but the fallacy of this assumption, in reference to locomotive engines, has been sufficiently explained in the foregoing remarks."—*Observations, etc. pp.* 6–8.

fixed engines, ropes, and machinery, until they had tested the powers of the locomotive, as recommended by their own engineer. Mr. Stephenson continued to urge upon them that the locomotive was yet capable of great improvements, if proper inducements were held out to inventors and machinists to make them; and he pledged himself that, if time were given him, he would construct an engine that should satisfy their requirements, and prove itself capable of working heavy loads along the railway with speed, regularity, and safety.

The directors were more bewildered than ever. Yet they had confidence in their engineer, and had but recently borne public testimony to his practical efficiency. They had seen him form a road which other engineers of high reputation had repeatedly declared to be impracticable; and it might be the same with the locomotive.

At length, influenced by his persistent earnestness not less than by his arguments, the directors, at the suggestion of Mr. Harrison, determined to offer a prize of 500*l.* for the best locomotive engine which, on a certain day, should be produced on the railway, and perform certain specified conditions in the most satisfactory manner. The conditions were these—

1. The engine must effectually consume its own smoke.

2. The engine, if of six tons weight, must be able to draw after it, day by day, twenty tons weight (including the tender and water-tank), at *ten miles* an hour, with a pressure of steam on the boiler not exceeding fifty pounds to the square inch.

3. The boiler must have two safety valves, neither of which must be fastened down, and one of them be completely out of the control of the engineman.

4. The engine and boiler must be supported on springs, and rest on six wheels, the height of the whole not exceeding fifteen feet to the top of the chimney.

5. The engine, with water, must not weigh more than six tons; but an engine of less weight would be preferred on its drawing a

proportionate load behind it; if of only four and a half tons, then it might be put on only four wheels. The Company to be at liberty to test the boiler, etc., by a pressure of one hundred and fifty pounds to the square inch.

6. A mercurial gauge must be affixed to the machine, showing the steam pressure above forty-five pounds per square inch.

7. The engine must be delivered, complete and ready for trial, at the Liverpool end of the railway, not later than the first of October, 1829.

8. The price of the engine must not exceed 550*l.*

It will be observed that the requirements of the directors as to speed were not excessive. All that they asked for was, that a speed of ten miles an hour should be maintained. Perhaps they had in mind the severe animadversions of the Quarterly Reviewer on the absurdity of traveling at a greater velocity, and also the remarks published by Mr. Nicholas Wood, whom they selected to be one of the judges of the competition, in conjunction with Mr. Rastrick of Stourbridge, and Mr. Kennedy of Manchester.*

It was now generally felt that the fate of railways in a great measure depended upon the issue of this appeal to the mechanical genius of England. When the advertisement of the prize for the best locomotive was published, scientific men began more particularly to direct their attention to the new power which was thus struggling into existence. In the meantime public opinion on the subject of railway working remained suspended, and the progress of the undertaking was watched with the most intense interest.

* Many persons of influence declared the conditions published by the directors of the railway chimerical in the extreme. One gentleman of some eminence in Liverpool, Mr. P. Ewart, who afterwards filled the office of government inspector of post-office steam packets, declared that only a parcel of charlatans would ever have issued such a set of conditions; that it had been *proved* to be impossible to make a locomotive engine go at ten miles an hour; but if it ever was done, he would eat a stewed engine-wheel to his breakfast!

CHAPTER XXII.

THE BUILDING OF THE "ROCKET."

We now return to the history of the locomotive factory commenced by Mr. Stephenson and his associates at Newcastle in the year 1824. Its establishment at that early period was a most important step in the progress of the railway system, and mainly contributed to the eventual triumph of the locomotive. Mr. Stephenson engaged skilled mechanics in the workshops, by whose example others were trained and educated. Having their attention especially directed to the fabrication of locomotives, they acquired a skill and precision in the manufacture of the several parts, which gave to the Stephenson factory a prestige which was afterwards a source of no small profit to its founders. It was a school or college, in which the locomotive workmen of the kingdom were trained; and many of the most celebrated engineers of Europe, America, and India, acquired their best practical knowledge in its workshops.

Several years, however, passed before the factory so much as paid expenses. For the first four or five years it was carried on at considerable loss; and Edward Pease wished to retire, but Mr. Stephenson could not provide the necessary money to buy him out. It must, therefore, be persevered in until the locomotive had established itself in public estimation as a practicable and economical motive power. And that time was now fast approaching.

It will be remembered that Robert Stephenson set out for the mines of Columbia, in South America, in the year 1824, during the time that the works of the Stockton and Darlington Railway were in progress. He remained there until the middle of 1827, when he received a letter from his father urging him to come home and take charge of the Newcastle works, as the time was coming when there would probably be a fair chance for the locomotive. Mr. Stephenson felt that he was now engaged in the greatest enterprise of his life; and he wanted some fast friend and helper to stand by him and aid him in developing his plans as to the locomotive railway system. He knew that he could rely upon the now matured judgment of his son, and he urged him to return home forthwith. Accordingly, Robert made immediate arrangements to leave Columbia for England, which he reached in December, 1827.

On his way home, Mr. Stephenson had a singular rencontre with a person well known in connection with the early history of the locomotive. He was waiting for a ship in which to embark for New York, at the small town of Cartagena, on the Gulf of Darien. No vessel being ready to sail, he was under the necessity of staying for some days in the place, then desolated by the ravages of the yellow fever. Sitting one day in the large, bare, comfortless room of the miserable hotel, of the almost deserted town, he observed two strangers, whom he at once perceived to be English. One of the strangers was a tall, gaunt man, with shrunken flesh, on which his shabby clothes hung loosely. On making inquiry, he found it was Trevethick! He was on his way from the gold mines of Peru, and was penniless! Still he was full of speculation, and was returning to England, where he proposed to organize a gold-mining company, that was to make the fortunes of thousands. Trevethick and his friend had lost everything in their journey across the country from Peru. They had forded rivers, and wandered through forests, leaving all their baggage behind them, and had reached thus far with only the clothes upon their backs. Their money was all spent, and they were only too happy to have arrived at Cartagena with their lives.

The adventures of Trevethick in connection with his gold-mining speculations, have almost the air of romance. It will be remembered that his high-pressure engine, adapted for traveling on roads, was invented as early as 1802. The model was beautifully finished, and found its way to London as a mechanical curiosity. There it remained until the year 1811, when M. Francois Uvillé arrived in England from Peru, for the purpose of obtaining steam machinery wherewith to clear the gold mines of water, by which some of the richest in that country had been totally drowned, and consequently fallen into decay. Uvillé, however, found little encouragement to pursue his plan. The rarity of the atmosphere in the lofty regions of the Cordilleras, and the impracticability of conveying large engines over almost inaccessible mountains, presented difficulties apparently too great to be surmounted. He was about to leave England in despair, when, one day, passing through a street leading out of Fitzroy-square, in London, he accidentally observed the model of a steam engine exposed for sale in the shop of a Mr. Roland. It was Trevethick's model of his locomotive engine. Uvillé was struck with its simplicity and excellence of construction, and bought it at once for twenty guineas. He carried the model with him to Lima, and tried its effects on the highest ridges of Pasco. The action of the engine exceeded even his sanguine expectations. An association was formed in Lima for the purpose of contracting with the proprietors of the flooded gold mines, to clear them of water, by powerful engines, similarly constructed; and M. Uvillé again embarked for England, to discover Trevethick, and enlist him in the speculation.

Trevethick's sanguine mind was inflamed by the prospects held out by his new friend. He entered into an engagement to provide nine pumping engines, made after his locomotive model, at a cost of about 10,000*l.*; and they were made and shipped for Lima, in September, 1814.

Trevethick was meanwhile engaged in providing further supplies of steam-engines, as well as in constructing coining apparatus for the Peruvian mint, and furnaces for purifying the silver ore by fusion. In October, 1816, he set sail for Lima, thinking no more of the locomotive engine, which was now safe in the hands of George Stephenson. Trevethick had a more immediate prospect before him of both fame and gain. On landing at Lima, he was received with public honors and rejoicings, was immediately presented to the Viceroy, and most graciously received. His advent was described as forming an epoch in the prosperity of Peru. The Viceroy ordered a guard of honor to attend him; and M. Uvillé, writing to his associates, declared that Heaven had sent them Don Ricardo Trevethick for the prosperity of the mines, and that "the Lord Warden had proposed to erect his statute in massy silver." His friends at home hailed with delight the triumphant success of Trevethick; and, in describing these transactions, they stated that his emoluments from the mines, taken at a moderate estimate, amounted to 100,000*l.* a year! *

Robert Stephenson's surprise may, therefore, be imagined, when he found this potent Don Ricardo in the inn at Cartagena, reduced almost to his last shilling, and unable to proceed further. Trevethick had realized the truth of the Spanish proverb, that a "silver mine brings misery, a gold mine ruin." Mr. Stephenson lent him 50*l.*, and thus helped him on his way back to England; but although Trevethick was heard of in England afterwards, he had no part in the ultimate triumph of the locomotive.†

* Geological Transactions of Cornwall, vol. i, p. 222.

† On the 12th of August, 1831, Mr. Trevethick appeared as a witness before the select committee of the House of Commons on the employment of steam-carriages on common roads. He said "he had been abroad a good many years, and had had nothing to do with steam-carriages until very lately. He had it now, however, in contemplation to do a great deal on common roads, and, with that view, had taken out a patent for an entirely new

Mr. Robert Stephenson, on his arrival in England, proceeded to take charge of the locomotive manufactory at Newcastle, thenceforward devoting himself assiduously to the development of his father's ideas of the locomotive; and, by the great additions made by him to its working powers, from time to time, as will afterwards be seen, he contributed in an eminent degree to the ultimate success of the railway system.

During the progress of the important discussion at Liverpool, with reference to the kind of power to be employed in working the railway, the father and son were in constant communication, and Robert made frequent visits to Liverpool, for the purpose of assisting his father in the preparation of his reports to the board on the subject. Mr. Swanwick remembers the vivid interest of the evening discussions which then took place between father and son as to the best mode of increasing the powers and perfecting the mechanism of the locomotive. He wondered at their quick perception and rapid judgment of each other's suggestions, at the mechanical difficulties which they anticipated and at once provided for in the practical arrangement of the machine; and he speaks of these evenings as most interesting displays of two actively ingenious and able minds, stimulating each other to feats of mechanical invention, by which it was ordained that the locomotive engine should become what it now is. These discussions became more frequent, and still more interesting, after the public prize had been offered for the best locomotive by the directors of the railway, and the working plans of the engine which they proposed to construct had to be settled.

One of the most important considerations in the new engine was the arrangement of the boiler and the extension of its heating surface to enable steam enough to be raised rapidly and continuously, for the purpose of maintaining high rates of speed—the effect of high-pressure engines being ascertained to depend

engine the arrangements in which were calculated to obviate all the difficulties which had hitherto stood in the way of traveling on common roads" mainly upon the quantity of steam which the boiler can generate, and upon its degree of elasticity when produced. The quantity of steam so generated, it will be obvious, must chiefly depend upon the quantity of fuel consumed in the furnace, and, by consequence, upon the high rate of temperature maintained there.

It will be remembered that in Mr. Stephenson's first Killingworth engines, he invented and applied the ingenious method of stimulating combustion in the furnace, by throwing the waste steam into the chimney, after performing its office in the cylinders, thus accelerating the ascent of the current of air, greatly increasing the draught, and consequently the temperature of the fire. This plan was adopted by him, as we have already seen, as early as 1815; and it was so successful that he himself attributed to it the greater economy of the locomotive as compared with horse power, and hence its continued use upon the Killingworth Railway. This arrangement was adopted, without exception, in all the locomotives subsequently constructed by Mr. Stephenson for the Killingworth, Hetton, and Stockton and Darlington Railways.

Though the adoption of the steam blast greatly quickened combustion and contributed to the rapid production of high-pressure steam, the limited amount of heating surface presented tc the fire was still felt to be an obstacle to the complete success of the locomotive engine. Mr. Stephenson endeavored to overcome this by lengthening the boilers, and increasing the surface presented by the flue tubes. He also further endeavored to meet the difficulty by doubling the flue, the last engine which he constructed for the Stockton and Darlington Railway, previous to the building of the "Rocket," being constructed with a double tube, which thus presented a considerably greater surface to the fire. The "Lancashire Witch," built by him for the Bolton and Leigh Railway, and employed in the completion of the Liverpool and Manchester Railway embankments, was also constructed with a double tube, each of which contained a fire, and passed longitudinally through the boiler. But this arrangement necessarily led to a considerable increase in the weight of these engines, which amounted to about twelve tons each; and as six tons was the limit allowed for engines admitted to the Liverpool competition, it was clear that the time was come when the Killingworth engine must undergo a further important modification.

For many years previous to this period, ingenious mechanics had been engaged in attempting to solve the problem of the best and most economical boiler for the production of high-pressure steam. As early as 1803, Mr. Woolf patented a tubular boiler, which was extensively employed at the Cornish mines, and was found greatly to facilitate the production of steam, by the extension of the heating surface. This boiler consisted of eight tubes placed horizontally in the centre of the longitudinal furnace; and they were so arranged that the whole current of the flame passed over them before it escaped into the chimney. Mr. Woolf stated the object of the arrangement to be, that "the tubes composing the boiler should be so combined and arranged, and the furnace so constructed, as to make the fire, the flame, and the heated air to act around, over, and among the tubes, embracing the largest possible quantity of their surface." In this arrangement the steam and water were *within* the tubes. Various modifications of this boiler were afterwards adopted. The ingenious Trevethick, in his patent of 1815, seems also to have entertained the idea of employing a boiler constructed of "small perpendicular tubes," with the object of increasing the heating surface. These tubes were to be closed at the bottom, opening into the common reservoir, from whence they were to receive their water, and into which the steam of all the tubes was to be united. It does not, however, appear that any locomotive was ever constructed according to this patent. Mr. W. H. James, a son of the first surveyor of the Liverpool and Manchester Railway, patented a new form of boiler in 1825, the object of which was to increase the heating surface by means of a series of annular tubes placed side by side, and bolted together, so as to form by their union a long cylindrical boiler, in the centre of which, at one end, the fireplace was situated. A model of this tubular boiler was shown by Mr. James to both Mr. Losh and Mr. Stephenson, about 1827. Losh expressed the opinion that, if such a boiler could be put to Stephenson's engine, there would be no limits to its power; and Mr. James spoke of a speed of from twenty to thirty miles an hour, at which Mr. Stephenson shook his head, remembering, as no doubt he did, his severe cross-examination and denunciation by counsel before the House of Commons, for venturing to say that twelve miles an hour might be achieved by the locomotive on railways; and he said that was a rate of speed they did not now dare to talk about. Mr. Goldsworthy Gurney, the persevering inventor of steam-carriages for traveling on common roads, also applied the tubular principle extensively in his boiler, the steam being generated within the tubes. Messrs. Summers and Ogle invented a boiler for their turnpike-road steam-carriage, consisting of a series of tubes placed vertically over the furnace, through which the heated air passed before reaching the chimney. The application of the same principle to the railway locomotive, it has been stated by a French author,* was first effected by M. Seguin, the engineer of the Lyons and St. Etienne Railway. He claimed to have patented a boiler, in 1828, in which he placed a series of horizontal tubes immersed in the water, through which the hot air passed in streamlets, thus greatly increasing the heating surface, and consequently the evaporative power. Two locomotives had been constructed at Mr. Stephenson's works in Newcastle, for the St. Etienne Railway, which were sent to France, in 1829. M. Seguin found that, by applying his invention to these engines in conjunction with the steam blast, he was at once enabled greatly to increase their power and speed. The same idea of a tubular boiler had occurred to Mr. Henry Booth, the secretary of the Liverpool and Manchester Railway, who strongly

* Lobet, *Des Chemins de Fer de France*, 1845.

urged its adoption by Mr. Stephenson in the construction of the "Rocket" engine.

On the subject of this important combination, we cannot do better than here quote the words of Mr. Robert Stephenson himself, in a statement with which he has favored us:

"After the opening of the Stockton and Darlington, and before that of the Liverpool and Manchester Railway, my father directed his attention to various methods of increasing the evaporative power of the boiler of the locomotive engine. Amongst other attempts, he introduced tubes (as had before been done in other engines), small tubes containing water, by which the heating surface was materially increased. Two engines with such tubes were constructed for the St. Etienne Railway, in France, which was in progress of construction in the year 1828; but the expedient was not successful—the tubes became furred with deposit, and burned out.

"Other engines, with boilers of a variety of construction, were made, all having in view the increase of the heating surface, as it then became obvious to my father that the speed of the engine could not be increased without increasing the evaporative power of the boiler. Increase of surface was in some cases obtained by inserting two tubes, each containing a separate fire, into the boiler; in other cases the same result was obtained by returning the same tube through the boiler; but it was not until he was engaged in making some experiments, during the progress of the Liverpool and Manchester Railway, in conjunction with Mr. Henry Booth, the well known secretary of the company, that any decided movement in this direction was effected, and that the present multitubular boiler assumed a practicable shape. It was in conjunction with Mr. Booth that my father constructed the 'Rocket' engine.

"At this stage of the locomotive engine, we have in the multitubular boiler the only important principle of construction introduced, in addition to those which my father had brought to bear at a very early age (between 1815 and 1821) on the Killingworth Colliery Railway. In the 'Rocket' engine, the power of generating steam was prodigiously increased by the adoption of the multitubular system. Its efficiency was further augmented by narrowing the orifice by which the waste steam escaped into the chimney; for by this means the velocity of the air in the chimney—or, in other words, the draught of the fire—was increased to an extent that far surpassed the expectations even of those who had been the authors of the combination.

"From the date of running the 'Rocket' on the Liverpool and Manchester Railway, the locomotive engine has received many minor improvements in detail, and especially in accuracy of workmanship; but in no essential particular does the existing locomotive differ from that which obtained the prize in the celebrated competition at Rainhill.

"In this instance, as in every other important step in science or art, various claimants have arisen for the merit of having suggested the multitubular boiler as a means of obtaining the necessary heating surface. Whatever may be the value of their respective claims, the public, useful and extensive application of the invention must certainly date from the experiments made at Rainhill. M. Seguin, for whom engines had been made by my father some few years previously, states that he patented a similar multitubular boiler in France, several years before. A still prior claim is made by Mr. Stevens, of New York, who was all but a rival to Mr. Fulton in the introduction of steam-boats on the American rivers. It is stated that as early as 1807 he used the multitubular boiler. These claimants may all be entitled to great and independent merit; but certain it is that the perfect establishment of the success of the multitubular boiler is more immediately due to the suggestion of Mr. Henry Booth, and to my father's practical knowledge in carrying it out."

The fitting of the copper tubes in the boiler of the "Rocket" so as to prevent leakage, was a work of some difficulty. They were manufactured by a Newcastle coppersmith, and soldered to brass screws which were screwed into the boiler ends, standing out in great knobs. When the tubes were thus fitted, and the boiler was filled with water, hydraulic pressure was applied; but the water squirted out at every joint, and the factory floor was soon flooded. Robert went home in despair; and in the first moment of grief, he wrote to his father that the whole thing was a failure. By return of post came a letter from his father, telling him that despair was not to be thought of—that he must "try again;" and he suggested a mode of overcoming the difficulty, which, singularly enough, his son had already anticipated and proceeded to adopt. It was, to bore clean holes in the boiler ends, fit in the smooth copper tubes as tightly as possible, solder up, and then raise the steam. This plan succeeded perfectly, the expansion of the copper tubes completely filling up all interstices, and producing a perfectly water-tight boiler, capable of withstanding extreme internal pressure.

The mode of employing the steam-blast for the purpose of increasing the draught in the chimney, was also the subject of numerous experiments. The increased effect obtained by contracting the orifice of the blast-pipe had by this time been ascertained, although doubts were expressed whether the greater draught thus secured was not counterbalanced in some degree by the negative pressure upon the piston. A series of experiments was made with blast-pipes of different diameters; and their efficiency was tested by the amount of vacuum that was produced in the smoke-box. The degree of rarefaction was determined by a glass tube fixed to the bottom of the smoke-box, and descending into a bucket of water, the tube being open at both ends. As the rarefaction took place, the water would of course rise in the tube; and the height to which it rose above the surface of the water in the bucket, was made the measure of the amount of rarefaction. These experiments proved that a considerable increase of draught was obtained by the contraction of the orifice; accordingly, the two blast-pipes opening from the cylinders into either side of the "Rocket" chimney, and turned up within it,* were contracted slightly below the area of the steam-ports; and before the engine left the factory, the water rose in the glass tube three inches above the water in the bucket.

The other arrangements of the "Rocket" were briefly these: The boiler was cylindrical with flat ends, six feet in length, and three feet four inches in diameter. The upper half of the boiler was used as a reservoir for the steam, the lower half being filled with water. Through the lower part, twenty-five copper tubes of three inches diameter extended, which were open to the fire-box at one end, and to the chimney at the other. The fire-box or furnace, two feet wide and three feet high, was attached immediately behind the boiler, and was also surrounded with water. The cylinders of the engine were placed on each side of the boiler, in an oblique position, one end being nearly level with the top of the boiler at its after end, and the other pointing towards the centre of the foremost or driving pair of wheels, with which the connection was directly made from the piston-road to a pin on the outside of the wheel. The engine, together with its load of water, weighed only four tons and a quarter; and it was supported on four wheels, not coupled. The tender was four-wheeled, and similar in shape to a wagon—the foremost part holding the fuel, and the hind part a water cask.

When the "Rocket" was completed, it was placed upon the Killingworth Railway for the purpose of experiment. The new boiler arrangement was found perfectly successful. The steam was raised rapidly and continuously, and in a quantity which then appeared marvelous. The same evening, a letter was dispatched to George Stephenson at Liverpool, informing him, to

* The alteration afterwards made in the blast of the "Rocket," after the competition at Rainhill, by which the two separate exit pipes were thrown into one, as in the original Killingworth engines, was adopted rather with the view of lessening the space occupied by them in the chimney than because of any increased effect thereby secured, though it is probable that the jet of steam is rather more efficient when thrown upwards in the exact centre of the chimney than when slightly on one side.

his great joy, that the "Rocket" was "all right," and would be in complete working trim by the day of trial. The engine was shortly after sent by wagon to Carlisle, and thence shipped for Liverpool.

The Rocket.

CHAPTER XXIII.

THE COMPETITION OF LOCOMOTIVES AT RAINHILL.

The time, so much longed for by George Stephenson, had now arrived, when the merits of the passenger locomotive were about to be put to the test. He had fought the battle for it until now almost single-handed. Engrossed by his daily labors and anxieties, and harassed by difficulties and discouragements which would have crushed the spirit of a less resolute man, he had held firmly to his purpose through good and through evil report. The hostility which he experienced from some of the directors opposed to the adoption of the locomotive, was the circumstance that caused him the greatest grief of all; for where he had looked for encouragement, he found only carping and opposition. But his pluck never failed him; and now the "Rocket" was upon the ground—to prove, to use his own words, "whether he was a man of his word or not."

Great interest was felt at Liverpool, as well as throughout the country, in the approaching competition. Engineers, scientific men and mechanics, arrived from all quarters to witness the novel display of mechanical ingenuity on which such great results depended. The public generally were no idle spectators either. The populations of Liverpool, Manchester and the adjacent towns felt that the successful issue of the experiment would confer upon them individual benefits and local advantages almost incalculable, whilst populations at a distance waited for the result with almost equal interest.

On the day appointed for the great competition of locomotives at Rainhill, the following engines were entered for the prize:

1. Messrs. Braithwaite and Erricson's "Novelty."
2. Mr. Timothy Hackworth's "Sans-pareil."
3. Messrs. Stephenson and Booth's "Rocket."
4. Mr. Burstall's "Perseverance."

Another engine was entered by Mr. Brandreth of Liverpool—the "Cycloped," weighing three tons, worked by a horse in a frame; but it could not be admitted to the competition. The above were the only four exhibited, out of a considerable number of engines which had been built in different parts of the country in anticipation of this contest, but which could not be satisfactorily completed by the day fixed for the competition.

The ground on which the engines were to be tried was a level piece of railroad, about two miles in length. Each engine was to make twenty trips, or equal to a journey of seventy miles, in the course of the day; and the average rate of traveling was to be not under ten miles an hour. It was determined that, to avoid confusion, each engine should be tried separately, and on different days.

The day fixed for the competition was the 1st of October; but to allow the engines sufficient time to get into good working order, the directors extended it to the 6th. The judges were Mr. Nicholas Wood, Mr. Rastrick and Mr. Kennedy. On the morning of the 6th, the ground at Rainhill presented a lively appearance, and there was as much excitement as if the St. Leger were about to be run. Many thousand spectators looked on, amongst whom were some of the first engineers of the day. A stand was provided for the ladies; and the "beauty and fashion" of the neighborhood were present, whilst the sides of the road were lined with carriages of all descriptions.

It was quite characteristic of Mr. Stephenson, that, although his engine did not stand first on the list for trial, it was the first that was ready; and it was accordingly ordered out by the judges for an experimental trip. The distance which it ran on that day was about twelve miles, performed in about fifty-three minutes.

The "Novelty" was next called out. It was a light engine, very compact in appearance, carrying the water and fuel upon the same wheels as the engine. The weight of the whole was only three tons and one hundred weight. A peculiarity of this engine was, that the air was driven or *forced* through the fire by means of bellows—an adoption of Trevethick's idea. The day being now far advanced, and some dispute having arisen as to the method of assigning the proper load for the "Novelty," no particular experiment was made, further than that the engine traversed the line by way of exhibition, occasionally moving at the rate of twenty-four miles an hour.

The "Sans-pareil," constructed by Mr. Timothy Hackworth, was next exhibited; but no particular experiment was made with it on this day. This engine differed but little in its construction, from the locomotives last supplied by Mr. Stephenson to the Stockton and Darlington Railway, of which Mr. Hackworth was the locomotive foreman. It had the double tube containing the fire, passing along the inside of the boiler and returning back to the same end at which it entered. It had also the steam-blast in the chimney; but, as the contraction of the orifice by which the steam was thrown into the chimney for the purpose of intensifying the draught, was a favorite idea of Mr. Hackworth, he had sharpened the blast of his engine in a remarkable degree. This was the only novel feature in the "Sans-pareil."

The contest was postponed until the following day; but before the judges arrived on the ground, the bellows for creating the blast in the "Novelty" gave way, and it was found incapable of going through its performance. A defect was also detected in the boiler of the "Sans-pareil;" and Mr. Hackworth was allowed some further time to get it repaired. The large number of spectators who had assembled to witness the contest were greatly disappointed at this postponement; but, to lessen it, Mr. Stephenson again brought out the "Rocket," and, attaching to it a coach containing thirty persons, he ran them along the line at the rate of from twenty-four to thirty miles an hour, much to their gratification and amazement. Before separating, the judges ordered the "Rocket" to be in readiness by eight o'clock on the following morning, to go through its definitive trial according to the prescribed conditions.

On the morning of the 8th of October, the "Rocket" was again ready for the contest. The engine was taken to the extremity of the stage, the fire-box was filled with coke, the fire lighted, and the steam raised until it lifted the safety-valve loaded to a pressure of fifty pounds to the square inch. This proceeding occupied fifty-seven minutes. The engine then started on its journey, dragging after it about thirteen tons weight in wagons, and made the first ten trips backwards and forwards along the two miles of road, running the thirty-five miles, including stoppages, in an hour and forty-eight minutes. The second ten trips were in like manner performed in two hours and three minutes. The maximum velocity attained by the "Rocket" during the trial trip was twenty-nine miles an hour, or about three times the speed that one of the judges of the competition had declared to be the limit of possibility. The average speed at which the whole of the journeys were performed was fifteen miles an hour, or five miles beyond the rate specified in the conditions published by the Company. The entire performance excited the greatest astonishment amongst the assembled spectators; the directors felt confident that their enterprise was now on the eve of success; and George Stephenson rejoiced to think that, in spite of all false prophets and fickle counselors, his locomotive system was now safe. When the "Rocket," having performed all the conditions of the contest, arrived at the close of its day's successful run, Mr.

Cropper—one of the directors favorable to the fixed-engine system—lifted up his hands, and exclaimed, "Now has George Stephenson at last delivered himself!"

Neither the "Novelty" nor the "Sans-pareil" were ready for trial until the 10th, on the morning of which day an advertisement appeared, stating that the former engine was to be tried on that day, when it would perform more work than any engine upon the ground. The weight of the carriages attached to it was only about seven tons. The engine passed the first post in good style; but in returning, the pipe from the forcing-pump burst, and put an end to the trial. The pipe was afterwards repaired, and the engine made several trips by itself, in which it was said to have gone at the rate of from twenty-four to twenty-eight miles an hour.

The "Sans-pareil" was not ready until the 13th; and when its boiler and tender were filled with water, it was found to weigh four hundred weight beyond the weight specified in the published conditions as the limit of four-wheeled engines; nevertheless, the judges allowed it to run on the same footing as the other engines, to enable them to ascertain whether its merits entitled it to favorable consideration. It traveled at the average speed of about fourteen miles an hour, with its load attached; but at the eighth trip the cold-water pump got wrong, and the engine could proceed no further.

It was determined to award the premium to the successful engine on the following day, the 14th, on which occasion there was an unusual assemblage of spectators. The owners of the "Novelty" pleaded for another trial; and it was conceded. But again it broke down. Then Mr. Hackworth requested the opportunity for making another trial of his "Sans-pareil." But the judges had now had enough of failures; and they declined, on the ground that not only was the engine above the stipulated weight, but that it was constructed on a plan which they could not recommend for adoption by the directors of the Company.

One of the principal practical objections to this locomotive was the enormous quantity of coke consumed or wasted by it—about 692 lbs. per hour when traveling—caused by the sharpness of the steam-blast in the chimney,* which blew a large proportion of the burning coke into the air.

The "Perseverance," of Mr. Burstall, was found unable to move at more than five or six miles an hour; and it was withdrawn at an early period from the contest. The "Rocket" was thus the only engine that had performed, and more than performed, all the stipulated conditions; and it was declared to be fully entitled to the prize of 500*l.*, which was awarded to its makers accordingly. And further to show that the engine had been working quite within its powers, Mr. Stephenson ordered it to be brought upon the ground and detached from all incumbrances, when, in making two trips, it was found to travel at the astonishing rate of thirty-five miles an hour.

The "Rocket" had thus eclipsed the performances of all locomotive engines that had yet been constructed, and outstripped even the sanguine anticipations of its constructors. Above all, it effectually answered the report of Messrs. Walker and Rastrick, and established the superiority of the locomotive for the working of the Liverpool and Manchester Railway, and indeed all future railways. The success of the experiment, as judged by the public, may be inferred from the fact that the shares of the Company immediately rose ten per cent., and nothing further was

* The importance of the contraction of the blast-pipe at the point of its opening into the chimney, was greatly overrated by Mr. Hackworth. The contraction of the pipe, in many of the best locomotives, is quite unnecessary, and indeed rather disadvantageous than otherwise; for, since the speed of the engines has been increased, the velocity of the eduction steam is quite sufficient to produce the needful rarefaction in the chimney, without any contraction whatever. In the early locomotives, when the speed of the piston was slow, the contraction was undoubtedly advantageous; but now that the boilers have been increased in size, and the heating surface thereby greatly extended, a considerably less intense blast is required. The orifices of the blast-pipes in many engines running at the present day are as large as the steam-ports; consequently they cannot be said to be contracted at all. In fact, the greater apparent efficiency of the steam-blast, as at present used, is entirely owing to the greater velocity of the piston.

heard of the proposed twenty-one fixed engines, engine-houses, ropes, etc. All this cumbersome apparatus had been effectually disposed of by the success of the "Rocket" at Rainhill.

Very different now was the tone of those directors who had distinguished themselves by the persistency of their opposition to Mr. Stephenson's plans. Coolness gave way to eulogy, and hostility to unbounded offers of friendship. Deeply though he had felt aggrieved by the conduct pursued towards him during this eventful struggle, by some from whom forbearance was to have been expected, Mr. Stephenson never entertained towards them in after life any angry feelings; on the contrary, he forgave all. But though the directors afterwards passed unanimous resolutions eulogizing "the great skill and unwearied energy" of their engineer, he himself, when speaking confidentially to those with whom he was most intimate, could not help distinguishing between his "foul-weather and fair-weather friends."

The immense consequences involved in the success of the "Rocket," and the important influence the above contest, in which it came off the victor, exercised upon the future development of the railway system, might have led one to suppose that the directors of the Liverpool and Manchester Railway would have regarded the engine with pride and cherished it with care, as warriors prize a trusty weapon which has borne them victoriously through some grand historical battle. The French preserve with the greatest care the locomotive constructed by Cugnot, which is to this day to be seen in the Conservatoire des Arts et Métiers, at Paris. But the "Rocket" was an engine of much greater historical interest. And what became of the "Rocket?" The directors of the Liverpool and Manchester Company sold it in 1837! Heavier engines were brought upon the road; and the old "Rocket" was regarded as a thing of no value. It was purchased by Mr. Thompson, of Kirkhouse, the lessee of the Earl of Carlisle's coal and lime works near Carlisle. He worked the engine on the Midgeholme Railway for five or six years, during which it hauled coals from the pits to the town. There was wonderful vitality in the old engine, as the following circumstance proves. When the great contest for the representation of East Cumberland took place, and Sir James Graham was superseded by Major Aglionby, the "Rocket" was employed to convey the Alston express with the state of the poll from Midgeholme to Kirkhouse. On that occasion the engine was driven by Mr. Mark Thompson, and it ran the distance of upwards of four miles in four and a half minutes, thus reaching a speed of nearly sixty miles an hour—proving its still admirable qualities as an engine. But again it was superseded by heavier engines; for it only weighed about four tons, whereas the new engines were at least three times the weight. The "Rocket" was consequently laid up in ordinary in the yard at Kirkhouse. It was afterwards purchased by Mr. Stephenson, and is now preserved in the works at Newcastle-upon-Tyne.

CHAPTER XXIV.

THE OPENING OF THE LIVERPOOL AND MANCHESTER RAILWAY.

THE directors of the Railway now began to see daylight. Doubts were being cleared up, and largely-debated questions one by one set at rest. A solid road had been formed over Chat Moss; and one "impossibility" had been accomplished. A locomotive had been constructed that could run at thirty miles an hour; and thus a second "impossibility" had been achieved. Difficulties, which at first appeared insurmountable, were being borne down by sheer determination, assisted by skill and labor.

The engineer brought the powers of the locomotive to bear in accelerating the progress of the works. Now, it is a common thing to employ such an agency in leading stuff to form the embankments of a railway; but then, it was an unheard-of expedient. After the competition at Rainhill, the "Rocket" engine was set to work on Chat Moss, to drag the gravel for finishing the permanent way—at the same time economizing horse labor, consolidating the road, and advancing the works towards completion.

About the middle of 1829 the tunnel at Liverpool was finished; and being lit up with gas, it was publicly exhibited one day in each week. Many thousand persons visited the tunnel, at the charge of a shilling a head—the fund thus raised being appropriated partly to the support of the families of laborers who had been injured upon the line, and partly in contributions to the

Manchester and Liverpool infirmaries. Notwithstanding the immense quantity of rain that fell during the year, great progress had been made; and there seemed every probability that one line of road would be laid complete between the two towns by the 1st of January, 1830.

As promised by the engineer, a single line was ready by that day; and the "Rocket," with a carriage full of directors, engineers, and their friends, passed over the entire length of Chat Moss, and also along the greater part of the road between Liverpool and Manchester. The coal traffic had already been commenced at different parts of the railway; but the passenger traffic was delayed until locomotives and carrying stock could be constructed, which involved a considerable additional expenditure. In consequence of the wetness of the season, the completion of the works was somewhat postponed; but in the meantime Mr. Stephenson and his son were engaged in improving and perfecting the locomotive, and in devising new arrangements in those which were in course of construction in their workshops at Newcastle for the purposes of the railway. It was soon found that the performances of the "Rocket" on the day of competition were greatly within the scope of her powers; and at every succeeding effort she excelled her previous feats. Thus, in June, 1830, a trial trip was made between Liverpool and Manchester and back, on the occasion of the board meeting being held at the latter town. A great concourse of people assembled at both termini, and along the line, to witness the spectacle. The train consisted of two carriages, filled with about forty persons, and seven wagons laden with stores—in all about thirty-nine tons. The "Rocket," light though it was as compared with modern engines, drew the train from Liverpool to Manchester in two hours and one minute, and performed the return journey in an hour and a half. The speed of the train over Chat Moss was at the rate of about twenty-seven miles an hour.

The public opening of the railway took place on the 15th of

September, 1830. Eight locomotive engines had now been constructed by the Messrs. Stephenson, and placed upon the line. The whole of them had been repeatedly tried, and with success, weeks before. A high paling had been erected for miles along the deep cuttings near Liverpool, to keep off the pressure of the multitude, and prevent them from falling over in their eagerness to witness the opening ceremony. Constables and soldiers were there in numbers, to assist in keeping the railway clear. The completion of the work was justly regarded as a great national event, and was celebrated accordingly. The Duke of Wellington, then prime minister, Sir Robert Peel, secretary of state, Mr. Huskisson, one of the members for Liverpool, and an earnest supporter of the project from its commencement, were present, together with a large number of distinguished personages. The "Northumbrian" engine took the lead of the procession, and was followed by the other locomotives and their trains, which accommodated about 600 persons.* Many thousands of spectators cheered them on their way—through the deep ravine of Olive Mount; up the Sutton incline; over the Sankey viaduct, beneath which a multitude of persons had assembled—carriages filling the narrow lanes, and barges crowding the river. The people gazed with wonder and admiration at the trains which sped along the line, far above their heads, at the rate of twenty-four miles an hour.

At Parkside, seventeen miles from Liverpool, the engines stopped to take in water. Here a deplorable accident occurred to one of the most distinguished of the illustrious visitors present, which threw a deep shadow over the subsequent proceedings of the day. The "Northumbrian" engine, with the carriage con-

* The engines with which the line was opened on the 15th of September, were the following: 1. The "Northumbrian," driven by George Stephenson; 2. The "Phœnix," by Robert Stephenson; 3. The "North Star," by Robert Stephenson, senior (brother of George); 4. The "Rocket," by Joseph Locke; 5. The "Dart," by Thomas L. Gooch; 6. The "Comet," by William Allcard; 7. The "Arrow," by Frederick Swanwick; 8. The "Meteor," by Anthony Harding

taining the Duke of Wellington, was drawn up on one line, in order that the whole of the trains might pass in review before him and his party on the other. Mr. Huskisson had, unhappily, alighted from the carriage, and was landing on the opposite road, along which the "Rocket" engine was observed rapidly coming up. At this moment, the Duke of Wellington, between whom and Mr. Huskisson some coolness had existed, made a sign of recognition, and held out his hand. A hurried but friendly grasp was given; and before it was loosened, there was a general cry from the bystanders of "Get in, get in!" Flurried and confused, Mr. Huskisson endeavored to get round the open door of the carriage, which projected over the opposite rail; but in so doing he was struck down by the "Rocket," and falling with his leg doubled across the rail, the limb was instantly crushed. His first words, on being raised, were, "I have met my death," which, unhappily, proved too true, for he expired that same evening in the neighboring parsonage of Eccles. It was cited at the time as a remarkable fact, that the "Northumbrian" engine conveyed the wounded body of the unfortunate gentleman a distance of about fifteen miles in twenty-five minutes, or at the rate of thirty-six miles an hour. This incredible speed burst upon the world with the effect of a new and unlooked for phenomenon.

The lamentable accident threw a gloom over the rest of the day's proceedings. The Duke of Wellington and Sir Robert Peel expressed a wish that the procession should return to Liverpool. It was, however, represented to them that a vast concourse of people had assembled at Manchester to witness the arrival of the trains; that report would exaggerate the mischief if they did not complete the journey; and that a false panic on that day might seriously affect future railway traveling, and the value of the company's property. The party consented accordingly to proceed to Manchester, but on the understanding that they should return as soon as possible, and refrain from further festivity.

The opening of the line was, however, accomplished; and the eloquent tribute afterwards paid by Lord Brougham to the skill and energy of its constructors, so strikingly represents the actual feeling and opinion of the time, that we cannot refrain from here quoting his words: "When I saw," said he, "the difficulties of space, as it were, overcome; when I beheld a kind of miracle exhibited before my astonished eyes; when I surveyed masses pierced through on which it was before hardly possible for man or beast to plant the sole of the foot, now covered with a road, and bearing heavy wagons, laden not only with innumerable passengers, but with merchandise of the largest bulk and heaviest weight; when I saw valleys made practicable by the bridges of ample height and length which spanned them; saw the steam railway traversing the water at a distance of sixty or seventy feet perpendicular height; saw the rocks excavated, and the gigantic power of man penetrating through miles of the solid mass, and gaining a great, a lasting, an almost perennial conquest over the powers of nature by his skill and industry; when I contemplated all this, was it possible for me to avoid the reflections which crowded into my mind—not in praise of man's great success; not in admiration of the genius and perseverance he had displayed, or even of the courage he had shown in setting himself against the obstacles that matter offered to his course—no! but the melancholy reflection that these prodigious efforts of the human race—so fruitful of praise, but so much more fruitful of lasting blessings to mankind—have forced a tear from my eye by that unhappy casualty which deprived me of a friend and you of a representative?"

It is scarcely necessary that we should here speak of the commercial results of the Liverpool and Manchester Railway. Suffice it to say that its success was complete and decisive. The anticipations of its projectors were, however, in many respects at fault. They had based their calculations almost entirely on the heavy merchandise traffic—such as coal, cotton, and timber—

relying little upon passengers; whereas the receipts derived from the conveyance of passengers far exceeded those derived from merchandise of all kinds, which, for a time, continued a subordinate branch of the traffic. In the evidence given before the Committee of the House of Commons, the promoters stated their expectation of obtaining about one-half of the whole number of passengers that the coaches then running could take, which was from 400 to 500 a day. But the railway was scarcely opened before it carried, on an average, about 1200 passengers a day; and five years after the opening, it carried nearly half a million of persons yearly.*

It was anticipated that the speed at which the locomotive could run upon the line, would be about nine or ten miles an hour; but the wisest of the lawyers, and the most experienced of the civil engineers, did not believe this to be practicable, and they laughed outright at the idea of an engine running twenty miles in the hour. But very soon after the railway was opened for traffic, passengers were regularly carried the entire thirty miles between Liverpool and Manchester in little more than an hour. Two Edinburgh engineers, who went to report upon the railway, expressed their wonder at the traveling being smoother and easier than any they had hitherto experienced, even on the smoothest turnpikes of Mr. Macadam. At the highest speed, of twenty-five miles an hour, they said, "we could observe the passengers, among whom were a good many ladies, talking to gentlemen with the utmost *sang froid*."† Such things were considered wonderful, then. It was regarded as quite extraordinary that men should be enabled, by this remarkable invention, to proceed to Manchester in the morning, do a day's business there, and return to Liverpool the same night. So successful, indeed, was the pas-

* In the first eighteen months, upwards of 700,000 persons, or about 1270 a day, were conveyed on the line without an accident. Formerly, the transit by coach had occupied four hours. The railway passenger trains performed the journey in an hour and a half on the average.

† [illegible] Grainger and Buchanan, in the *Scotsman* newspaper

senger traffic, that it engrossed the whole of the Company's small stock engines.

Although the bulk of the heavy goods continued to go by the canal, yet the opening of the railway immediately caused a large reduction in the price of coals, and in the rates for the carriage of merchandise. The annual saving to the public in money, not to speak of the great saving of its equivalent—time—was about 250,000*l.* a year. The net profit had been estimated by the projectors at 62,500*l.* a year, whereas the net profit actually realized during the first five years exceeded this by about 20,000*l.* The expense of executing the works had, however, been exceeded—the estimate having been 800,000*l.*, and the actual expenditure about 1,200,000*l.*

One of the curious results of the opening of the railway was its effect on the value of the adjoining land. Instead of the population being frightened away by the noise, fire and smoke of the locomotives, as had been predicted, there was a sudden demand for land in the neighborhood of the stations, and the price of property rose rapidly. One witness, who was examined before the Committee on the bill, painted in very black colors the horrors of the steam-engine—that it would destroy the grass on the neighboring estate, and ruin the owner by rendering the land worthless for building purposes; that "no man in his sober senses would build houses there, each to have a level line with locomotive engines running before them;" * and yet the land in question was shortly after covered with villas, and its value was enormously enhanced. Mr. Hardman Earle, who had opposed the line, afterwards declared before the Committee on the London and Birmingham Bill, that his fears on account of residential injury had been entirely unfounded; and that the passing of the locomotives, instead of being regarded as a nuisance, was actually regarded as an object of interest. The landlords who had driven

* Evidence of Mr. Thomas Dickenson before the Committee on the Liverpool and Manchester Railway Bill, p. 363

the surveyors from their grounds, and compelled the promoters of the railway to divert it from its original route, were shortly found complaining of the grievance of being deprived of the advantages of railway communication;* while those who were so fortunate as to have had the railway forced through their lands, were observed, when letting their farms, to advertise that the railway passed through the estate, or near it; and it was found that there was a quicker competition for farms so situated, and higher rents were obtained for them. When the Railway Company came again to these land owners to purchase additional land from them, they had invariably to "pay through the nose" —the improved value of the land, in consequence of its proximity to their own stations, being quoted against them. Even the most barren and unproductive land became of value. Chat Moss itself, which could scarcely, previous to the formation of the railway, afford footing for a strayed cow, promised soon to become covered with valuable farms. Mr. Baines, of Leeds, in conjunction with several other spirited gentlemen, bought a portion of the bog, near the Manchester end, laid down a private railway into it connected with the main line, and in the course of a few years, a comfortable farm-stead, surrounded with belts of wood and patches of arable land, stood smiling on the verge of the Moss. Since that time, cultivation has extended into it in all directions, and especially along the line of the railway.

* The following evidence was given by Mr. Moss, one of the directors of the Liverpool and Manchester Railway, before the Committee on the London and Birmingham Bill in 1833:

"Have you found owners, on the line between Liverpool and Birmingham, consent to the railroad there, who, nevertheless, opposed the Liverpool and Manchester line?" "Yes, several; among others, Lords Derby and Sefton."

"Did Mr. Heywood, of Manchester, oppose the Manchester Railroad?" "Yes."

"Did he afterwards complain of its not passing through his lands?" "Yes; he complained very much of it."

Lords Derby and Sefton, who, by their opposition, forced the line from their estates, and compelled Mr. Stephenson to take it over the worst part of Chat Moss, were afterwards found patronizing a second and rival line between Liverpool and Manchester, on condition that the line should pass through their property.

Mr. Stephenson did not rest satisfied with the success he had achieved in the construction of the "Rocket." He regarded it only in the light of a successful experiment; and every succeeding engine which he placed upon the line exhibited some improvement upon its predecessors. The engines were varied in their form, in their arrangement, in their weight and proportions, as the experience of each successive day, or week, or month suggested. No sooner were defects made apparent, than steps were taken to remedy them; and each quarter produced engines of such increased power and efficiency, that their predecessors were abandoned; not because they were worn out, but because they had been outstripped in the rapid march of improvement.

The "Planet" engine embodied most of the improvements made by Mr. Stephenson and his son between the construction of the "Rocket" and the opening of the railway on the 15th of September. The "Planet" was in the Mersey, but not landed, on that day. This engine exhibited in one combination nearly all the improvements which the inventors had by this time effected—the blast pipe, the tubular boiler, the horizontal cylinders inside the smoke-box, (a great improvement on the "Rocket,") and the cranked axle, together with a fire-box firmly fixed to the boiler. In the "Rocket" the fire-box was only screwed against the boiler, allowing a considerable leakage of air which had not passed through the fire. The tubes and furnace of the "Planet" gave a heating surface of 407¼ feet. The cylinder was 11 inches in diameter, with a 16 inch stroke; the boiler was 6⅛ feet long, by 3 feet in diameter; the four wheels were 5 and 3 feet in diameter, respectively.

On the 4th of December, the "Planet" took the first load of merchandise from Liverpool to Manchester, consisting of 18 wagon-loads of cotton, 200 barrels of flour, 63 sacks of oatmeal, and 34 sacks of malt. The total load, exclusive of the engine, was 80 tons, and it was taken to Manchester, in the face of a strong, adverse wind, in two hours and thirty-nine minutes, which was considered an exceedingly successful trip. Previous to this, however, the speed of the "Planet" had been tested in bringing up a cargo of voters from Manchester to Liverpool, on the occasion of the contested election there, when she performed the journey between the two places in sixty minutes.

The next important improvement in the locomotive was made in the "Samson," which was placed upon the line about the beginning of 1831. In this engine the plan of *coupling* the fore and hind wheels of the engine was adopted; by which means the adhesion of the wheels on the rails was more effectually secured, and thus the hauling force of the locomotive was made more available. This mode of coupling the wheels was found to be a great improvement, and it has since been adopted in all engines constructed for drawing heavy loads, where power is of greater consequence than speed. On the 25th of February, the "Samson" drew a train of thirty wagons, weighing 151 tons exclusive of the weight of the tender, between Liverpool and Manchester, at the rate of about twenty miles an hour on the level parts of the railway. In this engine the blast, the tubes and furnace were so contrived, that the consumption of coke was reduced to only about one-third of a pound per ton per mile.

The rapid progress thus made will show that Mr. Stephenson's inventive faculties were kept fully on the stretch; but his labors were amply repaid by the result. He was, doubtless, to some extent stimulated by the number of competitors who about the same time appeared as improvers of the locomotive engine. Of these the most prominent were the Messrs. Braithwaite and Ericsson, whose engine, the "Novelty," had excited such high expectations at the Rainhill competition. The directors of the railway, desirous of giving all parties a fair chance, ordered from those makers two engines on the same model; but their performances not proving satisfactory, they were finally withdrawn. One of them slipped off the rails near the Sankey viaduct, and was nearly thrown over the embankment. Their chief defect consisted in their inability to keep up a sufficient supply of steam for regular work; the steam-blast not being adopted in the engines. Indeed, the superiority of Mr. Stephenson's locomotives over all others that had yet been tried, induced the directors of the railway to require that the engines supplied to them by other builders should be constructed after the same model. It is now an invariable practice with railway companies to determine the kind of locomotive with which they are to be supplied by contractors; but in those days it was positively made a ground of complaint, against both the company and the engineer, that this salutary precaution was adopted. The Liverpool directors had given every opportunity for trials, from Dr. Booth's "Velocipede" (which knocked itself to pieces on the line) to the "Rocket;" and having ascertained by actual experience the best kind of engine for their purpose, they could not, amidst the bustle and responsibilities of a large and increasing traffic, allow their railway to be used as a practicing ground for the host of experimenters and inventors who were springing up on all sides. They therefore closed the line against further trials of new inventions.

It was afterwards made a ground of complaint against Mr. Stephenson in an influential publication,* that he had obtained a monopoly of the engines supplied to the Liverpool and Manchester Railway, as well as of the appointments of the workmen employed on the line. At the same time the writer admitted the rapidity of the improvements made in the locomotives, notwithstanding the alleged monopoly; for he stated that during the year and a half which followed the opening, "the engines have been constantly varied in their weight and proportions, in their magnitude and form, as the experience of each successive month has indicated: as defects became manifest they were remedied; improvements suggested were adopted; and each quarter produced engines of such increased power and efficiency, that their

* Edinburgh Review for October, 1832. Art. by Dr. Lardner.

predecessors were abandoned, not because they were worn out, but because they had been outstripped in the rapid march of improvement." What more than this *could* have been done? Granting, for a moment, that the alleged "monopoly" had any existence in point of fact—if it tended in any way to stimulate that rapidity in the improvement of the locomotive, which the reviewer so distinctly admitted to have been effected, its temporary adoption in favor of the indefatigable and industrious Stephensons would have been amply justified. But the simple truth was, that the Newcastle factory was at that time the only source from which efficient engines could be obtained. The directors were fully alive to the importance of inducing competition in this new branch of manufacture; and they offered every inducement to mechanical engineers, with the view of enlarging the sources from which they could draw their supplies of engines. And so soon as they could rely upon the quality of the article supplied to them by other firms, they distributed their orders indiscriminately and impartially.

Mr. Thomas Gray* also proclaimed his opposition to the Stephenson "monopoly," but on another ground. The Stephenson rails were smooth, and consequently the engines were adapted for traveling on them at high speeds; whereas Mr. Gray was still an adherent of the long-exploded cog-rail of Blenkinsop. He urged that the railroad should be greased, and cog-rails placed outside the smooth rails—the propulsive agency working in the former, while the burden of the engine traveled on the latter. "It will certainly," said he, "answer the private views of engineers, mechanics and others employed in manufacturing rails, steam-engines, etc., to recommend the application of numerous engines and the most costly machinery." And he added: "Had the recent grand feat, accomplished by the two new pon-

* Mechanics' Magazine, 1831, vol. xv, p. 167. The "Mechanics' Magazine" supported the cog-rail as opposed to the smooth rail, probably because the smooth rail was adopted by Stephenson. See vol. xv, p. 190.

derous engines, been performed by means of *cog-rails,* I do not hesitate to assert that the very same engines would have effected *five* times more;" which assertion serves further to prove, that the founding of the modern railway system could not have been effected by Thomas Gray.

The charge brought against Mr. Stephenson, as engineer of the Liverpool and Manchester Railway, of employing men under him to carry out his instructions, whom he knew, in preference to persons belonging to the parishes through which the line passed, whom he did not know, was of a piece with many other charges gravely advanced against him at the time. Even the drivers of stage-coaches were not then selected by the proprietors because they belonged to the respective parishes through which the coaches ran, but because they knew something of stage-coach driving. But in the case of the Liverpool and Manchester Railway, it was insisted that the local population had the first claim to be employed; * and the engineer was strongly censured "for introducing into the country a numerous body of workmen in various capacities, strangers to the soil and to the surrounding population, thus wresting from the hands of those to whom they had naturally belonged, all the benefits which the enterprise and capital of the district in this case conferred." But the charge was grossly exaggerated, and, for the most part, unfounded. As respected the working of the engines, it was natural and proper that Mr. Stephenson, who was responsible for their efficiency, should employ men to work them who knew something about their construction and mode of action. And as the only locomotive railways previously at work in England were those in the neighborhood of Newcastle, he of course sought there for engine drivers, stokers and other workmen of practical experience on railways, to work the Liverpool and Manchester line. But it was from the first one of Mr. Stephenson's greatest difficulties to find able workmen enough to make his engines as well as to con-

* Edinburgh Review for October, 1832, p. 130.

struct his roads. It was a saying of his that "he could engineer matter very well, and make it bend to his purpose, but his greatest difficulty was in engineering *men.*" Of the 600 persons employed in the working of the Liverpool line, not more than sixty had been recommended by him in his capacity of engineer, and of these a considerable proportion were personally unknown to him. Some of them, indeed, had been brought up under his own eye, and were men whose character and qualifications he could vouch for. But these were not enough for his purpose; and he often wished he could procure heads and hands on which he could rely, as easily as he could manufacture locomotives. As it was, Stephenson's engine-men were in request all over England, and they never were in want of remunerative employment. Indeed, for many years after, the Newcastle school of engineers, of which he was the head, continued to furnish the chief part of the locomotive superintendents and drivers on railways, not only in this country, but all over Europe; preference being given to them by the directors of these undertakings, in consequence of their previous practical experience, as well as their general excellent qualities as steady and industrious workmen. Mr. Stephenson had, no doubt, a warm heart for Northumberland men; and who will blame him for it? But that he ever permitted his love for canny Newcastle to bias his judgment or stand in the way of his duty to his employers in recommending the best men for appointment to the offices under him, those who knew him best most confidently deny.

Before leaving the subject of the Liverpool and Manchester railway, we may briefly mention that Mr. Stephenson's ingenuity continued for some time to be employed in perfecting the working arrangements of the line. The springs of the carriages were improved: buffers were contrived to prevent that hard bumping of the carriage ends, which was felt to be a very objectionable feature in the first passenger trains; and everything was done that was calculated to diminish friction or jerking, and make traveling comfortable and easy. Amongst Mr. Stephenson's other inventions of this time were his method of lubricating carriage axles, his spring frames for the carriages, his buffers and his railway breaks.

Like the engine power and the carriage arrangements, the road was for some time in an experimental state, and was gradually brought into a condition of practical efficiency. As the power and weight of the locomotives were increased, and the speed at which the trains traveled steadily advanced, it soon became clear to Mr. Stephenson that a considerable modification in the road was absolutely necessary. The fish-bellied rails, first laid down, were of the weight of only thirty-five pounds to the yard, and calculated only for horse traffic, or at most for engines like the "Rocket," of very light weight. In the course of a short time it was found necessary to have the road relaid with stronger rails of greater weight and improved form, though at a very considerable expense to the Company. Mr. Stephenson was determined, however, to the best of his power, to fulfill his promise to the Committee of the House of Commons, that he would make his railway as perfect as possible.

CHAPTER XXV.

EXTENSION OF THE RAILWAY SYSTEM—THE LONDON AND BIRMINGHAM LINE.

WHEN Mr. Stephenson had completed the Liverpool and Manchester Railway, and brought the locomotive engine, by means of which it was to be worked, into a state of practical efficiency, he may be said to have accomplished the great work of his life. By persevering study and observation—by treasuring up carefully the results of experience, neglecting no fact or suggestion howsoever insignificant it might at first sight appear—holding fast to his purpose, with a conviction that was never shaken, and a determination that was never baffled—he had established with but small assistance or encouragement, and in the face of every kind of difficulty and opposition, the superiority of the Locomotive system of railways. And it is perhaps not saying too much to aver, that in accomplishing this, Mr. Stephenson did more to advance the civilization of the world than any single individual of his age. Excepting only the discovery of Printing, no other invention will bear a comparison with that of Railway Locomotion, as affecting the destinies of mankind. In former times, the builder of a bridge, and the maker of a road, which brought towns and villages into communication with each other, were regarded as public benefactors. But how much greater a benefactor of his species was the man who invented the Locomotive Railway system, which unites nation with nation, and is now rapidly drawing the ends of the earth together!

It may be humiliating to our schools of science and learning to confess, that the men who brought the locomotive to perfection—George Stephenson above all—were comparatively unlettered and uneducated, possessing none of the advantages of scholastic or scientific culture. The educated men, and even the scientific engineers, were wholly opposed to the locomotive system, declaring it to be absurd and impracticable. The general public, where not actively hostile, were indifferent. With the performances of the "Rocket," however, all doubts upon the subject were in a great measure set at rest. What had been ridiculed as an impossibility, was now recognized as a fact. The "Rocket" showed that a new power had been born into the world, full of activity and strength, with boundless capability of work. It was the simple but admirable contrivance of the steam-blast, and its combination with the multitubular boiler with its large heating surface, that at once gave the high-pressure locomotive its vigorous life, and secured the triumph of the railway system. As has been well observed, this wonderful ability to increase and multiply its powers of performance with the emergency that demands them, has made this giant engine the noblest creation of human wit, the very lion among machines.

The practicability of Railway Locomotion being now proved, its extension was merely a question of time, money, and labor. A fine opportunity presented itself for the wise and judicious action of government in the matter. The improvement of the internal communications of a country seems to fall peculiarly within its province. The government was indeed at this very time directing its attention to the improvement of the old turnpike roads, and voting large sums of money to Mr. Macadam, for his so-called "discovery."

But here was a new system of internal communication invented, which was destined entirely to supersede the old macadamized roads. What was the action of the legislature in regard to it? They took no part except to retard and obstruct it; until at length their sluggish resistance was overborne, and the railway system was established, by the perseverance of private individuals. The opposition raised by the governing classes to the progress of railway bills in Parliament, would have damped the energy of any people less resolute than the English. But the leading men of industry throughout the kingdom had grasped a great idea, and would not let it go. They had the sagacity to perceive the value of railways, though the government had not; and when the legislature failed to enter, at this juncture, upon the grand enterprise of planning and executing railways upon a national system, there was a sufficient amount of active public spirit in the country to undertake the work on private risk, and to carry it into practical effect in the face of every opposition.

The mode of action was characteristic and national. The execution of the new lines was undertaken entirely by joint-stock associations of proprietors, after the manner of the Stockton and Darlington, and Liverpool and Manchester Companies. These associations are conformable to our national habits, and fit well into our system of laws. They combine the power of vast resources with individual watchfulness and motives of self-interest; and by their means gigantic enterprises, which elsewhere would be impossible to any but kings and emperors with great national resources at command, were carried out by associations of private persons. And the results of this combination of means and of enterprise have been truly marvelous. Within the life of the present generation, the private citizens of England engaged in railway enterprises, have, in the face of government obstructions, and without taking a penny out of the public purse, executed a system of railways, involving works of the most gigantic kind, which, in their total mass, their cost, and their eminent public utility, far exceed the most famous national constructions of any age or country.

Mr. Stephenson was of course actively engaged in the construction of the numerous railways now projected by the joint-stock companies. During the formation of the Manchester and Liverpool line, he had been consulted respecting many projects of a similar kind. One of these was a short railway, between Canterbury and Whitstable, about six miles in length. He was too much occupied with the works at Liverpool to give this scheme much of his personal attention. But he sent his assistant, Mr. John Dixon, to survey the line; and afterwards Mr. Locke to superintend the execution of the principal works. The act was obtained in 1826, and the line was opened for traffic in 1830. It was partly worked by fixed-engine power, and partly by Stephenson's locomotives, similar to the engines used upon the Stockton and Darlington Railway.

But the desire for railway extension principally pervaded the manufacturing districts, especially after the successful opening of the Liverpool and Manchester line. The commercial classes of the larger towns soon became eager for a participation in the good which they had so recently derided. Railway projects were set on foot in great numbers, and Manchester became a centre from which main lines and branches were started in all directions. The interest, however, which attaches to these later schemes is of a much less absorbing kind than that which belongs to the earlier history of the English railway, and the steps by which George Stephenson secured its eventual establishment. We naturally sympathize more with the early struggles of a great principle, its trials and its difficulties, than with its after stages of success; and, however gratified and astonished we may be at its permanent results, the secret charm of the interest is gone, and the excitement has ceased, when its ultimate triumph has become a matter of certainty.

The commercial results of the Liverpool and Manchester line were so satisfactory, and indeed so greatly exceeded the expectations of its projectors, that many of the abandoned projects of the speculative year 1825 were forthwith revived. An abundant crop of engineers sprang up, ready to execute railways of any extent. Now that the Liverpool and Manchester line had been made, and the practicability of working it by locomotive power had been proved, it was as easy for engineers to make railways and to work them, as it was for navigators to find America after Columbus had made the first voyage. George Stephenson had shown the way, and engineers forthwith crowded after him full of great projects. Mr. Francis Giles himself took the field as a locomotive railway engineer, attaching himself to the Newcastle and Carlisle, and London and Southampton projects. Mr. Brunel appeared, in like manner, as the engineer of the line projected between London and Bristol; and Mr. Braithwaite, the builder of the "Novelty" engine, as the engineer of a line from London to Colchester.

The first lines, however, which were actually constructed, subsequent to the opening of the Liverpool and Manchester Railway, were in connection with it, and principally in the county of Lancaster. Thus a branch was formed from Bolton to Leigh, and another from Leigh to Kenyon, where it formed a junction with the main line between Liverpool and Manchester. Branches to Wigan on the north, and to Runcorn Gap and Warrington on the south of the same line, were also formed. A continuation of the latter, as far south as Birmingham, was shortly after projected under the name of the Grand Junction Railway. The scheme of a line from Birmingham to London was also brought forward anew, and it was thus contemplated to bring the populous districts of Lancashire and the northwestern counties into direct railway communication with the metropolis. At the same time an important cross country railway was projected from Manchester to Leeds, traversing the populous manufacturing districts of East Lancashire and West Yorkshire, and bringing the chief towns of the two great northern counties into direct communication with each other. Of the principal lines projected in these districts, Mr. George Stephenson was appointed engineer; in some cases, in conjunction with his son. He was the engineer of the Grand

Junction, of the Manchester and Leeds, and other new lines, so that his hands were full of work.

The number of railway schemes which were thus projected by companies of private individuals, principally resident in the manufacturing districts, created considerable alarm in the minds of the country gentlemen, who were found everywhere up in arms against these "new-fangled roads." The farmers were thrown into a state of consternation at the idea of "fire-horses" running through their quiet fields and frightening their sheep and cattle while grazing. In remote country places the most extraordinary stories were propagated and believed respecting railway locomotives. On one occasion, Mr. Stephenson and some directors of the line projected from Chester to Birmingham, on coming into the neighborhood of Nantwich to obtain the consent of some land-owners, were told that the canal proprietors had been before them, and had told the farmers and land-owners that if a bird flew over the district when the locomotive passed, it would drop down dead!

The inhabitants of even some of the large towns were thrown into a state of consternation by the proposal to provide them with the accommodation of a railway. The line from London to Birmingham would naturally have passed close to the handsome town of Northampton, and was so projected. But the inhabitants, urged on by the local press, and excited by men of influence and education, opposed the project, and succeeded in forcing the promoters, in their resurvey of the line, to pass the town at a distance. The necessity was thus involved of distorting the line, which incurred the enormous expense of constructing the Kilsby Tunnel. Not many years elapsed before the very same inhabitants of Northampton became clamorous for railway accommodation, and a special branch was constructed for them. The additional cost involved by this forced deviation of the line could not have amounted to less than half a million sterling; a loss falling, not upon the shareholders only, but also upon the public at large, who are the eventual sufferers from all railway waste and extravagance.

But the most formidable opponents of the London and Birmingham Railway were the land-owners, whose position in the legislature gave them an overwhelming influence in determining the direction of railways, and the terms on which they were to be conceded. And as the history of the progress of the London and Birmingham scheme differs but little, in the main, from that of similar projects of the time, a brief statement of the leading facts in connection with it may not be out of place here.

Surveys of a line of railway from London to Birmingham had been made as early as the great speculative year, 1825, but the commercial crash which occurred stopped its further progress. It was, however, revived in 1830, when two committees were formed at Birmingham. One had for their consulting engineers the Messrs. Rennie, and the other Mr. Francis Giles. The line of the former was projected to pass by Oxford to London; and that of the latter by way of Coventry. There was at that early date less of the fighting spirit amongst rival railway projectors than unhappily prevailed at a subsequent period. The promoters were desirous of obtaining a good railroad to London, rather than of carrying on a costly warfare for the benefit of rival lawyers, surveyors, and engineers. So the two committees wisely determined to unite, and call to their aid the matured experience and judgment of Mr. George Stephenson, in adjudicating upon the merits of the respective lines. After a careful examination of the country, Mr. Stephenson reported in favor of the Coventry route; and the Lancashire gentlemen, having great confidence in his judgment, supported his decision, on which the line recommended by him was adopted.

At the meeting of gentlemen held at Birmingham to determine upon the appointment of the engineer for the railway, there was a strong party in favor of appointing as Mr. Stephenson's associate a gentleman with whom he had been brought into serious collision in the course of the Liverpool and Manchester undertaking. When the offer was made to him that he should be joint engineer with the other, he requested leave to retire and consider the proposal with his son. The two walked into St. Philip's churchyard, which adjoined the place of meeting, and debated the proposal. The father was in favor of accepting it: his struggle heretofore had been so hard, that he could not bear the idea of missing an opportunity of advancing himself. But the son, foreseeing the jealousies and heart-burnings which the joint engineership would most probably create, recommended to his father the answer which Mr. Bradshaw gave, when shares were offered to the Duke of Bridgewater's Trustees in the Liverpool and Manchester line—"All or none!" "Well, I believe you are right," said Mr. Stephenson; and, returning to the Committee, he announced to them his decision. "Then 'all' be it!" replied the Chairman; and he was at once appointed the engineer of the London and Birmingham Railway, in conjunction with his son.

The line, as originally laid out, was to have had its London terminus at Maiden Lane, King's Cross, the site of the present Great Northern Station: it passed through Cashiobury and Grove Parks, the seats of Lord Essex and Lord Clarendon, and along the Hemel Hempstead and Little Goddesden valleys, in Hertfordshire. This latter portion of the project excited a vehement opposition on the part of the land-owners, who formed a powerful confederacy against the bill. The principal parties who took an active part in the opposition were Lady Bridgewater and her trustees, Lord Essex and Sir Astley Cooper, supported by the Grand Junction Canal Company. By their influence the land-owners throughout the counties of Hertford and Buckingham were completely organized in opposition to the measure. The time for preparing the plans to be deposited with the several clerks of the peace, as required by the standing orders of Parliament, being very limited, the necessary documents were prepared in great haste, and were deposited in such an imperfect state as to give just grounds for presuming that they would not pass the ordeal of the Standing Orders Committee. It was also thought that alterations might be made in some parts of the railway which would remove the objections of the principal land-owners, and it was therefore determined to postpone the application to Parliament until the following session.

In the meantime the opponents of the bill out of doors were not idle. Public meetings were held in most of the districts through which the line was projected to pass, under the presidency of the nobility and gentry, when it was unanimously determined that railways were wholly unnecessary. Numerous pamphlets were published, calling on the public to "beware of the bubbles," and holding up the promoters of railways to ridicule. They were compared to Sir John Long, and similar quacks, and pronounced fitter for Bedlam than to be left at large. The canal proprietors, land-owners, and road trustees, made common cause in decrying and opposing the projected line. The failure of railways was still confidently predicted, notwithstanding the success of the Liverpool Railway; and it was industriously spread abroad that the locomotive engines, having proved a failure there, were immediately to be abandoned! — a rumor which the directors of the Liverpool and Manchester Company considered it necessary publicly to contradict.

The feeling of opposition excited in the districts through which the line was intended to pass, was so great that it was with difficulty the surveys could be made. At one point the vigilance of the land-owners and their servants was such, that the surveyors were effectually prevented making the surveys by the light of day; and it was only at length accomplished at night by means of dark lanthorns. Mr. Lecount mentions another instance of a clergyman, who made such alarming demonstrations of his opposition, that the extraordinary expedient was resorted to of surveying his property during the time he was engaged in the pulpit. This was accomplished by having a strong force of surveyors in readiness to commence their operations, and entering the clergyman's grounds on the one side at the same moment that they saw him fairly off them on the other; by a well-organized and systematic arrangement, each man concluded his allotted task just as the reverend gentleman concluded his sermon; so that, before he left the church, the deed was done, and the sinners had all decamped. Similar opposition was offered at many other points, but ineffectually. The perseverance of Mr. R. Stephenson (who, in examining the country to ascertain the best line, walked over the whole intervening districts between London and Birmingham upwards of twenty times), and the patient industry of his surveyors, under the direction of Mr. Gooch, overcame all obstacles; and by the end of 1831, the requisite plans were deposited preparatory to an application being made to Parliament in the ensuing session.

The principal alterations made in the new line were at the London end; the terminus being changed from Maiden Lane to a large piece of open land adjoining the Regent's Canal — the site of the present London and Northwestern Goods Station; and also at Watford, where the direction of the line was altered so as entirely to avoid the parks of Lords Essex and Clarendon. This diversion, however, inflicted upon the public the inconvenience of the Watford Tunnel, about a mile in length, and upon the company a largely increased outlay for its construction. The Hemel Hempstead and Goddesden valleys were also avoided, and the line proceeded by the towns of Berkhampstead and Tring. It was expected that these alterations would have the effect of mitigating, if not of entirely averting, the powerful opposition of the land owners; but it was found that, on the contrary, it was now more violent than ever, although all grounds of complaint in regard to their parks and residences had been entirely removed. The most exaggerated alarms continued to be entertained, especially by those who had never seen a railway; and, although there were a few country gentlemen who took a different view of the subject, when the bill for the altered line was introduced into Parliament in the session of 1832, the owners of nearly seven-eighths of the land required for the railway were returned as dissentients. It was, however, a noticeable fact, that Lords Derby and Sefton, who had so vehemently opposed the Liverpool Railway in all its stages, were found amongst the assentients to the London and Birmingham line. The scheme had, it is true, many warm friends and supporters, but these were principally confined to classes possessing more intelligence than influence. Indeed, the change which was rapidly taking place in public opinion on the subject of railways, induced the promoters to anticipate a favorable issue to their application, notwithstanding the hostility of the land owners. They drew a favorable augury from the fact that the Grand Junction Canal Company, although still opposing the measure as strenuously as ever, so far as the influence of its proprietors collectively and individually extended, and watching all the proceedings of the bill with a jealous eye, did not openly appear in the ranks of its opponents, and, what was of still greater significance, did not open their purse-strings to supply funds for the opposition.

When the bill went before the Committee of the Commons, a formidable array of evidence was produced; all the railway experience of the day was brought to bear in support of the measure, and all that interested opposition could do was set against it. The necessity for an improved mode of communication between London and Birmingham was clearly demonstrated; and the engineering evidence was regarded as quite satisfactory. So strong an impression was made upon the Committee, that the result was no longer doubtful so far as the Commons were concerned; but it was considered very desirable that the case should be fully brought out in evidence for the information of the public, and the whole of the witnesses in support of the bill, about a hundred in number, were examined at great length. The opponents confined themselves principally to cross-examination, without producing direct evidence of their own; reserving their main opposition for the House of Lords, where they knew that their strength lay. Not a single fact was proved against the great utility of the measure, and the bill passed the Committee, and afterwards, the third reading, in the Commons, by large majorities.

It was then sent to the House of Lords, and went into Committee, when a similar mass of testimony was again gone through during seven days. An overwhelming case was made out as before; though an attempt was made to break down the evidence of the witnesses on cross-examination. The feasibility of the route was doubted, and the greatest conceivable difficulties were suggested. Their lordships seemed to take quite a paternal interest in the protection of the public against possible loss by the formation of the line. The Committee required that the promoters should prove the traffic to be brought upon the railway, and that the profits derived from the working, would pay a dividend of from six to eight per cent. upon the money invested. A few years after, the policy of Parliament completely changed in this respect. When the landed interest found railway companies paying from six to ten times the marketable value of the land taken, they were ready to grant duplicate lines through the same districts, without proving any traffic whatever!

It soon became evident, after the proceedings had been opened before the Committee, that the fate of the bill had been determined before a word of the evidence had been heard. At that time the committees of the Lords were open to all peers; and the promoters of the bill found, to their dismay, many of the peers who were avowed opponents of the measure as land owners, sitting as judges to decide its fate. Their principal object seemed to be, to bring the proceedings to a termination as quickly as possible. An attempt at negotiation was made in the course of the proceedings in committee, but failed. One party offered to the promoters to withdraw their opposition on payment to them of 10,000*l.* This disgraceful proposal was scouted; the directors would not bribe high enough; and the bill was lost, on the motion of Earl Brownlow—"That the case for the promoters of the bill having been concluded, it does not appear to the Committee that they have made out such a case as would warrant the forcing of the proposed railway through the land and property of so great a proportion of dissentient land owners and proprietors."

The vote of the Committee confirming the resolution, though carried by a large majority, was far from unanimous; and, as the result had been foreseen, measures were immediately taken to neutralize its effect as regarded future operations. Not less than 32,000*l.* had been expended in preliminary and parliamentary expenses up to this stage; but the promoters determined not to look back, and forthwith made arrangements for prosecuting the bill in a future session. A meeting of the friends of the measure was held in London, attended by members of both Houses of Parliament, and by leading bankers and merchants; and a series of resolutions was passed, declaring their conviction of the necessity for the railway, and deprecating the opposition by which it had been encountered. Lord Wharncliffe, who had acted as the chairman of the Lords Committee, attributed the failure of the bill entirely to the land owners; and Mr. Glynn subsequently declared that they had tried to smother the bill by the high price which they demanded for their property. The result proved that the opposition had been really got up mainly for the purpose of being bought off; for the same bill, when brought before Parliament in the following session, passed silently and almost without opposition. The mystery was solved by the appearance of a circular issued by the directors of the company, in which it was stated, that they had opened "negotiations" with the most influential of their opponents; that "these measures had been successful to a greater extent than they had ventured to anticipate; and the most active and formidable had been conciliated." An instructive commentary on the mode by which these noble lords and influential landed proprietors had been "conciliated," is presented by the simple fact that the estimate for land was nearly trebled, and that the owners were paid about 750,000*l.* for what had been originally estimated at 250,000*l.* The total expenses of carrying the bill through Parliament amounted to the frightful sum of 72,868*l.*

The land owners having thus been "conciliated," the promoters of the measure were at length permitted to proceed with the formation of their great highway, and allowed to benefit the country by establishing one of the grandest public works that has ever been achieved in England, the utility of which may almost be pronounced unparalleled. Eighty miles of the railway were shortly under construction; the works were let (within the estimates) to contractors, who were necessarily, for the most part, new to such work. The business of railway contractors was not then so well understood as it has since become. There were no leviathans among them, as there are now, able to contract for the formation of a line of railway hundreds of miles in length; they were for the most part men of small capital and slender experience. Their tools and machinery were imperfect; they did not understand the economy of time and piece labor; the workmen, as well as their masters, had still to learn their trade; and every movement of an engineer was attended with outlays, which were the inevitable result of a new system of things, but which each succeeding day's experience tended to diminish.

The difficulties encountered by the Messrs. Stephenson, in the execution of the London and Birmingham Railway, were thus very great; but the most formidable of them originated in the character of the works themselves. Extensive tunnels had to be driven through unknown strata, and miles of underground excavation accomplished in order to form a level road from valley to valley under the intervening ridges. This kind of work was the newest of all to the contractors of that day. The experience of the Messrs. Stephenson in the collieries of the North, made them, of all living engineers, the best fitted to grapple with such difficulties; but even they, with all their practical knowledge, could not have foreseen or anticipated the formidable obstacles which were encountered in the execution of the Kilsby Tunnel.

It will be remembered that the opposition to the railway on the part of the inhabitants of Northampton had compelled the engineer to avoid that town, and to carry the line through the Kilsby ridge. A tunnel was thus rendered necessary of about 2400 yards in length, penetrating about 160 feet below the surface. The exact nature of the strata throughout could not be ascertained with precision, except by the expenditure of vast sums in boring. Before the contract was let, however, trial shafts were honestly sunk at different points, to enable the contractor to judge of the nature of the ground through which the excavation was to be carried. On this being, as it was supposed, sufficiently ascertained, advertisements for tenders were issued, and the work was let to a contractor for 90,000*l.* The result cannot be better described than in the words of Sir F. Head, in his interesting account of the London and Northwestern Railway:*

"The work was in busy progress, when, all of a sudden, it was ascertained that, at about 200 yards from the south end of the tunnel, there existed, overlaid by a bed of clay forty feet thick, a hidden quicksand, which extended 400 yards into the proposed tunnel, and which the trial shafts on each side of it had, almost miraculously, just passed without touching.

"The traveler in India could scarcely be more alarmed at the sudden sight of a crouching tiger before him, than the contractor was at the unexpected appearance of this invincible enemy. Overwhelmed at the discovery, he instantly took his bed, and though he was liberally, or, to speak more correctly, justly relieved by the company from his engagement, the reprieve came too late, for he actually died!

"The question then arose, whether, in the face of this tremendous difficulty, the execution of the Kilsby Tunnel should be

* "Stokers and Pokers." London: Murray, pp. 19–21.

continued or abandoned. The general opinion of the several eminent engineers who were consulted, was against proceeding, and certainly the amount of the difficulties which were subsequently incurred justified the verdict. But in science, as well as in war, the word 'IM*possible*' can occasionally, by cool and extraordinary exertions, be divested of its first syllable; and, accordingly, Mr. Robert Stephenson offering, after mature reflection, to undertake the responsibility of proceeding, he was duly authorized to do so.

"His first operation was, of course, to endeavor, by the power of steam-engines—the comrades of his life—to lower the water with which he had to contend; and although, to a certain degree, this attempt succeeded, yet by the draining of remote springs, and by the sinking of the water in wells at considerable distances, it was soon ascertained that the quicksand in question covered several square miles.

"The tunnel, thirty feet high by thirty feet broad, arched at the top as well as the bottom, was formed of bricks laid in cement, and the bricklayers were progressing in 'lengths' averaging twelve feet, when those who were nearest the quicksand, on driving into the roof, were suddenly almost overwhelmed by a deluge of water which burst in upon them. As it was evident that no time was to be lost, a gang of workmen, protected by the extreme power of the engines, were, with their materials, placed on a raft; and while, with the utmost celerity, they were completing the walls of that short length, the water, in spite of every effort to keep it down, rose with such rapidity that, at the conclusion of the work, the men were so near being jammed against the roof, that the assistant engineer, Mr. Charles Lean, in charge of the party, jumped overboard, and then, swimming with a rope in his mouth, he towed the raft to the foot of the nearest working shaft, through which he and his men were safely lifted up into daylight, or, as it is termed by the miners, '*to grass.*'

"The water now rose in the shaft, and, as it is called, 'drowned out' the works. For a considerable time all the pumping apparatus appeared to be insufficient. Indeed, the effort threatened to be so hopeless, that the directors of the company almost determined to abandon it; but the engineer-in-chief, relying on the power of his engines, prayed for one fortnight more. Before that period expired, science triumphed over her subterranean foe, and — thanks to the inventors of the steam-engine — the water gradually lowered.

"By the main strength of 1250 men, 200 horses, and thirteen steam-engines, not only was the work gradually completed, but during night and day, for eight months, the astonishing and almost incredible quantity of 1800 gallons per *minute* from the quicksand alone was raised by Mr. Robert Stephenson, and conducted away!

"The time occupied, from the laying of the first brick to the completion of the work, was thirty months. The number of bricks used was 36,000,000 — sufficient to make a good footpath from London to Aberdeen (missing the Forth) a yard broad!"

The cost of executing the Kilsby Tunnel was, in consequence of these formidable and unforeseen difficulties, increased from 90,000*l.* (the amount of the original estimate) to about 350,000*l.* Enormous sums were paid for land and compensation — far beyond the amounts originally estimated. Thus, 3000*l.* were given for one piece of land, and 10,000*l.* for consequential damages, when it was afterwards made clear that the land had been greatly improved in value by the formation of the railway. After compensation had been paid for land alleged to have been thus deteriorated, the company, on purchasing any further quantity, had almost invariably to pay a higher price, on the ground of its increased value! All sorts of payments were demanded on the most frivolous pretexts. The land owners discovered that they could demand accommodation bridges, which they did in large numbers. One originally demanded five, but afterwards came down to four, with an equivalent in the price of the bridge given up. Then he found he could do with three bridges, provided the company would pay him a further sum in hard cash, which they were ready to do; and, in like manner, he gave up the remaining bridges, on being paid a further round sum: in fact, the bridges were wholly unnecessary, and had only been insisted on as a means of extorting money from the company. To these causes of increased expense must be added the rise in the prices of labor and materials, which took place shortly after the letting of the works, by which many of the contractors were ruined, no fewer than seven of the contracts having been thrown upon the company's hands. The directors had then to purchase all kinds of implements and materials at great expense, in order to carry on the works and avoid heavier loss. But the energy of the engineers, cordially supported by the directory and proprietors, enabled them at length, after many years' anxiety, to bring the stupendous undertaking to a successful completion, though at a cost far beyond that which had been originally estimated.

The estimates laid by Mr. Robert Stephenson before Parliament amounted to 2,750,000*l.*; and it was then confidently expected that the works would have been completed within this sum. The most eminent engineers of the day were brought forward to give evidence on the subject, and those of the greatest experience stated their opinion to be that the estimates were altogether too high. Mr. Walker said the prices allowed were 30 per cent. higher than any he could remember. Mr. Locke considered them too high; and Mr. Rastrick objected to support the estimates for the same reason. Yet the result proved them to have been much too low. The works were, it is true, let to the contractors under the sum estimated, but in consequence of the adverse circumstances which occurred in the course of their execution, the expenditure had reached the immense amount of 5,000,000*l.*, or about double the original estimate, before the line was opened for public traffic.

Strong animadversions were made at the time upon this excessive expenditure; but the circumstances which we have stated — the obstacles encountered in the Kilsby and other tunnels, the rapid rise in the price of labor and materials, the extortions of the land owners (which it was impossible accurately to estimate), were sufficient, in a considerable degree, to account for the excess: in addition to which, it was a matter of the greatest difficulty for men of the very highest talent and experience then to form accurate estimates of the labor attending works of so stupendous a character, in the absence of the data since furnished by experience. Mr. Robert Stephenson, in his evidence before a Committee of the House of Commons in 1839, gave this further explanation: "The principal excess, or at least a very large item of the excess, arose from the stations on the line. The public required much larger accommodation at the stations than was originally contemplated. In fact, at the time the estimate of the London and Birmingham Railway was made, it was apprehended that something like 25,000*l.* or 30,000*l.* for a station at each end of the line was ample; but they have exceeded 100,000*l.* I have no hesitation in saying that the expense of stations has been eight or ten-fold beyond the parliamentary estimate. The plans were on much too small a scale in the stations originally contemplated." "But," he remarked on another occasion,* "let individuals who make observations as to the excessive cost of the works as compared with the estimates, look not at the commencement, but at their close. Let them recollect that those great works now spreading irresistibly, like network, all over the country, are exciting commercial enterprise, augmenting the national wealth, increasing our social comforts, and raising the nation in the scale of civilization. It is the end, therefore, that ought to be looked at, and not the beginning; and you, contractors, have all contributed your mite, as well as myself, to produce those glorious results."

* Speech of Mr. Robert Stephenson at the dinner given to him by the contractors for the London and Birmingham Railway, on the occasion of presenting him with a testimonial, November 16th, 1839.

It is probable, indeed, that had the projectors of the undertaking foreseen that it would cost as much as five millions sterling, they would have been deterred from entering upon it. As it was, however, the expenditure, though immense, was justified by the result; for the excess in the traffic beyond the estimates, was even greater in proportion than the excess in the capital expenditure. The line, of 112 miles in length, was opened on the 17th of September, 1838, and in the following year the receipts from passenger traffic alone amounted to 608,564*l.* The company was enabled to pay its proprietors a large dividend; and the results of the working were cited as sufficient grounds for pushing railways in all directions.

The magnitude of the works, which were unprecedented in England, was one of the most remarkable features in the undertaking. The following striking comparison has been made between this railway and one of the greatest works of ancient times. The great Pyramid of Egypt was, according to Diodorus Siculus, constructed by three hundred thousand—according to Heroditus, by one hundred thousand—men. It required for its execution twenty years, and the labor expended upon it has been estimated as equivalent to lifting 15,733,000,000 of cubic feet of stone one foot high. Whereas, if in the same manner the labor expended in constructing the London and Birmingham Railway be reduced to one common denomination, the result is 25,000,000,000 of cubic feet *more* than was lifted for the Great Pyramid; and yet the English work was performed by about 20,000 men in less than five years. And whilst the Egyptian work was executed by a powerful monarch, concentrating upon it the labor and capital of a great nation, the English railway was constructed, in the face of every conceivable obstruction and difficulty, by a company of private individuals, out of their own resources, without the aid of government or the contribution of one farthing of the public money.

CHAPTER XXVI.

ADVANCE OF PUBLIC OPINION IN FAVOR OF RAILWAYS.

NOTWITHSTANDING the decisive success of the Liverpool and Manchester project, the prejudices against railways and railway-traveling continued very strong. Their advantages were already fully known to the inhabitants of those districts through which they passed, for they had experienced their practical benefits in substantial reductions in the price of coal, in the carriage of merchandise of all kinds, and in the cheap and rapid transit of their persons from place to place. The Liverpool and Manchester Railway was regarded as a national wonder from the first; and strangers resorted to Lancashire from all quarters, to witness the trains, and to travel in the wake of the locomotive. To witness a railway train some five and twenty years ago, was an event in one's life.

But people at a distance did not see railways and railway traveling in the same light. The farther off, and the greater the ignorance which prevailed as to their modes of working, the greater, of course, was the popular alarm. The towns of the South only followed the example of Northampton when they howled down the railways. It was proposed to carry a line through Kent, by the populous county town of Maidstone. But a public meeting was held to oppose the project; and the railway had not a single supporter amongst the townspeople. The railway, when at length formed through Kent, passed Maidstone at a distance; but in a few years the Maidstone burgesses, like those of Northampton, became clamorous for a railway; and a branch was formed for their accommodation. Again, in a few years, they complained that the route was circuitous, as they had compelled it to be; consequently another and shorter line was formed, to bring Maidstone into more direct communication with the metropolis. In like manner, the London and Bristol (afterwards the Great Western) Railway was vehemently opposed by the people of the towns through which the line was projected to pass; and when the bill was thrown out by the Lords—after 30,000*l.* had been expended by the promoters—the inhabitants of Eton assembled, under the presidency of the Marquis of Chandos, to rejoice and congratulate themselves and the country on the defeat of the measure.

When Colonel Sibthorpe openly declared his hatred of "those infernal railroads," he only expressed in a strong manner the feeling which then pervaded the country gentry and many of the middle classes in the southern districts. That respectable nobleman, the late Earl of Harewood, when it was urged by the gentleman who waited upon him on behalf of the Liverpool and Manchester Company, that great advantages to trade and commerce were to be anticipated from the facilities which would be afforded by railways, refused to admit the force of the argument, as he doubted whether *any* new impetus to manufactures would be advantageous to the country. And Mr. H. Berkley, the intelligent member for Cheltenham, in like manner, strongly expressed the views of his class, when, at a public meeting held in that town, he declared his utter detestation of railways, and wished that the concoctors of every such scheme, with their solicitors and engineers, were at rest in Paradise! "Nothing," said he, "is more distasteful to me than to hear the echo of our hills reverberating with the noise of hissing railroad engines running through the heart of our hunting country, and destroying that noble sport to which I have been accustomed from my childhood." Colonel

Sibthorpe even went so far as to declare that he "would rather meet a highwayman, or see a burglar on his premises, than an engineer; he should be much more safe, and, of the two classes, he thought the former more respectable!"

Railways had thus, like most other great social improvements, to force their way against the fierce antagonism of united ignorance and prejudice. Public-spirited obstructives were ready to choke the invention at its birth, on the ground of the general good. The forcible invasion of property—the intrusion of public roads into private domains—the noise and nuisance caused by locomotives, and the danger of fire to the adjoining property, were dwelt upon *ad nauseam.* Then the breed of horses would be destroyed; country innkeepers would be ruined; posting towns would become depopulated; the turnpike roads would be deserted; and the institution of the English stage-coach, with its rosy-gilled coachman and guard, known to every buxom landlady at roadside country inns, would be destroyed forever. Fox-covers and game-preserves would be interfered with; agricultural communication destroyed; land thrown out of cultivation; land owners and farmers alike reduced to beggary; the poor-rates increased in consequence of the numbers of laborers thrown out of employment by the railways; and all this in order that Liverpool, Manchester and Birmingham manufacturers, merchants, and cotton-spinners, might establish a monstrous monopoly in railroads! However, there was always this consolation to wind up with—that the canals would beat the railroads, and that, even if the latter were made, the public would not use them, nor trust either their persons or their goods to the risks of railway accidents and explosions. They would thus prove only monuments of the folly of their projectors, whom they must inevitably involve in ruin and disaster.

Sanitary objections were also urged in opposition to railways; and many wise doctors strongly inveighed against tunnels. Sir Anthony Carlisle insisted that "tunnels would expose healthy people to colds, catarrhs, and consumption." The noise, the darkness, and the dangers of tunnel traveling were depicted in all their horrors. Worst of all, however, was "the destruction of the atmospheric air," as Dr. Lardner termed it. Elaborate calculations were made by that gentleman to prove that the provision of ventilating shafts would be altogether insufficient to prevent the dangers arising from the combustion of coke, producing carbonic acid gas, which, in large quantities, was fatal to life. He showed, for instance, that in the proposed Box Tunnel, on the Great Western Railway, the passage of a load of 100 tons would deposit about 3090 lbs. of noxious gases, incapable of supporting life! Here was an uncomfortable prospect of suffocation for passengers between London and Bristol. But steps were adopted to allay these formidable sources of terror. Solemn documents, in the form of certificates, were got up and published, signed by several of the most distinguished physicians of the day, attesting the perfect wholesomeness of tunnels, and the purity of the air in them.* Perhaps they went further than was necessary, in alleging, what certainly subsequent experience has not verified, that the atmosphere of the tunnel was "dry, of an agreeable temperature, and free from smell." Mr. Stephenson declared his conviction that a tunnel twenty miles long could be worked safely, and without more danger to life than a railway in the open air; but at the same time, he admitted that tunnels were nuisances, which he endeavored to avoid wherever practicable.

Meanwhile the extension of railways in various directions continued to be discussed; but the legislature took no directing part in the matter. Their *vis inertiæ* was indeed at length overcome; and by dint of repeated pressure from without, carried on at great cost, the railway system was gradually extended. Parliament

* See Report of Experiments made in the Primrose Hill Tunnel of the London and Birmingham Railway, signed by Drs. Paris and Watson, Mr. Lawrence, Mr. Phillips, and Mr. O. Lucas; and Report on the Leeds and Selby Tunnel, signed by Drs. Davy, Rothman, and Williamson.

could not disregard the urgent and repeated petitions of the commercial towns of the North for improved postal communication. But the legislature was dragged on; it did not by any means aspire to guide or direct. Whilst associations of private persons, mostly belonging to the trading classes, were endeavoring to force on the adoption of railways, the English Lords and Commons—unlike the government of Belgium, which early adopted the railway system—occupied themselves in discussing the improvement of the turnpike roads. The country gentlemen determined to mend and patch up the old highways as well as they could. Their motto was *stare super antiquas vias*. The macadamized system was becoming effete, but they did not know it. The surprising performances of the "Rocket" at Rainhill opened their eyes to the significance of the locomotive engine; but they could not yet rise above the idea of a macadamized road, and hence they hailed the proposal to apply the locomotive to turnpikes. In the year 1831 the House of Commons appointed a Committee to inquire into, and report upon—not the railway system—but the applicability of the steam-carriage to traveling on common roads. Before this Committee, Mr. Trevethick, Mr. Goldsworthy Gurney, Nathaniel Ogle, and others, were examined; and the Committee were so satisfied with their evidence, that they reported decidedly in favor of the road-locomotive system. Though railways were ignored, yet the steam-carriage was recognized.

But there are limits to the wisdom even of a parliamentary committee. Although many trials of steam-carriages were made by Sir Charles Dance, Mr. Hancock, Mr. Gurney, Sir James Anderson, and others, and though the House of Commons had reported in their favor, Mr. Stephenson's first verdict, pronounced upon them many years before—that they could never successfully compete with locomotive engines on railroads, nor even with horses on common roads—was fully borne out by the result; for the steam-carriage projects, after ruining many speculators and experimenters, were at length abandoned in favor of railways, which extended in all directions. Another attempt was, however, made in 1836, in favor of the common-road locomotive system; when a bill was passed through the House of Commons to repeal the acts imposing prohibitory tolls on steam-carriages. When the bill went into the Lords, it was referred to a committee, who took evidence on the subject at great length. Many witnesses were examined in support of steam-carriages, including Mr. Gurney, Mr. Hancock, and others, who strongly testified to their economy and efficiency.

Their lordships then called before them Mr. Stephenson, whose experience as a locomotive engineer entitled him to be heard on such a subject. "The steam-carriages," he said, "will never do any good on a common road: I do not see the slightest possibility of it." The principal difficulty, in his opinion, was the friction between the wheel and the road—so great, that it was as much as the road-engine could do to drag its own weight. Then, from the inevitable inequalities in common roads, the machinery of the road-engine would be liable to constantly-recurring accidents, which no springs yet invented would enable it to avoid. But even admitting that the road-engine could be made to go regularly, he was quite confident that it could not be made to go so as *to pay*, even though all the tolls were taken off. Besides these objections, there was the element of danger in the road locomotive; for its boiler could not be constructed so small and so light as to enable it to do any heavy work without risk of bursting. He then contrasted it with the railway locomotive. "Our engines," he said, "are from twenty to thirty horse power, whilst those on the common roads are not more than three or four horse power. The road locomotive must necessarily be limited, whereas the power of the railway locomotive can be increased to almost any extent. We have engines now constructed that can haul 400 tons on a level railway, taking a large ship-load of goods in one train, at fifteen miles an hour. I will engage to make a locomotive of a hundred horse power to run upon a railway. I have already made some of fifty horse power for Belgium and the United States."

His evidence was so strong and conclusive, that it could not fail to have great weight with their lordships; and in their report to the House, they said: "It appears that some experienced engineers, after a careful examination of the expense attendant upon it (the common-road steam-carriage), have been induced to abandon all hopes of its success as a profitable undertaking. It is probable, therefore, that any encouragement on the part of the legislature would only give rise to wild speculations, ruinous to those engaging in them, and to experiments dangerous to the public."* However unjust the prohibitory tolls on steam-carriages might be, there is no doubt that the decision of the committee as to the impracticability of the steam-carriage system was correct, and that there was no hope of its ever competing successfully on common roads with the locomotive railway. The highest speed which the promoters promised was ten miles an hour; but this would no longer satisfy the public requirements, now that the Liverpool and Manchester Railway had demonstrated the practicability and the safety of regular traveling at thirty and forty miles an hour. The House of Commons prophecy, that "a railway could never enter into successful competition with a canal, and that, even with the best locomotive engine, the average rate would be but three miles and a half per hour,"† was now laughed at, because so ludicrously at variance with every-day facts.

The opening of the great main line of railroad communication between London, Liverpool, and Manchester, in 1838, shortly proved the fallaciousness of the rash prophecies promulgated by the opponents of railways. The proprietors of the canals were

* Report of the Lords' Committee appointed to consider the Bill, entitled "An Act to repeal such Portions of all Acts as impose prohibitory Tolls on Steam-Carriages, and to substitute other Tolls on an equitable Footing with Horse-Carriages." Session 1836.

† Hansard, 2d series, vol. iv, p. 853.

astounded by the fact that, notwithstanding the immense traffic conveyed by rail, their own traffic and receipts continued to increase; and that, in common with other interests, they fully shared in the expansion of trade and commerce which had been so effectually promoted by the extension of the railway system. The cattle-owners were equally amazed to find the price of horse-flesh increasing with the extension of railways, and that the number of coaches running to and from the new railway stations gave employment to a greater number of horses than under the old stage-coach system. Those who had prophesied the decay of the metropolis, and the ruin of the suburban cabbage-growers, in consequence of the approach of railways to London,* were also disappointed. For, whilst the new roads let citizens out of London, they let country people in. Their action, in this respect, was centripetal as well as centrifugal. Tens of thousands who had never seen the metropolis could now visit it expeditiously and cheaply. And Londoners who had never visited the country, or but rarely, were enabled, at little cost of time or money, to see green fields and clear blue skies, far from the smoke and bustle of town. If the dear suburban-grown cabbages became depreciated in value, there were truck-loads of fresh-grown country cabbages to make amends for the loss: in this case, the "partial evil" was a far more general good. The food of the metropolis became rapidly improved, especially in the supply of wholesome meat and vegetables. And then the price of coals—an article which, in this country, is as indispensable as daily food to all classes—was greatly reduced. What a blessing to the metro-

* "The first practical effect," said the *John Bull*, in September, 1838, "of these unnatural forcings of humanity will be, the reduction in value of all property near London, and the proportionate increase of value in property more remote. All the delicate produce of the garden and the field, which round town is cultivated with the most assiduous care, and consequently sold at a high and remunerating price, will be excluded from our markets: fine fruit, fine vegetables, raised and produced at half, or less than half the cost, will be brought into competition with those which have hitherto been raised and ripened by a great expenditure in high wages, and carried to the place of sale by teams of horses kept at a considerable expense. All this must end."

politan poor is described in this single fact! And George Stephenson was not only the inventor of the system of internal communication by which coals were made cheaper in London, but he was also the originator of the now gigantic trade in coal conveyed to the metropolis by railway.

The prophecies of ruin and disaster to landlords and farmers were equally confounded by the opening of the London and Birmingham Railway. The agricultural communications, so far from being "destroyed," as had been predicted, were immensely improved. The farmers were enabled to buy their coals, lime, and manure for less money, whilst they obtained a readier access to the best markets for their stock and farm-produce.

Notwithstanding the predictions to the contrary, their cows gave milk as before, their sheep fed and fattened, and even skittish horses ceased to shy at the passing locomotive. The smoke of the engines did not obscure the sky, nor were farm-yards burnt up by the fire thrown from the locomotives. The farming classes were not reduced to beggary; on the contrary, they soon felt that, far from having any thing to dread, they had very much good to expect from the extension of railways.

Landlords also found that they could get higher rents for farms situated near a railway, than at a distance from one. Hence they became clamorous for "sidings." They felt it to be a grievance to be placed at a distance from a station. After a railway had been once opened, not a landlord would consent to have the line taken from him. Owners who had fought the promoters before Parliament, and compelled them to pass their domains at a distance, at a vastly-increased expense in tunnels and deviations, now petitioned for branches and nearer station accommodation.* Those who held property near towns, and had extorted

* Some landlords were slow in learning the advantages of railways. When, many years later, an important railway bill was before Parliament, a noble marquis compelled the company to pass his mansion at a distance of at least five miles, to do which it was necessary to construct two expensive tunnels When the line was opened, his lordship felt the exceeding inconvenience of being so far distant from a railway station, and requested

large sums as compensation for the anticipated deterioration in the value of their building land, found a new demand for it springing up at greatly advanced prices.* Land was now advertised for sale, with the attraction of being "near a railway station."

The prediction that, even if railways were made, the public would not use them, was also completely falsified by the results. The ordinary mode of fast traveling for the middle classes had heretofore been by mail-coach and stage-coach. Those who could not afford to pay the high prices charged for such conveyances went by wagon, and the poorer classes trudged on foot. George Stephenson was wont to say that he hoped to see the day when it would be cheaper for a poor man to travel by railway than to walk; and not many years passed before his expectation was fulfilled. In no country in the world is time worth more money than in England; and by saving time—the criterion of distance—the railway proved a great benefactor to men of industry in all classes. Many deplored the inevitable downfall of the old stage-coach system. There was to be an end of that delightful variety of incident usually attendant on a journey by road. The rapid scamper across a fine country on the outside of the four-horse "Express," or "Highflyer;" the seat on the box beside Jehu, or the equally coveted place near the facetious guard behind; the journey amid open green fields, through smiling villages and fine old towns, where the stage stopped to change horses and the passengers to dine—was all very delightful in its way; and many regretted that this old-fashioned and pleasant style of traveling was about to pass away. But it had its dark side also. Any one who remembers the journey by stage from Manchester to London will associate it with recollections and sensations of not unmixed delight. To be perched for twenty-four hours, exposed to all

the company to provide a branch for his accommodation. As he had already put them to enormous and unnecessary expense, they respectfully declined doing so, and he has since been under the necessity of himself constructing a branch at a cost of 160,000*l.* which he has requested the parent company to do him the favor of working for him.

weathers, on the outside of a coach, trying in vain to find a soft seat—sitting now with the face to the wind, rain, or sun, and now with the back—without any shelter such as the commonest penny-a-mile parliamentary train now daily provides—was a miserable undertaking, looked forward to with horror by many whose business called upon them to travel frequently between the provinces and the metropolis. Nor were the inside passengers more agreeably accommodated. To be closely packed up in a little inconvenient, straight-backed vehicle, where the cramped limbs could not be in the least extended, nor the wearied frame indulge in any change of posture, was felt by many to be a terrible thing. Then there were the constantly-recurring demands, not always couched in the politest terms, for an allowance to the driver every two or three stages, and to the guard every six or eight; and if the gratuity did not equal their expectations, growling and open abuse were not unusual. These *désagrémens*, together with the exactions practiced on travelers by inn-keepers, seriously detracted from the romance of stage-coach traveling; and there was a general disposition on the part of the public to change the system for a better.

The avidity with which the public at once availed themselves of the railways proved that this better system had been discovered. Notwithstanding the reduction of the coach fares between London and Birmingham to one-third of their previous rate, the public preferred traveling by the railway. They saved in time; and they saved in money, taking the whole expense into account. In point of comfort there could be no doubt as to the infinite superiority of the railway carriage. But there remained the question of safety, which had been a great bug-bear with the early opponents of railways, and was made the most of by the coach proprietors to deter the public from using them. It was predicted that trains of passengers would be blown to pieces, and that none but fools would entrust their persons to the conduct of an explosive machine such as the locomotive. It appeared, however, that during the first eight years not fewer than five millions of passengers had been conveyed along the Liverpool and Manchester Railway, and of this vast number only two persons had lost their lives by accident. During the same period, the loss of life by the upsetting of stage-coaches had been immensely greater in proportion. The public were not slow, therefore, to detect the fact, that traveling by railways was greatly safer than traveling by common road; and in all districts penetrated by railways the coaches were very shortly taken off from want of support.

Mr. Stephenson himself had a narrow escape in one of the stage-coach accidents so common twenty years ago, but which are already almost forgotten. While the Birmingham line was under construction, he had occasion to travel from Ashby-de-la-Zouche to London by coach. He was an inside passenger with several others; and the outsides were pretty numerous. When within ten miles of Dunstable, he felt, from the rolling of the coach, that one of the linch-pins securing the wheels had given way, and that the vehicle must upset. He endeavored so to fix himself in his seat, holding on firmly by the arm-straps, that he might save himself on whichever side the coach fell. The coach soon toppled over, and fell crash upon the road, amidst the shrieks of his fellow passengers and the smashing of glass. He immediately pulled himself up by the arm-strap above him, let down the coach window, and climbed out. The coachman and passengers lay scattered about on the road, stunned, and some of them bleeding, whilst the horses were plunging in their harness. Taking out his pocket knife, he at once cut the traces and set the horses free. He then went to the help of the passengers, who were all more or less hurt. The guard had his arm broken; and the driver was seriously cut and contused. A scream from one of his fellow-passenger "insides" here attracted his attention: it proceeded from an elderly lady, whom he had before observed to be decorated with one of the enormous bonnets in fashion at that time. Opening the coach door he lifted the lady out; and her principal lamentation was that her large bonnet had been crushed beyond remedy! Mr. Stephenson then proceeded to the nearest village for help, and saw the passengers provided with proper assistance before he himself went forward on his journey.

It was some time before the more opulent classes, who could afford to post to town in aristocratic style, became reconciled to railway traveling. The old families did not relish the idea of being conveyed in a train of passengers of all ranks and conditions, in which the shopkeeper and the peasant were carried along at the same speed as the duke and the baron—the only difference being in price. It was another deplorable illustration of the leveling tendencies of the age.* It put an end to that gradation of rank in traveling, which was one of the few things left by which the nobleman could be distinguished from the Manchester manufacturer and bagman. So, for a time, many of the old families sent forward their servants and luggage by railway, and condemned themselves to jog along the old highway in the accustomed family chariot, dragged by country post-horses. But the superior comfort of the railway shortly recommended itself to even the oldest families; posting went out of date; post-horses were with difficulty to be had along even the great highroads; and nobles and servants, manufacturers and peasants, alike shared in the comfort, the convenience and the dispatch of railway traveling. The late Dr. Arnold of Rugby regarded the opening of the London and Birmingham line as but another step accom-

* At a meeting of the Chesterfield Mechanics' Institute, at which Mr. Stephenson was present, one of the speakers said of him, "Known as he is wherever steam and iron have opened the swift lines of communication to our countrymen, and regarded by all as the Father of Railways, he might be called, in the most honorable acceptation of the term, *the first and greatest leveler of the age.*" Mr. Stephenson joined heartily in the laugh which followed this description of himself. Sir Humphry Davy was once similarly characterized; but the remark was somewhat differently appreciated. When traveling on the Continent, a distinguished person about a foreign court inquired who and what he was, never having heard of his scientific fame. Upon being told that his discoveries had "*revolutionized chemistry*," the courtier promptly replied, "I hate all revolutionists; his presence will not be acceptable here."

plished in the great march of civilization. "I rejoice to see it," he said, as he stood on one of the bridges, and watched the train flashing along, and away through the distant hedge-rows—"I rejoice to see it, and think that feudality is gone forever. It is so great a blessing to think that any one evil is really extinct."

It was long before the late Duke of Wellington would trust himself behind a locomotive. The fatal accident to Mr. Huskisson, which had happened before his eyes, contributed to prejudice him strongly against railways; and it was not until the year 1843 that he performed his first trip on the Southwestern Railway, in attendance upon Her Majesty. Prince Albert had for some time been accustomed to travel by railway alone; but in 1842, the Queen began to make use of the same mode of conveyance between Windsor and London, after which the antipathies of even the most prejudiced were effectually set at rest.

CHAPTER XXVII.

MR. STEPHENSON ENGINEER OF THE MANCHESTER AND LEEDS, AND MIDLAND RAILWAYS.

Mr. Stephenson resided in Liverpool until after the completion and opening of the Liverpool and Manchester Railway. He then removed to Alton Grange, near Ashby-de-la-Zouche, in Leicestershire, where he lived for several years. Whilst his son Robert was engaged as engineer in superintending the construction of the Leicester and Swannington Railway in 1830, his experience as a coal-viewer and practical geologist suggested to him that coal was to be found in the estate of Snibston, near Ashby, then advertised for sale, and lying in the immediate neighborhood of the line of railway. He mentioned the circumstance to his father, who inspected the ground, and came to the same conclusion.

The large manufacturing town of Leicester, about fourteen miles distant, had up to that time been exclusively supplied with coal brought by canal from Derbyshire; and Mr. Stephenson was quick to perceive that the railway under construction, from Swannington to Leicester, would furnish him with a ready market for any coals which he might find at Snibston. Having induced two of his Liverpool friends to join him in the venture, the Snibston estate was purchased in 1831; and Mr. Stephenson removed his home from Liverpool to Alton Grange, for the purpose of superintending the sinking of the pit. He traveled by gig with his wife—his favorite horse "Bobby" performing the journey by easy stages.

Sinking operations were immediately commenced, and proceeded satisfactorily until the old enemy, water, burst in upon the workmen, and threatened to drown them out. But by means of efficient pumping engines, and the skillful casing of the shaft with segments of cast iron—a process called "tubbing," which Mr. Stephenson was the first to adopt in the Midland counties—it was eventually made water-tight, and the sinking proceeded. When a depth of 166 feet had been reached, a still more formidable difficulty presented itself—one which had baffled former sinkers, and deterred them from further operations. This was a dyke of fused granite, which had been brought down by volcanic action from the adjacent Charnwood Forest range, and here overlapped the coal-bed of the district. Mr. Stephenson fell back upon his old motto, "Persevere:" he determined to go on boring; and down through the solid granite he went until, twenty-two feet lower, he came upon the coal measures. In the meantime, however, lest the boring at this point should prove unsuccessful, he had commenced sinking another pair of shafts about a quarter of a mile west of the "fault;" and after about nine months' labor he reached the principal seam, called the "main coal."

The works were then opened out on a large scale, and Mr. Stephenson had the pleasure and good fortune to send the first train of main coal to Leicester by railway. The price was immediately reduced there to about 8*s.* a ton, effecting a pecuniary saving to the inhabitants of the town of about 40,000*l.* per annum, or equivalent to the whole amount then collected in government taxes and local rates, besides giving an impetus to the manufacturing prosperity of the place, which has continued down to the present day. The correct and scientific principles upon which he conducted his mining operations at Snibston, offered a salutary example to the neighboring colliery owners. The numerous improvements which he introduced were freely exhibited to all, and they were afterwards reproduced in many forms all over the Midland Counties, greatly to the advantage of the mining interests.

At the same time Mr. Stephenson endeavored to extend the benefit of railways throughout the district in which he now resided. He suggested to Lord Stamford the importance of constructing a branch line from the Leicester and Swannington Railway through his property, principally for the purpose of opening out his fine granite quarries at Groby. The valuable advice was taken by Lord Stamford, and Mr. Stephenson laid out the line for him and superintended the works gratuitously. Another improvement which he effected for Lord Talbot proved of even greater pecuniary value. He contrived for his lordship, with no slight difficulty, a plan for "tubbing off" the fresh water from the salt at his mines near Tamworth, which enabled the salt works there to be subsequently carried on to a great profit, which had not before been practicable. Mr. Stephenson was less successful in his endeavors to induce the late Marquis of Hastings to consent to the Birmingham and Derby Railway, of which he was the engineer, passing through the mineral district of Ashby-de-la-Zouche. The Marquis was the principal owner of the colliery property in the neighborhood, and Mr. Stephenson calculated upon his lordship's influence in support of a scheme so certain to increase the value of his estate. But the marquis, like many others of his class, did not yet detect the great advantages of railways, and he threatened his determined opposition if the Derby line were attempted to be brought through his coal-field. The line was consequently taken further to the west, by way of Burton; and thus Ashby for a time lost the benefits of railway communication. Twenty years elapsed before Mr. Stephenson's designs for its accommodation were carried into effect.

Nor was Mr. Stephenson less attentive to the comfort and well-being of those immediately dependent upon him—the workpeople of the Snibston colliery and their families. Unlike many of those large employers who have "sprung from the ranks," he was one of the kindest and most indulgent of masters. He would have a fair day's work for a fair day's wages; but he never forgot that the employer had his duties as well as his rights. First of all, he attended to the proper home accommodation of his work-people. He erected a village of comfortable cottages, each provided with a snug little garden. He was also instrumental in erecting a church adjacent to the works, as well as church schools for the education of the colliers' children; and with that broad catholicity of sentiment which distinguished him, he further provided a chapel and a school-house for the use of the Dissenting portion of the colliers and their families—an example of benevolent liberality which was not without its salutary influence on the neighboring employers.

When at home, in the intervals of his now extensive business as a railway engineer, Mr. Stephenson delighted to snatch an occasional hour to indulge his love of rural life. When he could, he went bird-nesting in spring, and nutting in autumn; occasionally he did a little gardening, or took a rural ride on his favorite "Bobby," now growing old.* His uniform kindness and good temper, and his communicative intelligent disposition, made him a great favorite with the neighboring farmers, to whom he would volunteer much valuable advice on agricultural operations, drainage, ploughing, and labor-saving processes.

Shortly after Mr. Stephenson had settled down at Alton Grange, railway projects of great magnitude began to spring up all over England, and he was often called away for the purpose of making surveys, and conferring with committees of directors as to their parliamentary procedure. For several years he spent most of his time in traveling about on such business, besides frequently going down to Lancashire to watch over the working of

* "Bobby" was about twenty years old when he died, in 1845. During the last few years of his life he was a pensioner, living in clover and doing no work.

the Liverpool and Manchester line. His correspondence increased so much that he found it necessary to engage a private secretary, who accompanied him on his journeys. He was himself exceedingly averse to writing letters. The comparatively advanced age at which he learnt the art of writing, and the nature of his duties while engaged at the Killingworth colliery, precluded that facility in correspondence which only constant practice can give. He possessed, however, great facility in dictation, and was very particular and precise as to the terms in which his letters must be written. He also had the power of laboring continuously at dictation; the gentleman who acted as his secretary, in the year 1835, stating that during his busy season, he one day dictated not fewer than thirty-seven letters, several of them embodying the results of much close thinking and calculation. On another occasion, he dictated reports and letters for twelve continuous hours, until his secretary was ready to drop off his chair from sheer exhaustion, and at length he pleaded for a suspension of the labor. This great mass of correspondence, although closely bearing upon the subjects under discussion, was not, however, of a kind to supply the biographer with matter for quotation, or to give that insight into the life and character of the writer which the letters of literary men so often furnish. They were, for the most part, letters of mere business, relating to works in progress, parliamentary contests, new surveys, estimates of cost, and railway policy—curt, and to the point; in short, the letters of a man, every moment of whose time was precious.

Hence, also, there is very little record of Mr. Stephenson's private life during this busy period. For he had scarcely a moment that he could call his own. What with the business of his colliery, his locomotive manufactory, and the various railways of which he was the principal engineer, there was little time left for private intercourse. During the three years ending in 1837—perhaps the busiest years of his life—his secretary traveled with him by post-chaise alone upwards of twenty thousand miles, and yet six months of the whole time were spent in London. During this period, he was engaged in the survey of the North Midland, extending from Derby to Leeds; the York and North Midland, from Normanton to York; the Manchester and Leeds; the Birmingham and Derby, and the Sheffield and Rotherham Railways; the whole of these, of which he was principal engineer, having been authorized in 1836. Fortunately, Mr. Stephenson possessed a facility of sleeping, which enabled him to pass through this enormous amount of fatigue and labor without injury to his health. He had been trained in a hard school, and could bear with ease conditions which, to men more softly nurtured, would have been the extreme of physical discomfort. Many, many nights he snatched his sleep while traveling in his chaise; and at break of day he would be at work, surveying until dark, and this for weeks in succession. His whole powers seemed to be under the control of his will, for he could wake at any hour, and go to work at once. It was difficult for secretaries and assistants to keep up with such a man.

As an example of the nature of Mr. Stephenson's labors about this period, we give the following epitome of two of his journeys, upon which he entered immediately after the conclusion of the heavy parliamentary session of 1836:

First Journey. August 4th.—Traveled from Alton Grange to Burton, and on to the Foxhall summit on the Birmingham and Derby Railway; then to Ingestre Hall, to examine Lord Talbot's saltworks, and thence to Lichfield. August 5th.—Lichfield to Birmingham, to examine the ground for the terminal station of the Birmingham and Derby Railway; then on to Derby with Mr. Glynn (director), and Mr. Carter, (solicitor.) August 6th. Engaged at Derby all day with the corporation, conferring with them as to the site of the station for the Birmingham and Derby and Midland Railways; then examining the Holmes, and journey home by Burton.

Second Journey. August 9th.—Alton Grange to Derby and

Matlock; and forward by mail to Manchester, to meet the committee of the South Union Railway. August 10th.—Manchester to Stockport, to meet committees of the Manchester and Leeds Railway; then to Liverpool, to meet directors of the Chester and Birkenhead, and Chester and Crewe Railways. August 11th.—Liverpool to Woodside, to meet committee of the Chester and Birkenhead line; journey with them along the proposed railway to Chester; then back to Liverpool. August 12th.—Liverpool to Manchester, to meet directors of the Manchester and Leeds railway, and traveling with them over the works then in progress. August 13th.—Continued journey over the works, and arrival at Wakefield; thence to York. August 14th.—Meeting with Mr. Hudson at York, and journey from York to Newcastle. August 15th.—At Newcastle, working up arrears of correspondence. August 16th.—Meeting with Mr. Brandling as to the station for the Brandling Junction at Gateshead, and stations at other parts of the line. August 17th.—Newcastle to Carlisle, to inspect the Maryport line. August 18th.—Carlisle to Wigton and Maryport, examining the railway. August 19th.—Maryport to Carlisle, continuing the inspection. August 20th.—At Carlisle, examining the ground for a station; and working up correspondence. August 21st.—Carlisle to Dumfries by mail; forward to Ayr by chaise, proceeding up the valley of the Nith, through Thornhill, Sanquhar and Cumnock. August 22d.—Meeting with promoters of the Glasgow, Kilmarnock and Ayr railway, and journey along the proposed line; meeting with the magistrates of Kilmarnock at Beith, and journey with them over Mr. Gale's proposed line to Kilmarnock. August 23d.—From Kilmarnock along Mr. Miller's proposed line, to Beith, Paisley and Glasgow. August 24th.—Examination of site of proposed station at Glasgow; meeting with the directors; then from Glasgow, by Falkirk and Linlithgow, to Edinburgh, meeting there with Mr. Grainger, engineer, and several of the committee of the proposed Edinburgh and Dunbar Railway. August 25th.—Examining the site of the proposed station at Edinburgh; then to Dunbar, by Portobello and Haddington, examining the proposed line of railway. August 26th.—Dunbar to Tommy Grant's, to examine the summit of the country towards Berwick, with a view to a through line to Newcastle; then return to Edinburgh. August 27th.—At Edinburgh, meeting the provisional committee of the proposed Edinburgh and Dunbar Railway. August 28th.—Journey from Edinburgh through Melrose and Jedburgh to Horsley, along the route of Mr. Richardson's proposed railway across Carter Fell. August 29th.—From Horsley to Mr. Brandling's, then on to Newcastle; engaged on the Brandling Junction Railway. August 30th.—Engaged with Mr. Brandling; after which, meeting a deputation from Maryport. August 31.—Meeting with Mr. Brandling and others as to the direction of the Brandling Junction in connection with the Great North of England line, and the course of the railway through Newcastle; then on to York. September 1st.—At York; meeting with York and North Midland directors; then journeying over Lord Howden's property, to arrange for a deviation; examining the proposed site of the station at York. September 2d.—At York, giving instructions as to the survey; then to Manchester, by Leeds. September 3d.—At Manchester; journey to Stockport with Mr. Bidder and Mr. Bourne, examining the line to Stockport, and fixing the crossing of the river there; attending to the surveys; then journey back to Manchester, to meet the directors of the Manchester and Leeds Railway. September 4th.—Sunday at Manchester. September 5th.—Journey along part of the Manchester and Leeds railway. September 6th.—At Manchester, examining and laying down the section of the South Union line to Stockport; afterwards engaged on the Manchester and Leeds working plans, in endeavoring to give a greater radius to the curves; seeing Mr. Seddon about the Liverpool, Manchester and Leeds Junction Railway. September 7th.—Journey along the Manchester and Leeds line, then on to Derby. September 8th.

— At Derby; seeing Mr. Carter and Mr. Beale about the Tamworth deviation; then home to Alton Grange. September 10th. — At Alton Grange, preparing report to the committee of the Edinburgh and Dunbar Railway.

Such is a specimen of the enormous amount of physical and mental labor undergone by Mr. Stephenson during the busy years above referred to. He was no sooner home, than he was called away again by some other railway or business engagement. Thus, in four days after his arrival at Alton Grange from the above journey into Scotland, we find him going over the whole of the North Midland line as far as Leeds; then by Halifax to Manchester, where he stayed for several days on the business of the South Union line; then to Birmingham and London; back to Alton Grange, and next day to Congleton and Leek; thence to Leeds and Goole, and home again by the Sheffield and Rotherham and the Midland works. And early in the following month (October) he was engaged in the north of Ireland, examining the line, and reporting upon the plans, of the projected Ulster railway. Then he was called upon to inspect and report upon colliery works, salt works, brass and copper works, and such like, in addition to his own colliery and railway business. He usually also staked out himself the lines for which he was engineer, and which involved a good deal of labor since undertaken by assistants. And occasionally he would run up to London, to attend in person to the preparation and depositing of the plans and sections of the projected undertakings for which he was engaged as engineer.

It is pleasant to record that, in the midst of these engrossing occupations, his heart remained as soft and loving as ever. Thus, during one of his brief sojourns at Alton Grange, he found time to write to his son a touching account of a pair of robins that had built their nest within one of the empty upper chambers of the house. One day he observed a robin fluttering outside the windows, and beating its wings against the panes, as if eager to gain admission. He went up stairs, and there found, in a retired part of one of the rooms, a robin's nest, with one of the parent birds sitting over three or four young—all dead. The excluded bird outside still beat against the panes; and on the window-sill being let down, it flew into the room, but so exhausted that it dropped upon the floor. Mr. Stephenson took up the bird, carried it down stairs, and had it warmed and fed. The poor robin revived, and for a time was one of his pets. But it shortly died, too, as if unable to recover from the privations it had endured during its three days fluttering and beating at the windows. It appeared that the room had been unoccupied, and the window having been let down for some time, the robins had taken the opportunity of building their nest within it; but the servant having accidentally closed the window, the calamity befell them which so strongly excited Mr. Stephenson's sympathies. An incident such as this, trifling though it may seem, gives the true key to the heart of the man.

The amount of his parliamentary business having greatly increased with the projection of new lines of railway, Mr. Stephenson found it necessary to take an office in London during the session of 1836.* This office was the busy scene of railway politics for many years. There consultations were held, schemes were matured, deputations were received, and many projectors called upon our engineer for the purpose of submitting their plans of railway working. But Mr. Stephenson's principal business was in carrying through the projects for which he was professionally concerned as engineer-in-chief. He was also called upon to give evidence in support of many lines, such as the Great Western, with which he was not immediately connected. "In fact," as he said to the House of Commons' Committee, in 1841, "there is hardly a railway in England that I have not had to do with." In the session of 1836 alone, powers were obtained to

* His first office was at No. 9 Duke Street, Westminster, from which he removed to 30½ George Street, Westminster, in 1837.

construct 214 miles of new railway after Mr. Stephenson's designs, at an expenditure of upwards of five millions sterling.

Numerous other companies obtained their acts during the same session. The Midland Counties Act authorized the formation of a line from Rugby (on the London and Birmingham line) to Derby, there to join the North Midland, which, in conjunction with the Great North of England Railway, from York to Darlington, and the Durham Junction, and Branding Junction, already authorized, would complete the line of railway communication from London to Newcastle. At the same time, powers had been obtained to construct lines from London to Bristol, to Southampton, to Dover, and to Colchester; so that already measures had been adopted to place the metropolis in direct communication with the most important districts of the kingdom.

The rapidity with which railways were carried out, when the spirit of the country was fairly up, was indeed remarkable. This was, doubtless, in some measure owing to the increased force of the current of speculation, but chiefly to the desire which the public now entertained for the general extension of the system. Railways became the topic of conversation in all circles; they were felt to give a new value to time; their vast capabilities for "business" peculiarly recommended them to the trading classes; whilst the friends of "progress" dilated on the great benefits they would eventually confer upon mankind at large. It began to be seen that Mr. Edward Pease had not been exaggerating when he said, "Let the country but make the railroads, and the railroads will make the country!" They also came to be regarded as inviting objects of investment to the thrifty, and a safe outlet for the accumulations of inert men of capital. Thus new avenues of iron road were soon in course of construction in all directions, branching north, south, east, and west, so that the country promised in a wonderfully short space of time to become wrapped in one vast network of iron.

Although occasionally employed to survey lines and give evidence in favor of railways projected in the south of England, Mr. Stephenson's principal attention was directed to the development of the system in the northern counties, leaving the south to the energy of his son. Besides the Grand Junction, he was, shortly after the completion of the Liverpool and Manchester line, engaged in surveying and laying out a railway from Manchester to Leeds, with the object of forming a connection between the principal towns of Lancashire and Yorkshire. An attempt had been made to obtain an act for this purpose as early as the year 1831; but having been met by the powerful opposition of the land owners, aided by the canal companies, it was defeated, and was not revived until several years later. Mr. Stephenson, however, having carefully examined the entire district, had already determined in his own mind the route of the Manchester and Leeds line, and decided that no other was practicable, without the objectionable expedient of a tunnel three and a half miles in length under Blackstone Edge, and the additional disadvantage of heavy gradients. This line, as projected by him, and afterwards considerably improved, was somewhat circuitous, and the works were heavy; but on the whole the gradients were favorable, and it had the advantage of passing through a district full of manufacturing towns and villages, the teeming hives of population, industry and enterprise. The act authorizing the construction of the railway, was finally obtained in the session of 1836: it was greatly amended in the succeeding year; and the first ground was broken on the 18th of August, 1837.

An incident occurred while the second Manchester and Leeds bill was before the Committee of the Lords, which is worthy of passing notice in this place, as illustrative of Mr. Stephenson's character. The line which was authorized by Parliament in 1836, had been hastily surveyed within a period of less than six weeks; and before it received the Royal assent, Mr. Stephenson became convinced that many important improvements might be made in it, and communicated his views to the directors. They determined, however, to obtain the act, although conscious at the time that they would have to go for a second and improved line in the following year. The second bill passed the Commons in 1837, without difficulty, and promised in like manner to receive the sanction of the Lords' Committee. Quite unexpectedly, however, Lord Wharncliffe, who was interested in the Manchester and Sheffield line, which passed through his colliery property, in the South of Yorkshire, and conceived that the new Manchester and Leeds line might have some damaging effect, appeared as a strenuous opponent of the bill. He was himself a member of the Committee, and adopted the unusual course of rising to his feet, and making a set speech against the bill, while Mr. Stephenson was under examination. After pointing out that the bill applied for and obtained in the preceding session was one that the promoters had no intention of carrying out, that they had secured it only for the purpose of obtaining possession of the ground, and reducing the number of the opponents to their present application, and that in fact they had been practicing a deception upon the House, his lordship turned full upon the witness, and addressing him, said: "I ask you, sir, do you call that conduct *honest?*" Mr. Stephenson, his voice trembling with emotion, replied: "Yes, my lord, I *do* call it honest. And I will ask your lordship, whom I served for many years as your enginewright at the Killingworth collieries, when did you ever know me to do any thing that was not honest and honorable? You know what the collieries were when I went there, and you know what they were when I left them. Did you ever hear that I was found wanting when honest services were wanted, or when duty called me? Let your lordship but fairly consider the circumstances of the case, and I feel persuaded you will admit that my conduct has been equally honest throughout in this matter." He then briefly but clearly stated the history of the application to Parliament for the act, which was so satisfactory to the Committee that they passed the preamble of the bill without further objection. Lord Wharncliffe requested that the Committee would permit his observations, together with Mr. Stephenson's reply, to be erased from the record of the evidence, which, as an acknowledgment of his error, was permitted; Lord Kenyon and several other members of the Committee, afterwards came up to Mr. Stephenson, shook him by the hand, and congratulated him on the manly way in which he had vindicated himself in the course of the inquiry.

In conducting this project to a successful issue, Mr. Stephenson had much opposition and many strong prejudices to encounter. Predictions were confidently made in many quarters, that the line could never succeed. It was declared, that the utmost engineering skill could not construct a railway through such a country of hills and hard rocks; and it was maintained that, even if the railway were practicable, it could only be formed at so enormous a cost as to prevent it from ever remunerating the proprietors.

The croaking of all the prophets of evil and disaster reached its height in December, 1840, as the Summit Tunnel, near Littleborough, was fast approaching completion, when the alarming rumor was spread abroad in Manchester that the tunnel had fallen in and buried a number of workmen in the ruins. The last arch had been keyed in, and the work was all but finished, when the accident occurred which was thus exaggerated by the lying tongue of rumor. An invert had given way through the irregular pressure of the surrounding earth and rock at a part of the tunnel where a "fault" had occurred in the strata. A party of the directors accompanied the engineer to inspect the scene of the accident. They entered the tunnel's mouth preceded by upwards of fifty navvies, each bearing a torch. This extraordinary subterranean viaduct had occupied the labors of above a thousand men during nearly four years. Besides excavating the arch out of the solid rock, they had used 23,000,000 of bricks, and 8000 tons of Roman cement. Thirteen stationary engines, and about 100 horses, had also been employed in drawing the earth and stone out of the shafts. The entire length of the tnnnel was 2869 yards, or nearly a mile and three-quarters—exceeding the famous Kilsby Tunnel by 471 yards.

After walking a distance of about half a mile, the inspecting party arrived at the scene of the "frightful accident," about which so much alarm had been spread in Manchester. All that was visible was a certain unevenness of the ground, which had been forced up by the invert under it giving way; thus the ballast had been loosened, the drain running along the centre of the road had been displaced, and small pools of water stood about. But the whole of the walls and the roof were as perfect there as in any other part of the tunnel. Mr. Stephenson explained the cause of the accident: The blue shale, he said, through which the excavation passed at that point, was considered so hard and firm, as to render it unnecessary to build the invert very strong there. But shale is always a deceptive material. Subjected to the influence of the atmosphere, it gives but a treacherous support. In this case, falling away like quicklime, it had left the lip of the invert alone to support the pressure of the arch above, and hence its springing inwards and upwards. Mr. Stephenson directed the attention of the visitors to the completeness of the arch overhead, where not the slightest fracture or yielding could be detected. Speaking of the work, in the course of the same day, he said, "I will stake my character, my head, if that tunnel ever gives way, so as to cause danger to any of the public passing through it. The fracture that has taken place must, doubtless, be a disappointment to the directors, by delaying the opening of the line; but the fact is, that the invert is covered with material, so that we could not find it out till that material was taken away, so as to make the culvert through to carry the water from end to end; but I believe that if the invert were taken away altogether, the tunnel would stand firm. It is a question now with me, whether we ought to put the invert in again, or to strengthen the foot of the side walls. However, it being a work of such magnitude, it is perhaps safer to take a little more time to it, and make it perfect. With respect to the tunnel, taking it as a whole, I don't think there is such another piece of work in the world. It is the greatest work that has yet been done of this kind, and there has been less repairing than is usual. Indeed, no tunnel of such magnitude have I known with so little re-doing of the work. It is a great work—though one where an engineer might be beaten in his calculations, for he cannot beforehand see into those little fractured parts of the earth he may meet with. This is a dislocated part of a very high country, where the *débris* has come off at a time and in a place where we could have no chance of examining it, except by excavation. But this is the only weak part we have met with. It runs diagonally across the tunnel. It begins at one end of the fractured part and runs to its other end. It is a part that has chipped off from its neighbors, and not being so firmly fixed as the adjoining rocks on each side, when we took off the bottom it eased a little, and that has been the cause of the upper part throwing a little more pressure upon the invert." As Mr. Stephenson had promised, the invert was put in; the tunnel was made perfectly safe; and the traffic began to be carried over the entire length of the line early in the year 1841, and has continued without interruption ever since.

In 1838, Mr. Stephenson was acting as engineer for the Blackwall Railway, in conjunction with Mr. Bidder. In their united report of that year we find them recommending stationary engines for the working of that line, as being the more safe and economical, principally on the ground of the sharpness of the curves, the steepness of the gradients, and the shortness of the railway. Subsequent experience, however, of the powers of the locomotive, and of its economy in working as compared with fixed engines, induced the eventual abandonment of the latter power in favor of the former. It is worthy of notice that Mr. Stephenson, who was always ready to adopt improved modes of working railways, employed the electric telegraph at a very early period to regulate the working of that line; indeed, he was one of the first of the railway engineers who recognized its advantages for this purpose.

The North Midland Railway was a favorite line of Mr. Stephenson's for many reasons. Its works were of a formidable character; it passed through a rich mining district, in which it opened up many valuable coal-fields, and it formed part of the great main line of communication between London and Edinburgh, on the completion of which, by the East Coast line through Newcastle, Mr. Stephenson had anxiously set his heart. The North Midland Railway was originally projected by gentlemen interested in the London and Birmingham line. The intention was to carry the latter railway from Rugby to Leeds; but, finding themselves anticipated in part by the projection of the Midland Counties line from Rugby to Derby, they confined themselves to the district between Derby and Leeds. The projectors appointed Mr. Stephenson to examine the country, and lay out the best line; and after a careful and laborious investigation, in which he was ably assisted by his pupil Mr. Swanwick, he reported the result to a public meeting held at Leeds, in September, 1835; and the result was the approval of the line as laid out by him. A subscription list was at once opened, and Mr. John Marshall, one of the most public-spirited and influential manufacturers of Leeds, having put his name down for 35,000*l.*, the shares were soon taken, and the project was fairly launched. The act was obtained in 1836, and the first ground was broken in February, 1837. The execution of the works extended over a period of above three years, and the line was opened throughout in July, 1840.

Although the North Midland Railway was only one of the many great works of the same kind executed at that time, it was enough of itself to be the achievement of a life. Compare it, for example, with Napoleon's much-vaunted military road over the Simplon, and it will at once be seen how greatly it excels that work, not only in the constructive skill displayed in it, but also in its cost and magnitude, and the amount of labor employed in its formation. The road of the Simplon is 45 miles in length; the North Midland Railway 72½ miles. The former has 50 bridges and 5 tunnels, measuring together 1,338 feet in length; the latter has 200 bridges and 7 tunnels, measuring together 11,400 feet, or about 2¼ miles. The former cost about 720,000*l.* sterling, the latter above 3,000,000*l.* Napoleon's grand military road was constructed in six years, at the public cost of the two great kingdoms of France and Italy; while Stephenson's much more magnificent railway was formed in about three years, by a company of private merchants and capitalists out of their own funds, and under their own superintendence.* And if the name of the Chevalier Fabbroni has been honored for the design and construction of the military road across the Simplon, how much higher ought the name of George Stephenson to rank as the engineer and architect of the North Midland, the Manchester and Leeds, the Liverpool and Manchester, and many other equally gigantic works of great public utility!

Mr. Stephenson's strong sagacity, assisted by the experience he had gained in the northern coal districts, early detected the importance of the Midland Railway as opening up new markets for the vend of coal which abounded in the district through which it passed. At a time when everybody else was skeptical as to the possibility of coals being carried from the midland counties, and sold in London at a price to compete with sea-borne coals, he declared his firm conviction that the time was fast approaching when the London market would be regularly supplied with north-country coals led by railway. One of the greatest advantages of railways, in his opinion, was that they would bring coal and iron, the staple products of the country, to the doors of all England. "The strength of Britain," he would say, "lies in her coal-beds; and the locomotive is destined, above all other

* The number of men employed on the line, while the works were in full operation, was between 9000 and 10,000, assisted by eighteen stationary and several locomotive engines. The quantity of earthwork on the line amounted to 9,500,000 cubic yards.

agencies, to bring it forth. The Lord Chancellor now sits upon a bag of wool; but wool has long ceased to be emblematical of the staple commodity of England. He ought rather to sit upon a bag of coals, though it might not prove quite so comfortable a seat. Then think of the Lord Chancellor being addressed as the noble and learned lord *on the coal-sack!* I am afraid it wouldn't answer, after all."

To one gentleman he said: "We want from the coal-mining, the iron-producing, and manufacturing districts, a great railway for the carriage of these valuable products. We want, if I may so say, a stream of steam running directly through the country, from the North to London, and from other similar districts to London; speed is not so much an object as utility and cheapness." And at a meeting of railway proprietors at York, in 1840, he told them "there was little doubt in his mind that coals would in a very short time be supplied to the London market from that county by means of their line." * He proved his conviction by acting upon it, taking a lease of the Clay Cross Colliery, in anticipation of the demand for railway-led coals. In this, as in some other matters, Mr. Stephenson was rather ahead of his time; and though the Clay Cross Colliery did not prove a very successful venture, and he did not live to see his anticipations as to the supply of the London coal market fully realized, yet he was the first to point out, and, to some extent, to prove the practicability of establishing a profitable coal trade by railway between the northern counties and the metropolis. Since his time, his prediction has to a great extent been fulfilled, both on the Midland and the Great Northern Railways. The quantity of coal brought by railways to London, in 1855, from the Durham, Yorkshire, and other northern collieries, amounting to upwards of a million of tons. The Great Northern carried 547,602; the Midland and Northwestern, 339,656; the Eastern Counties, 145,327; and the Great Western, 80,950 tons.

* Meeting of the York and North Midland Company, 19th July, 1840.

About the same time that Mr. Stephenson entered upon his lease of the colliery at Clay Cross, he took up his abode at Tapton House, near Chesterfield, which continued his home until the close of his life. It was a central point on the Midland Railway, from which he could proceed north, south, and west, in his superintendence of the four important lines which were in progress of construction at the same time—the Midland, the York and North Midland, the Birmingham and Derby, and the Manchester and Leeds Railways.

The York and North Midland line extended from Normanton —a point on the Midland Railway—to York; it was a line of easy formation, traversing a comparatively level country. The inhabitants of Whitby, as well as York, were busy projecting railways as early as 1832; and in the year following, Whitby succeeded in obtaining a horse line of twenty-four miles, connecting it with the small market town of Pickering. The York citizens were more ambitious, and agitated the question of a locomotive line to connect them with the town of Leeds. A company was formed in 1833, and Mr. George Rennie was called upon to survey the line. About the same time, however, other engineers — Mr. Walker, Mr. Cundy, and Mr. Gibbs — were severally engaged in getting up the surveys of a direct main line from London to York. The local committee were perplexed by the conflicting views of the engineers, and at length called to their assistance Mr. George Stephenson, who had already been consulted by the provisional committee of the Midland Company as to the best line from Derby to Leeds. He recommended the York gentlemen to adopt their railway to that proposed line of communication, and they embraced his views. The company was formed, the shares were at once subscribed for, and Mr. Stephenson appointed his pupil and assistant, Mr. Swanwick, to lay out the line in October, 1835. The act was obtained in the following year, and the works were constructed without any difficulty under the superintendence of Mr. Cabrey, another of

Mr. Stephenson's pupils and assistants, brought up under his own eyes in the Killingworth workshops.

As the best proof of his conviction that the York and North Midland would prove a good investment, Mr. Stephenson invested in it a considerable portion of his savings, being a subscriber for 420 shares; and he also took some trouble in persuading several wealthy gentlemen in London and elsewhere to purchase shares in the concern. The interest thus taken in the line by the engineer was on more than one occasion specially mentioned by Mr. Hudson, then Lord Mayor of York, as an inducement to other persons of capital to join the undertaking; and had it not afterwards been encumbered and overlaid by comparatively useless, and therefore profitless branches, in the projection of which Mr. Stephenson had no part, the sanguine expectations which he early formed of the paying qualities of the line would have been even more than realized.

There was one branch, however, of the York and North Midland line in which he took an anxious interest, and of which he may be pronounced the projector—the branch to Scarborough; which proved to be one of the most profitable parts of the railway. He was so satisfied of its value, that, at a meeting of the York and North Midland proprietors,* he volunteered his gratuitous services as engineer until the company was formed, in addition to subscribing largely to the undertaking. At that meeting he took an opportunity of referring to the charges brought against engineers of so greatly exceeding the estimates: "He had had a good deal to do with making out the estimates of the North Midland Railway, and he believed there never was a more honest one. He had always endeavored to state the truth as far as was in his power. He had known a director who, when he (Mr. Stephenson) had sent in an estimate, came forward and said, 'I can do it for half the money.' The director's estimate went into Parliament, but it came out his. He could go

* Held at York in July, 1840.

through the whole list of the undertakings in which he had been engaged, and show that he had never had any thing to do with stock-jobbing concerns. He would say that he would not be concerned in any scheme, unless he was satisfied that it would pay the proprietors; and in bringing forward the proposed line to Scarborough, he was satisfied that it would pay, or he would have had nothing to do with it."

About this time, numerous lines, constructed under Mr. Stephenson's direction, were completed and opened for public traffic. The Sheffield and Rotherham Railway was opened on the 1st of November, 1838; the Birmingham and Derby in August, 1839, having been constructed in about two years, within the parliamentary estimates; and in the course of the year 1840, the Midland, the York and North Midland, the Chester and Crewe, the Chester and Birkenhead,* the Manchester and Birmingham, the Manchester and Leeds, and the Maryport and Carlisle Railways, were all publicly opened in whole or in part. Thus 321 miles of railway constructed under Mr. Stephenson's superintendence, at a cost of upwards of eleven millions sterling, were, in the

* At a meeting of the Chester and Birkenhead Company, held at Liverpool in October, 1845, the following circumstance, highly honorable to Mr. Stephenson, was related by W. Jackson, Esq., the chairman of the Company: "When this railway was first projected, or rather when a railway was first projected between Chester and Birkenhead, the Company failed in their efforts to get a bill. Mr. George Stephenson was the engineer. When the second measure was taken up, he was also the Company's engineer, as it was understood that the same engineer and the same surveyors should be employed, and that in the event of the bill being carried, they should receive their costs for the defeated measure. To several parties, their costs were paid. Mr. George Stephenson's amounted to 800*l.*, and he very nobly said: "You have had an expensive career in Parliament; you have had a great struggle; you are a young Company; you cannot afford to pay me this amount of money; I will reduce it to 200*l.*, and I will not ask you for that 200*l.* until your shares are at 20*l.* premium; for, whatever may be the reverses you will go through, I am satisfied I shall live to see the day when I can legally and honorably claim that 200*l.* when your shares will be at 20*l.* premium." The time had now arrived when Mr. Stephenson's foreboding proved true. The shares were selling at 60 in the market, and the new ones were at a high premium, and he (the chairman) thought, that in asking for a vote of 500*l.* for conduct so noble, he was asking only for what was amply due. He left the matter in the hands of the proprietors. The proprietors immediately voted the full amount of 800*l.* stated by the chairman as due to Mr. Stephenson.

course of about two years, added to the traffic accommodation of the country.

The ceremonies which accompanied the public opening of these lines were often of an interesting character. The adjoining population held general holiday; bands played, banners waved, and assembled thousands cheered the passing trains amidst the occasional booming of cannon. The proceedings were usually wound up by a public dinner; and on such occasions, Mr. Stephenson would often revert to his favorite topic—the difficulties which he had early encountered in the establishment of the railway system, and in proving, to the satisfaction of the public, the superiority of the locomotive. At the dinner which followed the opening of the Sheffield and Rotherham line, the Earl Fitzwilliam presided, and most of the notable personages of the district, including the Master Cutler, were present, and made speeches. When Mr. Stephenson's turn came to speak, he could not resist the opportunity of contrasting the recent success of railways with the obstacles which had early beset them, and the now proved efficiency of the locomotive with the former dismal prophecies of its failure. "He ventured to say that he might lay claim to some credit for what he had done with respect to locomotive engines. He had now fought their battles for twenty-five years, and for more than twenty years of that time single-handed. Though all other engineers had been against him, he still persevered. The most severe trials which he had to go through were in going to Parliament, where he had the barristers to encounter. When they put him into the witness-box, they generally looked about to measure their man. He was quite aware that they had certain tools to work with if he was not a good witness. They did not care a pin about a locomotive engine; their object was to put him off his guard, and then they could bring him down. He must say, that he had gone into the witness-box many and many a time with the utmost possible reluctance. The only thing which gave him courage was, that he knew he had nothing but truth to state. He knew enough of mechanics to know where to stop. He knew that a pound would weigh a pound, and that more should not be put upon a line than it would bear. He never was an advocate for unfavorable gradients — he wanted low levels. They had been passing that day upon a beautiful low level, and it was in a situation where no low level line would ever be brought to compete with it."

Mr. Stephenson always took great pleasure in alluding to the services rendered to himself and the public by the young men brought up under his eye—his pupils at first, and afterwards his assistants. No great master ever possessed a more devoted band of assistants and fellow-workers than he did. And, indeed, it was one of the most marked evidences of his own admirable tact and judgment that he selected, with such undeviating correctness, the men best fitted to carry out his plans. The ability to accomplish great things, to carry grand ideas into practical effect, depends in no small measure on an intuitive knowledge of character, which Mr. Stephenson possessed in a remarkable degree. Thus, on the Liverpool and Manchester line, he secured the able services of Messrs. Vignolles and Locke; the latter had been his pupil, and had laid down for him several coal-lines in the north.* John Dixon, trained by him on the Stockton and Darlington Railway, afterwards ably carried out his views on the Canterbury

* An unhappy difference afterwards occurred between Mr. Stephenson and Mr. Locke, on the latter being appointed the principal engineer of the Grand Junction Railway, during the progress of the works. Considerable personal feeling was thrown into the affair, which had no small influence upon the railway politics (so to speak) of the time; and in determining the direction of the new lines of railway between Manchester and the South. The projectors of the Manchester and Birmingham Railway—a rival line to the Grand Junction—at once invited Mr. Stephenson to act as their engineer; and it was alleged that a personal feeling actuated him in the professional support which he gave to the undertaking. The declared object of the promoters, however, was to secure a more direct communication between Manchester and London than was afforded by the circuitous route *via* Warrington. Mr. Crawshay, at one of their meetings, asserted, that he for one would never cease going to Parliament until they had got the nearest and best way to the metropolis. In like manner, the Trent Valley line, projected with the same object, had the strong support of the Manchester men; indeed, the project originated almost entirely with them.

and Whitstable, the Liverpool and Manchester, and the Chester Railways. Thomas Gooch was his able representative in superintending the execution of the formidable works of the Manchester and Leeds line. Swanwick on the North Midland, Birkenshaw on the Birmingham and Derby, and Cabrey on the York and North Midland, seconded him well and ably, and established their own reputation while they increased the engineering fame of their master. All these men, then comparatively young, became, in course of time, engineers of distinction, and were employed to conduct, on their own account, numerous railway enterprises of great magnitude.

At the dinner at York, which followed the partial opening of the York and North Midland Railway, Mr. Stephenson, as was his wont, prominently acknowledged the merit of his engineering pupils and assistants, and accompanied the recognition with many encouragements drawn from his own life and experience. On this occasion, he said "he was sure they would appreciate his feelings when he told them, that when he first began railway business, his hair was black, although it was now gray; and that he began his life's labor as but a poor ploughboy. He was only eight years old when he went to work, and he had been laboring hard ever since. About thirty years since, he had applied himself to the study of how to generate high velocities by mechanical means. He thought he had solved that problem. But when he afterwards appeared before a Committee of Parliament, and stated that, in his opinion, a locomotive machine might, with safety, travel upon a railway at a speed of ten miles an hour, he was told that his evidence was not worth listening to. That, however, did not prevent him going forward with his plans, and they had for themselves seen, that day, what perseverance had brought him to. He was, on that occasion, only too happy to have an opportunity of acknowledging that he had, in the later portion of his career, received much most valuable assistance, particularly from young men brought up in his manufactory. Whenever talent showed itself in a young man, he had always given that talent encouragement where he could, and he would continue to do so."

That this was no exaggerated statement, is amply proved by facts which redound to Mr. Stephenson's credit. He was no niggard of encouragement and praise when he saw honest industry struggling for a footing. Many were the young men whom, in the course of his useful career, he took by the hand and led steadily up to honor and emolument, simply because he had noted their zeal, diligence and integrity. One youth excited his interest while working as a common carpenter on the Liverpool and Manchester line; and before many years had passed, he was recognized as an engineer of distinction. Another young man he found industriously working away at his bye-hours, and, admiring his diligence, engaged him for his private secretary; the gentleman shortly after rising to a position of eminent influence and usefulness. Indeed, nothing gave Mr. Stephenson greater pleasure than in this way to help on any deserving youth who came under his observation, and, in his own expressive phrase, to "make a man of him."

CHAPTER XXVIII.

SURVEYS OF LINES TO SCOTLAND AND HOLYHEAD.

HAVING now supplied the more important districts of Yorkshire and Lancashire with efficient railway communication, connected with the metropolis by means of the London and Birmingham Railway, and the Midland lines, which radiated from it, Mr. Stephenson's attention was next directed to the completion of the system, so as to embrace Scotland on the north, and Ireland on the west, and place the capitals of those divisions of the United Kingdom in more direct communication with the great heart of the nation—the city of London.

He had already, with the assistance of his son, been instrumental in carrying the great main line of road as far northward as Newcastle-on-Tyne; and his advice was from time to time anxiously solicited as the best mode of completing the remaining links. As early as 1836, he had been called upon, by the committee of a proposed railway between Edinburgh and Dunbar, to inspect the route, and report thereon, with a view to the line being afterwards connected with Newcastle. He proceeded to comply with this request, and, at the same time, he personally examined the other routes by which such a line could pass from Edinburgh to the south—traversing the vale of the Gala, and the mountainous district of Carter Fell—while he also carefully inspected the coast route, by way of Berwick-upon-Tweed. In his report to the directors of the projected line, he stated his opinion to be in favor of the latter route, on account both of the more favorable nature of the gradients, and the less expensive character of the works.*

The project, however, slept until August, 1838, when Mr. Stephenson was requested to make a further careful inspection of the country between Newcastle and Edinburgh, and "report his opinion on the best line of railway between those places, upon levels to which locomotive steam power can be advantageously applied, preparatory to such line being more minutely surveyed, and ultimately adopted." After again making a careful inspection of the country, he sent in his report.† He went at great length into the comparative merits of the routes by Carter Fell and by Berwick, and expressed a decided opinion, as before, on the superiority of the latter route. As the report presented by him on this subject contains many points of interest, and may be taken as a fair specimen of the character of his railway reports, we venture to give the following extract:

"In laying out a line of railway from England to the two principal cities in Scotland, and as a great thoroughfare between the two countries, there are many circumstances to be taken into consideration. The first and most important of all, considering it as a great national work, and desirable for the convenience and advantage of the whole community, is to endeavor to obtain a railway with such inclinations as will secure a certain, speedy, and safe conveyance between the two countries, not merely for the conveyance of passengers, but more especially for the mails. We should endeavor to obtain a railway on which the engines should at all times be enabled to perform the duties required of them, without having to encounter steep inclined planes totally unfit for the profitable employment of the locomotive engine, and also without having to depend in a great measure upon the pecu-

* Report to the Directors of the Edinburgh and Dunbar Railway, dated Alton Grange, September 11th, 1836.

† Report, September 13th, 1838.

liar state of the atmosphere, in order to enable the engines to surmount such inclined planes at all.

"It is extremely desirable, in laying out a main line of railway like this, to avoid as much as possible passing through a high country, as in so doing you not only invariably meet with difficulties in the form of extensive works to be executed, and inclined planes to be overcome, but you also traverse a country much more subject to the inclemency of the weather, especially in winter, where in high countries the snow, a great impeder to railway traveling, remains so long a time upon the ground.

"In consequence of the line I propose to you running so near the coast, it is entirely free from those great disadvantages. It passes through a low country; it possesses levels of a most favorable nature; and in the neighborhood of the sea-coast the snow remains a very short time upon the ground. The line itself runs so near the coast, that it may be found of great advantage in conveying troops from station to station, and, in case of war, in conveying dispatches from the seat of government to any part of the North, and also for keeping up a communication with the sea. If it should be found necessary, the whole line, from Newcastle to Edinburgh, might be formed into one continuous battery, by erecting a mound in exposed places to protect the engines from any attack from the sea. The whole troops of the country might also by its means be concentrated in one spot on the shortest notice.

"The line of railway which I am proposing will constitute the last link in the great chain of railway communication from London to Edinburgh and Glasgow: in the whole of this chain there will not be between London and Edinburgh one inclination exceeding 20 feet a mile (except at the London and Birmingham station), and the characteristic inclination will be 16 feet a mile. The same description of engine will be enabled to work the whole of the lines included in this chain, so that, if it should be necessary, either from necessity or dispatch being requisite, or in case of accident, an engine may be transferred from one line to another, capable of performing the work. But, as I stated before, it appears to me that, both in a national and commercial point of view, the most important consideration in procuring easy inclinations is, that it insures a certain, speedy and punctual performance of the duties required from the engines.

"In looking at the subject in a local point of view, I may state that it has always been my practice to lay out main lines of railway through the lowest country, unless some important consideration, such as a large and populous town, induced me to diverge into a higher country. I consider that by adopting the low country I have many advantages which are lost by taking a high one. Considering the subject locally, I afford great facilities in procuring cheap branches from the main line into the interior of the country, and up the various valleys which run nearly at right angles to the main line; for instance, as regards the present railway, those productions, both agricultural and mineral, which are found in Northumberland and Scotland, may be conveyed on branch railways running up the valleys of the Blyth, the Wansbeck, the Coquet, and the Tweed, on declining railways from the places where they are produced to the main line of railway, when they can be carried north or south, as may be required.

"It is a very important consideration indeed, that branch railways should possess a falling inclination towards the main line, as the productions of the country are invariably conveyed either to the coast for shipment, or to populous towns through which the main railways of the kingdom are carried; and the traffic conveyed from populous towns and the coast into the interior of the country is generally of a light description, consisting of groceries, and what may be called the luxuries of life. There is, however, in this case, an exception, and that is the river Tweed. It will be a great advantage to the valley of the Tweed, inasmuch as the inhabitants will procure both lime and coal from Berwick at a cheap rate, and as that river is crossed at the height of 90 feet, and being a sluggish stream near its mouth, you will be enabled to have a level branch along the valley for many miles.

"The towns of Morpeth, Belford, Alnwick and Kelso may be easily accommodated by branches up the different valleys in which they are situated.

"I will now conclude this Report, congratulating you upon the favorable nature of the country, and the great facilities which exist for constructing the works on the coast line, with a firm conviction on my own mind that it is the only feasible and desirable line of railway, with levels to which locomotive steam power can be advantageously applied, between the town of Newcastle-upon-Tyne and the cities of Edinburgh and Glasgow."

The recommendations contained in this able Report were eventually adopted, although several years elapsed before the line was actually constructed. This delay was caused by unavoidable circumstances, to which we shall afterwards recur. In the meantime, the alternative route to Edinburgh by Carter Fell was not without its advocates, Mr. Nicholas Wood heading the opposition to Mr. Stephenson, and alleging that the east coast route by Berwick "could neither answer the purpose of the public in general nor the subscribers."*

Mr. Stephenson was also consulted with reference to the formation of a main line from Chester to Holyhead, with the view of improving the railway communication with Dublin, and Ireland generally. Mr. Giles and Mr. Vignolles were both engaged in surveying lines of railway to Holyhead in 1838, and they presented reports on the subject to their respective promoters. About the same time the directors of the Chester and Crewe Company called upon Mr. Stephenson to make a preliminary survey of the country between Chester and Holyhead, and inquire into the practicability of forming the line by Shrewsbury to Port Dynllaen, which had been suggested by the Irish Railway Commissioners in their published report, as compared with a line to

* Railway Times, 1839, p 372.

Holyhead passing through Chester. After a careful examination, Mr. Stephenson reported in very strong terms against the line adopted by the Irish Railway Commissioners, and by Mr. Vignolles, and in favor of the route by Chester, which, he alleged, could be formed for less money, and would be a shorter line, with much more favorable gradients.*

A public meeting was held at Chester on the 10th of January, 1839, in support of Mr. Stephenson's line, at which the Marquis of Westminster, Mr. Wilbraham, the member for the county, and other influential gentlemen, were present. Mr. Uniacke, the Mayor, in opening the proceedings, observed that it clearly appeared that the rival line through Shrewsbury was quite impracticable. "Mr. Stephenson, the first railway authority in the kingdom—in fact, the father of railways—had so characterized it; and, after that opinion, he did not think that any one could be found who would risk money in such a speculation. Their object was, to advance and carry the really practicable project; and he would take the opportunity of saying, that the dissemination of Mr. Stephenson's admirable report had satisfied the people of Ireland, not only that the project was practicable, but that it was the only one that was practicable, and worthy of general support." Mr. Stephenson, he added, was present in the room, ready to answer any questions which might be put to him on the subject; and "it would be better that he should be asked questions than required to make a speech; for, though a very good engineer, he was a bad speaker." One of the questions then put to Mr. Stephenson related to the mode by which he proposed to haul the passenger carriages over the Menai Bridge by horse power; and he was asked whether he knew the pressure the bridge was capable of sustaining. His answer was, that "he had not yet made any calculations; but he proposed getting data

* Report upon the proposed Railway Communications with Ireland, addressed to the Directors of the Chester and Crewe Railway Company, dated Newcastle-upon-Tyne, Dec. 19th, 1838.

which would enable him to arrive at an accurate calculation of the actual strain upon the bridge during the late gale. But he had no hesitation in saying that it was more than twenty times as much as the strain of a train of carriages and a locomotive engine. The only reason why he proposed to convey the carriages over by horses, was in order that he might, by distributing the weight, not increase the waving motion. All the train would be on at once; but distributed. This he thought better than passing them linked together by a locomotive engine."

Mr. Vignolles, in the course of the same month, published a defense of his mode of effecting a communication between London and Dublin, although he confessed that to impugn Mr. Stephenson's statements in reference to his measure, or to enter into a professional contest with such high authority, was almost "bearding the lion in his den." The Dublin Chamber of Commerce decided in favor of Mr. Stephenson's plan; and at a meeting of members of Parliament held in London in May, 1839, a series of resolutions was adopted in favor of the scheme. At that meeting Mr. Stephenson was present, and gave explanations on many of its essential points. Notwithstanding, however, these important demonstrations of opinion in its favor, Mr. Stephenson's plan of a railway from Chester to Holyhead, like many others projected about the same time, was allowed to drop; and it was not resumed until several years after, when it was taken up by his son, and brought to a successful completion, with certain modifications, including the grand original feature of the tubular bridge across the Menai Straits.*

The completion of a main line of railway communication between London and Glasgow by the western side of the island, was another of the great projects on which Mr. Stephenson was now engaged. In 1837, he was requested by the Caledonian Railway Committee, and also by the Whitehaven, Workington, and Maryport Railway Committee, to make an examination of

* The Chester and Holyhead Act was obtained in the session of 1844.

the country, and report to them as to the best line that could be formed. With this object, he made a careful survey of the entire country between Lancaster and Carlisle, by Ulverstone and Whitehaven, and also by Kirby, Lonsdale, and Penrith. As on the eastern coast, here also he reported in favor of the coast route. Besides the flatness of such a line, and the consequent superiority of the gradients—a point to which he always attached the greatest importance—the coast line could be formed at comparatively small expense; valuable iron mines would be opened out, from which a large traffic might be anticipated, while, as a collateral advantage, an extensive tract of valuable land would be reclaimed by the formation of his proposed embankment across Ulverston sands, at the head of Morecombe Bay. There would also be fifteen miles less of new railway to be constructed by the coast line than by the more direct inland route across Shap Fell. The latter route — planned by Mr. Locke — was twenty miles shorter between Lancaster and Carlisle; but the gradients were much heavier, and the works far more difficult and costly. It was, however, eventually preferred to the west coast line of Mr. Stephenson, which was, for a time, lost sight of. Nevertheless it has since been formed; the large traffic in iron ore which he anticipated has been obtained; and his favorite scheme of reclaiming the immense tract of land at the head of Morcombe Bay —from forty to fifty thousand acres in extent—by means of the railway embankment necessary to complete the connection with the Lancaster and Carlisle line, has recently been carried into effect in a modified form, and to some extent after his plans.*

The Leeds and Bradford Railway, surveyed by Mr. Stephenson in 1838, was a line of comparatively small extent, but of considerable importance in a local point of view, as connecting the two principal manufacturing towns of Yorkshire. The scheme was brought out in the following year, under very favorable

* See Reports by Mr. Stephenson on the subject, dated October 12th, 1836; March 13th, 1837; and August 16th, 1837.

auspices; but like most of the railway projects of the same period, it was suspended in consequence of the financial embarrassment of the country, which was to some extent caused by the large investments of capital in railways during the few preceding years.

The rapidity with which railways had been extended between the years 1836 and 1839 was extraordinary, although not to be compared with the railway mania of a subsequent period. There was quite a rush for railway acts in the sessions of 1836 and 1837. In the former year, thirty-four bills passed the legislature, authorizing the formation of 994 miles of new railway, at an estimated cost of 17,595,000*l.* The traffic cases got up by the promoters of some of the bills, were very strong. Traffic-taking had become a lucrative trade; and ingenious arithmeticians who devoted themselves to the art of getting up traffic, soon became able to "prove" whatever the promoters of railways wanted. Thus, the traffic case of the Eastern Counties Railway showed that there would be a clear profit on the outlay of 23½ per cent.! The North Midland "proved" a traffic which would yield them a profit of 10½ per cent.; the York and North Midland, of 13½; and the London and Cambridge, of 14½ per cent. Other companies made out equally "strong" traffic cases.

In the following session of 1837, not fewer than 118 notices of new railway bills were given. Seventy-nine of these were actually introduced to Parliament; and forty-two acts were obtained, the principal of which, however, were extensions of previous acts. Fourteen new companies were incorporated, and authorized to construct 464 miles of railway, at a cost of 8,087,000*l.* During this session the traffic-takers grew bolder, and reached their highest flights. Thus, the promoters of the Sheffield and Manchester Bill "proved" a traffic which was to yield a net profit of 18½ per cent. on the outlay. One of the fortunate shareholders in the company, in a letter to the "Railway Magazine," even went so far beyond the traffic-taker, as to calculate on a dividend of 80 per cent.!

But the prodigious extent of railway works already authorized was not enough to satisfy the rage for railway extension which still prevailed; for, by the end of 1837, notices were given of seventy-five new bills, to authorize the construction of some 1230 miles of additional railway, at an estimated cost of above nineteen millions sterling. By this time, thirty millions had actually been expended, and nearly 1500 miles of railway constructed and opened, in the course of a very few years; and several hundred thousand laborers and mechanics were still occupied in the making of railways and the manufacture of railway stock. It was estimated that the railways in course of construction would cost twenty-two millions more before they were ready for traffic. Heavy calls were made from time to time upon the holders of the shares to enable the works to proceed. The monetary pressure which had already set in, was thereby increased; shares fell in price; and the railway interest began to be severely discouraged. Railway extension was thus effectually checked for a time; and a sort of collapse ensued, which, together with the restrictions imposed by Parliament on the obtaining of new acts, placed a severe and indeed wholesome restraint upon speculation; and many of the most recent railway projects were consequently abandoned, or for a time lay dormant. Amongst this latter class, were Mr. Stephenson's East and West Coast lines to Scotland, the Chester and Holyhead Railway, and the line from Leeds to Bradford. During the two sessions of 1838 and 1839 only five new railway companies obtained acts of incorporation. In 1840, not a single railway act was obtained; and in 1841 only the Hertford and Ware branch, 5¾ miles in length, was authorized; and even that was not constructed. In 1842 the Newcastle and Darlington Railway (part of the original Great North of England, which could not be completed for want of capital) was authorized under this new name; and in the same session, the Yarmouth and Norwich and Warwick and Leamington branches were authorized. The year 1843 was also a quiet railway session, only a few new branches of established lines having been then authorized; and it was not until 1844 that the tide of railway enterprise suddenly rose again, and in the following year fairly burst all bounds, breaking out in the wildest fury of speculation.

CHAPTER XXIX.

MR. STEPHENSON AND THE NEW SCHOOL OF FAST ENGINEERS.

The general demand for railways which sprang up shortly after the successful opening of the Liverpool and Manchester line, brought into existence a large number of engineers of great ability, distinguished by their practical skill and their high standing as scientific men. In this country of free industrial competition, no sooner does the demand for a particular class of talent arise, than it is supplied as if by magic. The *laissez faire* course of action adopted by the government with reference to railways, though it led to much bungling and enormous expense, nevertheless gave full scope to the genius and enterprise of English engineers. So long as the prospect of dividends ranging from 8 to 15 per cent. was held out, there was to be found a numerous class of private capitalists ready to invest money in iron roads, and to find capital for the construction of new lines. Much rivalry thus arose, the engineers usually appearing as the leaders of the battle on opposing sides, when two or more lines were started between the same points. A considerable amount of personal feeling was occasionally evoked in these engineering contests, which were as often trials of individual ambition as of professional skill. Aspiring juniors sought to supplant their elder brethren at boards of directors, or to defeat their schemes before parliamentary committees; and many new men labored to mature and bring out railway projects more striking and original than anything that had before been proposed.

Whilst continental governments, early recognizing the great national advantages of railways, were appointing state engineers for the purpose of determining by preliminary surveys the most eligible lines of communication, leaving only the execution of the requisite works open to competition, the English government left it to joint-stock companies to project and construct our national highways. The first step usually taken was the formation of a provisional committee, which at once proceeded to appoint an engineer to lay out the line, and a solicitor to constitute the company and agitate public opinion on behalf of the scheme. But the chief responsibility unquestionably rested with the engineer, who had to find a practicable road, to survey the line, to plan the necessary work—tunnels, viaducts, bridges, cuttings and embankments—to form estimates of the cost, and, above all, to be prepared to stand the cross-examination of his opponents before Parliament.

This keen competition of professional ability tended rapidly to develop the peculiar qualities of the English Railway Engineer. His experience, it will be observed, must necessarily be of an exceedingly varied character, to enable him to stand the test of the parliamentary crucible. He must be conversant with land-surveying and leveling, and have considerable practical knowledge of the strength and qualities of materials—of iron work, masonry, tunneling and earth works. He must be something of an architect, a mathematician and a geologist. He must also be familiar with the structure of the steam-engine and its application to the purposes of locomotion; and he must have studied the principles of mechanical science, more especially the laws of gravity, friction and momentum. Thus, the practical education of the English Engineer included almost the entire field of natural science. Being often called upon to act in emergencies, he acquired a promptitude of action, and a facility in inventing

24

expedients to meet difficulties as they arose, which gave him a commanding superiority over the engineers of the continent. The works on foreign railways being for the most part under the control of Government, their engineers, though possessing the advantages of a much more scientific training, were trammeled and fettered in all that they did; and in cases of great practical difficulty, which required boldness and skill of contrivance, the English engineers—though they might, like George Stephenson, be entirely self-educated—were found greatly their superiors.

With all the wholesome rivalry and competition to which we have referred, and which tended to stimulate and strengthen their practical ability, there was a considerable admixture of jealousy and heartburning. It was long before Mr. Stephenson, notwithstanding the immense engineering works he had planned and executed, was recognized by the "regular" professional men as entitled to the *status* of a Civil Engineer. He had served no apprenticeship, and could show no indentures. Even the mechanical engineers connected with the manufacture of steam-engines regarded him as an interloper, denied him all merit, and pursued him with detraction in the pages of their "Mechanics' Magazine," long after the world had recognized his claims to distinction. This bitterness of spirit produced a similar spirit in himself; and he occasionally entertained a resentment towards his detractors which he could not and would not conceal.

The railway system, as established by Mr. Stephenson, was too new as yet to command that prestige which belongs to older institutions. It was but in its infancy; and the many able engineers who rose up, naturally supposed it to be imperfect, and capable of vast improvement. The scientific professional men employed to survey the numerous new lines of railway which radiated in all directions from the metropolis, exerted themselves to improve upon Mr. Stephenson's plans, and thereby to enhance their own reputation. Indeed, they were sometimes twitted by the press for following so closely in the footsteps of the comparatively uneducated men who had gathered their experience in the Newcastle coal-pits. Several of the new engineers therefore determined to be original. About the year 1838, they began to strike out many new lights, and to propound new plans, by way of improvement upon the Stephenson system.

These aspiring engineers did not want followers enough amongst railway speculators. In answer to the objections advanced against their plans, they cited the numerous predictions which had so recently been uttered against the practicability of working the locomotive itself upon railways. Give them an opportunity, and they would prove even the locomotive to be clumsy, and the existing system quite inferior to their own. And, indeed, so many "impracticable" and "impossible" things had within a very few years been proved to be both practicable and possible on railways, that the public became much less skeptical as to the plans of new projectors, and many were found ready to subscribe their capital for the purpose of bringing them into practical use.

Among the many novelties in railway engineering originated by the new school, the proposal of a pneumatic apparatus to supersede entirely the locomotive engine, was probably the most important. It was also proposed to adopt uneven railways, without much regard to gradients, as an improvement upon the flat lines so much insisted upon by Mr. Stephenson: this was scientifically designated "the undulating system." And some engineers, whilst retaining the locomotive as the tractive power, proposed to propel it at speeds which even Mr. Stephenson himself, sanguine and impracticable as he had so often been pronounced, had never dreampt of.

Another improvement which was much discussed for many years, and of which, unhappily, we have not yet heard the last, was the alteration of the gauge of railways from 4 feet 8½ inches to a greater width.

As already stated, the original width of the coal tramroads in the North had virtually determined the British gauge. It was the width of the ordinary road-track—not fixed after any scientific theory, but adopted simply from general use. Mr. Stephenson introduced it without alteration on the Liverpool and Manchester Railway; and the several lines subsequently formed in the same districts were laid down on the same system. Mr. Stephenson from the first anticipated the general adoption of railways throughout England; and one of the principles with which he started was, the essential importance of preserving such a uniformity as would admit of perfect communication between them. All the railways, therefore, laid down by himself and his assistants in the neighborhood of Manchester, extending from thence to London on the south and to Leeds on the east, were constructed on the Liverpool and Manchester or narrow gauge. While others were declaring that railroads would be effective only for passenger traffic and for the local accommodation of the largest towns, Mr. Stephenson foresaw and foretold that universal adoption of them in all places for the conveyance both of goods and passengers which the iron-road system has since attained; and he accordingly prepared the railways under his control for the eventual receipt of traffic from the cross roads and the by roads, as well as from the main roads of the kingdom.

When Mr. Brunel projected the Great Western line, he fixed upon a broader gauge; but he adopted a narrower view of the subject of railway extension than Mr. Stephenson had done. He assumed that the country would be divided into railway districts, under a sort of railway Heptarchy, each having little intercourse with the other, and adopting its own gauge according to circumstances. Mr. Brunel was an ingenious designer, and fond of doing things on a large scale, whether in forming railways or building a steam-ship. Unlike Mr. Stephenson, who, though no less bold in his original conceptions, adhered to opinions once formed with remarkable tenacity, and even seemed to acquire a certain fixity of ideas which precluded the consideration of plans at variance with his own—Mr. Brunel was ever looking forward to indefinite and continual improvement; he was restive under any restraint on invention, and could brook no limit to change. His railways were to be broader, his locomotives larger, and the speeds to be attained by them were to surpass those on all other railways. But even the speed of locomotives would not satisfy his ambition; and in their stead he would have a system of gigantic pneumatic tubes, along which trains of travelers were to be flashed with the speed of lightning. Mr. Stephenson was not so venturous, but, as events proved, he was wiser. His locomotives and his railways had alike been carefully designed; and he had so well adapted them to the practical purposes for which they were intended, that they held their ground amidst the brilliant inventions and improvements of the new school of engineers; and to this day they remain in all respects very much as he left them.

Mr. Stephenson was examined as a witness in favor of the Great Western Railway Bill; but the subject of an alteration in the gauge of the line had not then been mooted. It was in preparing the working plans, that Mr. Brunel conceived the idea of increasing the width of his gauge to seven feet. At that time, the directors of the London and Birmingham Railway had under their consideration a plan for joining the Great Western line at Oxford, and uniting with them in a joint metropolitan terminus. The proposed alteration of the gauge was referred by them to their engineer, Mr. Robert Stephenson, who reported decidedly against it. The Great Western directors, however, supported their own engineer; and the broad gauge was eventually adopted by them, but not without a lengthened discussion. In his report of 1838, Mr. Brunel represented to the proprietors, that the position of the Great Western line was such, that it could have no connection with any other of the main lines of railway, now that the London and Birmingham had obtained an independent access to the metropolis; that it held the exclusive command of its special district; that no inconvenience would result from the diversity of gauge, as that district was entirely isolated from the others; and, further, that no extension of the line towards the north would be required. It was even anticipated by Mr. Brunel that if other railways were formed, their exclusion from a connection with the Great Western line by the difference of gauge, would be of advantage to the company, by securing for it a monopoly of the traffic to and from South Wales and the West of England for all time to come. The Great Western Railway was thus to be independent of all other railways, and to stand apart from them in solitary grandeur. The engineer received the warm encomiums of the directors and proprietors, who considered it a bold and original thing to plan a railway which was to be more than two feet broader than any other, requiring works and plant on a corresponding scale, without regard to past example and experience. Provincial patriotism was also evoked in favor of the measure; and it was anticipated that Bristol would rival, if not far outstrip Liverpool, in its railway accommodation and facilities.

Mr. Stephenson was, from the first, opposed to the adoption of the broad gauge. He held that the gauge which had already been adopted on the northern lines was amply sufficient for the public accommodation; that it was wide enough to admit of the most effective arrangement of the machinery of the locomotive; that it was much safer to work over where the curves of the railway were at all sharp; that it was far more economical, taking into consideration the paying weight carried, in proportion to the dead weight in the shape of rolling stock; that it would cost considerably less to maintain, in consequence of the less weight to bear, and the smaller tear and wear of materials—not to mention the much smaller capital that was required to form a line upon the narrow gauge than upon the broad—the latter requiring more land, wider bridges and tunnels, broader embankments and viaducts, heavier rails, chairs and sleepers, and more expensive engines and carriages. But his principal objection was, that by forming the Great Western line on an exceptional gauge, the proprietors of the undertaking were virtually closing it against the public traffic from other parts of the kingdom, and rendering it a mere provincial railway or by-way, instead of part of a great national system. He would not believe, with Mr. Brunel, that railways were to be confined to particular districts, but he held that, before long, they must become the universal high-roads as well as by-roads for both goods and passengers; and that any break in the continuity of the system by a difference of gauge, would seriously detract from those great public advantages which their general adoption might reasonably be expected to confer. The contrary views, advocated with so much persuasiveness by Mr. Brunel, unhappily prevailed with his directors; and a subject fruitful in contentions and controversies was thus introduced into the railway world.

When the proprietors, however, observed the enormous expense that was involved in carrying out Mr. Brunel's designs, they became alarmed, and at length dissatisfied; and they invited Mr. Robert Stephenson to examine and report upon the new gauge. He declined, on the ground that his opinion was already known to be strongly unfavorable, on which Mr. Nicholas Wood and Mr. Hawkshaw were called upon to make an investigation into the subject. This they did in a very able manner, Mr. Hawkshaw's report being particularly clear and decisive. Their opinion was against the new gauge. Nevertheless, the majority of the proprietors determined to support Mr. Brunel, and to carry out his experiment to an issue. The Great Western road was formed, and set to work with the aid of George Stephenson's locomotives; and the public waited the result of the new system.

Its inconvenience was not felt so long as the Great Western line remained in the position anticipated by Mr. Brunel; but when, after the lapse of a few years, railways on the narrow gauge met it at various points, and a break of continuity occurred, involving the change of carriages both for passengers and goods, it was felt to be a great public nuisance, loudly calling for a remedy.

The same mistake was committed on the Eastern Counties Railway, on which a gauge of five feet had been adopted, Mr. Braithwaite, the engineer, being of opinion that an increase of three and a half inches in the width of his line, would give him better space for the machinery of his locomotive. But when the northern and eastern extension of the same line was formed, which was to work into the narrow gauge system of the Midland Railway, Mr. Robert Stephenson, its new engineer, strongly recommended the directors of the Eastern Counties line to alter their gauge accordingly, for the purpose of securing uniformity; and they wisely adopted his recommendation. Mr. Braithwaite himself afterwards justified the wisdom of this step, and stated that he considered the narrow gauge "infinitely superior to any other," more especially for passenger traffic.*

The Great Western Company, however, would not adopt a similar step; they held by the superiority of their gauge. The Company had invested a vast sum of money in constructing their line, and perhaps thought it was too late to remedy the admitted inconvenience of the want of continuity. The Birmingham manufacturers were the first to experience its evils, in consequence of the break of gauge at Gloucester, which involved great delay and loss from the transfer of goods. In 1844 they held a public meeting on the subject, and protested against it "as a commercial evil of the first magnitude." This formed the commencement of "The Battle of the Gauges." In the following session of Parliament, the London and Birmingham and Great Western Companies were competitors for the supply of railroad accommodation to the country between Oxford and Wolverhampton. The Board of Trade reported against the Great Western extensions, on account of the break of gauge. The House of

* Evidence before the Gauge Commission, 1845.

North-Western Railway Train.

Commons, however, stepped in and reversed the decision, determining nothing. Mr. Cobden then moved for a royal commission to ascertain "whether, in future private acts for the construction of railways, provision ought to be made for securing a uniform gauge; and whether it would be expedient and practicable to take measures to bring railways already constructed, or in progress of construction, into uniformity of gauge." The address was unanimously voted; and a commission was accordingly appointed, before which the principal engineers and railway men of the day were examined at great length. In 1846, they reported substantially against the broad, and in favor of the narrow, as the future national gauge of British railways. They also expressed their opinion as to the desirableness of adopting some equitable means of producing an entire uniformity of gauge on the lines already constructed. Mr. George Stephenson was not examined before the Gauge Commission, having by that time (1845) in a great measure retired from the active pursuit of his profession; but he was ably represented by his son, whose evidence in favor of the superiority of the gauge of railways which had been virtually settled by his father, was complete and conclusive.

Every day's successive experience has proved that the Stephenson gauge is sufficient for all purposes of public traffic, while it is, unquestionably, the most economical. Foreign engineers, who were not in the slightest degree trammeled by existing lines, laid down the narrow gauge in Belgium, in France, in Germany, and in Italy. Mr. Brunel was the engineer of the Genoa to Turin Railway; and there he had adopted the narrow gauge, with a view to the public convenience, as well as the interests of the undertaking itself. And the same considerations will, doubtless, sooner or later, induce the Great Western Company to place itself in connection with the national railway system of

England, instead of remaining, as at present, comparatively isolated.*

Another favorite idea of the Fast School of Engineers, was, as already mentioned, the substitution of atmospheric pressure for locomotive steam power in the working of railways. The idea of obtaining motion by atmospheric pressure originated with Papin, the French engineer; but it slept until revived by Mr. Medhurst, in 1810, who published a pamphlet to prove the practicability of conveying letters and goods by air. In 1824, Mr. Vallance of Brighton, took out a patent for projecting passengers through a tube large enough to contain a train of carriages; the tube being previously exhausted of its atmospheric air. The same idea was afterwards taken up, in 1835, by Mr. Pinkus, an ingenious American. Scientific gentlemen, Dr. Lardner and Mr. Clegg, amongst others, advocated the plan, and an association was formed to carry it into effect. Shares were created, and 18,000*l.* raised; and a model apparatus was exhibited in London. Mr. Vignolles took his friend Mr. Stephenson to see the model; and after carefully examining it, he observed emphatically, "*It won't do:* it is only the fixed engines and ropes over again, in another form." He did not think the principle would stand the test of practice, and he objected to the mode of applying the principle. Would it pay? He thought not. After all, it was only a modification of the stationary-engine plan; and every day's experience was proving that fixed engines could not compete with locomotives in point of efficiency and economy. He

* In Ireland, a peculiar gauge of five feet three inches has been adopted. The Irish Railway Commission did some remarkable things in its day. Amongst others, it recommended a gauge of six feet two inches; how they arrived at that precise width, no one can tell. The Ulster Railway was laid down for twenty-five miles on this gauge, whilst the Drogheda line, which ran from Dublin into the Ulster Railway, was laid down five feet two inches in width. General Pasley was appealed to, and after consulting all the leading authorities as to the proper gauge, he *struck an average*, and arrived at five feet three inches, which is now the Irish gauge.

stood by the locomotive engine; and subsequent experience proved that he was right.

Messrs. Clegg and Samuda afterwards, in 1840, patented their plan of an atmospheric railway; and they publicly tested its working on an unfinished portion of the West London Railway. The results of the experiment were so satisfactory that the directors of the Dublin and Kingstown line adopted it between Kingstown and Dalkey. The London and Croydon Company also adopted the atmospheric principle; and their line was opened in 1845. Great was the popularity of the atmospheric system; and still George Stephenson said, "It won't do; its only a gimcrack." Engineers of distinction said he was prejudiced, and that he looked upon the locomotive as a pet child of his own. "Wait a little," he replied, "and you will see that I am right."

Mr. Brunel approved of the atmospheric system; and had not his invention of the broad gauge proved him to be a man of genius? Mr. Cubitt, Mr. Vignolles, and Mr. James Walker, also men of great eminence, Dr. Lardner, and many others equally distinguished, as well as the Council of the Institute of Civil Engineers, approved of the atmospheric railway; and therefore it was becoming pretty clear that the locomotive system was about to be snuffed out. "Not so fast," said Mr. Stephenson. "Let us wait to see if it will pay." He never believed it would. It was ingenious, clever, scientific, and all that; but railways were commercial enterprises, not toys; and if the atmospheric railway could not work to a profit, it would not do. Considered in this light, he even went so far as to call it "a great humbug."

No one can say that the atmospheric railway had not a fair trial. The government engineer, General Pasley, did for it what had never been done for the locomotive—he reported in its favor, whereas a former government engineer, Mr. Telford, had inferentially reported against the use of locomotive power on railways. The House of Commons had reported in favor of the use of the steam-engine on common roads; and yet the railway locomotive had vitality enough in it to live through all. "Nothing will beat it," said George Stephenson, "for efficiency in all weathers, for economy in drawing loads of average weight, and for power and speed as occasion may require."

The atmospheric system was fairly and fully tried, and it was found wanting. It was admitted to be an exceedingly elegant mode of applying power; its devices were very skillful, and its mechanism was most ingenious. But it was costly, irregular in action, and, consequently, not to be depended upon. At best, it was but a modification of the stationary-engine system, which experience had proved to be so expensive that it was gradually being abandoned in favor of locomotive power. In fact, Mr. Stephenson's first verdict, "It won't do," proved correct; and, by the end of 1848, the whole of the atmospheric tubes were pulled up — including Mr. Brunel's immense tube on the South Devon Railway*—to make room for the locomotive engine.

About the year 1840, the fast school propounded another set of views respecting railways, which were entirely opposed to the practice and experience of Mr. Stephenson. They promulgated the idea that undulating railways of uneven, and even severe gradients, were as favorable for working as flat lines. Mr. Stephenson, throughout his professional career, was the unvarying advocate of level railways, in preference to more direct but uneven lines. His practice was to secure a road as nearly as possible on a level, following the course of the valleys when he could do so, and preferring to go round a difficulty rather than to tunnel through it or run over it—often making a considerable circuit in order to obtain good workable gradients. He studied so to lay out his lines, that minerals and merchandise, as well as passengers, could be hauled along them in heavy loads, at a comparatively small expenditure of locomotive power. He saw clearly that the longer flat line would eventually beat the shorter line of steep

* During the last half year of the atmospheric experiment on this line, there was an expenditure of 2,487*l.* beyond the gross income of 26,782*l.*, or about 9¾ per cent.

gradients, as respected paying qualities. It was perfectly clear to him that there must necessarily be a great waste of power in overcoming the irregularities of a heavy line. Thus, Mr. Stephenson had ascertained, by experiments made at Killingworth many years before, that the locomotive works at only half its power where it has a rising gradient of 1 in 260 to overcome; and when the gradient is so high as 1 in 100, not less than three-fourths of the propelling power of the engine is sacrificed in ascending the acclivity. Mr. Stephenson urged that, after all, the power of the locomotive was but limited; and, although he had done more to increase its working qualities than any other engineer, it provoked him to find that every improvement which he made in it was neutralized by the steep gradients which the fast school of engineers were setting it to overcome. On one occasion, when Mr. Robert Stephenson stated before a Parliamentary Committee that every improvement which they were making in the locomotive was being rendered virtually nugatory by the difficult and almost impracticable gradients proposed upon so many of the new lines, his father, on his leaving the witness box, went up to him and said, "Robert, you never spoke truer words than those in all your life."

In the case of passenger lines, where the load is light, and time an object of importance, short lines of comparatively heavy gradients are practicable—thanks to the great power which Mr. Stephenson and his son have given to the engine; but when the traffic consists, in any considerable proportion, of minerals or merchandise, experience has amply proved the wisdom of Mr. Stephenson's preference for level lines, though of greater length.

But engineers were growing bolder, and ambitious to do greater things. Among others, Dr. Lardner, who had originally been somewhat skeptical about the powers of the locomotive, now promulgated the idea that a railway constructed with rising and falling gradients would be practically as easy to work as a line perfectly level. Mr. Badnell went beyond him, for he held that an undulating railway was even much better than a level one for purposes of working.* For a time, this theory found favor, and the "undulating system" was extensively adopted; but Mr. Stephenson never ceased to inveigh against it; and experience has amply proved that his judgment was correct.

The engineers of the fast school were also becoming increasingly sanguine about the speed of railway traveling. Dr. Lardner considered that an average rate of a hundred miles an hour might be attained by the locomotive upon a railway, though he afterwards found cause to alter his opinion. Mr. Stephenson, who only a few years before was considered insane for suggesting a speed of twelve miles an hour, was now thought behind the age when he recommended that the rate of railway traveling should not exceed forty miles an hour. He said, "I do not like either forty or fifty miles an hour upon any line; I think it is an unnecessary speed; and if there is danger upon a railway, it is high velocity that creates it." † He had, indeed, constructed for the Great Western Railway an engine capable of running fifty miles an hour with a load, and eighty miles without one. But he never was in favor of a hurricane speed of this sort, believing it could only be accomplished at an unnecessary increase both of danger and expense. On this subject, he afterwards observed, "The first time I went to Parliament to give evidence on the locomotive engine, when I stated that I would make that machine travel at twelve miles an hour, I was thought to be mad. You will be surprised when I tell you that, during my recent examination before a Committee of the House of Commons on the management of railways, I stated, in my opinion, that the speed of the locomotive should not exceed forty miles an hour. I have been censured by many for giving that opinion. It is true that I have said the engine might be made to travel 100 miles an hour; but I always put a qualification on this, namely, as to what

* Treatise on Railway Improvements. By Mr. Richard Badnell, C. E.

† Evidence before the Select Committee on Railways, 27th May, 1841.

speed would best suit the public. I assure you I have been buffeted about in Parliament not a little on this question of railway speed."* Although Mr. Stephenson occasionally "girded" at Mr. Brunel and his high velocities, there is no doubt that the determination of the latter had the effect of spurring on the Stephensons to exert their ingenuity to the utmost in perfecting the narrow-gauge locomotive, and bringing it to the highest possible rate of speed. By the year 1845, Mr. Robert Stephenson had been enabled to construct the fastest locomotive that had yet run upon any railway—the celebrated "A" engine—which performed the forty-five miles between York and Darlington, with a train of seven carriages behind it, in about forty-seven minutes!

Mr. Stephenson's evidence before the Select Committee of 1841 bore chiefly upon the safer working of railways, and the means by which they might be improved. One of his suggestions was to the effect that a system of self-acting brakes should be adopted, so that a train might be more speedily and effectually stopped than by the ordinary system. He himself, he stated, had invented for the Liverpool and Manchester Railway a carriage-brake, which he had not patented, although, he understood, a patent for a similar machine had since been taken out. He proposed to fix to every carriage a brake so constructed that, on the moving power of the engine being taken off, every carriage should be brought into a state of sledge, and the rolling motion of the wheels thus interrupted. Mr. Stephenson would also have these brakes worked by the guard, by means of a connecting lever running along the whole of the carriages, by which they should at one and the same time be thrown out of gear. He also suggested, as an additional means of safety, that the signals should be self-acting, and worked by the engines as they passed along the line.

In opposing the views of the fast school of engineers, as to the alteration of the gauge, the employment of atmospheric pressure,

* Speech at Belper Mechanics' Institute, 6th July, 1841.

the formation of "undulating" lines, and the increase of speed, Mr. Stephenson was actuated by a just regard to the commercial part of the question. He had no desire to build up a reputation at the expense of railway shareholders, nor to obtain engineering *éclat* by making "ducks and drakes" of their money. He was persuaded that, in order to secure the practical success of railways, they must be so laid out as not only to prove of decided public utility, but also to be worked economically and to the advantage of their proprietors. They were not Government roads, but private ventures — in fact, commercial speculations. He therefore endeavored to render them commercially profitable; and he repeatedly declared that if he did not believe they could be "made to pay," he would have nothing to do with them. He frequently refused to act as the engineer for lines which he thought would not prove remunerative, or when he considered the estimates too low.* He was not ambitious to be thought a railway genius, but rather to be regarded as the engineer of useful and profitable railways; and the success which attended his arrangements fully proved the solidity of his judgment in this respect.

* In his evidence on the Great Western Bill, Mr. Stephenson said: "I made out an estimate for the Hartlepool Railway, which they returned on account of its being too high, but I declined going to Parliament with a lower estimate." Another engineer was employed. Then again: "I was consulted about a line from Edinburgh to Glasgow. The directors chalked out a line and sent it to me, and I told them I could not support it in that case." Another engineer was consequently employed to carry out the line which Mr. Stephenson could not conscientiously advocate.

CHAPTER XXX.

MR. STEPHENSON'S PARTIAL RETIREMENT FROM THE PROFESSION—PUBLIC RECOGNITION OF HIS SERVICES—AUTO-BIOGRAPHICAL SKETCHES.

The more laborious part of Mr. Stephenson's career in connection with railways was now over; and he frequently expressed a desire to retire from its troubles and anxieties into private life. At Blackburn, in 1840, he publicly intimated his intention of retiring from the more active pursuit of his profession; and, shortly after, he proceeded to resign the charge of several of the railways of which he was the chief engineer. He was succeeded, on the Midland and York systems, by his son Robert; on the Chester lines, by Mr. John Dixon; on the Manchester and Leeds lines, by Mr. Hawkshaw; and on the other railways, chiefly by his own pupils—all of whom, from his son downwards, did him honor.

He had removed his home from Alton Grange to Tapton House, in August, 1838; but the extent of his railway engagements had, up to this time, prevented his enjoyment of its comforts and retirement. Tapton House is a large, roomy brick mansion, beautifully situated amidst woods, upon a commanding eminence, about a mile to the northeast of the town of Chesterfield. Green fields dotted with fine trees slope away from the house in all directions. The surrounding country is exceedingly varied and undulating. North and south the eye ranges over a vast extent of lovely scenery; and on the west, looking over the town of Chesterfield, with its fine church and crooked spire, the extensive range of the Derbyshire hills bounds the distance. The Midland Railway skirts the western edge of the park in a deep rock cutting, and the shrill whistle of the locomotive sounds near at hand as the trains speed past. The gardens and pleasure grounds adjoining the house were in a very neglected state when Mr. Stephenson first went to Tapton; and he promised himself, when he had secured rest and leisure from business, that he would put a new face upon both. The first improvement he made, was in cutting a woodland footpath up the hillside, by which he at the same time added a beautiful feature to the park, and secured a shorter road to the Chesterfield station. But it was some years before he found time to carry into effect his contemplated improvements in the adjoining gardens and pleasure grounds.

He was a man of so active a temperament, had so long been accustomed to laborious pursuits, and felt himself still so full of work, that he could not at once settle down into the habit of quietly enjoying the fruits of his industry. There was, as we have seen, almost a complete lull in the railway world towards the end of 1837, principally caused by the monetary pressure; and this continued for several years. He had, for some time previously, been turning over in his mind the best mode of employing the facilities which railways afforded for the transport of coals to profitable markets; and, after careful consideration, he determined to enter as a master miner into the trade with which he had been familiar from his boyhood. Accordingly, early in 1838, conjointly with other parties, he had entered on a lease of the Clay Cross estate, for the purpose of working the coal which was known to exist there. He had an impression that a ready sale might be found for this coal at the stations of the Midland and London and Birmingham Railways, as far even as London itself. He invited, one day, to his house at Tapton a small party of gentlemen, consisting of Mr. Glyn, Sir Joshua Walmsley, Mr. Hudson, and Mr. Sandars, to take their opinion as to the qualities of the Derbyshire coal for household purposes. The coals were heaped upon the fire, and they burned so well, that all the gentlemen concurred in the opinion that a ready sale might be expected for coals of such a quality. Thus encouraged, sinking operations were commenced, a rich bed of coal was found, and the mineral was sent to market. The article, however, would not sell in the districts of the Midland Counties, where the people had been accustomed to use the Staffordshire coal—which is a much freer burning coal—though of this the above gentlemen, who had been accustomed only to the use of bituminous coal, such as that of the Clay Cross colliery, were not aware when they so decidedly pronounced their opinion as to the salable qualities of the latter. Then, the heavy tolls imposed upon coal by the Midland Railway Companies, at that early period, so enhanced the price of the article when conveyed to any considerable distance, that its sale in the metropolis, on which Mr. Stephenson had in a great measure relied, also proved a comparative failure. For some years, therefore, the Clay Cross undertaking did not prove successful; and it was not until new lines of railway had been made between the north and the south, and the tolls on coal were considerably reduced, that the owners of the colliery reaped the fruits of their enterprise.

Mr. Stephenson was not merely satisfied with the Clay Cross venture; but in 1841, he entered into a contract with the owners of lands in the townships of Tapton, Brimington and Newbold for the purchase of the whole of the coal thereunder, and commenced mining operations there also on an extensive scale. At the same time, he erected great lime-works close to the Ambergate station of the Midland Railway, from which, when in full operation, he was able to turn out upwards of 200 tons a day. The limestone was brought on a tramway from the village of Crich, about two or three miles distant from the kilns, the coal wherewith to burn it being supplied from his adjoining Clay Cross colliery. The works were on a scale such as had not before been attempted by any private individual engaged in a similar trade; and their success amply compensated the projector.

Mr. Stephenson's comparative retirement from the profession of railway engineer, led many persons interested in railways to moot the subject of presenting him with a testimonial, in consideration of the eminent services which he had rendered to the public, by contributing so greatly to the establishment of this new power. Railways had now been in full work for ten years, and, having struggled through trials and difficulties almost unparalleled, were now established as the chief mode of internal communication throughout Great Britain; they had also been largely adopted by Belgium, France, and the United States. Twenty-five hundred miles of railway, almost all of them double lines, had been laid down in these islands alone, connecting all the principal towns and provinces with the capital; joining in a more close and intimate union the various branches of the body politic, commercial and literary, with that great centre. Many new and important branches of industry had been entirely created by this new agency; and a stimulus had been given to all the existing departments of trade, as well as to the development of the bountiful resources of the soil, by which largely increased employment had been secured to the laboring classes. Some sixty millions of money had already been expended in forming railways; and this large investment was now returning about five millions yearly to the capitalists, for re-investment and further extension of the system. This vast iron revolution had been accomplished in a period of about ten years. So extraordinary a movement, powerfully affecting as it did all our social and commercial relations, and coming so closely home to the interests of every member of the community, had never before been experienced in our nation's history.

George Stephenson, above all others, had been the zealous propagandist of this great change. His ingenuity and perseverance had made the railway system practicable. His zeal and devotion had secured its success. What more natural than that some public mark of honor should be conferred upon him in recognition of his wonderful discovery? for such, in point of fact, it was. Had he been a Frenchman or a Belgian, the honors of the State would have been showered upon him. Had he invented a shell or a bullet to the satisfaction of the Board of Ordnance, the British Government might have recognized him. Perhaps, had he pointed out to the country gentlemen some improved mode of patching up the old common roads and preserving turnpike trusts, he might have been honored and rewarded as Macadam was. But who would now venture to compare the improver of turnpikes with the inventor of railroads, looking at the public benefits conferred by the respective systems? Yet Mr. Stephenson, though he had solved the great social problem of rapid and easy transit from place to place—the subject of so much parliamentary inquiry—not only remained without any parliamentary recognition of his distinguished public services, but almost the whole of his professional career was a prolonged struggle against the obstructiveness of the legislature. Certain it is, that he never contemplated receiving any reward or recognition from that quarter. Amidst all his labors, it was the last thing that would have crossed his mind; and it is well that our greatest men in England can undertake questions of public utility, and carry them to a successful issue in the face of stupendous difficulties, without the stimulus of an expected medal or riband, or any Government reward or recognition whatsoever. Mr. Stephenson was, however, on one occasion, offered a piece of Government patronage, thus recorded by his son:—"I remember my father once refusing to accept from the Government what they thought a piece of valuable patronage; and it was almost, if not absolutely, the only piece of patronage they ever offered him. It was the appointment of a walking postman between Chesterfield and Chatsworth, who was to walk eight miles there and eight miles back every day with the letter-bags, and who was to receive the immense stipend of twelve shillings a week!" *

A movement was made by some leading railway men, in February, 1839, under the presidency of Alderman Thompson, M. P., to offer to Mr. Stephenson some public testimonial in recognition of his distinguished services. A committee was formed, and an appeal was made to the public for subscriptions.

A list was opened, but filled slowly. Many other engineers, who had been his pupils, and numerous resident engineers, who had superintended the execution of the works planned by him, had received public recognition of their services in many forms. But it was, perhaps, felt, that while these were generally of a local character, it was fitting that the testimonial to Mr. Stephenson, if offered at all, should express, in some measure, the gratitude of the British nation. No active effort was, however, made by the committee calculated to evoke any such result. The scheme then dropped, and the Stephenson Testimonial was not resumed for several years.

But although no testimonial was presented to him, Mr. Stephenson was not without honor amongst his fellow citizens. His name was everywhere mentioned with admiration and respect. Thus Sir Robert Peel, in the address delivered by him on opening the public library and reading-room at Tamworth, prominently alluded to him as one of the most striking proofs that the heights of science are not inaccessible to even the humblest mechanic. "Look around," said he, "at this neighborhood. Look in this very town, and who is the man that is now engaged in extensive works, for the purpose of bringing coal and lime under your immmediate command? Mr. Stephenson, the engineer. Mr. Stephenson, I am assured, worked three years as a boy in the meanest capacity in a colliery at Newcastle. He saved 100*l.* by mending the watches of his fellow workmen for

* Reply of Robert Stephenson, Esq., M. P., President of the Institution of Civil Engineers, to Observations in the Second Report of the Postmaster-General, May 20th, 1856.

half-a-crown apiece; and he devoted that 100*l.* to provision for his indigent parents,* and set out with a light heart and conscience for the purpose of accumulating more. The result has been, that he presents a daily example of encouragement to our eyes, and is brought within our immediate contemplation in this very town."

From an early period Mr. Stephenson manifested a lively interest in the cause of Mechanics' Institutes. He could not but remember the difficulties which he had early encountered in gathering together his own scientific knowledge—the want of books from which he had suffered, and the miserable character of the only instruction then within the reach of the working classes in the smaller towns and villages. Since his youth, however, a new spirit had arisen on the subject of popular education. The exertions of Bell and Lancaster had led to the establishment of greatly improved agencies for the education of the children of the poor; and earnest efforts were also being made to admit the adult working classes to the benefits of elementary and scientific instruction by means of Mechanics' Institutes. There were thus few manufacturing towns into which the spirit of Birkbeck and Brougham had not, to some extent, penetrated, exhibiting itself in the establishment of Working Men's Institutions, with their organization of classes, lectures and libraries. While residing at Newcastle in 1824, shortly after he had commenced his locomotive foundry in Forth Street, Mr. Stephenson was requested to preside at a public meeting held in that town for the purpose of establishing a Mechanics' Institute. The meeting was held; but George Stephenson was a man comparatively unknown even in Newcastle at that time, and his name failed to summon an "influential" attendance. The local papers scarcely noticed the pro-

* This is not quite correct. Although Mr. Stephenson was not sparing in pecuniary assistance to his parents, the reason for his early thrift and industry in watch-cleaning was, as he himself stated, that he might be able to send his son to school, and furnish him with the elements of a sound education.

ceedings; yet the Mechanics' Institute was founded, and struggled into existence. Years passed, and George Stephenson had become a famous name. He had established a new power in the world, which the greatest were ready to recognize. Beyond the bounds of his own country, his genius was acknowledged. Belgium had given him a national welcome, and King Leopold had invested him with the Order of Knighthood of that kingdom. It was now, therefore, felt to be no small honor to secure Mr. Stephenson's presence at any public meetings held for the promotion of popular education. Amongst the Mechanics' Institutes in his immediate neighborhood at Tapton, were those of Belper and Chesterfield; and at their soirées he was a frequent, and always a highly welcome, visitor. On those occasions he loved to tell them of the difficulties which had early beset him through want of knowledge, and of the means by which he had overcome them —always placing in the first rank perseverance. This was his grand text—PERSEVERE. There was manhood in the very word. And he would remind them of their unspeakable advantages as mechanics, compared with the workmen of his early days. They had books; but he remembered the time "when a good library of books would have been worth worlds to him."

A new stimulus was given to the Mechanics' Institutes of Derbyshire in 1841, by the adoption of visits to each other by railway. The civilizing and educating influences of this great machine were thus carried on under Mr. Stephenson's own auspices, and almost at his very door. The Mechanics' Institution of Belper paid a visit, three hundred strong, to that of Chesterfield; and in a few weeks the latter returned the visit with interest. On both occasions Mr. Stephenson was the hero of the day. One after another the speakers acknowledged that to him, the most distinguished mechanic living, they had been indebted for the improved means of transit, which enabled them thus to hold intercourse with each other. Mr. Stephenson was, of course, a speaker on both occasions, and threw out many shrewd remarks and suggestions for the consideration of his friends, the young mechanics present. After describing the great difficulties which he had to encounter in connection with the locomotive, he said, "but that has been little, compared with the difficulty I have had in the management of man. I have found the engineering of railways to be light work, compared with the engineering of men." A favorite object of his observations at those mechanics' meetings was, the properties of the crank, and the mistakes which mechanics had so often made with respect to it. At Chesterfield he concluded with a piece of sound practical advice: "As an encouragement to young mechanics, I may state to them, that I commenced my mechanical career with very scanty means; and by close application and study, I have succeeded in establishing a manufactory which sends machinery to almost every kingdom in Europe. I may add, that nothing conduces, in my opinion, so much to the success in life of a thinking mechanic as sobriety, coupled with a steady and persevering application to his employment; never, however, in the midst of all his engagements, forgetting to contribute, by every means in his power, to the comfort of his wife and family." At both Belper and Chesterfield, Mr. Stephenson invited the members, at any time when they thought they had found out any new invention, to bring their discovery to him, and he would always be ready to give them his opinion and assistance. This invitation got into the newspapers, and the consequence was, that he was very shortly flooded with letters, soliciting his opinion as to inventions which his correspondents thought they had made. He soon found that he had set himself a formidable task, and had roused the speculative and inventive faculties of the working men of nearly all England. He was, however, ready on all occasions to give his advice; and he frequently subscribed sums of money to enable struggling inventors to bring their schemes to a fair trial, when he considered them to be useful and feasible.

Though Mr. Stephenson had retired from the more active pursuit of his profession, he was, in 1844, appointed engineer to the Whitehaven and Maryport Railway, in conjunction with his friend and former assistant, Mr. John Dixon. The line was actively promoted by Lord Lowther and the members for the county, and Mr. Stephenson consented to act—his name being regarded as a tower of strength in that district. This, however, was the only new project with which he was connected in that year.

He was also, about the same time, elected chairman of the Yarmouth and Norwich Railway, a line in which he took much interest, and had invested a good deal of money. At the meetings of the Company, he confessed that he felt he was more in his place as a railway engineer than as a railway chairman; but as he and his friends held about three-fourths of the shares in the concern, he felt bound to stand by it until its completion, which was effected in April, 1844. This line, like most others, was greatly fleeced by the land owners of the district, who sought to extort the most exorbitant prices for their land. One instance may be cited. A Mr. Tuck claimed 9000*l.* as compensation for severance, in addition to the very high price allowed for the land itself. After a careful investigation had been made by a jury, they awarded 850*l.*, or less than one-tenth of the amount claimed. One of the witnesses examined on the part of the land owners, was Mr. R. H. Gurney, the banker of Norwich, who exhibited a hatred of railways equalled only by that of Colonel Sibthorpe. On his cross-examination he said: "I have never traveled by rails; I am an enemy to them; I have opposed the Norwich Railway; I have left a sum of money in my will to oppose railroads!" Another witness, a Mr. Driver, admitted that, on a previous occasion, he had estimated the value of certain land required for a railway at from 35,000*l.* to 40,000*l.*, for which a jury had awarded only 2,000*l.* Such was the extortion to which those early railways were subjected, and which, in one way or another, has fallen ultimately upon the public.

Mr. Stephenson had been looking forward with much interest

to the completion of the East Coast route to Scotland as far as his native town of Newcastle-upon-Tyne. He had done much to form that route, both by constructing the lines from Derby to York, and by bringing before the public his plan for carrying the main line northward to Edinburgh. A bill with this object was again brought before Parliament in 1844. On the 18th of June, in that year, the Newcastle and Darlington line—an important link of the great main highway to the north—was completed and publicly opened—thus connecting the Thames and the Tyne by a continuous line of railway. On that day, Mr. Stephenson, Mr. Hudson, and a distinguished party of railway men, traveled by express train from London to Newcastle in about nine hours. It was a great event, and was worthily celebrated. The population of Newcastle held holiday; and a banquet held in the Assembly Rooms the same evening assumed the form of an ovation to Mr. Stephenson and his son. Thirty years before, George Stephenson, in the capacity of a workman, had been laboring at the construction of his first locomotive in the immediate neighborhood. By slow and laborious steps, he had worked his way on, dragging the locomotive into notice, and raising himself in public estimation. He had now, at length, established the great railway system, and came back amongst his townsmen to receive their greeting.

The Honorable Mr. Liddell, M. P., whose father, Lord Ravensworth, had helped and encouraged George Stephenson to make his first locomotive at Killingworth, appropriately occupied the chair, and, in introducing Mr. Stephenson to the meeting, alluded to the recent rapid progress of railroads, and especially to the last great event in their history—the opening of an uninterrupted railway communication from the Thames to the Tyne—whereby "he had been enabled to take part in the proceedings of the House of Commons at a late hour in the night, and to arrive at Newcastle in time for an early dinner on the following day. This wonderful achievement was the result of the capital, skill and enterprise of England; and if he (Mr. Liddell) felt proud of this new triumph of his country, what must be the feelings of that illustrious individual now sitting amongst them, who, though born in humble circumstances, had, by the force of his genius and industry, so distinguished himself as to hand down the name of Stephenson to everlasting fame! He would not have referred to the position from which Mr. Stephenson had sprung, were it not that he himself, so far from being ashamed of his origin, was in the habit of alluding to it; and if Mr. Stephenson took a pride in the humility of his birth, surely his countrymen might be proud of the obscurity of his youth, as compared with the prominence of his present position! He was happy to add, that, distinguished as he was by his genius and his deeds, his sterling honesty reflected higher honor upon George Stephenson than even those rare abilities with which he was endowed by the Almighty." Referring to the speech of Prebendary Townsend, Mr. Liddell stated that, "by the construction of a railway from London to Folkestone and Dover, thousands of persons had been enabled to spend their last Whitsuntide holidays at Calais and Boulogne, among their 'natural enemies;' and when such was the case, the two nations would in time be purged of their senseless antipathies, and learn to look upon each other, not as foreigners and foes, but members in common of the great human family. Mr. Stephenson, therefore, might be looked upon as the great pacificator of the age. And yet, a few years ago, he was but a working engineman at a colliery! But he was a man not only of talent, but of genius. Happily, also, he was a man of industry and of character. He constructed the first successful engine that traveled by its own spontaneous power over an iron railroad; and on such a road, and by such an engine, a communication had now been established between London and Newcastle. The author of this system of traveling had lived long enough for his fame, but not long enough for his country. He had reared to himself a monument more durable than brass or marble, and based it on a foundation whereon it would rest unshaken by the storms of time."

Mr. Stephenson, in replying to Mr. Liddell's complimentary speech, took occasion to deliver that memorable autobiography to which we have already referred; and, at the risk of repetition, we venture to insert it here in a more complete form, both on account of its extreme interest, and because of the valuable practical lessons it contains. "As the honorable member," said he, "has referred to the engineering efforts of my early days, it may not be amiss if I say a few words to you on that subject, more especially for the encouragement of my younger friends. Mr. Liddell has told you that in my early days I worked at an engine at a coal-pit. I had then to work early and late, and my employment was a most laborious one. For about twenty years I had often to rise to my labor at one and two o'clock in the morning, and worked until late at night. Time rolled on, and I had the happiness to make some improvements in engine work. The company will be gratified when I tell them that the first locomotive that I made was at Killingworth colliery. The owners were pleased with what I had done in the collieries; and I then proposed to make an engine to work upon the smooth rails. It was with Lord Ravensworth's money that my first locomotive was built. Yes, Lord Ravensworth and his partners were the first gentlemen to entrust me with money to make a locomotive. That was more than thirty years ago; and we first called it 'My Lord.' I then stated to some of my friends, now living, that those high velocities with which we are now so familiar, would, sooner or later, be attained, and that there was no limit to the speed of such an engine, provided the works could be made to stand; but nobody would believe me at that time. The engines could not perform the high velocities now reached, when they were first invented; but, by their superior construction, an immense speed is now capable of being obtained. In what has been done under my management, the merit is only in part my own. Throughout, I have been most ably seconded and assisted by my son. In the early period of my career, and when he was a little boy, I felt how deficient I was in education, and made up my mind that I would put him to a good school. I determined that he should have as liberal a training as I could afford to give him. I was, however, a poor man; and how do you think I managed? I betook myself to mending my neighbors' clocks and watches at night, after my daily labor was done. By this means I saved money, which I put by; and, in course of time, I was thus enabled to give my son a good education. While quite a boy he assisted me, and became a companion to me. He got an appointment as under-viewer at Killingworth; and at nights, when we came home, we worked together at our engineering. I got leave from my employers to go from Killingworth to lay down a railway at Hetton, and next to Darlington for a like purpose; and I finished both railways. After that, I went to Liverpool to plan a line to Manchester. The directors of that undertaking thought ten miles an hour would be a maximum speed for the locomotive engine; and I pledged myself to attain that speed. I said I had no doubt the locomotive might be made to go much faster, but we had better be moderate at the beginning. The directors said I was quite right; for if, when they went to Parliament, I talked of going at a greater rate than ten miles an hour, I should put a cross on the concern! It was not an easy task for me to keep the engine down to ten miles an hour; but it must be done, and I did my best. I had to place myself in the most unpleasant of all positions—the witness-box of a parliamentary committee. I was not long in it, I assure you, before I began to wish for a hole to creep out at. I could not find words to satisfy either the committee or myself; or even to make them understand my meaning. Some said, 'He's a foreigner.' 'No,' others replied; 'he's mad.' But I put up with every rebuff, and went on with my plans, determined not to be put down. Assistance gradually increased; great improvements were made in the locomotive; until to-day, a train which started from London in the morning, has brought me in the afternoon to my native soil, and enabled me to meet again many faces with which I am familiar, and which I am exceedingly pleased to see once more."

After the opening of this railway, the completion of the East Coast line, by effecting a connection between Newcastle and Berwick, was again revived; and Mr. Stephenson, who had already identified himself with the question, and was intimately acquainted with every foot of the ground, was called upon to assist the promoters with his judgment and experience.

By this time a strong popular opinion had arisen in favor of atmospheric railways. Many engineers avowedly supported them in preference to locomotive lines, and Mr. Brunel had considerable influence in determining the views of many members of Parliament on the subject. Amongst others, Lord Howick took up the question of atmospheric as opposed to locomotive railways, and, possessing great local influence, he succeeded, in 1844, in forming a powerful combination of the landed gentry of Northumberland in favor of an atmospheric line through that county. Mr. Stephenson could not brook the idea of seeing the locomotive, for which he had fought so many stout battles, pushed to one side by the atmospheric system, and that in the very county in which its great powers had been first developed. Nor did he relish the appearance of Mr. Brunel as the engineer of Lord Howick's atmospheric railway, in opposition to the line which had occupied his thoughts and been the object of his strenuous advocacy for so many years. When Mr. Stephenson first met Mr. Brunel in Newcastle, he good-naturedly shook him by the collar, and asked "what business he had north of the Tyne?" Mr. Stephenson gave him to understand that they were to have a fair stand-up fight for the ground, and shaking hands before the battle, like Englishmen, they parted in good humor. A public meeting was held at Newcastle in the following December, when, after a full discussion of the merits of the respective plans, Mr. Stephenson's line was almost unanimously adopted as the best.

The rival projects went before Parliament in 1845, and a severe contest ensued. The display of ability and tactics on both sides was great. Mr. Hudson and the Messrs. Stephenson were the soul of the movement in support of the locomotive, and Lord Howick and Mr. Brunel in behalf of the atmospheric system. The locomotive again triumphed: Mr. Stephenson's coast line secured the approval of Parliament, and the shareholders in the atmospheric company were happily saved from expending their capital in the perpetration of an egregious blunder; for, only a few years later, the atmospheric system was everywhere abandoned.

This was one of the very few projects in which Mr. Stephenson was professedly concerned in the mad railway session of 1845; and it was the last great parliamentary contest in which he took a prominent part. So closely was Mr. Stephenson identified with this measure, and so great was the personal interest which he was known to take in its success, that on the news of the triumph of the bill reaching Newcastle, a sort of general holiday took place, and the workmen belonging to the Stephenson Locomotive Factory, upwards of 800 in number, walked in procession through the principal streets of the town, accompanied by music and banners.

There was still another great work connected with Newcastle and the East Coast route, which Mr. Stephenson projected, but which he did not live to see completed—the High Level Bridge over the Tyne, of which his son Robert was the principal engineer. Mr. R. W. Brandling—to the public spirit and enterprise of whose family the prosperity of Newcastle has been in no small degree indebted, and who first brought to light the strong original genius of George Stephenson in connection with the safety lamp—is entitled to the merit of originating the idea of the High Level Bridge as it was eventually carried out, with a central terminus for the northern railways in the Castle Garth at Newcastle. He first promulgated the plan in 1841; and in the following year it was resolved that Mr. George Stephenson should be consulted as to the most advisable site for the proposed bridge. A prospectus of a High Level Bridge Company was issued in 1843, the names of George Stephenson and George Hudson appearing on the committee of management, Mr. Robert Stephenson being the consulting engineer. The project was eventually taken up by the Newcastle and Darlington Railway Company, and an act for the construction of the bridge was obtained in the session of 1845. The designs of the bridge were Mr. Robert Stephenson's; and the works were executed under the superintendence of Mr. Thomas Harrison, one of Mr. Stephenson's many able assistants. The High Level Bridge is certainly the most magnificent and striking of all the erections to which railways have given birth —more picturesque as an object than the tubular bridge over the Menai Straits, and even more important as a great public work. It has been worthily styled "the King of Railway Structures."

CHAPTER XXXI.

THE RAILWAY MANIA.

THE extension of railways had, up to the year 1844, been effected principally by men of the commercial classes, interested in opening up improved communications between particular towns and districts. The first lines had been bold experiments—many thought them exceedingly rash and unwarranted; they had been reluctantly conceded by the legislature, and were carried out in the face of great opposition and difficulties. At length the locomotive vindicated its power; railways were recognized by men of all classes, as works of great utility; and their vast social as well as commercial advantages forced themselves on the public recognition. What had been regarded as but doubtful speculations, and by many as certain failures, were now ascertained to be beneficial investments, the most successful of them paying from eight to ten per cent. on the share capital expended.

The first railways were, on the whole, well managed. The best men that could be got were appointed to work them. It is true, mistakes were made, and accidents happened; but men did not become perfect because railways had been invented. The men who constructed, and the men who worked the lines, were selected from the general community, consisting of its usual proportion of honest, practical, and tolerably stupid persons. Had it been possible to create a class of perfect men, a sort of railway guardian-angels, directors would only have been too glad to appoint them at good salaries. For with all the mistakes that may have been committed by directors, the jobbing of railway appointments, or the misuse of patronage in selecting the persons to work their lines, has not been charged against them. We have never yet seen a Railway Living advertised for sale; nor have railway situations of an important character been obtainable through "interest." From the first, directors chose the best men they could find for their purpose; and, on the whole, the system, considering the extent of its operations, worked satisfactorily, though admitted to be capable of considerable improvement.

The first boards of directors were composed of men of the highest character and integrity that could be found; and they almost invariably held a large stake in their respective undertakings, sufficient to give them a lively personal interest in their successful management. They were also men who had not taken up the business of railway direction as a trade, but who entered upon railway enterprise for its own sake, looking to its eventual success for an adequate return on their large investments.

The first shareholders were principally confined to the manufacturing districts—the capitalists of the metropolis as yet holding aloof, and prophesying disaster to all concerned in railway projects.* The stock exchange looked askance upon them, and it was with difficulty that respectable brokers could be found to do business in the shares. But when the lugubrious anticipations of the city men were found to be so completely falsified by the results, when, after the lapse of years, it was ascertained that railway traffic rapidly increased and dividends steadily improved, a change came over the spirit of the London capitalists: they then invested largely in railways, and the shares became a leading branch of business on the stock exchange. Speculation fairly

* The leading "city men" looked with great suspicion on the first railway projects, having no faith in their success. In 1835, the solicitorship of the Brighton Railway (then projected) was offered to a city firm of high standing, and refused—one of the partners assigning as a reason that "the coaches would drive the railway trains off the road in a month!"

set in; brokers prominently called the attention of investors to railway stock; and the prices of shares in the principal lines rose to nearly double their original value.

The national wealth soon poured into this new channel. A stimulus was given to the projection of further lines, the shares in the most favorite of which came out at a premium, and became the subject of immediate traffic on 'change. The premiums constituted their sole worth in the estimation of the speculators. As titles to a future profitable investment, the tens of thousands of shares created and issued in 1844 and 1845 were not in the slightest degree valued. What were they worth to hold for a time, and then to sell? what profit could be made by the venture?—that was the sole consideration.

A share-dealing spirit was thus evoked; and a reckless gambling for premiums set in, which completely changed the character and objects of railway enterprise. The public outside the stock exchange shortly became infected with the same spirit, and many people, utterly ignorant of railways, knowing and caring nothing about their great national uses, but hungering and thirsting after premiums, rushed eagerly into the vortex of speculation. They applied for allotments, and subscribed for shares in lines, of the engineering character or probable traffic of which they knew nothing. "Shares! shares!" became the general cry. The ultimate issue of the projects themselves was a matter of no moment. The multitude were bitten by the universal rage for acquiring sudden fortunes without the labor of earning them. Provided they could but obtain allotments which they could sell at a premium, and put the profit—often the only capital they possessed *—into their pockets, it was enough for them. The mania was not confined to the precincts of the stock exchange,

* The Marquis of Clanricarde brought under the notice of the House of Lords in 1845, that one Charles Guernsey, the son of a charwoman, and a clerk in a broker's office at 12*s*. a week, had his name down as a subscriber for shares in the London and York line, for 52,000*l* Doubtless, he had been made useful for the purpose by the brokers, his employers.

but infected all ranks throughout the country. Share markets were established in the provincial towns, where people might play their stakes as on a roulette table. The game was open to all—to the workman, who drew his accumulation of small earnings out of the savings' bank to try a venture in shares; to the widow and spinster of small means, who had up to that time blessed God that their lot had lain between poverty and riches, but were now seized by the infatuation of becoming suddenly rich; to the professional man, who, watching the success of others, at length scorned the moderate gains of his calling, and rushed into speculation. The madness spread everywhere. It embraced merchants and manufacturers, gentry and shopkeepers, clerks in public offices and loungers at the clubs. Noble lords were pointed out as "stags;" there were even clergymen who were characterized as "bulls;" and amiable ladies who had the reputation of "bears," in the share markets. The few quiet men who remained uninfluenced by the speculation of the time, were, in not a few cases, even reproached for doing injustice to their families, in declining to help themselves from the stores of wealth that were poured out all around.

Folly and knavery were, for a time, completely in the ascendant. The sharpers of society were let loose, and jobbers and schemers became more and more plentiful. They threw out railway schemes as mere lures to catch the unwary. They fed the mania with a constant succession of new projects. The railway papers became loaded with their advertisements. The post-office was scarcely able to distribute the multitude of prospectuses and circulars which they issued. For the time their popularity was immense. They rose like froth into the upper heights of society, and the flunky Fitz Plushe, by virtue of his supposed wealth, sat amongst peers and was idolized. Then was the harvest-time for scheming lawyers, parliamentary agents, engineers, surveyors and traffic-takers, who were alike ready to take up any railway scheme however desperate, and to prove any amount of traffic even where none existed. The traffic in the credulity of their dupes was, however, the great fact that mainly concerned them, and of the profitable character of which there could be no doubt. Many of them saw well enough the crash that was coming, and diligently made use of the madness while it served their turn.

Even men of reputed sagacity in commercial undertakings, who had accumulated their wealth patiently and honestly, and who seemed most unlikely to risk their capital in such a mania, were drawn into the irresistible vortex, and invested in the new schemes in the hope of realizing profits more rapidly, or obtain ing a higher interest for their money.

Parliament, whose previous conduct in connection with railway legislation was so open to reprehension, interposed no check —attempted no remedy. On the contrary, it helped to intensify the evils arising from this unseemly state of things. Many of its members were themselves involved in the mania, and as much interested in its continuance as were the vulgar herd of money-grubbers. The railway prospectuses now issued—unlike the original Liverpool and Manchester, and London and Birmingham schemes—were headed by peers, baronets, landed proprietors, and strings of M. Ps. Thus, it was found in 1845, that not fewer than 157 members of Parliament were on the list of new companies as subscribers for sums ranging from 291,000*l.* downwards! The projectors of new lines even came to boast of their parliamentary strength, and of the number of votes which they could command in "the House." The influence which landowners had formerly brought to bear upon Parliament in resisting railways when called for by the public necessities, was now employed to carry measures of a far different kind, originated by cupidity, knavery and folly. But these gentlemen had discovered by this time that railways were as a golden mine to them. They sat at railway boards, sometimes selling to themselves their own land at their own price, and paying themselves with the money of the unfortunate shareholders. Others used the railway mania as a convenient, and, to themselves, comparatively inexpensive mode of purchasing constituencies. It was strongly suspected that honorable members adopted what Yankee legislators call "log-rolling," that is, "You help me to roll my log, and I help you to roll yours." At all events, it is matter of fact, that, through parliamentary influence, many utterly ruinous branches and extensions projected during the mania, calculated only to benefit the inhabitants of a few miserable old boroughs accidentally omitted from schedule A, were authorized in the memorable sessions of 1844 and 1845.

This boundless speculation of course gave abundant employment to the engineers. They were found ready to attach their names to the most daring and foolish projects—railways through hills, across arms of the sea, over or under great rivers, spanning valleys at great heights or boring their way under the ground, across barren moors, along precipices, over bogs, and through miles of London streets. One line was projected direct from Leeds to Liverpool, which, if constructed, would involve a tunnel, or a deep rock cutting through the hills, twenty miles long. No scheme was so mad that it did not find an engineer, so called, ready to indorse it, and give it currency. Many of these, even men of distinction, sold the use of their names to the projectors. A thousand guineas was the price charged by one gentleman for the use of his name; and fortunate were the solicitors considered who succeeded in bagging an engineer of reputation for their prospectus.

Mr. Stephenson was anxiously entreated to lend his name in this way, but he invariably refused. Had he been less scrupulous, he might, without any trouble, have thus earned an enormous income; but he had no desire to accumulate a fortune without labor and without honor. He himself never speculated in shares. When he was satisfied as to the merits of any line, he subscribed for so much capital in the undertaking, and held on, neither buying nor selling. At a time when the shares in most of the lines in which he held, were selling at high premiums, some sagacious friends, foreseeing the inevitable panic, urged him to realize. His answer was, "No: I subscribed for those shares to hold during my lifetime, not to speculate with." Thus, all the railway stock that he had subscribed for, continued in his possession until his death, although much of it by that time had become greatly depreciated in value in consequence of over-speculation in railways. In 1844 and 1845 he conscientiously stood aloof, and endeavored, but in vain, to deter those who were imperiling the system which he had so laboriously worked out, from engaging in these rash and worthless schemes. Deputations, headed by lords and members of Parliament, waited upon him, and entreated him to act as consulting engineer for their lines. Instead of complying, he entreated them to desist, pointing out the ruinous consequences of their procedure.

During 1845, his son's offices in George Street, Westminster, were crowded with persons of various conditions seeking interviews, and presented very much the appearance of the levee of a minister of state. The Railway King, surrounded by an admiring group of followers, was often a prominent feature there; and a still more interesting person, in the estimation of many, was George Stephenson, dressed in black, his coat of somewhat old-fashioned cut, with square pockets in the tails. He wore a white neckcloth, and a large bunch of seals was suspended from his watch-ribbon. Altogether, he presented an appearance of health, intelligence and good humor, that rejoiced one to look upon in that sordid, selfish and eventually ruinous saturnalia of railway speculation.

Being still the consulting engineer for several of the older companies, he necessarily appeared before Parliament in support of their branches and extensions. In 1845, his name was associated with that of his son as the engineer for the Southport and Preston Junction. In the same session he gave evidence in favor of the Syston and Peterborough branch of the Midland Railway; but his principal attention was confined to the promotion of the line from Newcastle to Berwick, in which he had never ceased to take the deepest interest. At the same time he was engaged in examining and reporting upon certain foreign lines of considerable importance.

Powers were granted by Parliament, in 1845, to construct not less than 2883 miles of new railways in Britain, at an expenditure of about forty-four millions sterling! Yet the mania was not appeased; for in the following session of 1846 applications were made to Parliament for powers to raise 389,000,000*l.* sterling for the construction of further lines; and powers were actually conceded for forming 4790 miles (including 60 miles of tunnels), at a cost of about 120,000,000*l.* sterling! * During this session, Mr. Stephenson appeared as engineer for only one new line—the Buxton, Macclesfield, Congleton and Crewe Railway; and for three branch lines in connection with existing companies, for which he had long acted as engineer. During the same session, all the leading professional men were fully occupied, some of them appearing as consulting engineers for upwards of thirty lines each!

The course adopted by Parliament in dealing with the multitude of railway bills applied for during the prevalence of the mania, was as irrational as it proved to be unfortunate. The want of foresight displayed by both houses in obstructing the railway system so long as it was based upon sound commercial principles, was only equalled by the fatal facility with which they subsequently granted railway projects based on the wildest speculation. Parliament interposed no check, laid down no principle, furnished no guidance, for the conduct of railway projectors, but left every company to select its own locality, determine

* On the 17th November, 1845, Mr Spackman published a list of the lines *projected*, (many of which were not afterwards prosecuted), from which it appeared that there were then 620 new railway projects before the public, requiring a capital of 563,203,000*l.*

its own line and fix its own gauge. No regard was paid to the claims of existing companies, which had already expended so large an amount in the formation of useful railways. Speculators were left at full liberty to project and carry out lines almost parallel with theirs. In 1844, Lord Dalhousie, who then presided at the Board of Trade, endeavored, in a series of able reports, to give a proper direction to legislation on the subject of railways; but in vain. Both houses viewed with jealousy any interference with the powers of the committees; Lord Dalhousie's recommendations were entirely disregarded, and an unlimited scope was afforded to competition for railway bills. A powerful stimulus was thus given to the existing spirit of speculation, which rose to a fearful height, in 1845, turning nearly the whole nation into gamblers.

The House of Commons became thoroughly influenced by the prevailing excitement; and even the Board of Trade itself began to favor the views of the fast school of engineers. In the "Report on the Lines projected in the Manchester and Leeds District," * they promulgated some remarkable views respecting gradients, declaring themselves in favor of the "undulating system." Thus they cited the case of the Lickey incline on the Birmingham and Gloucester Railway, as "a conclusive proof that a gradient of 1 in 37½ for a length of two miles may be worked by the aid of an engine constructed for the purpose, without serious inconvenience to an extensive traffic;"—that "gradients of from 1 in 50 to 1 in 100 are perfectly practicable to the ordinary locomotive engine, with moderate loads;—that lines of an undulating character "which have gradients of 1 in 70 or 1 in 80 distributed over them in short lengths, may be positively *better* lines, *i. e.*, *more susceptible of cheap and expeditious working*, than others which have nothing steeper than 1 in 100 or 1 in 120!" They concluded by reporting in favor of the line which exhibited

* Dated the 4th February, 1845.

the most gradients and the sharpest curves, chiefly on the ground that it could be constructed for less money.

Sir Robert Peel took occasion, when speaking in favor of the continuance of the Railways Department of the Board of Trade, to advert to this Report in the House of Commons on the 4th of March following, as containing "a novel and highly important view on the subject of gradients, which, he was certain, never could have been taken by any Committee of the House of Commons, however intelligent;" and he might have added that the more intelligent, the less likely they were to arrive at any such conclusions. When Mr. Stephenson saw this report of the premier's speech in the newspapers of the following morning, he went forthwith to his son, and asked him to write a letter to Sir Robert Peel on the subject. He saw clearly that if these views were adopted, the utility and economy of railways would be seriously curtailed. "These members of Parliament," said he, "are now as much disposed to exaggerate the powers of the locomotive, as they were to under-estimate them but a few years ago." Mr. Robert Stephenson wrote a letter for his father's signature, embodying the views which he so strongly entertained as to the importance of flat gradients, and referring to the experiments conducted by him many years before, in proof of the great loss of working power which was incurred on a line of steep as compared with easy gradients. It was clear, from the tone of Sir Robert Peel's speech in a subsequent debate,* that he had carefully read and considered Mr. Stephenson's practicable observations on the subject; for he then took the opportunity of observing that "he thought there was too great a tendency to adopt the shortest lines without reference to gradients. Though, in recent instances, unfavorable gradients had been overcome by the construction of new engines, he doubted whether there was not an unprofitable expenditure of power in such cases—whether the

* Debate on Mr. Morison's resolutions, March 20th, 1845

mechanical action of locomotive engines was not materially interfered with by unfavorable gradients—and whether the exertions made to diminish the gradients, and to run as nearly as possible on a level, would not be amply repaid. He was alluding, not to the shortest lines merely with regard to *distance*, but to the shortest lines in point of *time*." On the whole, however, he declared himself favorable to direct lines, and cited the case of the Trent Valley Railway (which placed Tamworth on a main line) as one that "was about to be established by universal consent." Sir Robert's conclusions were not very decisive on the question; and it was not quite clear whether he was in favor of direct lines of unfavorable gradients, or somewhat longer lines of flat gradients. There was doubtless "much to be said on both sides;" and the committees were left to decide as they thought proper. Direct lines were very much in vogue at the time. There were "Direct Manchester," "Direct Exeter," "Direct York," and, indeed, new direct lines between most of the large towns. The Marquis of Bristol, speaking in favor of the "Direct Norwich and London" project, at a public meeting at Haverhill, said, "if necessary, they might *make a tunnel beneath his very drawing-room*, rather than be defeated in their undertaking!" How different was the spirit which influenced these noble lords but a few years before!

The Board of Trade, seeing clearly the disadvantages of the difference of gauge between the Great Western and the adjacent lines, recommended uniformity, and that the narrow gauge should be adopted as the national one. Again the House of Commons disregarded their advice. The Committee passed both broad and narrow gauge bills indiscriminately. The Board also reported against the atmospheric system of working. But Sir Robert Peel and other amateur railway men declared themselves strongly in its favor;* and numerous acts empowering the construction

* In the debate on Mr. Shaw's motion for a committee to inquire into the practicability of the atmospheric system, Sir Robert Peel, in supporting the resolution, said: "You will observe that my impression is strongly in favor of the atmospheric system. I deeply

of atmospheric lines were passed during the session. The result of the whole was, a tissue of legislative bungling, involving enormous loss to the public. Railway bills were granted in heaps. Two hundred and seventy-two additional acts were passed in 1846.* Some authorized the construction of lines running almost parallel to existing railways, in order to afford the public "the benefits of unrestricted competition." Locomotive and atmospheric lines, broad-gauge and narrow-gauge lines, were granted without hesitation. One of the grand points with the red-tapists, was compliance with standing orders. The real merits of the lines applied for, were of comparatively little moment. Committees decided without judgment, and without discrimination; it was a scramble for bills in which the most unscrupulous were the most successful. As an illustration of the legislative folly of the period, Mr. Robert Stephenson, speaking at Toronto, in Upper Canada, some years later, adduced the following instances: "There was one district through which it was proposed to run two lines, and there was no other difficulty between them than the simple rivalry that, if one got a charter, the other might also. But here, where the Committee might have given both, they gave neither. In another instance, two lines were projected through a

lament the loss of one of the gentlemen (Mr. Jacob Samuda) who were the patentees of this system, for his great acuteness tended much to the success of this very ingenious invention." March 14th, 1845.

* The following is a summary of the railway acts passed in the three sessions of 1844, 1845, and 1846:

Years.	Number of Acts passed.	Length of New Railways authorized.	New Railway Capital authorized
		Miles.	£
1844	48	797	14,793,994
1845	120	2,883	43,844,907
1846	272	4,790	121,500,000
Total,	440	8,470	180,138,901

barren country, and the Committee gave the one which afforded the least accommodation to the public. In another, where two lines were projected to run, merely to shorten the time by a few minutes, leading through a mountainous country, the Committee gave both. So that, where the Committee might have given both, they gave neither, and where they should have given neither, they gave both."

The frightful waste of money in conducting railway proceedings, before and after they reached the parliamentary committees, was matter of notoriety. An instance has been mentioned of an utterly impracticable line, which never got so far as the House of Commons, where the solicitor's bill for projecting and conducting the scheme amounted to 82,000*l.* It was estimated by Mr. Laing of the Board of Trade, and the estimate was confirmed by Mr. Stephenson, that the competition for new lines, many of which were sanctioned by Parliament under the delusion that railway traveling would be thereby cheapened, had led to the expenditure of about three hundred millions sterling, of which seventy millions had been completely thrown away in constructing unnecessary duplicate lines. But Mr. Stephenson further expressed himself of opinion, that this loss of seventy millions very inadequately represented the actual loss in point of convenience, economy, and other circumstances connected with traffic, which the public has sustained from the carelessness of Parliament in railway legislation.

The total cost of obtaining one act amounted to 436,223*l.* Another company expended 480,000*l.* on parliamentary contests in nine years. In another case, 57,000*l.* was expended in one session upon six counsel and twenty solicitors. One barrister, in good practice before the committees, pocketed 38,000*l.* in a single session.

Amongst the many ill effects of the mania, one of the worst was that it introduced a low tone of morality into railway transactions. The bad spirit which had been evoked by it unhappily extended to the commercial classes; and many of the most flagrant swindles of recent times had their origin in the year 1845. Those who had suddenly gained large sums without labor, and also without honor, were too ready to enter upon courses of the wildest extravagance; and a false style of living shortly arose, the poisonous influence of which extended through all classes. Men began to look upon railways as instruments to job with; and they soon became as overrun with jobbers as London charities. Persons, sometimes possessing information respecting railways, but more frequently possessing none, got upon boards for the purpose of promoting their individual objects, often in a very unscrupulous manner; land-owners, to promote branch lines through their property; speculators in shares, to trade upon the exclusive information which they obtained; whilst some directors were appointed through the influence mainly of solicitors, contractors, or engineers, who used them as tools to serve their own ends. In this way the unfortunate proprietors were, in many cases, betrayed, and their property was shamefully squandered, to the further discredit of the railway system.

Among the characters brought prominently into notice by the mania, was the railway navvy. The navvy was now a great man. He had grown rich, was a land-owner, a railway shareholder, sometimes even a member of Parliament; but he was a navvy still. He had imported the characteristics of his class into his new social position. He was always strong, rough, and ready; but withal he was unscrupulous. If there was a stout piece of work to be done, none could carry it out with greater energy, or execute it in better style according to contract—provided he was watched. But the navvy contractor was greatly given to "scamping." He was up to all sorts of disreputable tricks of the trade. In building a tunnel, he would, if he could, use half-baked clay instead of bricks, and put in two courses instead of four. He would scamp the foundations of bridges, use rubble instead of stone sets, and Canadian timber instead of

Memel for his viaducts; but he was greatest of all, perhaps, in the "scamping" of ballast. He had therefore—especially the leviathan navvy—to be very closely watched; and this was generally entrusted to railway inspectors at comparatively small salaries. The consequences were such as might have been anticipated. More bad and dishonest work was executed on the railways constructed in any single year subsequent to the mania, than was to be found on all the Stephenson lines during the preceding twenty years.

The mode of executing railway works, first adopted by Mr. Stephenson on the Stockton and Darlington Railway, and afterwards continued by himself and his son on the other lines with which they were connected, was this: The railway was divided into lengths of from ten to twenty miles, and an assistant engineer, usually an experienced man, on whom reliance could be placed, was appointed to the charge of each length. Under these were sub-engineers, generally young gentlemen who were Mr. Stephenson's apprentices or pupils, gathering valuable experience in his engineering school. Under them again were inspectors, generally of tunneling and masonry; these were, in most cases, experienced workmen. The contracts were let, in the lengths above mentioned, to the best contractors that could be found, according to a schedule of prices—the materials requisite to form the road, including girder bridges, etc., being provided by the company. The detailed plans of the works were prepared after consultation with the assistant engineer, under whose immediate superintendence they were to be executed. The levels were taken and the works set out by the sub-engineers; the greatest pains being taken to secure accuracy. The centres of bridges, and the moulds of difficult masonry, were struck out or tested by them and the inspectors. It was not considered correct, under this system, for the engineers to be on intimate terms with the contractors. They held an entirely independent position, and were free to reject and condemn inferior materials or bad workmanship, which they did not hesitate to do for their own credit's sake. In short, the most vigilant superintendence was maintained, and a high standard of perfection, both in design and execution, was aimed at. And the results were perceptible in the excellent character of the work executed under this system.

The other mode of forming railways became more general after the mania; and under that system the ingenuity of the navvy had full play. The line was let in much larger contracts; sometimes one of the leviathans undertook to construct an entire line of a hundred miles in length, or more. The projecting engineer, in such cases, retained in his own hands a greater share of nominal responsibility — he, himself, however, as well as the resident engineer, being free to engage in other undertakings. The assistant engineers were generally young and inexperienced men of inferior standing. The contractor was left more to himself, both as respected the quality of the materials and the workmanship. The navvy's great object was to execute the work so that it should pass muster, and be well paid for. The contractor in such cases was generally a large capitalist—a man looked up to even by the chief engineer himself. But the worst feature of this system was, that the principal engineer himself was occasionally interested as a partner, and shared in the profits of the contract. In passing the contractor's work, he was virtually passing his own; and in certifying the monthly pay bills, he was a party to the paying of himself. What security was there, under such a system, for either honest work or honest accounts? And what probability was there, that the small sub-engineer—even though cognizant of the facts—would carefully examine the works, or critically scrutinize the accounts which passed under his notice? The consequence was, that a great deal of slop-work was thus executed, the results of which, to some extent, have already appeared in the falling in of tunnels, and the premature decay and failure of viaducts and bridges.

Mr. Stephenson would never tolerate such a system; he put

his own character into his work; he would permit no dishonest scamping of a contractor to escape him; and he could point to his Midland, Manchester, and Leeds, and other great works, and honestly say that he was proud of them. He would even "offer his head," as he did to the Manchester directors, that his tunnel would stand; and he could honestly and without hesitation vouch for the soundness of all his structures.

CHAPTER XXXII.

MR. STEPHENSON'S CONNECTION WITH MR. HUDSON.

AMONGST the most prominent railway men of the day with whom Mr. Stephenson was necessarily brought into frequent and close connection—more especially with reference to the completion of the East Coast route from London to Edinburgh—was Mr. George Hudson of York, afterwards known to the public as "The Railway King." Mr. Stephenson, at the dinner which followed the opening of the York and Scarborough line, in June, 1845, thus described his first introduction to Mr. Hudson: "I happened," said he, "to be visiting Whitby; and whilst I was conversing with a gentleman of that town as to what might be done with regard to the formation of a line from Leeds to York, a few of the Whitby gentlemen came up to introduce me to Mr. Hudson and several York gentlemen. At that time Mr. Hudson was not to be led into a rapid movement with respect to railway speculations. He then looked very coolly at those undertakings; but in time he became so thoroughly convinced of the certainty of great results from improved railway communication, that he stretched out his gigantic arms, and was prepared to go north, south, east or west, wherever a line could be pointed out as being calculated to confer benefit upon the public and the proprietors of railways."

When the first line from Leeds to York was projected, Mr. Hudson was a respectable draper in the latter place. He was esteemed as a shrewd, practical man of business, had accumulated property, was a member of the corporation, and an active politician. As one of the managing directors of the Union Bank, he exercised considerable influence on the commercial affairs of his district. When a provisional committee was formed at York to promote a Leeds line, Mr. Hudson was requested to act as the deputy chairman, Mr. Alderman Meek being the chairman. The reputation which Mr. Stephenson had by this time acquired as a successful railway engineer induced the committee to invite him to act as their engineer. His report in favor of the line connecting York with the Midland system was adopted, and the act was obtained in 1835. When the railway was opened, in 1839, Mr. Hudson had become Lord Mayor of York, and was shortly after elected the chairman of the Company.

Mr. Hudson's views with respect to railways were, at first, extremely moderate, and his intentions were most honorable and praiseworthy. The York and North Midland line was only about thirty miles long; and he interested himself in it chiefly for the purpose of securing for York the advantages of the new system of communication which Mr. Stephenson had devised, and placing it in the most favorable position with reference to any future extension of the main line of railway, north and south. Viewed in this light, Mr. Hudson was one of the greatest local benefactors that the city of York had ever known, and entitled to the gratitude and respect of his fellow citizens.

The railway was not very prosperous at first; and during the years 1840 and 1841 its shares had greatly sunk in value. But Mr. Hudson, when chairman of the Company, somehow contrived to pay improved dividends to the proprietors, who asked no questions. He very soon exhibited a desire to extend the field of his operations, and proceeded to lease the Leeds and Selby Railway at five per cent. That line had been a losing concern; so its owners struck a bargain with Mr. Hudson and sounded his praises in all directions. He increased the dividends on the York and

North Midland shares to ten per cent., and began to be cited as the model of a railway chairman.

He next interested himself in the North Midland Railway, where he appeared in the character of a reformer of abuses. By this time he had secured the friendship of Mr. Stephenson, who had a high opinion of his practical qualities — his indefatigable industry and shrewdness in matters of business. He had abundance of pluck, and was exceedingly self-reliant. The North Midland shares had also gone to a great discount; and the shareholders were very willing to give Mr. Hudson an opportunity of reforming their railway. They elected him a director. His bustling, pushing, persevering character soon gave him an influential position at the board; and he shortly pushed the old directors from their stools. He labored hard, at much personal inconvenience, to help the concern out of its difficulties; and he succeeded. The new directors recognized his power, and elected him their chairman. He had thus conquered an important and influential position as a railway man.

Railway affairs generally revived in 1842; and public confidence in them as profitable investments steadily increased. Mr. Hudson had the benefit of this growing prosperity. The dividends in his lines improved, and the shares rose in value. The Lord Mayor of York began to be quoted as one of the most capable of railway directors. Stimulated by his success and encouraged by his followers, he struck out or supported many new projects—a line to Scarborough, a line to Bradford, lines in the Midland districts, and lines to connect York with Newcastle and Edinburgh. He was elected chairman of the Newcastle and Darlington Railway; and when—in order to complete the continuity of the main line of communication—it was found necessary to secure the Durham Junction, which was an important link in the chain, he and Mr. Stephenson boldly purchased that railway between them, at the price of 88,500*l.* It was an exceedingly fortunate purchase; the liability was afterwards undertaken by the parent Company, to whom it was worth double the money. This act was a successful stroke of policy, and was lauded as it deserved to be. Mr. Hudson, thus encouraged, purchased the Brandling Junction line for 500,000*l.*, in his own name—an operation at the time regarded as equally favorable, though he was afterwards charged with appropriating 1600 of the new shares created for the purchase, when worth 21*l.* premium each. The Great North of England line being completed, Mr. Hudson had thus secured the entire line of communication from York to Newcastle; and the route was opened to the public in June, 1844. On that occasion, Newcastle eulogized Mr. Hudson in its choicest local eloquence; and he was pronounced to be the greatest benefactor the district had ever known.

The adulation which now followed Mr. Hudson would have intoxicated a stronger and more self-denying man. He was pronounced to be the man of the age, and was hailed as THE RAILWAY KING. The grand test by which the shareholders judged him was the dividends that he paid, although subsequent events proved that these dividends were in many cases delusive, intended only "to make things pleasant." The policy, however, had its effect. The shares in all the lines of which he was chairman, went to a premium; and then arose the temptation to create new shares in branch and extension lines, often worthless, which were issued also at a premium. Thus he shortly found himself chairman of nearly 600 miles of railways, extending from Rugby to Newcastle, and at the head of numerous new projects, by means of which paper wealth could be created, as it were, at pleasure. He held in his own hands almost the entire administrative power of the companies over which he presided: he was chairman, board, manager, and all. His devoted admirers, for the time, inspired sometimes by gratitude for past favors, but oftener by the expectation of favors to come, supported him in all his measures. At the meetings of the companies, if any suspicious shareholder ventured to put a question about the accounts, he was summarily put down by the chair, and hissed by the proprietors. Mr. Hudson was voted praises, testimonials, and surplus shares, alike liberally; and scarcely a word against him could find a hearing. He was equally popular outside the circle of railway proprietors. His entertainments at Albert Gate were crowded; and he went his round of visits among the peerage like any prince.

Of course Mr. Hudson was a great authority on railway questions in Parliament, to which the burgesses of Sunderland had sent him. His experience of railways, still little understood, though the subject of so much legislation, gave value and weight to his opinions; and in many respects he was a useful member. During the first years of his membership, he was chiefly occupied in passing the railway bills in which he was more particularly interested. And in the session of 1845, when he was at the height of his power, it was triumphantly said of him, that "he walked quietly through Parliament with some sixteen railway bills under his arm." One of these bills, however, was the subject of a very severe contest—we mean that empowering the construction of the railway from Newcastle to Berwick. It was almost the only bill in which Mr. Stephenson was that year concerned. Mr. Hudson displayed great energy in support of the measure, and he worked hard to insure its success both in and out of Parliament; but he himself attributed the chief merit to Mr. Stephenson. Lord Howick, the leading supporter of the rival atmospheric line, proposed a compromise; but Mr. Stephenson urged its decided rejection. At a meeting of the York, Newcastle and Berwick Company, held shortly after the passing of the bill, Mr. Hudson thus acknowledged the services rendered to them by their consulting engineer: "This Company," said he, "is indeed under great obligations to Mr. Stephenson. Every shareholder, who is about to get his additional share, is almost entirely indebted to him for it. I know, and my brother directors know full well, the resolute and energetic manner in which he held us from any compromise in reference to the Berwick bill. He felt so strong in the integrity of his case, that whenever compromise was named, he always resisted the offer, and urged us to fight the battle on principle. By his indomitable perseverance and high tone of feeling, we were induced to do so, and thus at length we have so successfully accomplished our object."

Mr. Hudson accordingly suggested to the proprietors that they should present some fitting testimonial to Mr. Stephenson, as a recognition of the important services which he had rendered to them, as well as to the railway interest generally. With the same object, he appealed to the proprietors in the Midland, the York and North Midland, and the Newcastle and Darlington Companies, of which he was chairman, and they unanimously adopted resolutions, voting 2,000*l.* each for the erection of a statue of George Stephenson on the High Level Bridge at Newcastle, and the presentation to him of a service of plate, "in testimony of the deep obligations under which the above-mentioned Companies, in common with the whole country, feel themselves placed towards that eminent person." *

Mr. Ellis, M. P., then deputy chairman of the Midland, in seconding the resolution voting 2,000*l.* for the purpose indicated by Mr. Hudson, said, "it might appear to many strange that he should do so [statues not being recognized objects amongst the Society of Friends]; but he did so with all his heart. He believed he had the distinguished honor of having known George Stephenson longer than any one then present. Perhaps he could not say more of him than that he had always found in him an upright, honorable and honest man." †

At the meeting of the York and North Midland Company, the great benefits which Mr. Stephenson had conferred on the public,

* Resolution of the York, Newcastle and Berwick Company, unanimously adopted 31st August, 1845.

† Report of proceedings at the meeting of the Midland Railway Company, 25th July, 1845.

by opening up to them cheap and abundant supplies of fuel by means of railways, were strongly expressed; and Mr. Hudson, in concluding his observations, said: "By adopting this step, we shall show that we are not the sordid persons whom some have represented us to be—merely looking for our own pecuniary benefit; but that we are a body of men who know how to appreciate and admire genius and talent, and that we are not unmindful of the benefits which that talent has conferred upon us and upon mankind."* The resolution, like those passed by the other Companies, was adopted unanimously, and with "loud applause." But there ended the shareholders' appreciation of Mr. Stephenson's genius and talent; and Mr. Hudson's repudiation of sordid motives, on his part and theirs, thus proved somewhat premature. The contribution of subscriptions to present a testimonial to Mr. Hudson himself went on apace, and railway shareholders in all parts of the country, subscribed large sums of money to present him with a fortune for having already made one. But Mr. Stephenson pretended to fill no man's pocket with premiums. He was no creator of shares; he could not, therefore, work upon shareholders' gratitude for "favors to come;" and their testimonial accordingly ended with resolutions and speeches. Mr. Stephenson never asked for nor expected a testimonial. He had done the work of his life, and had retired from the field of railway enterprise, reposing upon his own sturdy independence.

Mr. Stephenson was afterwards somewhat indignant to find that, notwithstanding the "great obligations" which the chairman of the York, Newcastle and Berwick Company, had informed the proprietors they were under to their engineer for the labor and energy which he had devoted in their service, so much to their pecuniary advantage, the only issue of their fine resolutions and speeches was an allotment made to him of some thirty of the shares issued under the powers of the act which he had been mainly instrumental in obtaining. The chairman himself, it

* Report of proceedings at the York and North Midland Company, 29th June, 1845.

afterwards appeared, had at the same time appropriated not fewer than 10,894 of the same shares, the premiums on which were then worth, in the market, about 145,000*l.* The *manner* in which the gratitude of the Company and their chairman was thus expressed to their engineer, was strongly resented by Mr. Stephenson at the time, and a coolness took place between him and Mr. Hudson which was never wholly removed—though they afterwards shook hands, and Mr. Stephenson declared that all was forgotten.

Mr. Hudson's brief reign was now drawing rapidly to a close. The saturnalia of 1845 was followed by a sudden reaction. Shares went down faster than they had gone up; the holders of them hastened to sell, in order to avoid payment of the calls; and the fortunes of many were utterly wrecked. Then came sudden repentance, and professed return to virtue. The betting man, who, temporarily abandoning the turf for the share-market, had played his heaviest stakes and lost—the merchant who had left his business, and the doctor who had neglected his patients, to gamble in railway stock, and been ruined—the penniless knaves and schemers, who had speculated so recklessly, and gained so little—the titled and fashionable people, who had bowed themselves so low before the idol of the day, and found themselves so deceived and "done"—the credulous small capitalists, who, dazzled by premiums, had invested their all in railway shares, and now saw themselves stripped of everything—the Average Directors, who "never knew what was going on and thought all was right," but now found that all was wrong—the tradesmen who had sold their business to become sharebrokers, and had now reached the *Gazette*—were all grievously enraged, and looked about them for a victim. In this temper were shareholders, when, at a railway meeting in York, some pertinent questions were put to the Railway King. His replies were not satisfactory; and the questions were pushed home. Mr. Hudson became confused. Angry voices rose in the meeting. The monarch was even denounced. A committee of investigation was appointed, and the gilt idol of the railway world was straightway dethroned. A howl of execration rose from his deluded worshipers; and those who had bowed the lowest before him during his brief reign, hissed the loudest when he fell. The gold which he had put in their pockets might still be heard chinking there; but no one had yet found *them* out, and they joined in the chorus of popular indignation. Then committees of investigation were appointed on nearly all the railways; able reports by patriotic candidates for seats at boards were successively published; and, railways having been exorcised, and one of their evil spirits cast out, railway virtue was again supposed to be in the ascendant.

CHAPTER XXXIII.

MR. STEPHENSON'S CONNECTION WITH FOREIGN RAILWAYS—JOURNEYS INTO BELGIUM AND SPAIN.

LEOPOLD, King of the Belgians, was the first European monarch who discovered the powerful instrumentality of railways in developing the industrial resources of a nation. Having resided in England during the infancy of our railway enterprises, he had personally inspected the lines in operation, and satisfied himself of their decided superiority over all known modes of transit. He therefore determined at the earliest possible period to adopt them as the great high roads of his new kingdom.

Belgium had scarcely escaped from the throes of her revolution, and Leopold had only been a short time called to the throne, when by his command the first project of a Belgian railway was laid before him. It was a modest project it is true, a single line from Antwerp to Liege, requiring a capital of only 400,000*l.* But small though it was, his ministers even feared that the project was too ambitious, and that the king was about to embark his government in an enterprise beyond his strength. There was as yet only the experiment of the Liverpool and Manchester passenger railway to justify him; but in his opinion that had been complete and decisive.

The bill for the Antwerp and Liege line struggled with difficulty through the Chambers, and it became law in 1834. Before the measure received legislative sanction, the plan had been enlarged, and powers were taken to construct an almost entire system of lines, embracing the principal districts of Belgium; connecting Brussels with all the chief cities, and extending from Ostend eastward to the Prussian frontier, and from Antwerp southward to the French frontier. The total extent of railway thus authorized was 246 miles. The eventual success of this measure was mainly due to the energy and sagacious enterprise of the king. He foresaw the immense advantages of the railway system, and its applicability to the wants of such a state as Belgium. The country being rich in coal and minerals, had great manufacturing capabilities. It had good ports, fine navigable rivers, abundant canals, and a teeming, industrious population. He perceived railways were, of all things, the best calculated to bring the industry of the country into full play, and to render the riches of his provinces available to all the rest of the kingdom. King Leopold therefore openly declared himself the promoter of public railways throughout Belgium. The execution of the works was immediately commenced, the money being provided by the state. Every official influence was called into active exertion for the development of these great enterprises. And, in order to prevent the Belgian enterprise becoming in any sort converted into a stock-jobbing speculation, it was wisely provided that the shares were not to be quoted on the Exchange at Antwerp or Brussels, until the railway was actually completed.

Mr. George Stephenson and his son, as the leading railway engineers of England, were consulted by the King of the Belgians, as to the formation of the most efficient system of lines throughout his kingdom, as early as 1835. In the course of that year, Mr. Stephenson visited Belgium, and had some interesting conferences with King Leopold and his ministers on the subject of the proposed railways. On that occasion the king appointed him by royal ordinance a Knight of the Order of Leopold. Improvements of the system were recommended and adopted; and in 1837, a law was passed, authorizing the construction of additional lines—from Ghent to Mouscron on the French frontier—from Courtray to Tournai—from Brain-le-Comte to Namur—with several smaller branches. These, with the lines previously authorized, made a total length of 341 English miles.

Much diligence was displayed by the government in pushing on the works; the representatives of the people in the Chambers now surpassing even the king himself in their anticipation of the great public benefits to be derived from railways. The first twelve miles between Brussels and Malines were opened in 1835, a year after the passing of the law; and successive portions were opened from time to time, until the year 1844, when the entire national system was completed and opened, after a total outlay on works, stations, and plant, of about six and a half millions sterling. Never did any legislature expend public money in a wiser manner for the promotion of the common good. As the Belgian lines were executed as an entire system by the state, there was no wasteful parliamentary expenditure, and no construction of unnecessary duplicate lines; the whole capital invested was remunerative; and the Belgian people thus obtained the full advantages of railways at less than one half the average cost of those in England.

At the invitation of the king, Mr. Stephenson made a visit to Belgium in 1837, on the occasion of the public opening of the line from Brussels to Ghent. The event was celebrated with great ceremony. At Brussels there was a public procession, and another at Ghent on the arrival of the train. Mr. Stephenson and his party accompanied it to the Public Hall, there to dine with the chief ministers of state, the municipal authorities, and about five hundred of the principal inhabitants of the city; the English ambassador being also present. After the king's health and a few others had been drank, that of Mr. Stephenson was proposed; on which the whole assembly rose up, amidst great excitement and loud applause, and made their way to where he sat, in order to jingle glasses with him, greatly to his own amazement. On the day following, Mr. Stephenson dined with the king and queen at their own table at Laaken, by special invitation; afterwards accompanying his majesty and suite to a public ball given by the municipality of Brussels, in honor of the opening of the line to Ghent, as well as of their distinguished English guest. On entering the room, the general and excited inquiry was, "Which is Stephenson?" The English engineer had never before known that he was esteemed so great a man.

When the success of railways in Belgium was no longer matter of conjecture, capitalists were ready to come forward and undertake their formation, without aid from the government; and several independent companies were formed in England for the construction of new lines in the country. Mr. Stephenson was professionally consulted respecting several of these in the year 1845. The Sambre and Meuse Company having obtained the concession of a line from the legislature,* Mr. Stephenson proceeded to Belgium for the purpose of examining in person the district through which the proposed line was to pass. He was accompanied on this occasion by Mr. Sopwith and Mr. Starbuck: the former gentleman a highly distinguished Northumberland geologist, intimately conversant with the coal-bearing strata, who had already published an elaborate report on the nature and extent of the coal and mineral districts of the Sambre Meuse.

Mr. Stephenson went carefully over the whole length of the proposed line, as far as Couvin, the Forest of Ardennes, and Rocroi, across the French frontier. He examined the bearings of the coal-field, the slate and marble quarries, and the numerous

* The king, in his speech to the Chambers, in opening the session of 1845, said: "Ever since the National Railways have reached the French and German frontiers, the conveyance of goods and passengers, and the amount of the receipts, have rapidly and unceasingly advanced. The results obtained this year have surpassed my expectations. Your last session was distinguished, towards its close, by the vote of several projects of railways and canals. The favorable reception given to foreign capitalists has led to many demands for the concession of lines. Some of these demands, after being examined, will be submitted to your deliberation."

iron mines in existence between the Sambre and the Meuse, carefully exploring the ravines which extended through the district, in order to satisfy himself that the best possible route had been selected. He was delighted with the novelty of the journey, the beauty of the scenery, and the industry of the population. His companions were entertained by his ample and varied stores of practical information on all subjects; and his conversation was full of reminiscences of his youth, on which he always delighted to dwell when in the society of his more intimate friends and associates. The journey was varied by a visit to the coal-mines near Jemappe, where Mr. Stephenson examined with interest the mode adopted by the Belgian miners of draining the pits, their engines and brakeing machines, so familiar to him in his early life. At intervals of their journey, Mr. Stephenson prepared, in conjunction with Mr. Sopwith, the draft of a report embodying the result of their investigations, which was presented to the Sambre and Meuse Company, and afterwards published.

The engineers of Belgium took the opportunity of Mr. Stephenson's visit to their country to invite him to a magnificent banquet at Brussels. The Public Hall, in which they entertained him, was gaily decorated with flags, prominent amongst which was the Union Jack, in honor of their distinguished guest. A handsome marble pedestal, ornamented with his bust, crowned with laurels, occupied one end of the room. The chair was occupied by M. Massui, the Chief Director of the National Railways of Belgium; and the most eminent scientific men in the kingdom were present. Their reception of "the father of railways" was of the most enthusiastic description. Mr. Stephenson was greatly pleased with the entertainment. Not the least interesting incident of the evening was his observing, when the dinner was about half over, a model of a locomotive engine placed upon the centre table, under a triumphal arch. Turning suddenly to his friend Sopwith, he exclaimed, "Do you see the 'Rocket?'" It was indeed the model of that celebrated engine; and Mr. Stephenson prized the compliment thus paid him, perhaps more than all the encomiums of the evening.

The next day (April 5th) King Leopold invited him to a private interview at the palace. Accompanied by Mr. Sopwith, he proceeded to Laaken, and was very cordially received by his majesty. Nothing was more remarkable in Mr. Stephenson than his extreme ease and self-possession in the presence of distinguished and highly-educated persons. The king immediately entered into familiar conversation with him, discussing the railway project which had been the object of Mr. Stephenson's visit to Belgium, and then the structure of the Belgian coal-fields—the king expressing his sense of the great importance of economy in a fuel which had become indispensable to the comfort and well-being of society, which was the basis of all manufactures, and the vital power of railway locomotion. The subject was always a favorite one with Mr. Stephenson, and, encouraged by the king, he proceeded to describe to him the geological structure of Belgium, the original formation of coal, its subsequent elevation by volcanic forces, and the vast amount of denudation. In describing the coal-beds, he used his hat as a sort of model to illustrate his meaning; and the eyes of the king were fixed upon it as he proceeded with his interesting description. The conversation then passed to the rise and progress of trade and manufactures—Mr. Stephenson pointing out how closely they everywhere followed the coal, being mainly dependent upon it, as it were, for their very existence.

The king seemed greatly pleased with the interview, and at its close expressed himself obliged by the interesting information which Mr. Stephenson had given him. Shaking hands cordially with both the gentlemen, and wishing them success in all their important undertakings, he bade them adieu. As they were leaving the palace, Mr. Stephenson, bethinking him of the model by which he had just been illustrating the Belgian coal-fields, said to his friend: "By-the-bye, Sopwith, I was afraid the king would see the inside of my hat; it's such a shocking bad one!" Little could George Stephenson, when brakesman at a coal-pit, have dreampt that, in the course of his life, he should be admitted to an interview with a monarch, and describe to him the manner in which the geological foundations of his kingdom had been laid!

In the course of the same year Mr. Stephenson paid a second visit to Belgium, for the purpose of examining the direction of the proposed West Flanders Railway, and of suggesting any alterations which his judgment might point out. The results of his investigations were set forth in his report of August, 1845, in which he recommended several important alterations, with a view to facilitate the execution of the works, and to increase the traffic of the line. The inspection of the country lasted ten days. After the concession of this railway had been made to the English Company, other parties appeared in the field, and projected lines which, if carried out, would seriously affect the success of the West Flanders project. The government of King Leopold, however, on a representation to this effect having been made to them, at once distinctly stated that the lines already conceded would always be protected, and that no new lines would be granted, however little they might affect those already existing, without the proprietors of the latter being fully heard.

Mr. Stephenson had scarcely returned from this second visit to Belgium, before he was requested to proceed to Spain, for the purpose of examining and reporting upon a scheme then on foot for constructing "the Royal North of Spain Railway." He set out from London in the middle of September, accompanied by Sir Joshua Walmsley and several other gentlemen interested in the project. A concession had been made by the Spanish government of a line of railway from Madrid to the Bay of Biscay, and a numerous staff of engineers was engaged in surveying the proposed line. The directors of the Company had declined making the necessary deposits until more favorable terms had been secured, and the object of Sir Joshua Walmsley's journey was to press the Spanish government on the subject. Mr. Stephenson whom he consulted, was alive to the difficulties of the office which Sir Joshua was requested to undertake, and offered to be his companion and adviser on the occasion—declining to receive any recompense beyond the simple expenses of the journey. The railway mania was then at its height; and though Mr. Stephenson was not concerned in the multitude of new schemes which were daily coming out, he was engaged on some important measures, and, besides, had his own extensive collieries at Clay Cross to look after. He could, therefore, only arrange to be absent for six weeks, and he set out for England about the middle of September, 1845.

The party was joined at Paris by Mr. Mackenzie, the contractor for the Orleans and Tours Railway, then in course of construction, who took them over the works, and accompanied them as far as Tours. Sir Joshua Walmsley was struck during the journey by Mr. Stephenson's close and accurate observation. Nothing escaped his keen eye. The external features of the district passed through, every fissure or disruption in the mountain ridges, the direction of the rivers, the stratification and geological formation of the country, were carefully, though rapidly noted. The modes of farming were also observed; and he compared the herds of cattle, the horses and mules, with those which he had observed in his own and other countries. Nor did he fail to observe closely the agricultural products, and the fruits and flowers grown in the gardens of the villages through which they passed. Of course he was fully alive to any important engineering works which came in his way. Thus, in crossing the river Dordogne, on the road to Bordeaux, he was struck with the construction of the stupendous chain bridge which had recently been erected there. Not satisfied with his first inspection, he walked back, and again crossed the bridge. On reaching the shore, he said: "This bridge cannot stand; it is impossible that it can sustain the necessary pressure. Supposing a large body of troops to march over it, there would be so much oscillation as to cause the greatest danger; in fact, it could not stand." And he determined to write to the public authorities, warning them on the subject; which he did. His judgment proved to be quite correct, for only a few years after, no improvement having been made in the bridge, a body of troops marching over it under the precise circumstances which he had imagined, the chains broke, the men were precipitated into the river, and many lives were lost.

They soon reached the great chain of the Pyrenees, and crossed over into Spain. It was on Sunday evening, after a long day's toilsome journey through the mountains, that the party suddenly found themselves in one of those beautiful secluded valleys lying amongst the Western Pyrenees. A small hamlet lay before them, consisting of some thirty or forty houses and a fine old church. The sun was low on the horizon, and, under the wide porch, beneath the shadow of the church, were seated nearly all the inhabitants of the place. They were dressed in their holiday attire. The delightful bits of red and rich amber color of the women, and the gay sashes of the men, formed a striking picture, on which the travelers gazed in silent admiration. It was something entirely novel and unexpected. Beside the villagers sat two venerable old men, whose canonical hats indicated their quality of village pastors. Two groups of young women and children were dancing outside the porch to the accompaniment of a simple pipe; and within a hundred yards of them, some of the youths of the village were disporting themselves in athletic exercises; the whole being carried on beneath the fostering care of the old church, and with the sanction of its ministers. It was a beautiful scene, and deeply moved the travelers as they approached the principal group. The villagers greeted them courteously, supplied their present wants, and pressed upon them some fine melons, brought from their adjoining gardens. Mr. Stephenson used afterwards to look back upon that simple scene, and speak of it as one of the most charming pastorals he had ever witnessed.

They shortly reached the site of the proposed railway, passing through Irun, St. Sebastian, St. Andero, and Bilbao, at which places they met deputations of the principal inhabitants who were interested in the subject of their journey. At Raynosa, Mr Stephenson carefully examined the mountain passes and ravines through which a railway could be formed. He rose at break of day, and surveyed until the darkness set in; and frequently his resting-place at night was the floor of some miserable hovel. He was thus laboriously occupied for ten days, after which he proceeded across the province of Old Castile towards Madrid, surveying as he went. The proposed plan included the purchase of the Castile canal; and that property was also surveyed. He next proceeded to El Escorial, situated at the foot of the Guadarrama mountains, through which he found that it would be necessary to construct two formidable tunnels; added to which he ascertained that the country between El Escorial and Madrid was of a very difficult and expensive character to work through. Taking these circumstances into account, and looking to the expected traffic on the proposed line, Sir Joshua Walmsley, acting under the advice of Mr. Stephenson, offered to construct the line from Madrid to the Bay of Biscay, only on condition that the requisite land was given to the Company for the purpose; that they should be allowed every facility for cutting such timber belonging to the Crown as might be required for the purposes of the railway; and also that the materials required from abroad for the construction of the line should be admitted free of duty. In return for these concessions, the Company offered to clothe and feed several thousands of convicts while engaged in the execution of the earthworks. General Narvaez, afterwards Duke of Valencia, received Sir Joshua Walmsley and Mr. Stephenson on the subject of their proposition, and expressed his willingness to close with them; but it was necessary that other influential parties should give their concurrence before the scheme could be carried into effect. The deputation waited ten days to receive the answer of the Spanish government; but no answer of any kind was vouchsafed. Mr. Stephenson accordingly dissuaded his friend from making the necessary deposit at Madrid. Besides, he had by this time formed an unfavorable opinion of the entire project, and considered that the traffic would not amount to one-eighth of the estimate.

Mr. Stephenson was now anxious to be in England. During the journey from Madrid, he often spoke with affection of friends and relatives; and, when apparently absorbed by other matters, he would revert to what he thought might then be passing at home. Few incidents worthy of notice occurred on the journey homeward, but one may be mentioned. While traveling in an open conveyance between Madrid and Vittoria, the driver was urging his mules down hill at a dangerous pace. He was requested to slacken speed; but suspecting his passengers to be afraid, he only flogged the brutes into a still more furious gallop. Observing this, Mr. Stephenson coolly said, "Let us try him on the other tack; tell him to show us the fastest pace at which Spanish mules can go." The rogue of a driver, when he found his tricks of no avail, pulled up and proceeded at a moderate rate for the rest of his journey.

Urgent business required Mr. Stephenson's presence in London on the last day of November. They traveled, therefore, almost continuously, day and night; and the fatigue consequent on the journey, added to the privations voluntarily endured by the engineer while carrying on the survey among the Spanish mountains, began to tell seriously on his health. By the time he reached Paris, he was evidently ill; but he nevertheless determined on proceeding. He reached Havre in time for the Southampton boat; but when on board, pleurisy developed itself, and it was necessary to bleed him freely. During the voyage, he spent his time chiefly in dictating letters and reports to Sir Joshua Walmsley, who never left him, and whose kindness on the occasion he gratefully remembered. His friend was struck by the clearness of his dictated composition, which exhibited a vigor and condensation which to him seemed marvelous. After a few weeks' rest at home, Mr. Stephenson gradually recovered, though his health remained severely shaken.

On his report being presented to the shareholders in the projected "Royal North of Spain Railway," in the course of the following month, it was so decidedly unfavorable, that the project was abandoned and the Company forthwith dissolved.

CHAPTER XXXIV.

RESIDENCE AT TAPTON.

TOWARDS the close of his life, Mr. Stephenson almost entirely withdrew from the active pursuit of his profession as a railway engineer. He devoted himself chiefly to his extensive collieries and lime-works, taking a local interest only in such projected railways as were calculated to open up new markets for their products.

At home he lived the life of a country gentleman, enjoying his garden and his grounds, and indulging his love of nature, which, through all his busy life, had never left him. It was not until the year 1845, that he took an active interest in horticultural pursuits. Then he began to build new melon-houses, pineries, and vineries of great extent; and he now seemed as eager to excel all other growers of exotic plants in the neighborhood as he had been to surpass the villagers of Killingworth in the production of gigantic cabbages and cauliflowers some thirty years before. He had a pine-house built sixty-eight feet in length, and a pinery one hundred and forty feet. The workmen were never idle about the garden, and the additions to the forcing-houses proceeded until at length he had no fewer than ten glass forcing-houses, heated with hot water, which he was one of the first to introduce in that neighborhood. He did not take so much pleasure in flowers as in fruits. At one of the county agricultural meetings, he said that he intended yet to grow pineapples at Tapton as big as pumpkins. The only man to whom he would "knock under" was his friend Paxton, the gardener to the Duke of Devonshire; and he was so old in the service, and so skillful, that he could scarcely hope to beat him. Yet his "Queen" pines did take the first prize at a competition with the duke—though this was not until shortly after his death, when the plants had become more fully grown. His grapes also recently took the first prize at Rotherham, at a competition open to all England. He was extremely successful in producing melons, having invented a method of suspending them in baskets of wire gauze, which, by relieving the stalk from tension, allowed nutrition to proceed more freely, and better enabled the fruit to grow and ripen. Amongst his other erections, he built a joiner's shop, where he kept a workman regularly employed in carrying out his many ingenious contrivances of this sort.

He took much pride also in his growth of cucumbers. He raised them very fine and large, but he could not make them grow straight. Place them as he would, notwithstanding all his propping of them, and humoring them by modifying the application of heat, and the admission of light for the purpose of effecting his object, they would still insist on growing crooked in their own way. At last he had a number of glass cylinders made at Newcastle, for the purpose of an experiment; into these the growing cucumbers were inserted, and then he succeeded in growing them perfectly straight. Carrying one of the new products into his house one day, and exhibiting it to a party of visitors, he told them of the expedient he had adopted, and added gleefully, "I think I have bothered them noo!"

Mr. Stephenson also carried on farming operations with some success. He experimented on manure, and fed cattle after methods of his own. He was very particular as to breed and build in stock-breeding. "You see, sir," he said to one gentleman, "I like to see the *coo's* back at a gradient something like this," (drawing an imaginary line with his hand,) "and then the ribs or girders will carry more flesh than if they were so, or so." When he attended the county agricultural meetings, which he frequently did, he was accustomed to take part in the discussions, and he brought the same vigorous practical mind to bear upon questions of tillage, drainage, and farm economy, which he had been accustomed to exercise on mechanical and engineering matters. At one of the meetings of the North Derbyshire Agricultural Society, he favored the assembled farmers with an explanation of his theory of vegetation. The practical conclusion to which it led was, that the agriculturist ought to give as much light and heat to the soil as possible. At the same time, he stated his opinion that, in some cold soils, water contributed to promote vegetation, rather than to impede it, as was generally believed; for the water, being exposed to the sun and atmosphere, became specifically warmer than the earth it covered, and when it afterwards irrigated the fields, it communicated this additional heat to the soil which it permeated.

All his early affection for birds and animals revived. He had favorite dogs, and cows, and horses; and again he began to keep rabbits, and to pride himself on the beauty of his breed. There was not a bird's nest upon the grounds that he did not know of; and from day to day he went round watching the progress which the birds made with their building, carefully guarding them from injury. No one was more minutely acquainted with the habits of British birds, the result of a long, loving, and close observation of nature.

At Tapton he remembered the failure of his early experiment in hatching birds' eggs by heat, and he now performed it successfully, being able to secure a proper apparatus for maintaining a uniform temperature. He was also curious about the breeding and fattening of fowls; and when his friend Edward Pease of Darlington visited him at Tapton, he explained a method which he had invented for fattening chickens in half the usual time. The chickens were shut up in boxes, which were so made as to exclude the light. Dividing the day into two or three parts, the birds were shut up at each period after a heavy feed, and went to sleep. The plan proved very successful, and Mr. Stephenson jocularly said that if he were to devote himself to chickens he could soon make a little fortune.

Mrs. Stephenson tried to keep bees, but found they would not thrive at Tapton. Many hives perished, and there was no case of success. The cause of failure was a puzzle to Mr. Stephenson; but one day his acute powers of observation enabled him to unravel it. At the foot of the hill on which Tapton House stands, he saw some bees trying to rise up from amongst the grass, laden with honey and wax. They were already exhausted, as if with long flying; and then it occurred to him that the height at which the house stood above the bees' feeding ground rendered it difficult for them to reach their hives when heavy laden, and hence they sank exhausted. Mr. Stephenson afterwards stated the case to Mr. Jesse the naturalist, who concurred in his view as to the cause of failure, and was much struck by the keen observation which had led to its solution.

Mr. Stephenson had none of the in-door habits of the student. He read very little; for reading is a habit which is generally acquired in youth; and his youth and manhood had been for the most part spent in hard work. Books wearied him, and sent him to sleep. Novels excited his feelings too much, and he avoided them, though he would occasionally read through a philosophical book on a subject in which he felt particularly interested. He wrote very few letters with his own hand; nearly all his letters were dictated, and he avoided even dictation when he could. His greatest pleasure was in conversation, from which he gathered most of his imparted information; hence he was always glad in the society of intelligent conversable persons.

It was his practice, when about to set out on a journey by railway, to walk along the train before it started, and look into the carriages to see if he could find "a conversable face." On one of these occasions, at the Euston Station, he discovered in a carriage a very handsome, manly, and intelligent face, which he shortly found belonged to the late Lord Denman. He was on his way down to his seat at Stony Middleton, in Derbyshire. Mr. Stephenson entered the carriage, and the two were shortly engaged in interesting conversation. It turned upon chronometry and horology, and Mr. Stephenson amazed his lordship by the extent of his knowledge on the subject, in which he displayed as much minute information, even down to the latest improvements in watchmaking, as if he had been bred a watchmaker and lived by the trade. Lord Denman was curious to know how a man whose time must have been mainly engrossed by engineering, had gathered so much knowledge on a subject quite out of his own line, and he asked the question. "I learnt clockmaking and watchmaking," was the answer, "while a working man at Killingworth, when I made a little money in my spare hours by cleaning the pitmen's clocks and watches; and since then I have kept up my information on the subject." This led to further questions, and then Mr. Stephenson told Lord Denman the interesting story of his life, which held him entranced during the remainder of the journey.

Many of his friends readily accepted invitations to Tapton House to enjoy his hospitality, which never failed. With them he would "fight his battles o'er again," reverting often to his battle for the locomotive; and he was never tired of telling, nor were his auditors of listening to, the lively anecdotes with which he was accustomed to illustrate the struggles of his early career. Whilst walking in the woods or through the grounds, he would arrest his friends' attention by allusion to some simple object—such as a leaf, a blade of grass, a bit of bark, a nest of birds, or an ant carrying its eggs across the path—and descant in glowing terms upon the creative power of the Divine Mechanician, whose contrivances were so exhaustless and so wonderful. This was a theme upon which he was often accustomed to dwell in reverential admiration, when in the society of his more intimate friends.

One night, when walking under the stars, and gazing up into the field of suns, each the probable centre of a system, forming the Milky Way, a friend said to him: "What an insignificant creature is man in sight of so immense a creation as that!" "Yes!" was his reply, "but how wonderful a creature also is man, to be able to think and reason, and even in some measure to comprehend works so infinite!"

A microscope, which he had brought down to Tapton, was a source of immense enjoyment to him; and he was never tired of contemplating the minute wonders which it revealed. One evening, when some friends were visiting him, he induced each of them to puncture his skin so as to draw blood, in order that he might examine the globules through the microscope. One of the gentlemen present was a teetotaler, and Mr. Stephenson pronounced his blood to be the most lively of the whole. He had a theory of his own about the movement of the globules in the blood, which has since become familiar. It was, that they were respectively charged with electricity, positive at one end and negative at the other, and that thus they attracted and repelled each other, causing a circulation. No sooner did he observe any thing new, than he immediately set about devising a reason for it. His training in mechanics, his practical familiarity with matter in all its forms, and the strong bent of his mind, led him first of all to seek for a mechanical explanation. And yet he was ready to admit that there was a something in the principle of *life*—so mysterious and inexplicable—which baffled mechanics, and seemed to dominate over and control them. He did not care much, either, for abstruse mechanics, but only for the experimental and practical, as is usually the case with those whose knowledge has been self-acquired.

Even at this advanced age, his spirit of frolic had not left him. When proceeding from Chesterfield Station to Tapton House with his friends, he would almost invariably challenge them to a race up the steep path, partly formed of stone steps, along the hill-side. And he would struggle, as of old, to keep the front place, though by this time his "wind" had greatly failed. He would even invite an old friend to take a quiet wrestle with him on the lawn, in memory of former times. In the evening, he would sometimes indulge his visitors by reciting the old pastoral of "Damon and Phyllis," or singing his favorite song of "John Anderson my Joe." But his greatest glory amongst those with whom he was most intimate, was "a crowdie!" "Let's have a crowdie night," he would say; and forthwith a kettle of boiling water was ordered in, with a basin of oatmeal. Taking a large bowl, containing a sufficiency of hot water, and placing it between his knees, he then poured in oatmeal with one hand, and stirred the mixture vigorously with the other. When enough meal had been added, and the stirring was completed, the crowdie was made. It was then supped with new milk, and Mr. Stephenson generally pronounced it "capital!" It was the diet to which he had been accustomed when a working man, and all the dainties with which he had been familiar in recent years had not spoiled his simple tastes. To enjoy crowdie at his years, besides, indicated that he still possessed that quality on which no doubt much of his practical success in life had depended — a strong and healthy digestion.

He would also frequently invite to his house the humbler companions of his early life, and take pleasure in talking over old times with them. He never assumed any of the bearings of a great man on these occasions, but treated such visitors with the same friendliness and respect as if they had been his equals, sending them away pleased with themselves and delighted with him. At other times, needy men who had known him in youth, would knock at his door, and they were never refused access. But if he had heard of any misconduct on their part, he would rate them soundly. One who knew him intimately in private life has seen him exhorting such backsliders, and denouncing their misconduct and imprudence, with the tears streaming down his cheeks. And he would generally conclude by opening his purse, and giving them the help which they needed "to make a fresh start in the world."

Young men would call upon him for advice or assistance in commencing a professional career. When he noted their industry, prudence, and good sense, he was always ready. But, hating foppery and frippery above all things, he would reprove any tendency to this weakness which he observed in the applicants. One day, a youth, desirous of becoming an engineer, called upon him, flourishing a gold-headed cane. Mr. Stephenson said: "Put by that stick, my man, and then I will speak to you." To another extensively-decorated young man, he one day said: "You will, I hope, Mr. ——, excuse me; I am a plain-spoken person, and am sorry to see a nice-looking and rather clever young man like you disfigured with that fine-patterned waistcoat, and all these chains and fang-dangs. If I, sir, had bothered my head with such things when at your age, I would not have been where I am now."

Mr. Stephenson's life at Tapton during his later years was occasionally diversified with a visit to London. His engineering business having become limited, he generally went there for the purpose of visiting friends, or "to see what there was new going on." He found a new race of engineers springing up on all hands—men who knew him not; and his London journeys gradually ceased to yield him real pleasure. A friend used to take him to the opera, but by the end of the first act, he was generally observed in a profound slumber. Yet on one occasion he enjoyed a visit to the Haymarket, with a party of friends, on his birth-day, to see T. P. Cooke, in "Black-eyed Susan;"—if that can be called enjoyment which kept him in a state of tears during half the performance. At other times he visited Newcastle, which always gave him great pleasure. He would, on such occasions, go out to Killingworth and seek up old friends, and if the people whom he knew were too retiring and shrunk into their cottages, he went and sought them there. Striking the floor with his stick, and holding his noble person upright, he would say in his own kind way, "Well, and how's all here to-day?" To the last Mr. Stephenson had always a warm heart for Newcastle and its neighborhood.

Sir Robert Peel, on more than one occasion, invited Mr. Stephenson to his mansion at Drayton, where he was accustomed to assemble round him men of the greatest distinction in art, science, and legislation, during the intervals of his parliamentary life. The first invitation, Mr. Stephenson declined. Sir Robert invited him a second time, and a second time he declined: "I have no great ambition," he said, "to mix in fine company, and perhaps should feel out of my proper place among such high folks." But Sir Robert a third time pressed him to come down to Tamworth early in January, 1845, when he would meet Buckland, Follett, and others well known to both. "Well, Sir Robert," said he, "I feel your kindness very much, and can no longer refuse: I will come down and join your party."

Mr. Stephenson's strong powers of observation, together with his native humor and shrewdness, imparted to his conversation at all times much vigor and originality, and made him, to young and old, a delightful companion. Though mainly an engineer, he was also a profound thinker on many scientific questions; and there was scarcely a subject of speculation, or a department of recondite science, on which he had not employed his faculties in such a way as to have formed large and original views. At Drayton, the conversation often turned upon such topics, and Mr. Stephenson freely joined in it. On one occasion an animated discussion took place between himself and Dr. Buckland on one of his favorite theories as to the formation of coal. But the result was, that Dr. Buckland, a much greater master of tongue-fence than Stephenson, completely silenced him. Next morning before breakfast, when he was walking in the grounds deeply pondering, Sir William Follett came up and asked what he was thinking about? "Why, Sir William, I am thinking over that argument I had with Buckland last night. I know I am right, and that if I had only the command of words which he has, I'd have beaten him." "Let me know all about it," said Sir William "and I'll see what I can do for you." The two sat down in an arbor, where the astute lawyer made himself thoroughly acquainted with the points of the case; entering into it with all the zeal of an advocate about to plead the dearest interests of his client. After he had mastered the subject, Sir William rose up, rubbing his hands with glee, and said, "Now I am ready for him." Sir Robert Peel was made acquainted with the plot, and adroitly introduced the subject of the controversy after dinner. The result was, that in the argument which followed, the man of science was overcome by the man of law; and Sir William Follett had at all points the mastery over Dr. Buckland. "What do *you* say, Mr. Stephenson?" asked Sir Robert, laughing. "Why," said he, "I will only say this, that of all the powers above and under the earth, there seems to me to be no power so great as the gift of the gab."

One day, at dinner, during the same visit, a scientific lady asked him the question: "Mr. Stephenson, what do you consider the most powerful force in nature?" "Oh!" said he, in a gallant spirit, "I will soon answer that question: it is the eye of a woman for the man who loves her; for if a woman look with affection on a young man, and he should go to the uttermost ends of the earth, the recollection of that look will bring him back: there is no other force in nature which could do that."

One Sunday, when the party had just returned from church, they were standing together on the terrace near the Hall, and observed in the distance a railway train flashing along, throwing behind it a long line of white steam. "Now, Buckland," said Mr. Stephenson, "I have a poser for you. Can you tell me what is the power that is driving that train?" "Well," said the other, "I suppose it is one of your big engines." "But what drives the engine?" "Oh, very likely a canny Newcastle driver." "What do you say to the light of the sun?" "How can that be?" asked the doctor. "It is nothing else," said the engineer: "it is light bottled up in the earth for tens of thousands of years — light, absorbed by plants and vegetables, being necessary for the condensation of carbon during the process of their growth, if it be not carbon in another form — and now, after being buried in the earth for long ages in fields of coal, that latent light is again brought forth and liberated, made to work, as in that locomotive, for great human purposes." The idea was certainly a most striking and original one: like a flash of light, it illuminated in an instant an entire field of science.

During the same visit, Mr. Stephenson one evening repeated his experiment with blood drawn from the finger, submitting it to the microscope in order to show the curious circulation of the globules. He set the example by pricking his own thumb; and the other guests, by turns, in like manner gave up a small portion of their blood for the purpose of ascertaining the comparative liveliness of their circulation. When Sir Robert Peel's turn came, Mr. Stephenson said he was curious to know "how the blood globules of a great politician would conduct themselves." Sir Robert held forth his finger for the purpose of being pricked; but once, and again, he sensitively shrunk back, and at length the experiment, so far as he was concerned, was abandoned. Sir Robert Peel's sensitiveness to pain was extreme, and yet he was destined, a few years after, to die a death of the most distressing agony.

From these visits to distinguished persons, Mr. Stephenson went back to Tapton with an increased love for home and its pleasures. He must see after his garden, his birds, and his favorite animals. There were also his thousand workpeople to be looked after, at Tapton and Clay Cross; and Mechanics' Institutes to be visited, and many other things to be attended to. One of the subjects that gave him most pleasure during the later years of his life was, the encouragement of educational institutes for the working classes, in which he took the deepest interest. He had many discussions on the subject with his intimate friend Mr. Binns, the manager of the extensive works at Clay Cross. A large population had now settled down at that place, and the original hamlet, consisting of about twelve cottages, had assumed the dimensions of a town. Iron smelting furnaces had been added to the colliery, and decided prosperity at length promised to attend Mr. Stephenson's original enterprise. How were these workpeople to be morally and intellectually improved, and their children efficiently educated? Such was the question which occupied the attention of Mr. Stephenson and his friend. Small beginnings were made, educational institutes of all kinds growing but slowly; but at length a system was established, so admirable and calculated to be so beneficial to all parties concerned, employers and workpeople alike, that we think the institution at Clay Cross may be cited as a model for general imitation by large employers of labor in all districts. It is briefly as follows:

It is made a condition of employment at the works that every man and boy shall pay a fortnightly rate for educational and other purposes. Every married man pays a shilling a fortnight, every single man eight pence, every boy five pence. Of these respective contributions, two pence a fortnight from each is appropriated exclusively for education. It is further made a condition, that the funds shall be administered by the manager of the works; the concentration of the power in his hands insuring efficiency to the system.

In return for these contributions, the following important benefits are conferred: 1. Free education in day schools for all the children of the workpeople. 2. Free education in night schools for all the boys and young men desiring instruction. 3. Free access to a Workmen's Institute, with its lectures, reading room supplied with daily and weekly newspapers, and library of 1600 volumes. 4. Free medical and surgical attendance to all the workpeople and their families. 5. Relief at the rate of 4*s.* a week during sickness, and 5*s.* a week during disablement by accident, to all the workpeople. 6. Free access to a fortnightly dance in the large hall, attended by the workpeople and their families. 7. A band of instrumental music, a drum and fife band, a choral society, and a cricket club, are maintained out of the rate. 8. Between thirty and forty pounds are yearly granted out of the rate as prizes for the best cottage garden vegetables; the competion for which is held three times a year in the Public Hall.

Such is the admirable institution now existing at Clay Cross. The number of persons employed on the works is about fifteen hundred; and the amount of good daily effected by agencies of the character thus briefly stated can be better imagined than described. Schools, with a fine public hall, and a handsome church, have been erected at a cost of many thousand pounds, towards the expenses of which the Clay Cross Company have munificently contributed; but the main element of success in the Institution unquestionably consists in the truly philanthropic action of the manager, Mr. Binns, who was for so many years the private secretary of George Stephenson, and in whom his spirit strongly lives and nobly works.

"The *good* men do, lives after them," happily holds true quite as often as the converse maxim embodied in Shakspeare's well-known couplet.* The example and influence exercised by a good man upon his fellows, as by George Stephenson at Clay Cross during his life, is never lost; but goes on fructifying into good, long after his body has mouldered into dust.

* "The evil that men do, lives after them;
The good is often interred with their bones."
JULIUS CÆSAR.

CHAPTER XXXV.

CLOSING YEARS.

WHILE thus occupied in his country house at Tapton, many persons continued to seek Mr. Stephenson's advice on subjects connected with mechanical engineering. Inventors sent their plans to him, and his approval was regarded as a passport to success. He was always ready to consider the plans thus submitted. Sometimes it was a paddle-boat for canals, or a new break for railway trains, or a steam-gauge, or a patent axle. If his reply proved favorable, the inventor occasionally seized the opportunity of circulating or advertising it, often without asking his permission.

One gentleman requested his opinion respecting his "anti-friction wheeled carriages," to which a very civil letter was sent in reply containing some useful hints, and offering to subscribe towards having a carriage properly constructed after a carefully prepared model, but cautioning the inventor against being over-sanguine. "If I can be the means of helping you," said he, "I shall be glad to do so; but I should not be justified in leading you or any other person to spend money without any chance of getting it back again." This letter was immediately published in the railway papers, by the happy inventor, with a quantity of doggerel appended; but if the proposed wheel ran no smoother than the rhymes, it could not have been worth much.*

* Take the following specimen:

"I saw your son Robert, oh fie! oh fie!
He looked upon me with disdain;

Another inventor induced a mutual friend to write requesting his opinion respecting an improved steamboat for the working of canals. He wrote in reply, commending the plan of the boat, but at the same time expressing his belief that "no boat can be made now to work against the locomotive." When Beale's Rotatory Engine came out, although entertaining a strong opinion against it, he nevertheless subscribed a sum of money for the purpose of having it fairly tried. A boat was fitted up with the engine, and the trial came off at Yarmouth. After describing the experiment at a meeting of the Mechanical Engineers, he said: "When the engine was put to work, we could not get the boat to move forward, and the experiment failed. We managed, indeed, to get the boat to sea, but it cost me and the party 40*l.* to bring her back again."

While Mr. Stephenson was in the full tide of railway business in London, these frequent applications of inventors to submit their plans for his consideration had not always been so favorably received. They broke in upon him at a time when every moment was precious, preëngaged by railway companies with large interests at stake. Absorbed by work, and his mind full of the business in hand, it was scarcely to be expected that he should listen with patience to plans fifty times before proposed and rejected—to crude and wild theories believed in only by their projectors. But when he had secured leisure, and could call his time his own, he was always ready to give an ear to those who consulted him upon such subjects. Thus, when Mr. Smith of Nottingham, an ingenious person in humble life, waited upon him with his invention of a steam-gauge, for the purpose of obtaining his patronage

His father could see, with half an eye,
Far more than I could explain.

"He wouldn't allow me to leave him my models,
Or a drawing, nor yet read my rhyme;
For many came to him with crack'd noddles,
Which occupied half of his time."

and assistance, Mr. Stephenson at once saw its uses, and said: "Oh! I understand it altogether; it will do very well." Overjoyed with this approval, and with the practical suggestions with which it was accompanied, the inventor said: "Before I leave, will you be pleased to tell me what is your charge?" "Charge!" replied Mr. Stephenson, "oh, nonsense, I make no charge; but I'll tell you what you must do.* Send your instrument down to my works, and I'll attach it to one of my boilers and prove it. I will do more; I will put it in the papers for you, and invite the public to come and examine it at work, and afterwards purchase it myself, if it answers as I expect it will do." He was as good as his word; for he shortly after published the following letter in the daily papers, dated Tapton House, Chesterfield, Oct. 15th, 1847: "A most important invention has been submitted to me for my approval, patented by a Mr. Smith of Nottingham, and intended to indicate the strength of steam in steam-engine boilers. It is particularly adapted for steamboats, and can be placed in the cabin, on deck, or on any other part of the vessel, where it may be seen by every passenger on board. It may also be fixed in the office of every manufactory where a steam-engine is used, at a considerable distance from the boiler. I am so much pleased with it that I have put one up at one of my own collieries; it is some distance from the boiler, in another house, and works most beautifully, showing the rise and fall of the steam in the most delicate manner. The indicator is like the face of a clock, with a pointer, making one revolution in measuring from 1 lb. to 100 lbs. upon the square inch of the pressure of steam; it is quite from under the control of the engineer, or any other person, so that its indications may be relied upon; and the construction is so simple, that it is scarcely possible for it to get out of order. I might give a full explanation of the machine, but I think it

* The last two lines state a fact beyond dispute. The number of inventions in connection with railways thrust upon the Messrs. Stephenson for their opinion during the railway mania, was almost beyond computation.

best to leave that to the inventor himself. The numerous and appalling accidents which have occurred from the bursting of steamboat boilers have induced me to give you these observations, which I think desirable to be laid before the public. I may state that I have no pecuniary interest in the scheme; but being the first person to whom it has been shown, and the first to make use of it, I feel it a duty I owe to the inventor, as well as the public, to make it as universally known as possible. The indicator is put up at Tapton colliery, near Chesterfield, and may be seen any day, by any respectable person."

Mr. Stephenson also occupied some of his spare time, while at Tapton, in devising improvements in locomotive engines and railway carriages, still aiming at perfecting the great system which he had originated. Thus, in 1846, he brought out his design of a three-cylinder locomotive—the two outside cylinders acting together in the same plane, the third cylinder, with a crank in the middle of the axle, acting at right angles to the plane and crank pins of the two other cylinders. The middle cylinder was double the diameter of the others; and its compensating action neutralized the tendency to oscillate, which was a defect in the long-boiler outside-cylinder engines as originally constructed. Although this new engine was very ingenious, and acted with great power, it has not come into general use, in consequence of the somewhat greater expense of its construction and working. The oscillation, also, of the outside-cylinder engines, which this invention was designed to correct, has since been obviated by an improvement in their design and structure. A three-cylinder engine was, however, constructed by way of experiment for the Northeastern Railway, on which line it still continues in efficient work.

Shortly after, Mr. Stephenson invented a new self-acting brake, after a plan which had occupied his attention for many years, and which had been partially adopted on the Liverpool and Manchester Railway during the time that he was its acting engineer. He now communicated a paper on the subject, accompanied by a beautiful model, to the Institute of Mechanical Engineers at Birmingham, of which he was president. The great recommendation of the plan was its simplicity and cheapness. "Any effectual plan," he said, "for increasing the safety of railway traveling is, in my mind, of such vital importance, that I prefer laying my scheme open to the world to taking out a patent for it; and it will be a source of great pleasure to me to know that it has been the means of saving even one human life from destruction, or that it has prevented one serious concussion."*

In 1847, the year before his death, Mr. Stephenson was invited to join a distinguished party at Sir Robert Peel's mansion at Drayton Manor, and to assist in the ceremony of formally opening the Trent Valley Railway, which had been originally designed and laid out by him many years before. The first sod of the railway was cut by the Prime Minister himself, in November, 1845, during the time when Mr. Stephenson was abroad on the business of the Spanish railway. The formal opening took place on the 26th of June, 1847, the line having thus been constructed in less than two years.

What a change had come over the spirit of the landed gentry since the time when George Stephenson had first projected a railway through that district! Then they were up in arms against him, characterizing him as a devastator and spoiler of their estates; now he was hailed as one of the greatest benefactors of the age. Sir Robert Peel, the chief political personage in England, welcomed him as a guest and a friend, and spoke of him as the chief of our practical philosophers. A dozen members of Parliament, seven baronets, with all the landed magnates of the district, assembled to celebrate the opening of the railway. The clergy were there to bless the enterprise, and to bid all hail to railway progress, as "enabling them to carry on with greater facility those operations in connection with religion which were calculated to

* See the "Practical Mechanic's Journal," Vol. 1, p. 53, for a description of the Self-acting Brake.

be so beneficial to the country."* The army, speaking through the mouth of General A'Court, acknowledged the vast importance of railways, as tending to improve the military defenses of the country. And representatives from eight corporations were there to acknowledge the great benefits which railways had conferred upon the merchants, tradesmen, and working classes of their respective towns and cities. Amongst those present who could not fail to contrast the now triumphant success of railways with the dismal forebodings uttered twenty years before, was Mr. William Yates Peel, one of the earliest supporters of the Liverpool and Manchester Railway.

Sir Robert Peel made a capital speech on the occasion, pointing out that, at a remote period in the history of British high roads, 2000 years ago, Julius Agricola, who united in his person both engineer and contractor—being the Stephenson and Brassey of his day—had formed a direct line of communication between London and Chester, though with unfavorable gradients. As to the immense advantages of railways, there could be no manner of doubt; they were, in his judgment, "destined to effect a greater social revolution than any invention since the art of printing was discovered;" tending, as they did, to promote the moral and social welfare, and to advance the political security of the kingdom, to establish new bonds of connection between England and Ireland, and to develop the industrial energies and resources of both countries. Sir Robert, in the course of his speech, invited "the lions of the broad and narrow gauge" to forget the memory of all former grievances for that day, even if, unfortunately, they were doomed to be revived again on the morrow.

Mr. Stephenson, however, was so strongly convinced of the great mistakes which had been committed of late years—mistakes which had, in no small measure, been encouraged by Sir Robert Peel himself, greatly to the damage of railway property—that he would not omit the opportunity, as he said, of "giving him a

* Speech of Archdeacon Hodson at the opening of the Trent Valley Railway.

rub" on the occasion, and speaking out his mind freely on the subject of direct lines, steep gradients, and the atmospheric "humbug," all of which had at one time been patronized by Sir Robert, when Premier. In the course of his reply, he said: "When I look back to the time when I first projected a locomotive railway in this neighborhood, I cannot but feel astonished at the opinions which then prevailed. We were told, even by celebrated engineers, that it would be impossible ever to establish railways. Judge, then, how proud must now be the feelings of one who, foreseeing the results of railways, has risen from the lower ranks on their success! I may venture to make a reference to what the right honorable baronet said relative to Julius Agricola and a direct line. If Julius Agricola laid down the most direct lines, it must be recollected that he had no heavy goods trains to provide for, and gradients were of no consequence. The line that general took was probably very good for his troops, where the hills would serve to establish his watches; but such lines would be in no way applicable at the present day, where the road is covered with long goods trains propelled by the locomotive. What we require now is a road with such gradients that locomotives shall be able to carry the heaviest loads at the least expense. The right honorable baronet will excuse me if I say that to have a line that is direct is not the main thing. Had he studied the laws of practical mechanics as I have done, he would, doubtless, have regarded good gradients as one of the most important considerations in a railway. I will also venture to say a word as to the broad gauge. I am afraid that this is another misconception, almost as great as the atmospheric railway; only they have had the advantage of my engines to drag them through. The Great Western commenced operations by endeavoring to have everything different from us—a different gauge and different engines. They put the boiler on one carriage and the engine on another, and they used ten feet wheels, which were to go at a hundred miles an hour. But what became of those engines?

They required porters to help them out of the station; and then they would not work. Luckily, however, we had sent them one engine from Newcastle, called the 'North Star,' to carry on the traffic; and though, like a horse, an engine requires rest, yet it was continually being called out to bring in the trains, thereby doing double duty in conducting the traffic for which the original broad gauge engines were found incapable."

Nothing had occurred to weaken his confidence in the locomotive; it had gone on increasing in power and efficiency, perfected by the labors of a succession of eminent engineers, chief amongst whom was his son; and he regarded it as more than ever the king of machines. Doubtless, he had a strong bias in favor of his own engine—his mind having, like all others, become almost exclusively impressed with the idea which it had exclusively pursued. Nevertheless, continued experience only served to confirm the soundness of his opinion as to the superiority of the locomotive. That his views on the subject of gauge and gradients were equally sound, is now, we believe, generally admitted by railway managers and engineers.

Shortly after the triumphant celebration of the success of the railway system at Tamworth, Mr. Stephenson was invited to be present at an interesting assemblage of railway men in Manchester, at which a testimonial was presented to Mr. J. P. Westhead, the former chairman of the Manchester and Birmingham Railway. The original Liverpool and Manchester line had swelled into gigantic proportions. It formed the original nucleus of the vast system now known as the London and Northwestern Railway. First one line, and then another, of which Mr. Stephenson had been engineer, became amalgamated with it, until the main line extended from London to Lancaster, stretching out its great arms to Leeds in one direction and Holyhead in the other, and exercising an influence over other northern lines as far as Glasgow, Edinburgh and Aberdeen. On the occasion to which we refer, Mr. Stephenson, the father of railways, was not forgotten. It was mainly his ingenuity, energy and perseverance that had called forth the commercial enterprise which issued in this magnificent system of internal communication; and the railway men who assembled to do honor to Mr. Westhead, did not fail to recognize the great practical genius through whose labors it had been established. He was "the rock from which they had been hewn," observed Mr. Westhead—the father of railway enterprise—and the forerunner of all that had been done to extend the locomotive system throughout England and throughout the world.

This was the last railway meeting that Mr. Stephenson attended, and the last occasion on which he appeared in public, with the exception of a soirée of the Leeds Mechanics' Institute, in December, 1847. The words which he then addressed to the young men at Leeds were highly characteristic. Though crowned with honors, the architect of the railway system, and the constructor of some of the greatest works of his time, "he stood before them," he said, "but as an humble mechanic. He had risen from a lower standing than the meanest person there; and all that he had been enabled to accomplish in the course of his life had been done through perseverance. He said this for the purpose of encouraging youthful mechanics to do as he had done—to persevere." The words were simple, but forcible and pregnant with life and instruction for all men.

In the spring of 1848, Mr. Stephenson was invited to Whittington House, near Chesterfield, the residence of his friend and former pupil, Mr. Swanwick, to meet the distinguished American, Emerson. It was interesting to see those two remarkable men, so different in most respects, and whose lines of thought and action lay in such widely different directions, yet so quick to recognize each other's merits. Mr. Stephenson was not, of course, acquainted with Mr. Emerson as an author; and the contemplative American might not be supposed to be particularly interested beforehand in the English engineer, whom he knew by reputation only as a giant in the material world. But there was in both an equal aspiration after excellence, each in his own sphere—the æsthetic and abstract tendencies of the one complimenting the keen and accurate perceptions of the material of the other. Upon being introduced, they did not immediately engage in conversation; but presently Mr. Stephenson jumped up, took Emerson by the collar, and giving him one of his friendly shakes, asked how it was that in England we could always tell an American? This led to an interesting conversation, in the course of which Emerson said how much he had everywhere been struck by the haleness and comeliness of the English men and women; and this diverged into a further discussion of the influences which air, climate, moisture, soil, and other conditions exercised upon the physical and moral development of a people. From this the conversation was directed upon the subject of electricity, upon which Mr. Stephenson launched out enthusiastically, explaining his views by several simple and striking illustrations. From thence it diverged into the events of his own life, which he related in so graphic a manner as completely to rivet the attention of the American. Afterwards, Emerson said, "that it was worth crossing the Atlantic to have seen Stephenson alone; he had such native force of character and vigor of intellect." Although Emerson does not particularly refer to this interview in the interesting essay afterwards published by him, entitled "English Traits," embodying the results of the observations made by him in his journeys through England, one cannot help feeling that his interview with such a man as Stephenson must have tended to fix in his mind those sterling qualities of pluck, bottom, perseverance, energy, shrewdness, bravery, and freedom, which he so vividly depicts in his book as the prominent characteristics of the modern Englishman.

The rest of his days were spent quietly at Tapton, amongst his dogs, his rabbits, and his birds. When not attending to the extensive works connected with his collieries, he was engaged in horticulture and farming. He continued proud of his flowers, his fruits and his crops; and the old spirit of competition still lived strong within him. Although he had for some time been in delicate health, and his hand shook from nervous affection, he appeared to possess a sound constitution. Emerson had observed of him that he had the lives of many men in him. But perhaps the American spoke figuratively, in reference to his vast stores of experience. It appeared that he had never completely recovered from the attack of pleurisy which seized him shortly after his return from Spain. As late however as the 26th of July, 1848, he felt himself sufficiently well to be able to attend a meeting of the Birmingham Institute, and to read to the members his paper "On the Fallacies of the Rotary Engine." It was his last appearance before them. Shortly after his return to Tapton, he had an attack of intermittent fever, from which he seemed to be recovering, when a sudden effusion of blood from the lungs carried him off, on the 12th of August, 1848, in the sixty-seventh year of his age.

His remains were followed to the grave by a large body of his workpeople, by whom he was greatly admired and beloved. They remembered him as a kind master, who was ever ready actively to promote all measures for their moral, physical, and mental improvement. The inhabitants of Chesterfield evinced their respect for the deceased by suspending business, closing their shops, and joining in the funeral procession, which was headed by the corporation of the town. Many of the surrounding gentry also attended the funeral. The body was interred in Trinity Church, Chesterfield, where a simple tablet marks the great engineer's last resting-place.

The statue of George Stephenson, which the Liverpool and Manchester and Grand Junction Companies had commissioned, was on its way to England when his death occurred; and the statue served for a monument, though his best monument will always be his works. The Liverpool Board placed a minute on their books, embodying also the graceful tribute of their secretary,

Mr. Henry Booth, in which they recorded their admiration of the life, and their esteem for the character of the deceased. "The directors," they say, "on the present occasion look back with peculiar interest to their first connection with Mr. Stephenson, in the construction of the Liverpool and Manchester Railway; to a period now twenty years past, when he floated their new line over Chat Moss, and cut his way through the rock-cutting at Olive Mount. Tracing the progress of railways from the first beginning to the present time, they find Mr. Stephenson foremost in urging forward the great railway movement; earning and maintaining his title to be considered, before any other man, the author of that universal system of locomotion which has effected such mighty results—commercial, social, and political—throughout the civilized world. Two years ago, the directors entrusted to Mr. Gibson, of Rome, the duty and the privilege of producing a statue that might do honor to their friend, then living amongst them. They did not anticipate that on the completion of this work of art the great original would be no more — that they should be constrained to accept the marble effigy of the engineer in lieu of the living presence of the man." * The statue here referred to was placed in St. George's Hall, Liverpool. A full-length statue of the deceased, by Bailey, was also erected a few years later, in the noble vestibule of the London and Northwestern Station, in Euston Square. A subscription for the purpose was set on foot by the Society of Mechanical Engineers, of which he had been the founder and president. A few advertisements were inserted in the newspapers, inviting subscriptions; and it is a notable fact that the voluntary offerings shortly received included an average of two shillings each from 3,150 working men, who embraced this opportunity of doing honor to their distinguished fellow-workman.

George Stephenson had a shrewd, kind, honest, manly face.

* Minutes of the Liverpool Board of the London and Northwestern Railway Company, 6th Sept., 1848.

Statue of Stephenson at Euston Square.

His fair, clear countenance was ruddy, and seemingly glowed with health. The forehead was large and high, projecting over the eyes; and there was that massive breadth across the lower part, which is usually observed in men of eminent constructive skill. The mouth was firmly marked; and shrewdness and humor lurked there as well as in the keen gray eye. His frame was compact, well-knit, and rather spare. His hair became gray at an early age, and towards the close of his life it was of a pure silky whiteness. He dressed neatly in black, wearing a white neck-cloth; and his face, his person, and his deportment at once arrested attention, and marked the gentleman.

CHAPTER XXXVI.

HIS CHARACTER.

The life of George Stephenson, though imperfectly portrayed in the preceding pages, will be found to contain many valuable lessons. His was the life of a true man, and presented a striking combination of those sterling qualities which we are proud to regard as essentially English.

Doubtless he owed much to his birth, belonging as he did to the hardy and persevering race of the north—a race less supple, soft, and polished than the people of the more southern districts of England, but, like their Danish progenitors, full of courage, vigor, ingenuity, and persevering industry. Their strong, guttural speech, which sounds so harsh and unmusical in southern ears, is indeed but a type of their nature. When Mr. Stephenson was struggling to give utterance to his views upon the locomotive before the Committee of the House of Commons, those who did not know him supposed he was "a foreigner." Before long the world saw in him an Englishman, stout-hearted and true—one of those master minds who, by energetic action in new fields of industry, impress their character from time to time upon the age and nation to which they belong.

The poverty of his parents being such that they could not give him any, even the very simplest education, beyond the good example of integrity and industry, he was early left to shift for himself, and compelled to be self-reliant. Having the will to learn, he soon forced for himself a way. No beginning could have been more humble than his; but he persevered: he had determined to learn, and he did learn. To such a resolution as his, nothing really beneficial in life is denied. He might have said, like Sebastian Bach, "I was industrious; and whoever is equally sedulous will be equally successful."

The whole secret of Mr. Stephenson's success in life was his careful improvement of time, which is the rock out of which fortunes are carved and great characters formed. He believed in genius to the extent that Buffon did when he said that "patience is genius;" or as some other thinker put it, when he defined genius to be the power of making efforts. But he never would have it that he was a genius, or that he had done any thing which other men, equally laborious and persevering as himself, could not have accomplished. He repeatedly said to the young men about him: "Do as I have done—persevere!" He perfected the locomotive by always working at it and always thinking about it.

Every step of advance which he made was conquered by patient labor. When an engineman, he systematically took his engine to pieces on Saturday afternoons, while the works were at a stand, for the purpose of cleaning it thoroughly, and "gaining insight." He thus gradually mastered the mechanism of the steam-engine, so that, when opportunity offered, he was enabled to improve it, and to make it work even when its own maker was baffled. He practically studied hydraulics in the same plodding way, when acting as plugman; and when all the local pump doctors at Killingworth were in despair, he stepped in, and successfully applied the knowledge which he had so laboriously gained. A man of such a temper and purpose could not but succeed in life.

His long labor to invent the perpetual motion was not lost. The attempt did him good, stimulating his inventiveness and mechanical ingenuity. He afterwards used to lament this loss of time, and said that if he had enjoyed the opportunity which young men of this day have, of knowing from books what others had done before them, he would have been spared much labor and mortification. Sometimes he thought he had hit upon discoveries, which he afterwards found were but old fallacies long since exploded. Yet the very effort to overcome difficulty was of itself an education. By wrestling with it, he strengthened his judgment and sharpened his skill. Being in earnest in his struggle, he was compelled to consider the subject in all its relations; and this would not suffer him to be superficial. He thus acquired practical ability through his steadfast efforts even after the impracticable; and, like other inventors, he gained his knowledge of what will do, by successive trials of what will not do.

Whether working as a brakesman or an engineer, his mind was always full of the work in hand. He gave himself thoroughly up to it. Like the painter, he might say that he had become great "by neglecting nothing." Whatever he was engaged upon, he was as careful of the details as if each were itself the whole. He did all thoroughly and honestly. There was no "scamping" with him. When a workman, he put his brains and labor into his work; and when a master, he put his conscience and character into it. He would have no slop-work executed merely for the sake of profit. The materials must be as genuine as the workmanship was skillful. The structures which he designed and executed were distinguished for their thoroughness and solidity; his locomotives were famous for their durability and excellent working qualities. The engines which he sent to the United States in 1832 are still in good condition;* and even the engines built by him for the Killingworth colliery, upwards of thirty years ago, are working steadily there to this day. All his work was honest, representing the actual character of the man.

* In 1852, Major-General MacNeil (U. S.) said: "Their best engines were imported from England Those supplied in 1832, by Stephenson & Co., were still in excellent working order."—*Discussion at the Institution of Civil Engineers, April 27th*, 1852.

The battle which Mr. Stephenson fought for the locomotive—and he himself always spoke of it as a "battle"—would have discouraged most other men; but it only served to bring into prominence that energy and determination which formed the back-bone of his character. "I have fought," said he, "for the locomotive single-handed for nearly twenty years, having no engineer to help me until I had reared engineers under my own care." The leading engineers of the day were against him, without exception; yet he did not despair. He had laid hold of a great idea, and he stuck by it; his mind was locked and bolted to the results. "I put up," he says, "with every rebuff, *determined* not to be put down." When the use of his locomotive on the Liverpool and Manchester line was reported against, and the employment of fixed engines recommended instead, Mr. Stephenson implored the directors, who were no engineers, only to afford a fair opportunity for a trial of the locomotive. Their common sense came to his rescue. They had immense confidence in that Newcastle engine-wright. He had already made steadfast friends of several of the most influential men amongst them, who valued his manly uprightness and integrity, and were strongly disposed to believe in him, though all the engineering world stood on the one side, and he alone on the other. His patient purpose, not less than his intense earnestness, carried them away. They adopted his recommendation, and offered a prize of 500*l.* for the best locomotive. Though many proclaimed the Liverpool men to be as great maniacs as Stephenson, yet the result proved the practical sagacity of the directors and the skill of their engineer; but it was the determined purpose of the latter which secured the triumph of the locomotive. His resolution, founded on sound convictions, was the precurser of what he eventually achieved; and his intense anticipation was but the true presentiment of what he was afterwards found capable of accomplishing.

He was ready to turn his hand to anything—shoes and clocks, railways and locomotives. He contrived his safety-lamp with the object of saving pitmen's lives, and periled his own life in testing it. Whatever work was nearest him, he turned to and did it. With him, to resolve was to do. Many men knew far more than he; but none was more ready forthwith to apply what he did know to practical purposes.

Sir Joshua Walmsley mentions, that when examining the works of the Orleans and Tours Railway, Mr. Stephenson, seeing a large number of excavators filling and wheeling sand in a cutting, at a great waste of time and labor, after the manner of foreign navvies, he went up to the men and said he would show them how to fill their barrows in half the time. He showed them the proper position in which to stand so as to exercise the greatest amount of power with the least waste of strength; and he filled the barrow with comparative ease again and again in their presence, to the great delight of the workmen. When passing through his own workshops, he would point out to his men how to save labor and to get through their work skillfully and with ease. His energy imparted itself to others, quickening and influencing them as strong characters always do—flowing down into theirs, and bringing out their best powers. He was the zealous friend of Mechanics' Institutes, and often addressed them in his homely but always interesting style—cheering young men on by the recital of his own difficulties, which he had overcome through perseverance.

His deportment towards the workmen employed under him was familiar, yet firm and consistent. As he respected their manhood, so did they respect his masterhood. Although he comported himself towards his men as if they occupied very much the same level as himself, he yet possessed that peculiar capacity for governing others which enabled him always to preserve amongst them the strictest discipline, and to secure their cheerful and hearty services.

One of the most beautiful features of Mr. Stephenson's character, was the affectionate interest which he took in the education of his son, stinting himself when only a poor working man in order to provide his boy with useful learning. He was not satisfied till he had obtained for him the advantages of a University course. Then he found him a most valuable fellow-worker.

From the opening of the Liverpool and Manchester Railway, the works of the father and the son can scarcely be separated. In their great engineering enterprises, and in the successive improvements effected by them in the arrangement and construction of the locomotive, their names are indissolubly united. Of the distinguished works of the son, it would be out of place to speak at length. But the London and Birmingham Railway, the Tubular Bridge over the Menai Straits, and the High Level Bridge at Newcastle, are works which future generations will point to as worthy of the greatest engineer of his day, and as noble results of George Stephenson's self-denying determination to educate his son to the fullest extent of his ability.

We cannot, however, refrain from mentioning the manner in which Mr. Stephenson's son has repaid the obligations which both were under to the Newcastle Literary and Philosophical Institute, when working together as humble experimenters in their cottage at Killingworth. The Institute was, until quite recently, struggling under a debt of 6,200*l.*, which seriously impaired its usefulness as an educational agency. Mr. Robert Stephenson offered to pay one half of the entire sum, provided the local supporters of the Institute would raise the remainder; and conditional also on the annual subscription being reduced from two guineas to one, in order that the usefulness of the institution might be extended. The generous offer was accepted, and the debt extinguished.

Probably no military chiefs were ever more beloved by their soldiers than were both father and son by the army of men who, under their guidance, worked at labors of profit, made labors of love by their earnest will and purpose. True leaders of men and lords of industry, they were always ready to recognize and encourage talent in those who worked for and with them. It was pleasant at the openings of the Stephenson lines, to hear the chief engineers attributing the successful completion of the works to their able assistants; whilst the assistants, on the other hand, ascribed the entire glory to their chiefs.

A fine trait in Mr. Stephenson's character was his generosity, which would not permit an attack to be made upon the absent or the weak. He would never sanction any injustice of act or opinion towards those associated with himself. On one occasion, during the progress of the Liverpool and Manchester works, while he had a strong party to contend with at the Board, the conduct of one of his assistants was called in question, as he thought unjustly, and a censure was threatened. Rather than submit to this injustice to his assistant, Mr. Stephenson tendered his resignation; but it was not accepted, and the censure was not voted. The same chivalrous protection was on many occasions extended by him to the weaker against the stronger. Even if he were himself displeased with any one engaged about him, any attack from another quarter would rouse him in defense, not in the spirit of opposition, but from a kind and generous impulse to succor those in difficulty.

Mr. Stephenson, though a thrifty and frugal man, was essentially unsordid. His rugged path in early life made him careful of his resources. He never saved to hoard, but saved for a purpose, such as the maintenance of his parents or the education of his son. In latter years, he became a prosperous and even a wealthy man; but riches never closed his heart, nor stole away the elasticity of his soul. He enjoyed life cheerfully, because hopefully. When he entered upon a commercial enterprise, whether for others or for himself, he looked carefully at the ways and means. Unless they would "pay," he held back. "He would have nothing to do," he declared, "with stock-jobbing speculations." His refusal to sell his name to the schemes of the railway mania—his survey of the Spanish lines without remuneration—his offer to postpone his claim for payment from a poor company until their affairs became more prosperous—are instances of the unsordid spirit in which he acted. "No mere pecuniary interest," it has been well said, "could have led George Stephenson to persevere in his onward course from boyhood, when he toiled as a slave to the great steam-engine of the mine, up to the period when he had forced his way through all the difficulties, natural and artificial, of the Manchester and Liverpool way. No mere calculation of percentages and dividends wrought this work. It was the high heroic soul, the strong English spirit, the magnificent will, the indomitable energy, that accomplished this world-enduring labor." *

Another marked feature in Mr. Stephenson's character was his patience. Notwithstanding the strength of his convictions as to the great uses to which the locomotive might be applied, he waited long and patiently for the opportunity of bringing it into notice; and for years after he had completed an efficient engine he went on quietly devoting himself to the ordinary work of the colliery. He made no noise nor stir about his locomotive, but allowed another to take credit for the experiments on velocity and friction made with it by himself upon the Killingworth railroad.

By patient industry and laborious contrivance, he was enabled to do for the locomotive what James Watt had done for the condensing engine. He found it clumsy and inefficient; and he made it powerful, efficient and useful. Both have been described as the improvers of their respective engines; but, as to all that is admirable in their structure or vast in their utility, they are rather entitled to be described as their inventors. While the invention of Watt increased the power, and at the same time so regulated the action, of the steam-engine, as to make it capable of being applied alike to the hardest work and to the finest manufactures, the invention of Stephenson gave an effective power

* Westminster Review, Sept. 1844.

to the locomotive, which enabled it to perform the work of teams of the most powerful horses, and to outstrip the speed of the fleetest. Watt's invention exercised a wonderfully quickening influence on every branch of industry, and multiplied a thousand fold the amount of manufactured productions; and Stephenson's enabled these to be distributed with an economy and dispatch such as had never before been thought possible. They have both tended to increase indefinitely the mass of human comforts and enjoyments, and to render them cheap and accessible to all. But Stephenson's invention, by the influence which it is daily exercising upon the civilization of the world, is even more remarkable than that of Watt, and is calculated to have still more important consequences. In this respect, it is to be regarded as the grandest application of steam power that has yet been discovered. The locomotive, like the condensing engine, exhibits the realization of various capital, but wholly distinct, ideas, promulgated by many ingenious inventors. Stephenson, like Watt, exhibited a power of selection, combination and invention of his own, by which—while availing himself of all that had been done before him, and superadding the many skillful contrivances devised by himself—he was at length enabled to bring his engine into a condition of marvelous power and efficiency. He gathered together the scattered threads of ingenuity which already existed, and combined them into one firm and complete fabric of his own. He realized the plans which others had imperfectly formed; and was the first to construct, what so many others had unsuccessfully attempted, the practical working locomotive.

In his deportment, Mr. Stephenson was simple, modest and unassuming, but always manly. He was frank and social in spirit. When an humble workman, he had carefully preserved his sense of self-respect. His companions looked up to him, and his example was worth even more to many of them than books or schools. His devoted love of knowledge made his poverty respectable, and adorned his humble calling. When he rose to a more elevated station, and associated with men of the highest position and influence in Britain, he took his place amongst them with perfect self-possession. They wondered at the quiet ease and simple dignity of his deportment; and men in the best ranks of life have said of him that "He was one of Nature's gentlemen."

If he was occasionally impatient of the opposition of professional brethren, it is scarcely to be wondered at when we look at the simple earnestness of his character, and consider that his sole aim was the establishment of his own well-founded convictions. No wonder that he should have been intolerant of that professional gladiatorship against which his life had been one prolonged struggle. Nor could he forget that the engineering class had been arrayed against him during his arduous battle for the locomotive, and that, but for his own pluck and persistency, they would have strangled it in its cradle.

Mr. Stephenson's close observation of nature provided him with a fullness of information on many subjects, which often appeared surprising to those who had devoted to them a special study. In passing through a country, nothing escaped his attention—the trees, the crops, the birds, the farmers' stock—in short, everything in nature afforded him an opportunity for making some striking observation, or propounding some ingenious theory. This rendered him a highly instructive and amusing companion at all times. On one occasion the accuracy of his knowledge of birds came out in a curious way at a convivial meeting of railway men in London. The engineers and railway directors present knew each other as railway men and nothing more. The talk had been all of railways and railway politics. Mr. Stephenson was a great talker on these subjects, and was generally allowed, from the interest of his conversation and the extent of his experience, to take the lead. At length, one of the party broke in with "Come now, Stephenson, we have had nothing but railways; can not we have a change, and try if we can talk a little about something else?" "Well," said Mr. Stephenson, "I'll give you a wide range of subjects—what shall it be about?" "Say *birds' nests!*" rejoined the other, who prided himself on his special knowledge of this subject. "Then birds' nests be it." A long and animated conversation ensued; the bird-nesting of his boyhood, the blackbird's nest which his father had held him up in his arms to look at when a child at Wylam, the hedges in which he had found the thrush's and the linnet's nests, the mossy bank where the robin built, the cleft in the branch of the young tree where the chaffinch had reared its dwelling—all rose up clear in his mind's eye, and led him back to the scenes of his boyhood at Callerton and Dewley Burn. The color and number of the bird's eggs, the period of their incubation, the materials employed by them for the walls and linings of their nests—were described by him so vividly, and illustrated by such graphic anecdotes, that one of the party remarked that, if George Stephenson had not been the greatest engineer of his day, he might have been one of the greatest naturalists.

It is Goethe, we believe, who has said that no man ever receives a new idea, at variance with his preconceived notions, after forty. But this observation, though it may be generally, is not invariably true. There are many great minds which never close. Mr. Stephenson, to the last, was open to the reception of new ideas, new facts, new theories. He was a late learner; but he went on learning to the end. He shut his mind, however, against what he considered humbugs—especially mechanical humbugs. Thus, he said at Tamworth, that he had not been to see the atmospheric railway because it was a great humbug. He had gone to see Pinkus's model of it, and that had determined him on the subject. He then declared the atmospheric system to be "a rope of sand;" it could never hold together, and he would not countenance it.

When he heard of Perkins's celebrated machine, which was said to work at a tremendous pressure, without steam, but with water in the boiler almost at red heat, he went with his son to see it. The engine exhibited was of six-horse power, and the pressure was said to be not less than 1500lbs. to the square inch. Mr. Stephenson said he thought it humbug; but he would test its power. Taking up a little oakum, and wrapping some round each hand, he firmly seized hold of the piston rod and held it down with all his strength. The machine was at once brought to a stand, very much to Mr. Perkins's annoyance. But the humbug had been exploded to Mr. Stephenson's satisfaction.

Towards the close of his life he frequently went down to Newcastle, and visited the scenes of his boyhood. "I have been to Callerton," said he one day to a friend, "and seen the fields in which I used to pull turnips at twopence a day; and many a cold finger, I can tell you, I had."

His hand was open to his former fellow-workmen whom old age had left in poverty. He would slip a five-pound note into the hand of a poor man or a widow in such a way as not to offend their delicacy, but to make them feel as if the obligation were all on his side. To poor Robert Gray, of Newburn, who acted as his bridesman, on his marriage to Fanny Henderson, he left a pension for life, which continues to be paid him.

About the beginning of 1847, Mr. Stephenson was requested to state what were his "ornamental initials," in order that they might be added to his name in the title of a work proposed to be dedicated to him. His reply was characteristic. "I have to state," said Mr. Stephenson, "that I have no flourishes to my name, either before or after; and I think it will be as well if you merely say 'George Stephenson.' It is true that I am a Belgian knight, but I do not wish to have any use made of it. I have had the offer of knighthood of my own country made to me several times, but would not have it. I have been invited to become a Fellow of the Royal Society, and also of the Civil Engineers' Society, but objected to the empty additions to my name. I am a member of the Geological Society; and I have consented to become President of, I believe, a highly respectable Mechanics' Institution at Birmingham."

As the founder of the school of modern engineers, it might have been expected that Mr. Stephenson would have been invited to join the Civil Engineers' Institute; and, indeed, he himself desired to do so. But there were two obstacles to his being admitted to membership. The first was, that Mr. Stephenson had served no regular apprenticeship to the profession; and the second was the composition of a probationary essay in proof of his capacity as an engineer. Mr. Stephenson could not comply with the first condition, and he would not comply with the second. The council of the institute were willing to waive the former, but not the latter point. But Mr. Stephenson said, if he went in at all, he would go in upright, not stooping one inch; and he did think it was too much to ask of him, that he should undergo the probationary test required from comparatively unknown juniors, and write an essay in proof of his knowledge of engineering, for the approval or criticism of a society, many of whose members had been his own pupils or assistants. He therefore turned his back, though reluctantly, on the Institute of Civil Engineers, and accepted the office of President of the Institution of Mechanical Engineers at Birmingham, which he held until his death.

Sir Robert Peel made him the offer of knighthood more than once; but Mr. Stephenson had no desire to hang on the outskirts of the titled class, or to get perched into high places of any kind. Arago, in his *Eloge*, complained that Watt was not made a baron. But what lustre would such a title have added to the name of either Watt or Stephenson? Thank Heaven, the strongest and best men of England do their work without hope of any such reward. Never were men less the creatures of government or of patronage than James Watt and George Stephenson; and, as representing the genius of the people from whom they sprang, we would rather have their simple names descend to posterity unadorned, than disguised and hidden under any unmeaning title borrowed from the middle ages.

As respects the immense advantages of railways to mankind, there cannot be two opinions. They exhibit, probably, the grandest organization of capital and labor that the world has yet seen. Although they have unhappily occasioned great loss to many, the loss has been that of individuals; whilst, as a national system, the gain has already been enormous. As tending to multiply and spread abroad the conveniences of life, opening up new fields of industry, bringing nations nearer to each other, and thus promoting the great ends of civilization, the founding of the railway system by George Stephenson must be regarded as one of the most important events, if not the very greatest event, in the first half of this nineteenth century.

To quote his own modest words, in conclusion, as expressed at a meeting of engineers in Birmingham towards the close of his career, "I may say," he observed, "without being egotistical, that I have mixed with a greater variety of society than perhaps any man living. I have dined in mines among miners, and I have dined with kings and queens, and with all grades of the nobility, and have seen enough to inspire me with the hope that my exertions have not been without their beneficial results — that my labors have not been in vain."

RÉSUMÉ

OF THE

RAILWAY SYSTEM AND ITS RESULTS.

RÉSUMÉ

OF THE

RAILWAY SYSTEM AND ITS RESULTS.

BY ROBERT STEPHENSON, ESQ., M. P.

[As a fitting conclusion to the life of George Stephenson, we append the following *résumé* of the Railway System and its Results, as delivered by his distinguished son before the Institution of Civil Engineers, on taking the chair after his election as their President, in January, 1856, and which we republish from the Minutes of Proceedings of that Institution, by permission of the Council.]

OUR BRITISH RAILWAYS present a fertile theme for observation, and in considering them, in their varied relations, my chief object will be to suggest topics for communications and discussion at the meetings over which I hope to have the honor of presiding.

The general extent and scheme of the network of railways stretching from beyond Aberdeen in the north, to Portsmouth in the south; and between Yarmouth and Milford Haven on the east and west of the United Kingdom, are well known to you. To these must be added the Irish lines, now becoming very extensive and exercising the most beneficial influence on that portion of the Empire.

Let us look, in the first instance, to the length of these railways. At the end of 1854, the total length of the lines authorized by Parliament was 13,983 miles; but as 1,177 miles had been abandoned, and there still remained about 4,752 miles to be constructed, the aggregate length of railways opened in Great Britain and Ireland at that time measured about 8,054 miles—about the diameter of the globe, and nearly 500 miles more than the united lengths of the Thames, the Seine, the Rhone, the Ebro, the Tagus, the Rhine, the Elbe, the Vistula, the Dneiper, and the Danube, or the ten chief rivers of Europe.

Of these 8,054 miles completed, 1,962 miles are single lines. Taking double and single lines together, the total length of railway in the kingdom is, therefore, 14,146 miles.

To this must be added the very considerable extent of rails laid for sidings, which, on an average, may be said to be equal in length to one-third of the total mileage. Add, then, say 4,000 miles for sidings, there is a total of 18,000 miles of railway in Great Britain and Ireland.

These 18,000 miles have been the work of only twenty-five years, and in that short space of time there have been laid rails, within these islands, far more than are sufficient to "put a girdle round about the earth!"

It will naturally be asked, what amount of capital has been required for the construction of these vast works? The amount authorized by Parliament to be raised for railway works, amounted, at the end of 1854, to £368,000,000. Of that amount £286,000,000 has absolutely been raised. It is difficult to realize to the imagination what is £286,000,000 sterling. Let us try to test the importance of the amount by some familiar comparisons. It is more than four times the amount of the annual value of all the real property of Great Britain. It is more than one-third of the entire amount of the national debt. We have, indeed, already spent nearly a third of this sum, in two years, in the prosecution of the war in which this country is engaged; but it is impossible not to reflect that if nearly £100,-000,000 expended by the State has only gained for us the advantage of occupying one side of the city, which the valor of England and France has doomed to destruction, the expenditure of £286,000,000 by the people has secured to us the advantages of internal communication all but perfect—of progress in science and arts unexampled at any period of the history of the world—of national progress almost unchecked, and of prosperity and happiness increased beyond all precedent.

In considering the results produced, it is impossible to pass over the magnitude of the works. Our tunnels have traversed hills and penetrated beneath mountains to the extent of nearly seventy miles. Of our viaducts,

I am not able, at present, to give the precise extent; but some estimate may be formed from the fact of there being, in London and the suburbs, nearly eleven miles of viaduct, passing through the streets. Of railway bridges there must have been built at least twenty-five thousand; far more than all the bridges ever previously known in England. But perhaps the magnitude of the railway works undertaken in this country will be still more clearly exhibited, if you consider the extent of the earth-works. Taking them at an average of 70,000 cubic yards to a mile, they will measure 550,000,000 cubic yards. What does this represent? We are accustomed to regard St. Paul's as a test for height and space; but by the side of the pyramid of earth these works would rear, St. Paul's would be but as a pigmy by a giant. Imagine a mountain half a mile in diameter at its base, and soaring into the clouds one mile and a half in height; that would be the size of the mountain of earth which these earth-works would form; while St. James' Park, from the Horse Guards to Buckingham Palace, would scarcely afford space for its base.

It is computed, that no less than 80,000,000 miles are annually traversed on our railways. Now, to run 80,000,000 miles per annum, 2½ miles of railway, at least, must be covered by trains, during every second of time, throughout the entire year.

To work our railways, even to their present extent, there must be at least 5,000 locomotive engines; and supposing an engine with its tender to measure only 35 feet, it will be seen, that the whole number required to work our railway system would extend, in one straight line, over 30 miles, or the whole distance from London to Chatham. But these are only the engines and tenders. The number of vehicles of every sort employed cannot be much less than 150,000. Taking the length of each vehicle at 20 feet, you will find that, could 150,000 be linked together in one train, they would reach from London to Aberdeen, or a distance of 500 miles.

Has any one present considered the value of this railway stock? Take the cost of each engine and tender at £2,000, and the average cost of each carriage, truck and wagon at £100, and you have a total exceeding £25,000,000 invested in rolling stock alone.

But these are far from being all the startling facts connected with railway enterprise. There are as many as 2,416 railway stations in the United Kingdom — one at least for every 45,000 passengers. The various Companies have, in their direct employment, not less than 90,409 officers and servants. The consumption of coke by railway engines amounts to not less than 1,300,000 tons of that fuel, representing upwards of 2,000,000 tons of coals; so that in every minute of time, throughout the year, 4 tons of coals are consumed, and 20 tons of water are flashed into steam of high elasticity. What does this represent? The water would afford a supply to the population of Liverpool at the rate of 22 gallons per head per diem, and the steam evolved is adequate to the maintenance of stationary engines of more than 130,000 horse power. The consumption of fuel is almost equal to the amount of coal exported from Great Britain to foreign countries, and is more than one half the whole consumption of the Metropolis. If to this be added the amount that must be used in producing the rails and other iron required for the whole system, the value of railways to the coal-owner must be evident.

Ten years ago, in 1845, the entire number of passengers carried upon railways was 33,791,000 in the year. The railway system was, at that time, thought to be pretty well developed, at least as regarded the main channels of communication. Five years afterwards, in 1850, the number of passengers conveyed was 72,854,000, and in 1854, the number conveyed was 111,206,000. Thus the number of passengers has been more than trebled in ten years; and assuming an average of 14 persons to a ton, there would be a gross weight of upwards of 8,000,000 tons of passengers conveyed annually.

The average distance which these passengers are conveyed appears to be about 12 miles. The average number carried per day is about 300,000. Under the old coach system it was assumed, that on an average 10 passengers could be carried by each coach; therefore, to carry 300,000 passengers a day, 12 miles each, at least 10,000 coaches and 120,000 horses would be necessary. The national saving will be forcibly illustrated, if you consider the cost of running these coaches and maintaining these horses, against the fact that locomotive expenses on railways do not, on an average, exceed 9½*d.* per mile.

The railway receipts for passengers have been in the following proportions:

In 1845 - - - - - - -	£3,976,000
1850 - - - - - - -	6,827,000
1854 - - - - - - -	9,174,000

The total receipts for goods, passengers, and from all other sources, were for the same years:

In 1845 - - - - - - -	£6,209,000
1850 - - - - - - -	13,204,000
1854 - - - - - - -	20,215,000

There has been no instance in the annals of any railway, where the annual traffic has not been of continuous growth. Some remarkable facts illustrate this truth. At one period the Midland Railway had the monopoly of the whole traffic to the North; that line being "the route" to the North of England and to Scotland. When the Caledonian was opened, some years ago, the Northwestern Railway, working in conjunction with it, was able to abstract the bulk of the Scotch traffic from the Midland line. Nevertheless, the Midland traffic continued to increase. At a later period the Great Northern was opened, affording almost a direct route to Nottingham, to Leeds, to York and to Edinburgh. The Scotch traffic of the Midland was thereby annihilated, and its trade to the large towns named almost entirely abstracted; yet, with all this, the Midland receipts continued to increase largely, chiefly in consequence of its local growth and the development of its mineral traffic.

This is one only of the many illustrations that might be offered of the rapid progress of a system which is now producing a gross annual revenue exceeding TWENTY MILLIONS STERLING.

Looking at all the circumstances of a railway, the nature of its component parts, and the enormous amount of traffic over it, the constant depreciation necessarily becomes a source of serious consideration.

A permanent way may be said to consist of sleepers, chairs and rails. The rails, it has been already stated, are 30,000 miles in length; which, at a reasonable average weight, will give about 2,225,000 tons of iron laid down in rails alone; resting upon not less than 50,000,000 iron chairs, weighing nearly 750,000 tons. So that you have, in the whole, not less than 3,000,000 tons of iron on the permanent ways of the United Kingdom.

Estimating the waste of iron, from wear and tear, oxidation and loss in remanufacture at (say) half a pound per yard annually, there cannot be less than 20,000 tons of iron to be every year replaced, and 200,000 tons of rails to be rerolled. The sleepers, of which there are not less than 26,000,000 on our lines of railway, perish still more rapidly. What with decay from wet and other causes, the sleepers disappear at the rate of 2,000,000 per annum, at the least, and require to be wholly replaced every twelve or fourteen years. It is curious to consider the effect of this annual demand for sleepers. To provide 2,000,000 of new sleepers, 300,000 trees must every year be felled, supposing that each tree will yield as many as six good sleepers. Now 300,000 trees can scarcely attain growth and maturity on less than 5,000 acres of forest. Consequently, 5,000 acres of forest must be annually cleared of timber to provide sleepers for our lines of railway.

A very important question presents itself as to the mode of meeting this heavy annual depreciation. The practice of some Railway Companies has been to set aside a fund, to make good the waste of material in the permanent way. With many Companies the amount which has been, or which ought to be thus set aside, as a Renewal Fund, has frequently occasioned great conflict of opinion. Among engineers there is, no doubt, much discussion on the details and various bearings of the question. Perhaps, however, it may be well to consider whether there really is any good argument for a Renewal Fund at all.

When a railway is first opened, everything being new, the annual depreciation will for some time go on in an increasing ratio. But it is obvious, that there must be a period in the age of the railway, when that annually-increasing ratio of depreciation must cease, and when the sum required for regular restoration and repair must become fixed and (except under extraordinary circumstances) almost certain. This may be illustrated by the case of an Insurance Company. Probably in the first year of the existence of such a company it sustains no loss by death, and in the second and third years only one or two lives drop. For some succeeding years the losses from this source increase in an augmenting ratio. But a period arrives, when the annual decrement of life becomes fixed, and except in the case of pestilence or other extraordinary occurrence, nearly certain. As it is with humanity, so it is with rails and sleepers. The depreciation, small at first, increases gradually, until at length it arrives at an average, and becomes fixed and nearly certain every year. This being so, why should an extraordinary special fund be set aside to provide for renewals and repairs? Those renewals and repairs are, under such circumstances, as well established a charge as the salaries of officers or the cost of fuel. If there is to be a Renewal Fund, the true principle would seem to be, to set aside a considerable sum in the earlier years of a railway, until the period when the average is reached, after which time the repairs should be a regular charge upon receipts.

The argument by which a Renewal Fund is supported, is the assumed desirability of equalizing dividends; but it has been already stated, that there has never been a case where the gross annual receipts of a railway have diminished. The growth of a railway is, and must be, progressive, save under very exceptional circumstances. Not only does the very existence of a railway furnish excitement for trade and create taste for travel, but our population increases at the rate of 15 per cent. in every decade, which of itself affords assurance that, apart from transitory causes of disturbance, the traffic of railways must increase. The ground for a Renewal

Fund is removed by these considerations; and if Railway Companies would only honestly and fairly keep their roads in sound and substantial condition, the better system, probably, would be to make the annual costs of repairs a charge on revenue, and to entirely dispense with such a Renewal Fund.

Let it be observed, that the arguments which apply to the permanent way, apply equally to the rolling stock of railways. Accountants and Committees of Investigation have been in the habit of calling for annual valuations of rolling stock, as if such valuations threw any light upon the real state of the affairs of a Company. The truth would seem to be, that a valuation of rolling stock is a fallacy. Suppose a Railway Company commences with one hundred engines, costing £2,500 a piece, its locomotive stock will be of the value of £250,000. At starting, these one hundred engines are, of course, in complete order; but from the day they begin running, deterioration commences. At the end of four or five years, probably twenty or twenty-five of them are always in the workshop. If the traffic of a line requires one hundred engines to do its work, it is obvious that the Company must at that time provide twenty or twenty-five new engines, to supply the place of those which are undergoing repairs. But having done this, they are only just in the same position as they were in at starting; that is to say, they have one hundred effective engines at work. Let them continue to keep this number of engines in good working order, as a current expenditure for a like amount of traffic, and it is clear that the machinery of the railway requires nothing more. As for a money valuation, such a proceeding must obviously be unproductive of beneficial results. Not only do engines depreciate, like everything else, but their price varies with the supply and the demand, with invention and its application, and from many other causes. Within the last ten years, the market value of engines has fluctuated about twenty-five per cent.; so that a railway which had engines valued at £100,000 in January, 1850, might have found those same engines valued at £75,000 in January, 1851, even although they had not worked an hour. Or, to put the case the other way: a stock valued at £75,000 in 1851, might have been revalued at £100,000 in 1852. In either case, it is obvious that, for any practical purpose, the valuation must be fallacious, and that to allow it to affect the dividends, with which it has no concern, must be wrong in principle. The truth would appear to be, that the only useful valuation is that of the condition of the engines for working purposes, in order to show the extent to which they may have deteriorated by working within a given length of time.

But it may be urged, that this argument presupposes the same class of engines and the same weight of rails to be continued forever on a railway; whereas, owing to the demands of increasing traffic, and for high rates of speed, heavy rails are obliged to be substituted for light, and engines of greater for those of less power. The real question then is, what portion of the cost of such improvements should be charged to capital? In respect to these improvements many fallacies have undoubtedly crept into railway accounts. The only sound and rational principle seems to be, not to charge the whole sum to capital, but simply the difference. If, for example, a rail weighing 100 lbs. per yard be substituted for one weighing 70 lbs., the fair proportion to charge the capital would be, not the entire cost of the 100 lbs. of iron, but the cost of the 30 lbs. additional weight. The same with the engines. If an engine of improved construction be purchased to replace a less effective one, or for the purposes of increased traffic, capital should bear the proportion of cost which is due to its future efficiency, or to the accommodation of increased traffic, and that proportion only. It may be further urged, that there are extraordinary circumstances under which the average repairs of permanent way and works will be disturbed; and, no doubt, inevitable fluctuations must occur over which the greatest experience and foresight cannot exercise control. But here, again, the question arises, is a Renewal Fund, in the form it is now made to assume, necessary to meet such cases? Surely, perfect security might be attained with respect to such causes of disturbance, by setting aside an Equalizing or Differential Fund, of small amount, whence the casual excess of expenditure required might be drawn. Whatever system may be devised, by the most skillful accountant, to place this question upon an unexceptional basis, it must be borne in mind, that the feelings of shareholders and the opinions of directors will always practically control the effect of any such suggestions. Influenced, therefore, by the recollection of what has so repeatedly occurred in board rooms and at meetings of shareholders, I have arrived at the conviction that the only sound policy will be to adhere rigidly to the suggestions here made respecting Renewal Funds. But whatever may be determined on this point, undoubtedly, the only method of keeping railway accounts on a proper basis, must be to make them show whether the annual revenue is made to bear its fair charge of upholding the permanent way and rolling stock in complete efficiency; and it would appear that this would be most effectually accomplished when Renewal Funds were almost entirely dispensed with, and the charges for repairs and improvements were treated as standing charges against revenue.

It may be thought that, with respect to fares, the interests of Railway Companies and of the public are antagonistic. Regarding the question, however, with a more enlarged view, it will be readily seen that, so far from those interests being opposed, they are in all respects identical. Fares should be regulated by directorates exclusively by a consideration of the circumstances which produce the largest revenue to the Companies; and the circumstances which produce the largest revenue, are those which most induce travelers to avail themselves of railway facilities. As regards the public, it may be easily shown, that nothing is so desirable, for their interests, as to take advantage of all the opportunities afforded by railways. As regards railways, it is certain, that nothing is so profitable, because nothing is so cheaply transported, as passenger traffic. Goods traffic, of whatsoever description, must be more or less costly. Every article conveyed by railway requires handling and conveyance beyond the limit of the railway station; but passengers take care of themselves, and find their own way, at their own cost, from the terminus at which they are set down. It is true, that passengers require carriages somewhat more expensive in their construction than those prepared for goods; but this expense is compensated for by the circumstance that they are capable of running, and do run, a much greater number of miles—that the weight of passengers is small in proportion to the weight of goods—and that consequently the cost for locomotive power is less. It has been shown that 111,000,000 passengers, weighing 8,000,000 tons, have been conveyed, during the past year, over an average distance of twelve miles; yielding a revenue of more than £9,000,000 sterling. This gives, at the least, 2*s.* per ton per mile for the weight of passengers conveyed. Coals are conveyed, in some instances, at one halfpenny per ton per mile. It is to be recollected that trains are usually capable of transporting at least two or three times the number of passengers ordinarily traveling by them, and that the weight of the passengers, in all cases, is in extremely small proportion to the gross weight of a train, as, on an average, there will be fourteen passengers to every ton, and each train will readily convey two hundred passengers. The cost of running a train may be assumed, in most cases, to be about 15*d.* per mile, therefore one hundred passengers, at five-eighths of a penny per mile per passenger, would give 5*s.* 2½*d.* per train per mile, which may be taken as about the average of train earnings throughout the year. It is obvious, therefore, that any thing beyond five-eighths of a penny per mile per passenger may be rendered profitable, even if the passenger train is only half filled. Hence all directorates should look to the maximum amount of gross revenue to be derived from large passenger traffic, which maximum amount is only to be obtained by affording enlarged public facilities and temptations to travel. It results, then, that the interests of the public and of the Companies are identical, and not antagonistic.

It is not necessary to this argument to conclude, that in all cases fares should be fixed at a minimum rate. On the contrary, they should be regulated by local circumstances and considerations of public convenience and facility. In London and other parts of the kingdom where the population is dense, and where millions desire conveyance over short distances, say of from two to ten miles, low fares are indispensable, and wherever they have been tried, have proved thoroughly successful. As the average railway fare throughout the kingdom does not exceed 1*s.* 6*d.* per passenger, or the cost of conveyance in a first-class carriage from London to Wimbledon, a distance of seven miles and a half, it will be seen how preponderating a proportion of railway receipts arises entirely from local traffic; that local traffic can be most completely developed, wherever there are centers of public attraction and interest; and that whether to a crystal palace, or to a country fair, or market, a low fare for a short distance, on the return-ticket principle, or otherwise, is sure to pay. It is the lowness of price, in these cases, which is the real temptation to the population, and the fare should be regulated by that consideration. But there are other cases in which the lowness of price will not be the consideration. In a journey, for instance, from London to Edinburgh, or to Aberdeen, the amount of time consumed is necessarily so large, that, however low the fare, the great bulk of the public could not abandon other avocations for a sufficient interval to undertake the journey. No mere inducement of low fare, therefore, would be likely greatly to increase the traffic on so long a route. The public who have to perform so long a journey, want, in such cases, high rates of speed, together with those increased comforts and conveniences which are the more needed by travelers in proportion to the length of their journey. Provided these are afforded, liberal fares may be demanded from the public for these longer routes. And from this argument it may be deduced, that an invariable policy of either high or low fares is equally vicious, if applied to all cases; that every case ought to be treated upon consideration of its local circumstances; and that a system which, under one condition of things would be fatal, may, under another state of circumstances, be developed with success.

The facilities afforded by railways to the post-office are, no doubt, of the highest public consequence. The speed which is attained in the transmission would appear at first to be the greatest item in the catalogue of those facilities; but it may be doubted if it is the most important. What is really of the greatest value to the post-office, is the facility afforded for conveying bulk. It is not too much to say that, without railway facilities, the excellent plans of Mr. Rowland Hill, for the reduction of the rates of postage, could not have been carried out to their full extent. The first essential to the success of those plans would have been wanting ; for there would have been no sufficient means of conveying the greatly increased mass of correspondence necessary to be carried, in order to render the reduced rates of postage profitable. The old mail coaches were never planned for bulk, which would, indeed, have been fatal to that regularity and speed upon which the post-office could alone rely, as the means of securing to the government the monopoly of the letter-carriage of the nation. The aggregate weight of the evening mails dispatched from London in 1838, in twenty-eight mail-coaches, amounted, as was shown by the Report of the Select Committee on Postage, to only four tons six cwt., or an average of about three and one-fourth cwt. per coach. But now, on a Friday night, when so many thousands of weekly papers are sent into the country, the post-office requires, on the London and Northwestern Railway, not only the use of the traveling post-office, which is provided for its convenience, but it occupies also six or eight additional vans. It is obvious, therefore, that if the existing system of the post-office had been in operation, with the present results, in the days of mail-coach communication, not one mail alone, but fourteen or fifteen mails, such as were used in those days, would have been needed to carry on, with regularity, the post-office traffic between (say) London and Birmingham. Nearly every coach that ran in 1830, between Birmingham and London, would now have been needed for post-office purposes, if the London and Northwestern Railway had not been brought into existence. The expenses would, consequently, have been so large, that a universal penny postage would have entailed a certain loss. For the great blessing, therefore, derived from cheap postal communication, the nation is, in a great degree, indebted to the facilities offered by railways.

It must be borne in mind, here, that the boon conferred upon the public is not limited to written correspondence. Viewed in reference to the postal facilities they afford, the railways are the great public instructors and educators of the day. Contrast the size of "The Times" in 1830 and 1856. Do you suppose that the huge mass of paper, which you are permitted to forward by to-night's post, would have been conveyed upon the same terms, if the means of conveyance had remained limited to the mail and its four horses? Look at the immense mass of Parliamentary reports and documents, now distributed every session amongst all the constituencies of the empire, at almost a nominal charge. To what do the public owe the valuable information embodied in those documents, but to railways? Except as parcels by wagons, or by canal boats, they never could have been conveyed, prior to the existence of the railway system; and if they never could have been distributed, we may rely upon it that they never would have been printed. The reasoning which applies to "The Times" and to State papers, applies to newspapers generally, and to the distribution of the Prices Current of merchants, and of magazines, monthly publications, and bulky parcels of every description. Without railway facilities they would probably never have been circulated at all—certainly they never could have been circulated to the extent necessary to make them profitable. Hence, the railway, as before observed, is the great engine for the diffusion of knowledge.

Bearing these things in mind, it is obviously the duty of the government and of the Legislature to deal with railways upon an enlarged and liberal basis, in respect to all matters relating to postal communication. It is, no doubt, of the highest importance to the public, that the advantages railways are capable of affording to the post-office should be secured. Looking to the public interest, it is difficult, if not altogether impossible, to contend against any act of Parliament that peremptorily insists upon postal facilities being afforded, to the full extent they may be required for the public interest. At the same time whilst we may admit that railways have a duty to perform to the nation, in facilitating postal communication, it is clear that the peculiar and extraordinary advantages they afford in that respect, entitle them to a large share of consideration and to very liberal compensation for the work which they perform. It does not, however, altogether appear that the Companies have, hitherto, always been met by the post-office in the way in which they conceive themselves entitled to be treated. No fault, on this account, attaches to the post-office officials, who execute their arduous and important labors with very commendable zeal and with all possible courtesy; but the system of the government has been to require heavy service, and to allow the Companies little or no profit for its performance. A rent is paid, amounting to a fair rate of interest upon cost, for the carriages and vans which are employed upon a line; with, in addition, the exact amount of haulage and other special current expenses, which can be proved to be entailed by the conveyance of the mails; but should it chance, that upon any line the ordinary trains do not suit post-office purposes, the Companies may be compelled to put on trains at suitable hours for the mails, for which, ordinarily, very little remuneration is allowed, beyond the absolute outlay which the running of such trains can be proved to have entailed.

The effect of this must naturally be to make Railway Companies indifferent to postal traffic. It is needless to point out how seriously this must be to the public disadvantage. If Railway Companies had an interest in developing postal as well as passenger communication, what facilities might not be afforded to the people! It is beginning to be found, from the great bulk of correspondence requiring delivery, especially in London, that uncertainty, irregularity and delay, are becoming more and more frequent at the post-office. If Railway Companies were interested in postal intercourse, nothing would be easier for them than to make arrangements, whereby the deliveries, being rendered much more frequent, might entail much less duty at one given hour. Increased rapidity, certainty and regularity, would be thereby obtained; advantages which, with the means now at the disposal of the post-office, and with its vastly and rapidly increasing business, there seems but little prospect of the government alone being able to secure.

The post-office has recently absolutely entered into competition with the Railway Companies. As carriers, the Companies derived considerable profit from parcels. The post-office, finding that railways afford the means of carrying any quantity of bulk, has seen fit to undertake the conveyance of books and other parcels at very reduced postal rates. If the post-office should extend its operations a little further, it must be brought into absolute antagonism with the Companies. Books are heavier articles than laces or muslins, or many other fabrics, the conveyance of which enter largely into railway receipts. The post-office having made book parcels profitable, may try to turn to account the conveyance of other, whether lighter or heavier, articles of trade. It might be thought advisable to carry a small valuable parcel to Aberdeen for *2d.*, a rate at which railway Companies, having to pay interest on capital, certainly cannot hope to compete with a department which insists on the right of traveling on their roads at the mere actual cost. You will not, therefore, fail to see, that the post-office arrangements may be carried to a point at which great injustice would be done to Railway Companies.

Little more than a quarter of a century has elapsed, since Parliament first began to legislate for railways. In that period a multitude of laws have been placed upon the statute-book, which will certainly excite the wonder, if they fail to be the admiration, of future generations. The London and Northwestern Railway alone is regulated, as is shown by a return of Mr. Hadfield's, by no less than one hundred and eighty-six different acts! Of these the greater part were passed in the present reign.

But it is not so much the number of the statutes regarding railways, that excites surprise. The extraordinary feature of the parliamentary legislation and practice consists in the anomalies, incongruities, irreconcilabilities, and absurdities, which pervade this mass of legislation. A commission was appointed a few years since for the consolidation of the statute law. If ever that commission should have to deal with railway law it will indeed find itself in a dilemma. It will find, that the legislation for railways, both in principle and in detail, is utterly irreconcilable ; and that the only way of escaping the difficulties of the position would be to sweep the whole from the statute-book and legislate afresh.

Not only is the legislation irreconcilable, but throughout the quarter of a century during which attention has been given to this branch of legislation, the acts of the Parliament have been wholly at variance with its own principles. To illustrate this : Several different select committees have, at various times, deliberately reported against the possibility of maintaining competition between railways, and to this principle Parliament has as often assented. Yet the practical operation of the laws, which have received legislative sanction, has been throughout and at the same time directly to negative this principle, by almost invariably allowing competition to be obtained, wherever it has been sought! Parliament, therefore, has been adding to the capital of Railway Companies, whilst it has been sanctioning measures to subdivide the traffic. The decline of dividends was an inevitable consequence.

Again, in 1836, the House of Commons required its Committees upon Railway Bills specially to report as to the probability of railways paying. This principle has, however, been gradually departed from, until such inquiry is now considered and treated as utterly unimportant. Legislative sanction having been given to a line, it might be supposed that Parliament would also grant adequate protection, exacting from the railway certain public facilities and advantages, in return for the rights afforded to it. But, instead of doing this, the practice has been precisely the reverse. Whilst the legislature and the government have exacted facilities and advantages even beyond what they had a fair right to demand, so far from protecting the interests of those to whom they conceded the right of making the line, they have allowed—nay, they have encouraged—every description of competition! What has been the result? As regards the completeness and perfectness of the line first made, obviously it must have been most injurious ; as regards the profits of shareholders, no doubt, it has been, in many cases, most disastrous. But how does the case stand as regards the public? Why, whatever may have been the effect for the time, the competition, which Parliament has permitted, has invariably been terminated by combination—so that the public have been left precisely where they were.

But the incongruities are by no means the worst feature of the parliamentary legislation now under consideration. Mr. Hadfield's return has been spoken of. That return, in itself exceedingly incomplete, and affording no information of any sort respecting forty-five Railway Companies, for which acts have been obtained, shows that the amount expended by existing Railway Companies, in obtaining the Acts of Parliament by which they are empowered, has been no less, in parliamentary, legal, and engineering costs, than FOURTEEN MILLIONS sterling! No sooner was that fact placed on record, than a universal outcry burst from the alarmists. "See," it was said, "how shareholders have been plundered; see how their money has been squandered; look at this vast amount of waste, and consider how much better it would have been in your own pockets!" But, in no one case did those who made these bitter comments attribute the monstrous result to the proper cause. Railway directors and officials have been held responsible for what has been the fault, solely and exclusively, of Parliament itself. What interest can directors and officers have in Group Committees, wherein counsel must be feed for attendance during, perhaps, ten or twenty days, when they are never heard nor wanted? What interest can directors or officers have in keeping crowds of witnesses in London, at great expense, awaiting the pleasure of a Committee, which is engaged upon another measure, and which can rarely foresee or indicate when those witnesses will be required? The ingenuity of man could scarcely devise a system more costly, than that of getting a Railway Bill through the legislature. But who devised that system? Parliament itself. Who have begged, and prayed, and implored for alteration unavailingly? Directors and officers of Companies. An illustration may show more graphically how Parliament has entailed expense upon Railway Companies, by the system it has set up. Here is a striking one. The Trent Valley Railway was, under other titles, originally proposed in the year 1836. It was, however, thrown out by the Standing Orders Committee, in consequence of a barn, of the value of about £10, which was shown upon the general plan, not having been exhibited upon an enlarged sheet. In 1840 the line again went before Parliament. It was proposed by the Grand Junction Railway (now part of the Northwestern). No less than four hundred and fifty allegations were made against it before the Standing Orders sub-Committee. That sub-Committee was engaged twenty-two days in considering those objections; they ultimately reported that four or five of the allegations were proved; but the Standing Orders Committee, nevertheless, allowed the bill to be proceeded with. Upon the second reading it was supported by Sir Robert Peel, and had a large majority in its favor. It then went into Committee. The Committee took sixty-three days to consider it, and ultimately Parliament was prorogued, before the Report could be made. Such were the delays and consequent expenses which the forms of the House occasioned in this case, that it may be doubted if the ultimate cost of constructing the whole line was very much more than the amount expended in obtaining permission from Parliament to make it.

This example will show the delays and difficulties with which Parliament surrounds railway legislation. Another instance will illustrate the tendency of its proceedings to encourage competition. In 1845 a bill for a line now existing went before Parliament with no less than eighteen competitors, each party relying on the wisdom of Parliament to allow their bill at least to pass a second reading! Judged by such a case, the policy of Parliament really would seem to be to put the public to expense, and to make costs for lawyers, and fees for officers. Is it possible to conceive any thing more monstrous, than to condemn nineteen different parties to one scene of contentious litigation? Bear in mind that every additional bill received by Parliament entailed additional expense, not only on the promoters of that one bill, but on all the other eighteen competitors. They each and all had to bear the costs, not of parliamentary proceedings upon one bill, but of the parliamentary proceedings upon nineteen bills. They had to pay not only the costs of promoting their own line, but also the costs of opposing eighteen other lines! And yet, conscious as Government must have been of this fact, Parliament deliberately abandoned the only step it ever took, on any occasion, of subjecting railway projects to investigation by a preliminary tribunal.

Railways have suffered by parliamentary legislation from other causes. During every one of the twenty-five years that Parliament has legislated on the subject, it has always had a crotchet. One of these will be remembered by every civil engineer under the name of the "Datum point," which, for many years, offered a fatal objection to scores of projects. Perhaps some of the best proposals ever made for the benefit of the public fell through, because Parliament insisted on its "Datum point." Yet there is not an engineer in the kingdom who does not laugh at the idea. The "Datum point" is the crotchet of some theoretical red-tapist. Every practical man knows that it is not of the slightest real value in checking levels, or for any other practical purpose. The consequence of these crotchets is, that the Standing Orders are loaded with a number of useless forms which are not now rigidly enforced; and recording, as they do, the exploded crotchets of the House of Commons, they are become almost a nullity, except in so far as they occasionally involve expense or trouble.

But having passed a bill, how does Parliament treat the railway on which it has conferred powers? In the first place, it affords extraordinary facilities to land owners to make extraordinary demands for compensation. Having given them these facilities, it then makes the legal steps by which such demands can be resisted so expensive, that, in a money point of view, it is frequently difficult to decide whether, if all the desired reduction can be made, the cost of obtaining the saving will not exceed the whole amount that can be saved. This is so well understood, that acute surveyors and solicitors, after making fair estimates of value, always add an amount to their estimate, for charges which may be entailed by resisting claims.

Of the £286,000,000 of railway capital expended, it is believed that nearly one-fourth has been paid solely for land and conveyancing; and yet it is well known that, except in regard to the houses which have been actually demolished, nearly every piece of property which is intersected, undergoes improvement in value, in consequence of the construction of the lines. In towns and villages, the land abutting on the railway becomes frontage; and even in the country, land near stations becomes available for building purposes. The millions which have been paid by Railway Companies to land owners for their property, may therefore be said to be so much absolutely put into their pockets. Considering, in addition to this profit upon the land taken, the increased value of the land left, it is clear that the gain to the land owners by railways must, in the aggregate, have been enormous.

Now here again the one-sided character of parliamentary legislation is exhibited. Parliament has never, on any occasion, permitted improvement to be considered as an element in favor of a railway; but it has always been ready to tax the Railway Company, on account of possible depreciation. The extent to which claims on account of depreciation have been carried, is well known. Great was the ingenuity of the agent who discovered the use of the word "SEVERANCE." To Railway Companies constant repetition has made that term but too familiar. In every case in which the line passes through an estate, a claim is set up for compensation, on account of "severance;" which means simply, that the property having previously been in what is called a ring-fence, it becomes, by the passage of a railway through it, less convenient for purposes of cultivation. Let it be observed, that the depreciation upon which this claim is based, is ordinarily imaginary and ideal. It is utterly untrue, that an estate is necessarily rendered less convenient for cultivation, by the passage through it of a railway; indeed, in the majority of cases, it is capable of proof that the result is the reverse. The Railway Companies are therefore mulcted for an idea. No agent has yet been able to reduce to figures the practical value of this alleged inconvenience. Care is always taken that a railway shall supply facilities of communication; and when bridges and crossings are constructed, severance ceases in reality to exist. No one has ever been able to show, arithmetically, that, by the mere passage of a railway through an estate, loss is sustained; yet the practical result of the legislation of Parliament is this, that whereas a railway takes land from a land owner of the value of some £500 or £600, a claim for severance is often made and allowed to the extent of nearly as many thousands. Agents of the highest respectability make the claim, on the ground that it is customary, admitting that there is no substantial reason whatever for it. In one recent case, a claim for compensation for severance was made by the owner of some marsh land in Essex, whose whole estate was taken by a Company, but who claimed for "severance," on the ground that the loss of his marsh land on the Thames was injurious to an arable farm which he possessed many miles distant! This illustration will show the extent to which this doctrine is carried, and how this system of spoliation, permitted by Parliament, has become legalized by custom.

It may be asked, What is the proper remedy for the state of things which has been thus described? The remedy which has suggested itself to some practical minds, is one which, it is to be feared, the government of our day is unlikely to grant. If, instead of leaving the decision of these subjects to inexperienced tribunals, a mixed commission could be organized, of practical men, of acknowledged legal, commercial, and mechanical ability, there might be hope for us. What we want is a tribunal upon these subjects competent to judge, and willing to devote its attention to railway subjects only. We do not impute to Parliament that it is dishonest; but we impute that it is incompetent. Neither its practical experience, nor its time, nor its system of procedure, are adapted for railway legislation. Both Houses, indeed, admit their incompetency, by referring the consideration of every question to Select Committees. But go into a Select Committee, and observe how it is composed. Observe the list of subjects committed to it for investigation—including, as it does, not only railway bills, but gas bills, water bills, canal bills, navigation bills, drainage bills, and burial bills It is most unnatural to suppose that such tribunals can be satisfactory to those who have embarked hundreds of millions of money in the greatest enterprises of the age.

What we ask is knowledge. "Give us," we say, "a tribunal competent to form a sound opinion. Commit to that tribunal, with any restrictions you think necessary, the whole of the great questions appertaining to our system. Let it protect private interests apart from railways; let it judge of the desirability of all initiatory measures, of all proposals for purchases, amalgamations, or other railway arrangements: delegate to it the power of enforcing such regulations and restrictions as may be thought needful to secure the rights of private persons, or of the public; devolve on it the duty of consolidating, if possible, the Railway Laws, and of making such amendments therein as the public interests, and the property now depending upon the system, may require; give it full delegated authority over us in any way you please; all we ask is, that it shall be a tribunal that is impartial, and that is thoroughly informed; and if impartiality and intelligence are secured, we do not fear for the result."

It is to be apprehended that there is no probability of a government of routine, such as we have in England, conceding this, or any other departure from their system, however badly that system may be found to work. If a concession were made in any form, it is to be still further apprehended, that neither in the selection of the persons presumed to be competent for the fulfillment of such functions, nor in the remuneration the government would consent to award to them, would there be adequate security for the proper fulfillment of the high duties which they would have to perform. But it is not too much to insist that, in some shape or other, a new tribunal of this sort must be created, if the railway system of England is to work with advantage to those who have undertaken its development, without risk to the public, and without prospect of further legislative interference to its disadvantage.

From the very circumstances of the position in which they are placed by Parliament, Railway Managements are, and must be, anomalous in their character. Parliament has legislated for railways simply as public highways, to be passed over by the whole world, upon payment of a certain toll. It has placed managements, therefore, in the position of mere toll-takers; and mere toll-takers they would be, if the practical and actual necessities of their system did not compel them to become traders and carriers—to distribute goods, and to possess wagons, horses, and warehouses, for the purpose of carrying on their traffic.

Every energetic railway direction, controlled by men of business, embarks in enterprises which are, apparently, wholly foreign to the parliamentary objects of the railway itself. But then, unfortunately for all parties, this very necessity of doing an act, in itself irreconcilable with the intention of Parliament, produces serious dilemmas. So long as dividends are kept up, a directorate, however illegal may be its acts, or however inefficient its management, is certain to enjoy, with its shareholders, the highest meed of popularity; but only let the dividends fall, and however wise, however energetic, however prudent may have been the direction, it is immediately found that it has exceeded the limits of the duty devolved upon it by the Acts of Parliament; that it has embarked the Company in rash and unwise speculations; and that its members, collectively and individually, deserve to be impeached. Even one-half per cent. has been known to make all the difference in the popularity of the management. Let that popularity fall, and Committees of Investigation are forthwith appointed, charges are raked up and bandied about, affecting the character of the individuals who have got into disfavor, no matter how high those individuals may be in station, how honorable they may be known to be in principle, or how much soever their direction may have been hitherto advantageous to the Company. And, as it is with shareholders, so it is with the public. Local circumstances necessitate some alteration in the times of a train, or the rates of fares. The convenience, or the caprice, or the pocket of some contentious individual is thereby interfered with. Rejoicing that he has a grievance — in the phraseology of the day — he "writes to the Times." The press, necessarily ill-informed as to the actual facts, receives, as correct, the ex parte statement. Leading articles depict, in powerful language, the errors and abuses of management. Columns are filled with letters from all who have a petty grievance to complain of, or a private pique to gratify; and Companies are instructed as to all the minutiæ of management, by those who, except as travelers, are probably wholly uninformed as to railway affairs. The consequence of all this is, great injustice, and frequently great injury, to the Railway Companies; for no directorate feels itself safe, at least as to character, that does not restrict itself within the closest interpretation of the law, and that does not make concessions to the, presumed, public demands; but, in so doing, the certain result is, that the interests of the Company are lost sight of.

The period has arrived when these things, pressing heavily upon the most enlightened and enterprising railway managers, have caused serious reflections as to the way in which such difficulties are to be avoided. Many right-minded shareholders, also, feeling the force of the errors which are too often committed to their detriment, have attentively considered in what way the present system of management may be altered, so as to avoid these evils. Various suggestions have been made, some of which, undoubtedly, seem only calculated to increase the difficulty; whilst others in no degree alleviate it. Looking at the question in a broad point of view, the consideration occurs, whether it might not be possible, by some operation analogous to that of a trading company under the Limited Liability Act, to give an entirely new and greatly improved character to the relations between shareholders and managers. Suppose a limited number of men of business, varying, say, from ten to twenty, and capable of giving good security, agreed together to take a line from the shareholders, at a fixed rental. They might depute their management to two or three of their own body; or, even if the line was short, to one gérant. Under such circumstances, there would be no clamor from shareholders at half-yearly meetings—no sudden changes of directorates, involving ruinous alterations of policy—no cabals between one set of directors against another—and no mischievous interferences with the development of the system. The managers, free from the apprehension of being saddled, personally, with all the responsibility and liability, would be able to embark in enterprises, not comprehended in the terms of the Act of Parliament, but essential to the prosperity of their line. They might undertake business which, under the existing systems, the most enterprising directors would not dare to contemplate, however lucrative it might be. The managers of the line would have something more to look to than their position as directors. They would be free from apprehensions as to the liabilities they incurred; and whilst they would not be turned from their course of policy by the outcry of any discontented individual able to make his voice heard through any public channel, they would give practical security that the public interests would be consulted, because the interests of the public and those of the managers would be, in every respect, identical.

No doubt any system of this sort must be subject to restrictions, both for the interest of the public and the security of shareholders. Those restrictions are, however, matters of detail which it is needless at present to discuss. Presuming that leases were taken on good terms, and regarding the saving usually accruing from individual as compared with general management, it seems probable that an arrangement of this sort would be valuable alike to owners and to lessees, a large profit would accrue to those who took the line on safe and well considered terms, and who managed it with enterprise, vigor and economy. On the other hand, the shareholders would derive great advantages from the certainty of receiving fixed dividends, and from the present and prospective enhancement of the value of their property.

Upon other points of management, it is only needful here to say, that no railway can be efficiently or well conducted without thorough unity amongst the heads of all the great departments. Upon the superintendents of ways and works, of the locomotive department, of the out-door arrangements, and of traffic, devolve the most onerous and responsible duties. Where they fail to act together, or when any one of them ceases to enjoy the full confidence of the board, everything must go wrong. Having selected men of the best class, confiding in their integrity and assured of their competency, one of the principal duties of a railway direction is to support its officers. Any directoral interference with details must weaken their efficiency, upon which must mainly depend the ultimate success of the Company they serve.

No paper on railway subjects could be regarded as complete which did not offer some observations on the Electric Telegraph. The telegraph was, doubtless, an offspring of railways, and continues to be their indispensable companion. The first really practical application of the telegraph was to enable the stationary engine system on the Blackwall Railway to be worked with certainty and dispatch; but at this moment there are few lines of railway which do not employ the telegraph for every possible purpose. The total length of telegraph laid down in Great Britain is now about 7,200 miles; and the average number of wires being five, there is a total of 36,000 miles of wire, weighing 7,200 tons, and having cost upwards of £200,000. No less than three thousand people are constantly employed in transmitting messages and maintaining the works; and upwards of a million of public messages flow annually along this "silent highway."

Great as is the value of the electric telegraph to the public, there can be no doubt that it is far greater to the Railway Companies. On the Eastern Counties Line, three years ago, the number of messages transmitted on the special business of the Company was no less than 120,000 in one year. On that portion of the Northwestern Line where the traffic is largely concentrated, the progress of every train is now regulated, throughout its whole journey, by the operation of the telegraph. The system there employed may be thus described: The line is divided into convenient lengths of (say) from three to five miles. At each station there is a telegraph instrument in connection with a semaphore, which gives two signals only. If the needle of the instrument inclines to the right, it means that the line is clear; if it inclines to the left, it indicates that the line is blocked. Should it be observed that the needle rests upon the card vertically, this, though not a signal in the ordinary sense, is the most important indication of all, for it shows that the wire has been broken, either by some accident, which may possibly affect the line itself, or by some engine-driver or guard, whose train has met with a serious casualty, and whose first duty, in such an event, is to cut the wire.

Now, the great value of this system is, that whenever the needle rests vertically, or inclines to the left, the officers at the stations are immediately informed that something is wrong upon the line, and that no train must be allowed to pass, until the line is cleared. A collision, with such precautions, is all but physically impossible. And so far from this arrangement operating to delay the progress of a train, as might be supposed, experience proves that the traffic of a railway is immensely facilitated by it.

The automatic working of the telegraph shows the officers at every station, that for a considerable number of miles in advance of the station, whether up or down, the line of way is clear. This knowledge, imparted instantaneously, and comprehended by a glance, enables the officers to augment very materially the traffic over the portion of the line to which their duty may apply. The telegraph, in fact, does the work of an additional line of rails to every Company that uses it, and does it at a cost perfectly infinitesimal in comparison with the cost of constructing another line.

At one period of its history, the Northwestern Railway appeared to be so overcrowded with traffic, that additional lines for its relief were believed to be indispensable; but at the very moment when the demands upon the system were beginning to outgrow the machinery for safety, this remarkable invention came to its relief, and the capacity of the line for traffic has consequently been immensely increased. The very first use made of the telegraph was to enable the Company to meet the difficulty of a strike among the artisans. During the Great Exhibition of 1851, when 750,000 passengers were conveyed to London by the Northwestern excursion trains alone, the whole of the extraordinary traffic of the line was conducted by means of the electric telegraph. At the present moment, the ordinary traffic is double what it was when the telegraph was invented, and there is a greater capacity for increase than at any period since the line was opened.

Moreover, it must be observed that, great as is this saving to a Railway Company, it is not the only economy effected by the use of the electric telegraph. On every line where it is thoroughly employed, it effects a very material saving in the expensive element of rolling stock. The officers of a Company are enabled, the first thing every morning, to consider the wants and requirements of the day. They find that on one portion of their line there is likely to be extra traffic, whilst at some other station, during the previous day or night, there has been an accumulation of passenger carriages or vans. By the use of the electric telegraph, nothing is so easy as to supply the wants of one station from the surplus stock at the other, whilst the probabilities are, that without the facility afforded by the telegraph the stock at one place would have been lying idle, although it was urgently needed at another. Probably most lines would require fully twenty per cent. more carriage stock than they now possess, if it were not for the telegraph.

Whilst the value of the electric telegraph is very little understood, the means of working it are, probably, still less properly comprehended. It is generally supposed, that by some action of a handle at one station, the electric current is sent through a wire to another. But the fact is, that the success which the telegraph has obtained has been owing to the adoption of an opposite principle. Signals are now made, not by sending a current through a wire, but by the interception of the current which is continuously maintained; and this application is especially valuable, not only on account of the increased facility, but also on account of the increased security afforded. To signal, without a current through the wire, requires a machine in the hands of a skilled person; but to signal with a constant current through the wire, only requires that the wire should be broken, which can be accomplished on any spot by the most uninformed. The most unskillful, therefore, in case of accident, are fully able to use the electric telegraph, so as to give notice of difficulty or danger, and so as to receive immediate aid and assistance from the nearest stations, in both directions. Nor can there be any doubt, in such case, as to the indications of the telegraph. Alarm, misinterpretation, or other causes, might prevent a message from traveling or being read correctly, if it were dependent upon the use of a machine and the skill of both the sender and the interpreter; but where nothing more is needed than to intercept the flow of the current, by the rudest method, there can be no doubt either as to the operation or as to its effect. Of course this cutting of the wire applies solely to that which is called the "train wire," so that the messages of the public are in no way interrupted.

Recent projects gave promise of another, and not an unimportant improvement in the telegraph. Great, it might be supposed, would be the confusion, if two opposite currents of electricity met in one wire; but by a new adaptation, it is contemplated, that messages shall pass in opposite directions without the smallest interference with each other. The means employed are simply mechanical. The system would have been some time since in operation in England, but for the difficulty to be overcome from the variableness of the insulation of the wires, occasioned by the humidity of our climate. But already several beautiful modifications have been devised, in order to overcome this difficulty, and there is daily hope that the improvement will be perfected.

So much as regards railways. As regards the public, the electric telegraphs of England have been rapidly growing in importance, although, comparatively, we are still very backward in taking advantage of the facilities they afford. It is only a little more than eight years since the telegraph was first worked in this country. During the first quarter of 1848, the receipts of the Electric Telegraph Company were only £160; in the second quarter they increased to £240; in the third to £320; in the fourth to £400; and the receipts, despite the fact that other companies have grown up, and that the charges are now only one third of the amount originally demanded, have now reached £3,000 per week! The growth has thus been fifty fold in seven years; a progress unexampled in commercial annals, except in association with railway intercourse.

One of the original grounds of opposition to railways was the dangerous character of the traffic. A writer in one of our most popular reviews thus expressed, some years ago, the common opinion upon the danger of railway traveling:

"It is certainly some consolation to those who are to be whirled at the rate of eighteen or twenty miles an hour, by means of a high-pressure engine, to be told that there is no danger of being sea-sick while on shore; that they are not to be scalded to death, nor drowned, nor dashed to pieces by the bursting of a boiler; and that they need not mind being struck by the scattered fragments, or dashed in pieces by the flying off or breaking of a wheel. But, with all these assurances, we should as soon expect the people of Woolwich to suffer themselves to be fired off upon one of Congreve's ricochet rockets as to trust themselves to the mercy of such a machine, going at such a rate."

It is curious, occasionally, to contrast prediction and event. The last return of the Government Railway Department shows that the number of passengers killed, in proportion to the number conveyed upon railways in the United Kingdom, was, for the first half year of 1854, one in 7,195,343! Can it be assumed—would any life insurance company in the world assume—that to English gentlemen and ladies sitting at home at their ease by their firesides, fatal accidents would only occur, during half a year, in the proportion of one in seven millions? In the active performance of the duties of life, it is impossible to find a case in which the proportion of fatal accidents is so small. But nevertheless, whenever an accident does occur upon a railway, the public are sure to find it regarded as "Another Fatal Railway Accident," just as if such accidents were constant, instead of being, as the government statistics prove, most rare and extraordinary.

In comparison with deaths by railway accidents, how many are the accidents to persons walking in the streets! How fearful are the misadventures met with by those "who go down to the sea in ships!" Yet Parliament saw fit to provide, specially, for the smallest class of accidents arising from locomotion, and to afford only scanty redress for the greatest. Such has been the character of legislation for railways. The Merchant Shipping Law Consolidation Act, 1854, (17 and 18 Vict., c. 104,) recognizes in some sort the liability of shipowners in cases of loss of life, or of personal damage to passengers. But this act only exemplifies still more strongly the partial character of legislation as against the Railway Companies. For, whilst the damages in the case of accident upon a railway are unlimited, this act expressly limits the amount, which can be recovered under its operation, to £30 per head. Still further, if a crowded emigrant ship should be wrecked, and all the lives on board lost, the liability of the shipowner would be limited to the value of the ship and the amount due or accruing to him on account of freight in the voyage during which the accident occurred, so that, practically, the deodand amounts to nothing more than a first charge upon the insurance effected by the shipowner upon the ship and cargo. A shipowner might thus send his vessel to sea, her condition unseaworthy, her compasses ill-adjusted, inefficiently commanded, and with a disorderly or incapable crew. The ship might be wrecked the same night, or be run down, for want of proper vigilance, by some steamer in the channel. In such cases there would be only very partial redress against the shipowner, whatever might be his culpability. But let a railway carriage be thrown off a line in a dark night by a stone, or a log of wood carelessly or willfully placed upon it—let a fatal accident occur in consequence of some wanton act, not of the Railway Company, but of all that public who ought to guard and protect one another—and the Railway Company, although suffering severe loss of property, without having any pecuniary redress, even on the legal conviction of the perpetrator of the deed, which may have been prompted either by a diabolical desire to wreak a petty vengeance, or for the gratification of a malicious disposition, is liable to be mulcted in the heaviest penalties, for the accidental loss of life the misfortune may occasion. Can it be said that this is equitable legislation, or that it is calculated to protect the public from the class of accidents against which protection is most required?

Lord Campbell's Act not only creates a new and ill-adjusted liability, but it is also an exceedingly unfair act, in its application to different classes of society. The value of life is measured under this act by a class standard. A high public functionary may take a ticket for a journey of six miles at the cost of one shilling. In the same train there may be a working-man, who intends to travel one hundred miles, and who has paid ten shillings. The train meets with an accident, and both are killed. It is shown that, being a rich man, in the enjoyment of high posts, honors, and emoluments, his life was worth £20,000 to his family. The jury give the full amount claimed. But what do the family of the poor man get? The widow, not being able to establish any pecuniary loss, by reason of the accident which befel her husband, has charitably awarded to her, by the jury, £10, as a matter of feeling; and the attorney probably applies that amount to the payment of his costs. As regards the railway, therefore, this law is unequal; and it is still more so as regards the public.

The practical effect of this law is to retard the full adoption of low fares on railways. The Railway Companies, driven to become insurers of the lives of the public traveling on their lines, obviously must, in one form or another, have premiums to meet compensation. Hence, proposals to reduce fares to their minimum are constantly met by the consideration that the larger the number of passengers, the greater the liability to accident, and to the pecuniary loss incidental to it. It is, indeed, fortunate for the public that the proportion of accidents is so small. If the proportion was large, fares must no doubt be raised. And let it be observed that the Companies, thus driven to insure their passengers, are obliged to do so apart from all proper apportionment of premium to the risk incurred. A man traveling one hundred miles obviously incurs more risk than a man traveling six miles; yet, as we have seen, the family of the latter may get enormous compensation from the Company, whilst that of the former gets nothing. Nothing can be less equitable, or more opposed to every sound commercial principle. If Railway Companies are to be taxed in this way at all, the proper course would be, that each passenger should declare the value of his life, when he takes his ticket, and be charged in proportion to the distance he is traveling. But no consideration can be expected from those who have thought themselves justified in applying special legislation to a case in which that law applies only in the proportion of 1 to every 7,195,343!

Having now directed attention to the principal and more important topics of this great subject, it is desirable, before bringing this address to a close, to endeavor to lay before you some of the general results of the system.

You have heard that there are more than 90,000 men directly employed by the railways of the United Kingdom. Collaterally, in the manufacture of iron, the felling and transport of timber, the production of stores, the erection and improvement of buildings, etc., these lines give employment to at least 50,000 more men. Now, 140,000 men represent, with their wives and children, a population of more than half a million of souls. The result therefore is, that no less than 1 in 50, of the total population of these realms, is directly dependent on its railways! Having regard to this most startling fact, you will not be disposed to think that this is an interest which should be neglected, or be harshly treated by the legislature, or which should be the subject of imperfect and unsatisfactory legislation.

The financial results of railways will occasion no less surprise, when they are considered. In the gross, £20,000,000 of revenue are now realized annually by the Railway Companies of the United Kingdom—an amount nearly equal to one half the ordinary revenue of the state. Now, consider how the national wealth is affected by this large amount received from the people by the Railway Companies. Suppose that to-morrow there was a stoppage of all the railways—a cessation of the existing railway means of transporting human beings, merchandise, and animals. In the first place, it is certain that the traffic, represented by £20,000,000, could not be accommodated at all. But assume that it could be, it is certain that the accommodation could only be offered at more than three times the charge now made by the railways. The result then is, that upon the existing traffic of the nation, railways are effecting a direct saving to the people of not less than £40,000,000 per annum; and that sum exceeds by about 50 per cent. the entire interest of our National Debt. It may be said, therefore, that the railway system neutralizes to the people the bad effects of the debt with which the state is encumbered. It places us in as good a position as if the debt did not exist. And here the doubt arises as to which would be the most advantageous condition—a nation without a national debt and also without a railway system; or a nation hampered by a national debt, but having the advantage of cheap internal intercourse by railway.

Again, "Time is money." At least 111,000,000 passengers travel every year by our railways an average of 12 miles each. They perform the journey in half an hour. At the average rate of speed of the stage-coach, a journey of 12 miles would have occupied an hour and a half. Here is a direct saving of one hour upon every average journey performed by 111,000,000 of persons annually. These 111,000,000 hours saved are equal to 14,000,000 days, or 38,000 years, supposing the working man to labor eight hours a day; and allowing at the rate of 3*s*. a day for his labor, the annual saving to the nation, on this low average scale, is not less than £2,000,000 per annum.

Regard some of the moral results of the railway system. Observe how it operates in equalizing the value of land. Railways enable the farmer in Scotland to send his beasts to Smithfield, and gardeners in the west of England to send their early fruits to Covent Garden. Distant properties, therefore, become as valuable as those nearer to the centers of consumption. Nor is this all. Railways, by facilitating the transit of artificial manures, enable the farmers of poor land to compete with those who till superior soils; thus tending still further to equalize the value of the land, and thereby giving increased employment to, and improving the condition of, all classes of the population.

People are too apt to think and talk of railways as mere machines, whereby the speed of conveyance from one point to another is increased. You have seen them to-night in other and more important points of view. Let us look at them in other phases.

As stimulating national industry, perhaps the most familiar illustration will be the hard-metal trade. Look at the boiler-plate manufacture—comparatively insignificant before iron vessels and steam locomotion came into existence, and now one of the most important elements of the trade to which it appertains. Such is the extent of this branch of manufacture, that, extensive as they are, the iron-works are not even yet able to render the supply equal to the demand.

Again, before railways existed, the inland counties of England were unsupplied with fish from the coast. Now, fresh sea-fish enters into the consumption of almost every family of the middle class, in every considerable town. In the fish trade, indeed, railways have caused and are causing a prodigious revolution. Large fishing establishments have been formed at different parts of the east coast. Before the Norfolk Railway was constructed, the conveyance of fish from Yarmouth to London was entirely conducted in light vans with post-horses, and was represented by a bulk of about 2,000 tons a year. At present 2,000 tons of fish are, not unfrequently, carried on the Norfolk Railway, not in a year, but in a fortnight.

But perhaps there is no respect in which railways contribute so greatly to the public advantage as in the inland coal traffic; still in its infancy, but becoming most rapidly developed. The wagons which carry chalk from one county, return home laden with coals from another. Large reductions are being effected in the price of this prime necessary of life. Districts in which the peasantry, only a few years since, made their fires with a few scanty sticks gathered from a hedge, are now abundantly and cheaply supplied with the fuel which is so important to comfort and civilization. Railways have been already presented to you as public educators; here you have them as agents of benevolence and ameliorators of the condition of the human race; for it may be safely said that there is no contribution to the social comfort of society equal to warmth. Comfort, indeed, implies warmth; and warmth, chemically considered, is an addition to the supply of food.

Before railways were brought into existence, the internal communication of this country was restricted by its physical circumstances. Canals, apparently, allow an infinite series of boats to pass along them; but it must be borne in mind, that Nature opposes a practical limit to that description of transit. Every canal-boat has to pass a summit more or less abundantly supplied with water. Without a steam-engine at every lock, the extent of the traffic by this inland navigation must, therefore, be dependent upon the supply of water which can be commanded at the summits to be traversed. But, more than this, all canals are subject to the vicissitudes of dry seasons, which may occur at periods when the traffic is at a maximum, and to the frost of severe seasons, during which Nature may compel a total cessation of traffic for several weeks. In comparison with these difficulties, railway communication has none; and hitherto, whatever barriers NATURE has opposed, SCIENCE has entirely surmounted.

Before concluding this address, I am desirous of adding a few words by way of practical application of the great subject we have been considering.

I have directed attention to our railway system as it is. I have endeavored to show you the importance of that system, as regards the works which have been executed, the capital invested, and the multitudes to whom it gives employment. I have endeavored to point out some of the defects of the system, and to indicate the causes from which those defects arise. I have shown you the magnitude and importance of the results attained, and that the system under which they have been achieved must inevitably be progressive. There is, however, a great duty still unperformed, which devolves less upon myself than upon you. It should be one of the most earnest efforts of civil engineers to improve and perfect this vast and comprehensive system.

It is not merely upon works of magnitude that your attention should be fixed; the railway system is so vast, that every item, however minute in itself, becomes of the greatest importance, when multiplied by the extent of work performed. You must consider that every farthing saved upon the train mileage of our country represents to the railways no less an aggregate than £80,000 per annum. This fact may help to realize to you how important it is that your attention should be directed carefully to every department of the railway system. The perfection of the permanent way, its maintenance in sound condition, the durability of materials of construction, the simplification and improvement of locomotives, the economy of fuel—even the consumption of grease and cotton waste—all these are items in which economical arrangements may be turned to the highest advantage.

There are other points which will, doubtless, suggest themselves to many who are present; and I can only say, for my own part, that nothing will afford me higher satisfaction, than to feel that any observations I have addressed to you may elicit practical suggestions for the improvement of the system with which my name, chiefly in consequence of my father's works, is so intimately associated. For it is my great pride to remember, that whatever may have been done, and however extensive may have been my own connection with railway development, all I know and all I have done is primarily due to the parent whose memory I cherish and revere.

When I consider how intimately associated is the railway system with the profession to which I have the honor to belong—when I reflect, not only how much that system owes to the profession, but also how much the profession owes to railways, I cannot doubt that the civil engineers of England will fulfill their duty. For, looking around to-night, who can doubt that, whilst railways owe their construction to civil engineers, they, in return, owe to railways a large proportion of that improved position, that increased intelligence, and that familiar knowledge of abstract science, which, within the last twenty years, has so largely developed itself, both within and without these walls? Our business from a craft, has become a profession; and that profession, I rejoice to say, is daily exhibiting itself, not only as one of increased importance, but also as one of increasing cordiality and coöperation. There was a time, amid the many exciting competitions occasioned by railway enterprise, when the spirit of rivalry amongst the civil engineers of England was carried so far as to occasion some feelings of estrangement. I am happy to think that those feelings have given way to more friendly and confidential relations amongst us all; that our intercourse is now characterized by mutual forbearance and conciliation; and that, if rivalry does exist, it is no longer entertained in an unbecoming spirit, but is an honorable competition in the path of enterprise, and for the fair rewards of successful skill. To this Institution, and to the opportunities afforded by these meetings, we are mainly indebted for this improved spirit.

THE END.

www.ingramcontent.com/pod-product-compliance
Lightning Source LLC
LaVergne TN
LVHW021303110826
845150LV00003B/463

* 9 7 8 1 4 2 5 5 6 0 0 7 2 *